THE ENGLISH TEXT OF THE
ANCRENE RIWLE

EDITED FROM
MAGDALENE COLLEGE, CAMBRIDGE
MS. PEPYS 2498

EARLY ENGLISH TEXT SOCIETY

No. 274

1976

Ancren riwle

THE ENGLISH TEXT
OF THE
ANCRENE RIWLE

EDITED FROM
MAGDALENE COLLEGE, CAMBRIDGE
MS. PEPYS 2498

BY

A. ZETTERSTEN

Published for
THE EARLY ENGLISH TEXT SOCIETY
by the
OXFORD UNIVERSITY PRESS
LONDON   NEW YORK   TORONTO
1976

Oxford University Press, Walton Street, Oxford OX2 6DP

OXFORD LONDON GLASGOW NEW YORK
TORONTO MELBOURNE WELLINGTON CAPE TOWN
IBADAN NAIROBI DAR ES SALAAM LUSAKA ADDIS ABABA
KUALA LUMPUR SINGAPORE JAKARTA HONG KONG TOKYO
DELHI BOMBAY CALCUTTA MADRAS KARACHI

ISBN 0 19 722276 5

© *The Early English Text Society*

*Printed in Great Britain
at the University Press, Oxford
by Vivian Ridler
Printer to the University*

PREFACE

IN 1960 I undertook to edit the Pepys version of the *Ancrene
Riwle* for the Early English Text Society. Since that time
Ancrene Riwle scholarship has advanced considerably. Three of
the most important manuscripts, MSS. Corpus, Titus and
Cleopatra, have been edited for the Society and E. J. Dobson's
study of the affiliations of the *Ancrene* Riwle manuscripts was
published in 1962. These publications have greatly facilitated
my own work on the present edition. Also scholarship concerning the Pepys manuscript has made recent progress. Thanks to
the painstaking inventory of Middle English manuscripts in
England carried out by Angus McIntosh and M. L. Samuels,
two more manuscripts in the same hand as Magdalene College,
Cambridge, MS. Pepys 2498, have been identified.

The present text is edited in conformity with the principles
laid down by the Society for the editing of the manuscripts of
the *Ancrene Riwle*. I am indebted to the Master and Fellows of
Magdalene College, Cambridge, for their kindness in permitting
me to prepare the text for the press and to reproduce photo-
graphic facsimiles of pages of their manuscript. I also wish to
express my thanks to the Librarian of the Pepys Library, Dr.
Robert Latham, who has always been most generous in devoting
extra time to matters concerning MS. Pepys 2498, particularly
discussions of different handwritings.

In all my work on *Ancrene Riwle* manuscripts I have always
been greatly encouraged by Professor Norman Davis and
Professor Eric Dobson. I thank them both sincerely for valuable
advice in connection with my work on the Pepys MS. My
thanks are also due to Mr. John Bromwich, who has read my
introduction and notes in manuscript and contributed many
useful suggestions. For helpful advice on various points I am
further indebted to Professor Olof Arngart, Mr. R. W. Burch-
field, the former secretary of the Society, Dr. Pamela Gradon

and Dr. Anne Hudson, the present secretaries of the Society, Mr. Neil Ker, Professor Angus McIntosh, Dr. Raymond Page, Mr. D. Pepys Whiteley, Professor M. L. Samuels, and Professor G. V. Smithers.

ARNE ZETTERSTEN

Cambridge 1975

CONTENTS

PLATES

INTRODUCTION

1. *The Manuscript: Contents*

MAGDALENE COLLEGE, CAMBRIDGE, MS. PEPYS 2498 is written on vellum, each leaf measuring *c.* 340 × 240 mm. The manuscript, which is a large folio, contains 232 leaves. There are two paper flyleaves at the beginning and two at the end of the volume. The manuscript is written in two columns of 52–4 lines throughout the book, each column measuring *c.* 290 × 100 mm. All the quires except three consist of 8 leaves, as indicated by catchwords. The collation is: 1–2⁸; 3⁶; 4–23⁸; 24⁴ wants 4 blank; 25–29⁸; 30⁸ wants 8 blank. The quires are numbered in pencil at the bottom of the page in a modern hand. The manuscript is numbered by pages from 1 to 464. This pagination is followed in the description of the manuscript below, 'a' and 'b' being added to indicate the column.

The ruling of the pages is essentially the same throughout the whole volume. Besides the usual horizontal lines in thin ink, two parallel vertical lines are drawn for each column so as to form a frame for the writing. Sometimes the ruling has faded away completely. The scribe starts writing below the first ruled line of the page.

The upper parts of certain top lines are missing. This is because, when Pepys started the so-called Adjustment of his books in 1693, all books were placed and numbered in order of size so as to fit his presses perfectly, and the edges of many of the books were cut, or adjusted with a wooden plinth disguised with gilt leather.[1] This 'Adjustment' has affected particularly pp. 413–14, 431–2, and 451–6. Tears, cracks, stitchholes, etc., have been recorded in the footnotes.

There are no illuminations in MS. Pepys 2498. The first six items of the book are, however, characterized by a richly decorated initial at the beginning of each item. Those on pp. 1, 45, 212, and 371, are coloured blue, red, and violet, while those on pp. 226 and 263 are left uncoloured.

A. C. Paues drew attention to the contents of the volume in

[1] See A. Hobson, *Great Libraries* (London, 1970), p. 214.

1902. She published her description of the manuscript in 'A XIVth Century Version of the *Ancrene Riwle*', *Englische Studien*, xxx (1902), 344–6, and in *A Fourteenth Century English Biblical Version* (1902), lxv–lxix. M. R. James's description of the manuscript was published in *Bibliotheca Pepysiana, A Descriptive Catalogue of the Library of Samuel Pepys*, Part III (1923).

(i) *Binding*. The manuscript is bound in brown leather. In accordance with Samuel Pepys's will,[1] his crest was stamped on the front cover by his nephew, John Jackson, who was instructed in the will to make a general review of the whole library. This was done by Jackson in 1703–5 after Pepys's death on 26 May 1703. Jackson renumbered all the books of the library in red figures, and stamped Pepys's name, arms, crest, motto, and description of his official position on the covers.

Thus we find on the front cover, besides Pepys's crest, the following inscription:

SAM. PEPYS

CAR. ET IAC.

ANGL. REGIB.

A SECRETIS

ADMIRALIÆ.

On the back cover there are Pepys's crest and his family arms with the motto:

MENS CUJUSQUE IS EST QUISQUE

The volume was rebacked in the twentieth century, and at the same time the present shelf-mark, 'MS. 2498', was stamped at the bottom. The panel with the words 'WICKLEEF'S SERMON'S MS' is, however, from Pepys's period.

The inside cover bears the following note in red ink probably by John Jackson (or his clerk): 'N° 2498.' In the top left corner the following characters in black ink appear:

x

2

13

---

[1] Samuel Pepys's original will is dated 2 August 1701. The following paragraph is from the codicil added on 12 May 1703: '7^{thly} That my Arms or Crest or Cypher be Stampt in Gold on the outsides of the Covers of every booke admitting thereof.' See *The Diary of Samuel Pepys*, Supplementary volume, *Pepysiana* (London, 1899), ed. H. B. Wheatley, p. 266.

(ii) *First flyleaf.* On the recto the shelf-numbers '1376.B.' and '1369B.' (below the first number) in Pepys's own hand in black ink are crossed out in black ink. The number '1552.' in black ink to the right of '1369B.' is also in Pepys's hand. It has been crossed out in red ink, probably by Jackson or his clerk when the whole collection was renumbered. The same crossing out in red ink can be found in Pepys's *Catalogue of Michaelmas* (1700). In all the three different parts of this catalogue, the 'Numerical Catalogue' (p. 133), the 'Alphabet Catalogue' (p. 259), and 'Appendix Classica' (p. 174) the previous number '1552' in black was crossed out in red, and the new number '2498' inserted in red. The flyleaves are numbered in pencil at the bottom of the rectos in a modern hand.

On the verso of the first flyleaf there is a note by Daniel Waterland (1683–1740)[1] saying: 'These Sermons are not Wickliff's. Neither Matter, nor Style, nor Manner are at all like his: neither was the Author any Wicklevite. Indeed, the Language Seems to be older than Wickliff.'

(iii) *Second flyleaf.* On the recto is a list of contents in Daniel Waterland's hand, the last line of which refers to the *Ancrene Riwle.* The list runs as follows:

The Contents

1. The History of the Life of Christ, with a comment thereupon. p. 1.
2. The Mirrour. being a comment or Sermons[2] upon the Gospels, throughout the year. p. 45.
3. Sayings of wise men. 212.
4. The ten Commandments. 217.
5. A Comment upon the Apocalypse. 227.
6. The Psalter in English. with Gregory's Comment. 263.
7. The Canticle, <u>Confitebor tibi</u> &c. 361.
8. The Song moses. p. 362.
9. The Canticle of Isaiah. 364.
10. The Song of Zachary.[3] 368.

---

[1] Daniel Waterland was admitted to Magdalene College in 1699 and later became Fellow and Master of the College. He was Master when Pepys's books were presented to the College. I was able to study Waterland's hand from his letters, kept in the Master's Book, through the kindness of Mr. D. Pepys Whiteley. On Waterland see his *Works,* i (Oxford, 1823), 8 ff., and *DNB.*
[2] 'or Sermons' written above and marked for insertion.
[3] A word crossed out. 'Zachary.' added above.

11. The Magnificat.–368
12. The nunc dimittis. 368.
13. The Athanasian Creed. 369.
14. The Canticle upon the Mass. 371. 373.
    Several Old Rules. 371 &c.

On the verso of this leaf there is the book-plate (showing a portrait of Pepys) which appears in all the books of the Pepys Library. A copy of the portrait used for this book-plate is now in the Pepys Library. The portrait was painted by G. Kneller and the engraving made by R. White, as is indicated below the picture by the words: 'G. Kneller pinx. R. White sculp.'[1]

In the carved oval of this portrait there is the inscription which appears on the front cover. Pepys's motto is given below the picture on a riband.

(iv) pp. 1a–43a. *The Harmony of the Gospels*, edited by M. Goates for the Early English Text Society in 1923 under the title of *The Pepysian Gospel Harmony*. The right half of p. 43 is cut off, the manuscript of the Gospels ending on p. 43a.

(v) p. 44b. This page contains the following lines by Stephen Batman[2] (d. 1584):

> Brycrys gezet aramen
> Let reason Rule the, y[t] this booke shall reede:
> Miche good matter shalt thou finde in deede/
> Thowghe some bee ill, doo not the reste dispize
> Consider of the tyme, else thow art not wize

Anna Paues first suggested that this hand, which occurs in several places in the volume, was Stephen Batman's. This was also the opinion of M. R. James in *Bibliotheca Pepysiana, A Descriptive Catalogue of the Library of Samuel Pepys*, Part III (1923), pp. 106–10, and as far as I can judge there is no doubt that it is right. In the first three lines of the above text Batman tries to imitate earlier letter forms.

(vi) pp. 45a–212b. At the top of p. 45 the following title of the

---

[1] Cf. J. Charrington, *A Catalogue of the Engraved Portraits in the Library of Samuel Pepys* (Cambridge, 1936), p. 137, and *Pepysiana*, ed. Wheatley, p. 63.

[2] Stephen Batman (or Bateman) was domestic chaplain to Archbishop Parker and employed by him in collecting his library which is now in Corpus Christi College, Cambridge. Through the kindness of the Librarian of the college, Dr. Raymond Page, I have been able to study specimens of Batman's handwriting in the library. On Batman see *DNB*.

manuscript was written by Batman: 'Mirror, or glasse to Looke in;'. The Middle English *Mirror* has not been edited. Part of the Hunterian MS. of it was studied by T. G. Duncan in an unpublished Oxford B.Litt. thesis (1965). See also his article 'Notes on the language of the Hunterian MS of the *Mirror*', *Neuphilologische Mitteilungen*, lxix (1968), 204–8.

The prologue of the *Mirror* comprises pp. 45a–46a, l. 22. The main part of the *Mirror* begins on p. 46a, l. 23 and the various sermons on p. 50a. The item ends with the following verse (212b, ll. 22–4):

> Of þe holy omelies now i wil blynne.'
> God bringe vs to þat blisse.' þere ioye is euere inne.

(vii) pp. 212b–226b. This item begins with the following words in red ink (212b, ll. 25–8):

> Here bigynnen good techinges of wise Men wiþ þe ten
> hestes afterward. distinctelich expouned.

This item has not been edited. It ends with the following verse in red ink (226b, ll. 7–10):

> þe comaundementz expouned.' here enden i ȝou seie,
> vnto þe blis of heuene.' god vs wisse þe weie.

(viii) pp. 226b–263b. An English version of the *Apocalypse*. The English *Apocalypse* was edited in 1961 by E. Fridner in *An English Fourteenth Century Apocalypse Version with a Prose Commentary* (Lund Studies in English, 29). The edition was based on MS. Harley 874 with variants from ten other manuscripts including Pepys.

The *Apocalypse* begins with the following verse in red ink (226b, ll. 9–10):

> þapocalips on englissh.' makeþ here gynnyng
> After þis synful lyf.' god graunt vs good wonyng

It ends with the following verse in red ink (263b, ll. 11–12):

> þe Apocalips on englissch.' here now makeþ ende,
> Vnto þe blis of heuen.' god graunte vs grace to wende.

(ix) pp. 263b–370a. A version of the English prose psalter. The prose psalter was edited from two other manuscripts by K. D. Bülbring. Part I appeared as E.E.T.S. o.s. 97 (1891), but the second part of the edition, in which a collation of the Pepys manuscript was to have been included, was never completed.

The item begins with the following verse in red ink (263b, ll. 13–14):

> Of þe sautere on englisch: here is þe gynnynge,
> Wiþ þe latyn bifore: ᴣ Gregories expounynge

The Latin parts are in red ink. There are some Latin glosses underlined in black ink. The Canticles begin on p. 361. The item ends with the following lines in red (370a, ll. 46–7):

> Ter quinquagenos cantat dauid ordine psalmos,
> Versus bis mille. sex centum. sex canit ille.

(x) p. 370b. This column contains twenty-four lines in Stephen Batman's hand. Here Batman makes some of his characteristic imitations of early English script. The first twenty lines are versified.

> :ᴣif euer thys booke, don take his flight.
> on Stephan batman let it liᴣhte;
> ᴣit came to passe, and yt is trwe
> I will not change yt, for no newe/
>
> A learned pastor, this booke did make
> and in those daies. taken for great sapiens
> the vewe dooth vrge a Christian too quake
> the sight of souch blinde ignorance.
> Who wolde not but wayle souch a blindnes
> that hathe benne the cavse of mvche wretchednes
>
> The first part is veri good
> thowghe a worde or two doo varie
> The second is not sound
> smaule truthe dooth carie
> Yet as the one. without the other thow cannot bee
> Else falshod with trwthe mixed thow cannot see,
>
> To answer the ennemy thow maiste be boulde
> When theire owen penns svch errowres have tolde
> Teare not this book. but kepe it in store,
> thow maiest else misse for knoweng of more.

Finally there are four lines in prose containing information about the date of the manuscript: 'The age of this book. by

conferring with an other coppy, was wretten when k henry the
.4. had busines agayste the welshmen. Anº / 1401 / .'

(xi) pp. 371a–449a. *Ancrene Riwle*. For the analysis of this see
below pp. xviii–xxi. The text was edited in 1911 by J. Påhlsson
under the title of *The Recluse*, in *Lunds Universitets Årsskrift*,
N.F. Afd. 1, Bd. 6, Nr. 1, and reprinted with introduction and
textual notes in 1918.

(xii) pp. 449a–459b. This portion begins on p. 449a, l. 35.
Above the last two lines of the preceding item there is the following note in Batman's hand: 'the passion; Caulid the complainte of oure Lady'. The item begins with the following
verse in red ink (449a, ll. 35–6):

> Of oure lefdy Marie.' bigynneþ now here þe pleynt
> þat of þe passion of hir son sche telde with hert feynt

The whole item ends with the following verse (459b, ll. 16–17):

> þe passioun as oure lefdy seiþ.' of Ihesu endeþ here,
> In to þe blisse of heuen.' vs bringe it alle in fere.

(xiii) pp. 459b–463b. *The Gospel of Nicodemus*, which is the
earliest prose version. It was edited by W. H. Hulme in *The
Middle English Harrowing of Hell and Gospel of Nicodemus*,
E.E.T.S. E.S. 100 (1907). The work has a heading, '*Nicodemus
Gospel*;' written in Batman's hand. The item ends with the
following verse (463b, ll. 36–7):

> Of þe vprist of Crist.' as Nichodemus gan telle,
> Here now make ich ende.' god schilde vs alle from helle

(xiv) pp. 463b–464b. Five prayers in English beginning

(*a*) SWete fader of heuene . . .
(*b*) SWete lorde Ihesu crist goddes son of heuen . . .
(*c*) SWete lorde Ihesu crist fader ⁊ son ⁊ holy gost . . .
(*d*) LEfdi seint Marie als wis as þou art Moder of mercy . . .
(*e*) ALle halewen i biseche ȝou for Ihesu cristes loue . . .

On p. 464b below the text a modern reproduction of Pepys's
anchor-plate (always found at the end of Pepys's books) has been
inserted. This book-plate shows the initials 'S P' with two an-
chors and ropes intertwined and the motto on a riband above.

(xv) On the first of the two flyleaves at the end of the volume, the following notes on the contents in Waterland's hand can be read:

Priests, their duty and privileges. p. 103, 104.
Baptism, its cermonies. 117.
Testament-making p. 122.—
Obedience of wives. 127. buxom.—
Sacramental Body and Blood of *Christ* p. 168.
Purgatory. p. 213.
Canonical Hours. 376.

The last flyleaf is blank.

2. *History*

The first reference to the manuscript in print is found in *Catalogi Librorum Manuscriptorum Angliae et Hiberniae*, ii (1697), 207 ff. We know from a letter from Samuel Pepys to Dr. Arthur Charlett dated 4 August 1694[1] that he had given a description of his own collection of manuscripts for that catalogue. The collection was called 'Librorum Manuscriptorum viri sapientissimi *Samuelis Pepysii*, Curiae Admiraliae nuper a secretis, varii quidem argumenti, sed praecipue de re navali, quae est Anglorum gloria ac Praesidium, Thesaurus inaestimabilis'.

This catalogue has seven subdivisions, our manuscript being recorded under 'Religious' books, p. 208. The manuscript, wrongly attributed to Wycliffe, has the following entry: 'No. 6754. (35) His Sermons, Pergam. fol.'

References in his Diary from 1666[2] show that Pepys was engaged in cataloguing his collections as early as that. One catalogue, known as the 'Adjustment' of 1693, no longer exists. Pepys's oldest manuscript catalogue is his *Catalogue of Michaelmas (1700)*. In the 'Numerical Catalogue' (p. 133) the manuscript is recorded as follows: 'Wickliffe's Sermons upon the Epistles, Gospels & Psalms, MSS—1400.' After the entry the shelf-number '1552' is crossed out and replaced by '2498.'. See p. xi

---

[1] See *Academy*, xxxviii (London, 1890), 110. On Pepys's interest in the collecting of books and manuscripts see J. R. Tanner, *Mr. Pepys. An Introduction to the Diary together with a Sketch of his Later Life* (London, 1925), pp. 113–21, 276–9.
[2] See *The Diary of Samuel Pepys*, ed. R. Latham and W. Matthews, vii (London, 1972), p. 412 (17 December 1666).

above. '1552' seems to have been the manuscript number in the catalogue of 1700, and '1369B', crossed out on the first flyleaf, that of the 1693 catalogue. The third number crossed out on this flyleaf, '1376.B', is the earliest shelf-number of the volume known. It is not known when and where Pepys obtained the manuscript, but it was undoubtedly before 1693.

Samuel Pepys (1633–1703) lived most of his life in London. From 1679 his house with his library had been in York Buildings in Westminster. It is clear that he was adding considerably to his library after his retirement in 1689.[1] When he died in 1703 he bequeathed his library to John Jackson, his nephew, on the condition that it should be presented to Magdalene College, Cambridge, after Jackson's death. Jackson died in 1723, and the next year Pepys's library of c. 3,000 volumes was removed to the college.

Various suggestions have been made about the provenance of MS. Pepys,[2] but a considerable step forward was made when Professors M. L. Samuels and A. McIntosh in their inventory and dialectal mapping of all Middle English manuscripts realized that Pepys 2498, Bodleian MS. Laud Misc. 622,[3] and

---

[1] Cf. *The Diary*, i (1970), xxxviii–xxxix.

[2] Cf. the following opinions: A. C. Paues, *A Fourteenth Century English Biblical Version*, p. lxviii: 'The Dialect of our version presents a strange medley of Southern and Midland, even Northern forms, but the vocabulary is mainly Southern...'; Hulme, op. cit., p. xliii: 'The dialect, though by no means pure, is in the main a Southern variety of East Midland'; G. C. Macaulay, 'The Ancren Riwle', *MLR* ix (1914), 147: 'The dialect is Midland, but with some South-western characteristics'; J. Påhlsson, *The Recluse*, p. 334, agreeing with A. C. Paues, says: 'The language, however, cannot by any means be called a homogeneous dialect...'; R. Jordan, *Handbuch der mittelenglischen Grammatik* (2nd ed., Heidelberg, 1934), p. 11: 'Nottingham'.

[3] The following items are contained in this manuscript:

(i) ff. 71^v–72^v, 1^r–21^v: *The Siege of Jerusalem*.

(ii) ff. 21^v–26^v: *The Vision of St. Alexius*.

(iii) ff. 26^v–27^r: Adam Davy, *Five Dreams about Edward II*.

(iv) ff. 27^v–64^r: *Kyng Alisaunder*.

(v) ff. 64^r–64^v: Note of remarkable things and places seen on the pilgrimage to the Holy Land.

(vi) ff. 65^r–70^v: An incomplete *Temporale*.

(vii) ff. 70^v–71^r: Fifteen Tokens before the Day of Judgement.

(viii) ff. 71^r–71^v: Lines on the Birth of Christ.

Kyng Alisaunder was edited in 1952 and 1957 by G. V. Smithers in E.E.T.S. 227 and 237. The manuscript is described in vol. ii, pp. 1 ff. Items ii, iii, vii, viii, and a part of item vi were edited by F. J. Furnivall in *Adam Davy's 5 Dreams about Edward II*, etc., E.E.T.S. o.s. 69 (1878).

b

British Museum MS. Harley 874[1] are in one and the same hand.[2] Moreover, these three manuscripts, together with four others, belong to a group of fourteenth-century manuscripts which represent the earliest of the three types of early London English that can be distinguished, according to Samuels.[3] The closest linguistic description of a single item in this group of manuscripts so far made is G. V. Smithers's study of the Laud MS. in his edition of *Kyng Alisaunder*. His conclusion, based on a critical analysis of the rhymes in MS. Laud, is that the language is London English (p. 56). According to the Samuels–McIntosh Survey[4] the provenance of the three manuscripts is the Waltham Abbey area, about twelve miles north-north-east of the City of London in west Essex.

3. *The* ANCRENE RIWLE *text*

The part of the manuscript containing the *Ancrene Riwle* is divided thus:

Quire xxv: pp. 371a–386b. Catchwords at foot of p. 386b.
Quire xxvi: pp. 387a–402b. Catchwords at foot of p. 402b.
Quire xxvii: pp. 403a–418b. Catchwords at foot of p. 418b.
Quire xxviii: pp. 419a–434b. Catchwords at foot of p. 434b.
Quire xxix: pp. 435a–450b. The *Ancrene Riwle* ends on p. 449a.

The traditional dividing of the *Ancrene Riwle* into 'parts' is specifically indicated only in Parts I, III, VI, and VII. The Pepys version is divided into parts as follows:

Part I: pp. 371a–377b. On Devotions. This part ends with: *Here endeþ þe first Book.* (17: 16).
Part II: pp. 377b–387b. On the Custody of the Senses.
Part III: pp. 387b–402b. On the Custody of the Heart. This part begins with: *þis is now þe [þ]ridd dale of ʒoure booke.*(42: 18).
Part IV: pp. 402b–425a. On Temptations.

[1] This manuscript consists of the following items:
(i) ff. 2ʳ–31ᵛ: The Middle English Apocalypse.
(ii) f. 31ᵛ: An unfinished poem on the Universe.
The manuscript of the Apocalypse was edited in 1961 by Elis Fridner (see p. xiii above).
[2] Professor Samuels kindly informed me of this discovery in a letter of 1962.
[3] See 'Some Applications of Middle English Dialectology' (1963) reprinted in R. Lass, *Approaches to English Historical Linguistics* (New York, 1969), pp. 409–10. Cf. also M. L. Samuels, *Linguistic Evolution* (Cambridge, 1972), p. 166.
[4] Professor Samuels kindly tells me this in a letter of 1972.

Part V: pp. 425a–434b. On Confession.

Part VI: pp. 434b–441b. On Penance. This part is introduced at the end of the preceding part with the following words: *After schrift fallep to speken of penaunce pat dude bote ⁊ pis is pe sext dele of oure book.* (150: 31–3). The book ends with: *Here is pe sext dele of pis book.* (166: 22).

Part VII: pp. 441b–446a. On Love. This part ends with: *Pis is pe seuenpe dele of pis book.* (177: 29).

Part VIII: pp. 446a–449a. On the Outer Rule.

The whole manuscript is written in one hand. The writing can be attributed to the second half of the fourteenth century.[1] It is a clear, firm, uniform book-hand. The scribe used a good, deep black ink which occasionally turns brownish. As a rule Latin quotations are in red ink. Red ink is also used for headings, marginal notes, and occasional English words. All these are indicated in the footnotes to the text.

The initial at the beginning of the *Ancrene Riwle* is the letter R written in blue and red and picked out in red. The background of the letter is a network of thin red lines, on which a pattern of leaves stands out beautifully. Some thin lines of decoration in violet are found at the left and right sides of the letter. The whole ornamented letter measures *c.* 55 × 60 mm.

The initials of the subdivisions of *Ancrene Riwle* are coloured blue and decorated inside and outside the letter with red strokes. These initials are usually the height of two lines of the manuscript. The capital thorns can, however, cover more lines, for example at 105: 13, no less than twelve lines. The red strokes decorating these initials often form extensive patterns in the left margins and between the two columns of the page. Thorns covering more than two lines are found at the following places: 40: 31 (11 lines), 89: 9 (8 lines), 92: 21 (8 lines), 92: 33 (7 lines), 93: 12 (5 lines), 93: 24 (8 lines), 94: 10 (7 lines), 94: 16 (8 lines), 97: 11 (8 lines), 98: 20 (4 lines), 104: 7 (9 lines), 104: 14 (9 lines), 105: 13 (12 lines), 108: 1 (8 lines), 169: 11 (9 lines), 172: 15 (3 lines), 178: 18 (12 lines), 179: 24 (8 lines), 179: 31 (8 lines) 180: 21 (3 lines), and 183: 6 (11 lines).

Between 1: 14 and 11: 36 and at 17: 27, 45: 29, 30, 46: 2, 48: 24, 60: 6, 81: 7, 84: 20, 106: 23, 112: 1, 113: 24, 145: 14

---

[1] Mr. Neil Ker kindly tells me that he thinks that 'middle of the second half of s. xiv would do very well for this hand'.

and 167: 29, the Latin quotations in red ink begin with initials in blue only one line high. In some cases this type of blue initial is also used to introduce paragraphs in the English text (6: 11, 6: 25, 9: 31, 10: 1, 11, 16, 22, 25, 32, 11: 1, 7, 31, 36, 12: 18, 30, 13: 4, 14, 24 and 14: 33). The blue initials are marked by extra large one-line capitals in this edition.

Sometimes, for example on p. 371, in addition to ordinary capitals, some uncapitalized initial letters as well as Tironian notae are picked out in red. The paragraph marks in the *Ancrene Riwle* (indicated by (in this edition) are in blue ink. These marks as well as the capitals were inserted after the text was written; this is indicated by the existence of slanting guide-lines and guide-letters respectively. The guide-lines are not marked in the present edition.

The original marginal notes usually indicating the sources of the quotations are in red ink. In many cases these names have been cut off at the edge of the margin. Expansions of these marginal notes are included in square brackets in the footnotes. The only hand in the margin that can be identified is Stephen Batman's (always in black ink). Besides occurring on p. 370b (before the *Ancrene Riwle* starts) it appears on pp. 371, 373, 375, 377, and 449. All marginal notes, catchwords, drawn hands, etc., are recorded in the footnotes.

The text contains numerous errors due to the scribe's carelessness. Misspellings, omissions, examples of attraction, dittography, etc., are frequent; sometimes mistakes have been corrected by expunction, transposition marks, erasures, etc. The scribe seems to have made more mistakes when copying the *Ancrene Riwle* than when copying MSS Laud Misc. 622[1] and Harley 874[2]. The numerous blunders and alterations made in the transcription of the *Ancrene Riwle* lead to the conclusion that the manuscript is far removed from the original (see further section 4 below). Although some of the errors must have

---

[1] G. V. Smithers says of the Laud transcription (*Kyng Alisaunder*, ii. 9): 'Corruption in B is neither serious nor extensive . . . In fact B and its antecedents are the work of scribes who were intelligent and who scrupulously refrained from rewriting difficult passages.'

[2] E. Fridner, *Apocalypse*, p. xxxiii, when discussing the Harley transcription, remarks: 'judging from several scribal mistakes, it was preceded by a number of copies'.

been inherited from intervening manuscripts, the scribe must have been himself responsible for most of the mistakes.

There are a great number of additional passages in the Pepys version which contribute to make the manuscript very different from its original (see p. xxii, n. 4). Further the Pepys version is meant to be addressed to both men and women in contrast to the original Rule addressed to three women only. Personal references to three women or a larger community of women are thus avoided, masculine words being sometimes substituted for feminine ones, etc. For example, the sentence in Corpus, *For þi mine leoue sustren þe leaste þe ȝe eauer mahen luuieð ower þurles.* (12b: 21–3) is followed by the other early manuscripts, Cleopatra, Nero, and Titus, while MS. Pepys gives: *Forþi my leue breþeren and sustren. witeþ wel ȝoure eiȝen . . .* (18: 2–3).

Another significant passage is the reference to the order of St. James. The following sentence occurs in Corpus: *þus sein iame descriueþ religiun ⁊ ordre. þe leatere dale of his sahe limpeð to reclusen.* (3a: 13–14). This is followed by Cleopatra and Nero, the relevant passage not appearing in Titus.

The corresponding passage in MS. Pepys runs as follows: *And þus descryueþ seint iame Ordre and riȝth Religioun. And þe laste deel to onelich men ⁊ wymmen. ⁊ to alle oþere þat willeþ kepen hem clene out of synne ⁊ fram þe werlde* (4: 18–21).

Finally, the prayer *Saluas fac ancillas tuas.* (MS. Corpus 11b: 18; similarly Cleopatra and Nero) has been extended to *Saluos fac seruos tuos ⁊ Ancillas tuas.* in MS. Pepys 14: 20–21 (similarly Titus.)

The suppression of references to the sisters noted by Frances M. Mack in her edition of MS. Titus[1] is even more marked in MS. Pepys. The same kind of carelessness or uncertainty in the use of personal pronouns mentioned by Dr. Mack is likewise characteristic of MS. Pepys. On the connection between Titus and Pepys see below, p. xxii.

4. *MS. Pepys 2498 in relation to the other manuscripts of the* ANCRENE RIWLE

When J. Påhlsson published his edition very little was known about the affiliations of the manuscripts. Only J. Morton's

[1] E.E.T.S. 252 (1963), pp. xv–xvii.

edition of the Nero MS. (with very few variant readings from
MSS. Cleopatra and Titus) was available in print at the time.
When a reprint of the Pepys version was published by Påhlsson
in 1918, he added a substantial section containing textual notes
as well as some 'General Remarks' about the *Ancrene Riwle*.
By that time G. C. Macaulay's collation of the manuscripts of
the *Ancrene Riwle* had been published.[1] This gave Påhlsson a
more extensive collection of variant readings, but the only con-
secutive text available to him was still the Nero MS. with all its
shortcomings, innovations, and misconceptions. It was pointed
out by E. J. Dobson in 1962[2] that of the early manuscripts, Nero
is furthest removed from the original. Dobson has also shown
conclusively (p. 134) that Pepys has close connections with
Titus, although not derived from it. Påhlsson had noted the
'obvious affinity between the versions handed down in MSS. *P.*
and *T.*' (p. 329), but Dobson has clearly defined the arrange-
ment of the main manuscript groups as well as the likely cross-
links between individual manuscripts. The so-called ε-group is
clearly divided into two main subgroups, characterized by the
difference between Nero and Titus. Pepys, which is described
by Dobson as a 'late and extensively rewritten version' has also,
close though it is to Titus, distinctive agreements with Nero.[3]

From what has been said above, it is obvious that Påhlsson—
though he made few errors in the presentation of the diplomatic
text—was seriously hampered in his critical notes and in his
discussion of the interpolations in Pepys,[4] because he had access
only to the Nero MS.

---

[1] *MLR* ix (1914), 63–78, 145–60, 324–31, and 463–74.

[2] 'The affiliations of the manuscripts of *Ancrene Wisse*', *English and
Medieval Studies presented to J. R. R. Tolkien* (London, 1962), p. 133.

[3] See Dobson, p. 145. In his edition of the Cleopatra MS. (E.E.T.S.
267, 1972), xi, Dobson notes the influence of Cleopatra on the manuscripts
of the ε-group and draws the important conclusion that the original nucleus
of the ε-group and its immediate descendants 'must have been made at an
early date, probably before 1240'.

[4] On these interpolations see E. Colledge, '*The Recluse*. A Lollard inter-
polated version of the *Ancren Riwle*', *RES* xv (1939), 1–15, 129–45'. The
thirty-two longest and most important interpolations are listed by Colledge
on pp. 13–14.

5. *Editorial method*

The text of the Pepys version is reproduced from the manuscript without emendation. The capitalization, punctuation, and word division of the manuscript are retained. However, capitalization presents one complication: in the case of *a, i, ʒ, m, þ,* and *w* it has been especially difficult to distinguish between capitals and small letters. In such cases it is impossible to be sure whether the scribal intention has been followed or not. The scribe uses three different forms of the letter *a*: a small *a*, a semicapital *a*, and a capital *a*. For practical reasons the semicapital *a* has been printed as a capital, since it occurs many times at the beginning of a sentence. The initial *ff* has been represented by *F*.

Contractions are normally expanded without italics. The abbreviation for *et cetera* is usually expanded in full except for a few cases where, for typographical reasons, it has been expanded as *etc.* The Tironian nota, which is crossed (ᷓ), has been left unexpanded.

The hyphens at the end of lines in the printed text have been introduced by the printer. These words are not divided in the manuscript. Dots sometimes occur before and after *I* (*i*) (e.g. at 10: 17). They are usually much more lightly made than the points used as punctuation and have not been included in this edition. The points with a hair-line flourish used at the end of paragraphs have been represented by full stops. A sign consisting of the upper part only of a *punctus elevatus* occurs after *seist* at 124: 11.

The page references are given in the margin of the text as well as the references to Morton's edition of the Nero MS., as in all the other texts of the Society's *Ancrene Riwle* series. The Pepys version does not always incorporate all the contents of the corresponding page of the Morton edition.

ANCRENE RIWLE

Magdalene College, Cambridge, MS. Pepys 2498

p. 371a
(M. 2)

REcti diligunt te, In canticis canticorum. sponsa ad sponsum. Est rectum gramaticum. rectum geometrioum. rectum theologium, ⁊ sunt differencie totidem regularum. De recto theologio sermo nobis est cuius regule due sunt: una circa cordis directionem, Altera versatur circa exteriorem rectificacionem, 5 Recti diligunt te, Lorde seiþ goddes spouse to her derworþe spouse. þe riȝth louen þe. Hij ben riȝth þat lyuen after riȝth reule. Many dyuers reules. þere ben. Ac two þere ben among alle þat ich wil now speken of at þis tyme þorouȝ þe grace of god ⁊ of his dere moder Marie. þat on reuleþ þe hert and makeþ it 10 euene wiþ oute knoost and doþe of þouȝth inwiþ and bywraieþ þe. ⁊ seiþ to þe. here þou synnest oiþer wise ne may it nouȝth ben. þis reule is euere inwiþ þe ⁊ reuleþ þe hert as it auȝth to done. Hec est caritas illa quam describit apostolus de corde puro. ⁊ consciencia bona. ⁊ fide non ficta. ⟨ þis reule is charite of 15 schire hert and clene inwiþ and trewe byleue, Misericordiam tuam scientibus te per fidem non fictam. iustam viam id est vite rectitudinem. hijs qui recti sunt corde qui omnes voluntates suas dirigunt ad regulam diuine voluntatis. Isti dicuntur noui
(M. 4) atthonomasice. Vnde Psalmista. Benefac domine bonis ⁊ rectis 20 corde. Isti dicuntur vt glorientur testimonia. videlicet bone consciencie Gloriamini omnes recti corde Quos silicet rectificauit regula illa supprema, rectificans omnes. de qua Augustinus

At top of page in Stephen Batman's hand in black ink: The Canticle vpon the Masse, worth the keping, to answer their wilfull blindnes. & svmwhat strainge
2 gramaticum: *thin vertical cut in MS. between* a¹ *and* m¹. geometrioum, *sic for* geometricum. 3 theologium, *sic for* theologicum. theologio, *sic for* theologico. 8 *Full stop after* reules *in the red ink that is used on page 371 to ornament certain initial letters.* 11 doþe of þouȝth inwiþ: *Corpus has* dolc of woh inwit *1a:16.* 13 inwiþ, *sic for* inwit. 15 ficta: *between* i *and* c *traces of erased letter.* reule: le *partially erased.* is: s *partially erased.* 17 iustam viam, *sic for* iusticiam tuam. 18 recti, *sic for* recto. 19–20 noui atthonomasice, *sic for* boni antonomastice. 21 Isti dicuntur, *sic for* Istis dicitur. testimonia, *sic for* testimonio. 22 silicet, *sic for* scilicet.

dicit. Nichil petendum nisi regula magisterij. ⁊ Apostolus.
omnes in eadem regula permaneamus. et cetera. ⟨ þat oþer is
al wiþ outen ⁊ reuleþ þe body þat techeþ hou men schullen
beren hem. Wiþ outen howe, eten. dryken. wirchen. liggen and
fasten. bidden ⁊ stodien.   5
Hec est exercicio corporis que iuxta Apostolum modicum valet
hec est regula recti Mechamici quod sub geometrio recto con-
tinetur. ⟨ þis reule nys nouȝth bot forto seruen þat oþer. for
þat oþer is as lefdy of house. and þis reule is as þiften forto
seruen hir to wille and forto reulen þe hert wiþinne. Now to 10
onelich men ⁊ wymmen ⁊ to alle oþer þat desiren forto seruen
god what þat is ȝoure reule ȝe schulleþ riȝth wel witen. boþe þe
inner ⁊ þe vtter for hir sake. as vche man ⁊ vche womman may
best seruen þe inner. for alle men ⁊ wymen moten holde o
reule wiþinne.   15
Quantum ad puritatem cordis circa quod versatur tota religio.
⟨ þat is. alle men owen to holden on clennesse of hert ⁊ on porte⸴
þat is to louen god ouer al þinge. ⁊ þine euene cristen as þi
p. 371b seluen. þat is wille hem come to blisse wiþ þe and | helpe hem
bodilich ȝif þou may and gostlich. and bidde fast for hem. ⁊ 20
teche hem ȝif þou canst bettre þan hij. Ac ȝif it be a wicked man
oiþer a womman of lyf holde þe out of his compaignye bot ȝif it
be forto amenden hym. ⁊ elles he takeþ synne of hym. as seint
Poule seiþ and setteþ an ensample and seiþ. riȝth as a gret fat
ful of doghȝe takeþ souryng of a lytel gobett⸴ riȝth so doostou of 25
hym. And ȝif it be a man þat þou moste lyue by hym and
erne þi sustenaunce of hym⸴ bidde fast for hym þat god amende
hym ȝif it be his wille. and keepe þine hert clene ⁊ schire inwiþ
⁊ wiþ oute. clene ⁊ white fram synne. And ȝif þine hert wiþny-
meþ þe of any synne⸴ go ⁊ amende it wiþ schryft. For noþing ne 30
makeþ þe hert wronge bot synne one. Forto riȝthten hir ⁊
maken hir smeþe. þat longeþ to vche ordre ⁊ to vche religioun.
(M. 6) þe goode ⁊ alle þe strengþe. þis reule nys nouȝth of mannes fyndels. Ac it is of goddes hestes. ⁊ þerfore it most þe better ben ykept.
⁊ wiþ þe more bisynesse. And þerfor it is euere inwiþ ⁊ reuleþ 35
þe hert and seiþ to þe here þou synnest it ne may be non oþere.

---

1 regula: ul *touched up in black ink.* l *on erasure.*   magisterij: *first* i
written above an expuncted e.   Apostolus: *first 5 letters touched up in black*
ink. First o *on erasure.*   4 dryken, *sic for* drynken.   6 exercicio, *sic for* exercitacio.   modicum: di *partially erased.*   7 Mechamici,
sic for Mechamici.   geometrio, *sic for* geometrico.

Quantum silicet ad obseruancias corporales, etc. ⟨[þat is bodilich keepynges after þe vtter reule ⁊ þis is mannes fyndels. ⁊ for
nouȝth nys it ymade bot forto seruen þe inner to maken hire to
suffren hardeschipes. wakyng. fastyng. wirchyng ⁊ oþer penaunces
to done. Ac many ne may nouȝth suffren harde als wel as many. 5
And þerfore þis vtter reule mote be chaunged after vche mannes
manere as he may serue god best. For summe beþ stronge ⁊
summe beþ vnstronge of complexioun ⁊ of body boþe. and
mowen paye god ful wel. summe wiþ lesse penaunce þan summe
mowen. Summe is clerk oiþer clergesse. and þerfore hij moten 10
þe more wirchen þan þe lewed ⁊ siggen. Summe ben olde ⁊
nouȝth louelich. And summe ben ȝonge ⁊ louelich. ⁊ moten
haue þe better warde. ⁊ þe better ⁊ þe bisilier ben aboute forto
kepen hem seluen. And forþi schal vchone holde þe vtter reule
after schriftes rede of gostlich men ⁊ wyse. And þe seruauntes 15
þat knowen þe manere of hem ⁊ witen her strengþe. þeiȝ hij
schullen seruen hem hij mowen þe vtter reule chaungen after
wisdom. Ac by my red noman schal make none avow to do
noþing bot do als wel as he may. For ȝif he make avow and
breke it.ꞌ he synnes dedlich. And þerfore do þat he may as he 20
hadde made avow. And þeiȝ he ne do it nouȝth. he ne synnes
nouȝth dedlich Bot ȝif he wil make Professioun to lyue onelich
lyf. to þre þinges he moste make auow. To done obedience to
his bisshope. And to chastite. And to helde þe stede stille þere
his bisschop hym doþe þat he ne schal neuere þenne bot for 25
nede one, | For who so bihoteþ god a þing. he it wil asken as
biheste. And ȝif it be nouȝth bihoten.ꞌ hij mowen do at her lykynge of mete. ⁊ drynk. ⁊ werynge. bedes bidden so many as hym
lyst. oiþer on þis wyse. þise ben alle in free wille. Ac charite þat
is loue and lowenesse. lete litel of oure seluen, trewelich helden 30
þe ten hestes. schrift ⁊ penaunce. þis is þe moste penaunce þat
man may do. forsake synne. For þere ben many þat done
penaunce þat ne forsaken nouȝth her synne. Ac þat no stondeþ
in no stede forto haue any mede in þe blis of heuene. Do penaunce and oþer goode werkes. þat god haþ comaunded boþe in 35
þe olde lawȝe ⁊ in þe newe. And þerfore vche man it mote
holden for þise reulen þe hert. And of her reulyng is almest al

. 372a

M. 8)

---

1 silicet, *sic for* scilicet   2 *second Tironian sign ornamented in red.*   16
manere: *irregular stroke connecting lower parts of minims of* n.   37 al:
!*partially erased.*

þat i wil wryte. Bot in þe formest of þis boke ᷿ in þe last endynge.
In þe first deel ichil wryte ȝoure seruise to onelich men ᷿ wymmen ᷿ to alle þat it wil vsen and may goode it is. ȝif any man
askeþ of what ordre ȝe ben as mamy foles willen⸴ Ansuereþ on
þis manere ᷿ seiþ þat ȝe ben of seint Iames ordre þat for his   5
holynesse was cleped goddes broþer. And þan askeþ hym of
what ordre he is. ᷿ where he fyndeþ ordre in holy wrytt ᷿ riȝth
Religioun. Ac seint iame seiþ and makeþ ofte þis ensaumple.
þe gnatte foloweþ þe flesche. þat is to saye. Many maken mychel
strengþe þere leste is seint iame seiþ. Religio munda ᷿ inma-   10
(M. 10) culata apud deum patrem hec est: Visitare Pupillos ᷿ viduas in
tribulacione. ⟨ þis is. riȝth religioun ᷿ wiþoute wemme is þat.
þat can helpen faderles children ᷿ widewen. Hij ben faderles
childer þat han forlorne þe fader of heuene for synne And hij
ben widewen þat hane forlorne her spouse Ihesu crist þorouȝ   15
dedlich synne. Also þan he þat can fede þise wiþ holy lore and
þorou holy techynge brynge hem aȝein to her fader and to her
spouse. þis is þe heiȝest Religioun þat is. And þus descryueþ
seint iame Ordre and riȝth Religioun. And þe laste deel to onelich men ᷿ wymmen. ᷿ to alle oþere þat willeþ kepen hem clene   20
out of synne ᷿ fram þe werlde For seint Austyn seiþ A gaderyng
of wicked folk þat he clepeþ þe werlde. þat god biddeþ vs forsake. Ac nouȝth þe goodes of þe werlde. For none ne may wel
lyuen and seruen god bot ȝif hij han her sustenaunce And better
is to ernen it þan to bidden it. bot ȝif were a Prechoure ᷿ preched   25
goddes woord fram toun to toun so þat ne myȝth nouȝth for
stody ernen it And ȝutt Peter ᷿ Poule erneden her mete wiþ her
hondes and preched fram cite to cite. For Poule seiþ. þat he ne
ete neuere mannes mete bot ȝif it were his vnþonkes. Ac I nott ȝif
þere be any man þat wil haue heiȝer lyf in þe blisse of heuene þan   30
p. 372b   hij han. þan it is slik he take an heiȝer lyf in þe | blisse of heuene
þan hij han had. Ac euer be vche man þat he ne bigile nouȝth
seluen as he may ful liȝthlich forto desire so holy lyf. Ac biseeke

---

4 mamy, *sic for* many.   6 holynesse: l *partially erased.*   7 fyndeþ: eþ *crammed together at end of line.*   9 gnat *crossed out and
expuncted after* þe *at end of line.*   foloweþ: f *partially effaced.*   is: s
partially erased.   16 lore: l *partially erased.*   17 *second* her: e
partially erased.   18 þis: *thin cut on the curl of* s (*erasure?*).   22
first þat: t *partially erased.*   god: *MS.* godde *with* de *expuncted.*   25
Erasure between ȝif *and* were. *Space for* 2–3 *letters* (he?).   26 *Erasure
between* þat *and* ne. *Space for* 2–3 *letters* (he?).   31–2 heiȝer . . . han:
repetition of heiȝer . . . han 30–1.

he god þat he sette hym þere þat it is best for hym. ꝛ kepe hym
þan from Meridiane þe deuel þat wil schewe hym to hym as a
goode Aungel. ꝛ so bigileþ he many. And Poule clepeþ hym
Aungel of liȝth. þere ben two manere of wymmen þat ben
trewe prelates and prechoures. þise two hane þe heiȝest dale in 5
heuene. And ȝef he be proude. coueitouse oiþer leccherous and
loseniour. als longe as he vseþ any of þise synnes. he is a fals
prophete and heretike and ypocrite. ꝛ on of antecristes prophetes
and his prechoure seint Iohn þe ewangelist it seiþ in þe Apocalips. And þerfor vche man þat wil queme god kepe hym from 10
swich. þat oþer dale is to alle men þat kepeþ hem hem clene out
of synne ꝛ þus seint iame distinkteþ ordre noiþer white ne blak
Ac ofte he seiþ in þis booke þe gnat sweloweþ þe flee. Poule þe
first onelich man. nouȝth Poule þe Apostle. Aresine. Makeryne.
Sare. Sincletice and many oþer wiþ her grete Matten þat hij 15
layen inne ꝛ hard hayren. neren nouȝth þise of goode ordre.
Many wenen þat þe ordre sitteþ in þe couel oiþer in þe kirtel.
nay it nys nouȝth so. Ac hij mowen boþe wel weren And goddes
spouse sitteþ by hym seluen and syngeþ. Nigra sum set formosa.
℟ Ich am blak and fair. Foul wiþ outen ꝛ vnworþi to þe werlde. 20
briȝth ꝛ schene wiþinne. And þus ansuereþ to þe askers and
M. 12) seiþ þat ȝe ben blake þorouȝ þe grace of god ꝛ of seint Iames
ordre þat he wrott last.
Inmaculatum se custodire ab hoc seculo. ℟ þat is he þat kepeþ
hym clene ꝛ vnwemmed fram þe filþe of þis werlde þat is riȝth 25
ordre Ac þere many ben to gedre ꝛ ben cloþed in o cloþing in
tokne þat hij schulden be of on wille ꝛ on loue. ꝛ vche wil as oþer
wil And þus it is in couent. Looke now þat hij ne leiȝe nouȝth
And ȝif þat hij ne beþ nouȝth so. it nys bot treccherie ꝛ gyle,
Hem were better to kepen swyne oiþer gees. Michee þe pro- 30
phete askeþ what is ordre and ansuereþ hym self þerto ꝛ seiþ
þus.
Indicabo tibi o homo quid sit bonum. ꝛ quid deus requiret a te
vtique facere iudicium ꝛ iusticiam ꝛ solicite ambulare cum
domino deo tuo. ℟ Ichil seie þe he seiþ what god askeþ of þee 35
man do wele ꝛ deme þat euere þi seluen be þe werst. ꝛ folowȝe
god in loue ꝛ in drede. And þere þis is. þere is riȝth ordre ꝛ

7 loseniour: l *blotted.*   11 hem hem, *sic dittography.*   14 Aresine, *sic for* Arsenie.   20 vnworpi: wo *partially erased.*   27 wil: wi
probably on erasure.   30 oiþer *on erasure.*   35 he: h *partially erased.*

p. 373a riȝth religioun ⁊ elles it nys non ordre | ne no Religioun seint
Mathew seiþ.
Ve vobis Scribe. Pharisei. Ypocrite. qui mundatis quod deforis
est calicis ⁊ par aspidis. intus autem pleni omni spurcicia similes
sepulchris dealbatis.   5
℄ Seint Matheu seiþ in þe godspel. Acursed be ȝe ypocrites þat
maken fair wiþouten and ben þornes wiþinne. for ȝe ben liche
þe beriels þat is whited wiþ outen and roten þing wiþinne. Al
þat euere goode religious doþe oiþer wereþ it is goode for it is
bot a stole to tymber wiþ þe innere reule þat reuleþ þe hert.   10
Now ich to deele þis booke on viij distynctiouns þat ich clepe
(M. 14) parties. and vchone spekeþ by hym self of sunderlich þinges. ⁊
vchone falleþ after oþer. ⁊ þe latter ytied euere to þe first þe
first deel spekeþ of ȝoure seruise. þat oþer is hou ȝe schulle wiþ
fyue wittes witen wel ȝoure hert þat ordre ⁊ riȝth Religioun ⁊   15
soule lyf liþe inne. And in þise parties beþ chapiters fyue after
þe fyue wittes þat witeþ þe hert as wakemen þat ben trewe. þe
þridde deel is of al manere filþes. And þe fierþe deel of fleschlich
fondynges and gostlich boþe and confort aȝeins hem ⁊ salue. þe
fift deel is of schrift. þe sexte of Penaunce. þe seuenþe of schire 20
hert whi men owen to loue god ⁊ hou. þe eiȝtteþ deel is al of þe
vtter reule. hou eten. hou drynken. and þat falleþ þerto. ⁊ what
þinges ȝe mowen vnderfonge ⁊ helden ⁊ haue. þere after of cloþes
⁊ of ȝoure werkes. as schauynge. polling and bloode letynge.
Amorowe whan ȝe ariseþ. blisseþ ȝou ⁊ seiþ. In nomine patris 25
⁊ filij ⁊ spiritus sancti Amen, And bigynneþ onon. Veni creator
(M. 16) spiritus, wiþ þe versett. ⁊ þe orisoun wiþ vp heueande honden ⁊
eiȝen toward þe heuen. bowȝeand on knewes. þere after als ȝe
diȝtte ȝou seiþ alway. Domine ihesu christe fili dei viui miserere
nobis qui de virgine dignatus es nasci miserere nobis. ℄ And 30
seiþ þise woordes al way til þat ȝe ben diȝth. ⁊ haueþ þise wordes
mychel in vse wheþer ȝe gon or ȝe sitten. als often as ȝe may
þenchen þere vpon. And whan ȝe ben al diȝth. springeþ on ȝou
haly water ȝif ȝe it haue And þencheþ on goddes flesche and his

1 *At the top of page in Stephen Batman's hand in black ink*: An olde supersticius
rule which requireth wisely too be readd / of the Masse. & purgatorie.
3 Matheus *in left margin in red ink.*   4 par aspidis, *sic for* parapsidis.
10 a stole, *sic for* as tole.   *After this paragraph in Stephen Batman's hand
in black ink*: Weray trim, to qualifye a Papist   15 hert: *thin cut (erasure?)*
between e *and* r.   16 þise parties, *sic.*   18 al manere filþes: *Corpus has*
anes cunnes fuheles *4b: 1.*   31 diȝth: *long vertical downstroke under* ȝ.

derworþi bloode whan ȝe comen toforne an autere and siggeþ
þise gretynges, ⁊ ȝif ȝe haue none autere makeþ an autere of
ȝoure hert as god biddeþ makeþ myne autere of erþe.
Aue principium nostre creacionis.   Tu esto nostrum gau-
Aue precium nostre redempcionis.   dium qui es futurus   5
Aue viaticum nostre peregrinacionis. premium. sit nostra in te
Aue premium nostre expectacionis. gloria per cuncta semper se-
Aue gaudium nostre glorificacionis. cula. Amen. Mane no-
biscum domine noctem obscuram remoue omne delictum ablue. |

p. 373b   piam medelam tribue. Gloria tibi domine qui natus es de vir-   10
gine cum patre ⁊ sancto spiritu in sempiterna secula Amen.
⟨ And also seiþ þise atte leuacioun of þe Messe. ⁊ also after
ȝoure Confiteor. whan ȝe ben yhouseled. And after falleþ on
knewes bifore þe heiȝe roode wiþ þise gretynges in monyinge of
þe fyue woundes þat he suffred for ȝou.   15

(M. 18)   Adoramus te domine ⁊ benedicimus tibi quia per sanctam
crucem tuam redemisti mundum Tuam crucem adoramus. qui
passus es pro nobis. Salue crux sancta. O crux lignum. ⟨ And
wiþ þise woordes beteþ ȝoure breest, Et quod non valet vis
humana sit in tuo nomine, And who so ne cunne þe fyue·' seie þe   20
first Adoramus til he cunne þe oþer fyue. fyue siþes kneleande.
⁊ blisse ȝou wiþ vchone of þise gretynges. ⁊ wiþ þise woordes.
Miserere nostri qui passus es pro nobis, beteþ ȝoure breest ⁊
kysseþ þe erþe ⁊ croyce it wiþ ȝoure þombe. And þere after
greteþ oure lefdy wiþ fyue Auees. And after to alle Halewen.   25
And þo halewen þat ȝe han most sett ȝoure hert vpon. vnto þe
auter þe raþer ȝif it is yhalewed. And þere after onon riȝth
siggeþ oure lefdy Matyns on þis wise. Ȝif it is werkeday falleþ to
þe erþe. And ȝif it is haly day boweþ sumdel dounward wiþ þe.
Pater noster. ⁊ þe. credo. and þe. Aue Maria. And þan hastilich   30
riȝtteþ ȝou vpward att. Domine labia mea Aperies, And makeþ
on ȝoure mouþ a croice wiþ þe þombe. ⁊ att. Deus in adiutorium,
a large croice wiþ þe þombe ⁊ wiþ two fyngers from þe forhede
doun to þe breest. And falleþ to þe erþe ȝif it is werkeday wiþ.
Gloria patri, ⁊ ȝif it is haliday boweþ dounward. ⁊ þus doþe at   35
(M. 20)   vche. Gloria patri. and at þe gynnyng of þe. Venite, ⁊ att. Venite
adoremus. ⁊ att Aue maria, ⁊ whare ȝe hereþ her name kneleþ or
louteþ. and att. Ihesu. also. ⁊ att vche. Pater noster, þat falleþ to

---

3 myne: *the scribe first wrote* n *for* y. *Irregular [stroke on left minim of* n.
21 fyue¹, *sic for* foure.   26 most: o *and* s *crammed together*.

þe houres ⁊ euerych tyde. and atte last vers of euerylch psalme ⁊
of euerylch ympne wiþ outen o psalme. Benedicite,. . At alle
þise ʒif it is haly day bowʒeþ adounward ⁊ ʒif it is werkeday
falleþ to þe erþe ⁊ at euerylch tyde att. Deus in adiutorium,
makeþ a croice as i haue seide. ⁊ wiþ. Memento, falleþ euere 5
adoune. ⁊ wiþ þise woordes. Nascendo formam sumpseris. ⁊
kysseþ þe erþe. and also in Te deum laudamus. att. non abhor-
ruisti virginis vtcrum. and in þe Messe crede. at. ex Maria
virgine and att. homo factus est, kisseþ þe erþe and seiþ ʒoure
tydes sunderlich as forþ as ʒe may. In his tyme. Matyns by 10
niʒth in wynter. In somer in þe daweynge, þe wynter bigynneþ
at holy roode tyde in heruest and lasteþ vnto ester. Pryme in
wynter erlich. In somer by forþe Mornes and. Preciosa. þere
after. ʒif ʒe haue nede to speken ʒe may siggen it biforne onon
p. 374a after Matyns ʒif it so nedeþ ⁊ elles nouʒth, | Onon after mete 15
whan ʒe hane sleptte while þe Somer lasteþ ⁊ in wynter also
seiþ þe tyde of None at þe nynþe houre. And euere att o psalme
sitteþ ⁊ att anoþer stondeþ ʒif ʒe ben in eise þerto forto done it
(M. 22) whan ʒe eten twies. ⁊ euere wiþ. Gloria patri. Ariseþ oiþer
kneleþ ⁊ att euerych tyde seiþ a. Pater noster. atte gynnynge and 20
an. Aue. and att þre tydes seiþ ʒoure. Crede, Att Matyns. Att
Pryme. ⁊ att complyn. with þe. Pater noster. And after. Preciosa.
holdeþ silence ʒif ʒe may. ne spekeþ bot to god oiþer of hym to
hem þat hane wille to heren it. ⁊ of his Moder Marie. saieþ
ʒoure Placebo tofore complyn And Dirige after wiþ þre lessons. 25
⁊ ʒif ʒe ben on eyse seiþ alle nyne. And namelich ʒif it be haly
day ⁊ feste of ix lessons. Vche niʒth for alle cristene soules and
for ʒoure frendes soules. ⁊ þere ʒe schulden seie Gloria patri. ʒe
schullen seie. Requiem eternam etc., Att. Placebo. sitteþ. att.
Magnificat. stondeþ. ⁊ atte Dirige, sitteþ bott atte Lessons ⁊ 30
Miserere mei deus. ⁊ fram. Deus misereatur nostri stondeþ al out.
⁊ att. Benedictus. ⁊ atte Orisouns. on niʒth oiþer in þe Mornynge
after þe suffrages seiþ þe commendacioun, sittande. kneleande.
oiþer stoondande þe Orisouns, þe seuen psalmes seiþ kneleande
oiþer stondende wiþ þe Letany, att vndertyde. oiþer whan þe 35
preestes done parisch Messe ⁊ þe fiftene psalmes ʒif ʒe willeþ

---

16 sleptte: *irregular sign above* p.   22 Pater: Pa *probably on erasure.*
23–4 to hem *written above line and marked for insertion.*   26 nyne
on erasure.   30 Dirige: D *partially erased.*   31 misereatur: isereatur
on erasure.   33 commendacioun: commen *on erasure.*

oiþer whan ȝe comeþ in to chirche as oure lefdy dude. þere
were fyftene Greces in þe comynge in to þe Temple. ⁊ att
vchone sche seide a psalme at hire comynge in to þe Temple.
þan seiþ þem on þis wise. þe first fyue for ȝoure seluen. þe
oþer fyue for holy chirche þat is for alle cristen men. And þe 5
þridde fyue. for alle þe soules þat ben in Purgatorie. þe first
fyue wiþ. Gloria patri. Kyrie eleyson. christe eleyson. Kyrie
eleyson. Pater noster. Saluos fac seruos tuos ⁊ ancillas tuas
M. 24) et cetera. oracio. Deus cui proprium est misereri semper ⁊
parcere et cetera, þat oþer fyue wiþ. kyrie eleyson. christe eley- 10
son. kyrie eleyson. Pater. Aue. Domine fiat pax in virtute tua.
oracio Ecclesie tue quesumus domine preces placatus admitte,
etc. þe þridde fyue. wiþ Requiem eternam. Kirie eleyson christe
eleyson. Kyrie eleyson. A porta inferi. Erue domine animas
eorum. oracio. Fidelium deus omnium conditor. et cetera. Alle 15
Religiouse auȝtten to ben in bedes in þat vche tyme þat ihesus
crist suffred pyne for vs, on þis wise ȝe may ȝif ȝe wil sigge
M. 26) ȝoure pater nostres Al miȝtty god fader ⁊ son ⁊ holy gost as ȝe
ben þre Persones in o god and as ȝe ben of miȝth. of wisdom. ⁊
of loue. ⁊ þat miȝth in holy wrytt is turned to þe fader. ⁊ wisdom 20
p. 374b to þe son. ⁊ loue to þe holy gost ȝiue me o reule | in þise þre
þinges. myȝth forto serue þe. wisdom forto knowe þe. loue ⁊
wille forto doute þe. myȝth þat ich may do wisdom þat ich
cunne do. loue þat ich wil do al þat þe leeuest is. as þou art
floure of al goodenesse. And also wisse as þere nys no godenesse 25
wane þere þise þre ben. myȝth. wisdom. ⁊ looue. yfestned to
gedres. þat þo ȝeete in me þe holy Trinete. þre. Pater nostres.
and þre. Auees. Versiculus. Benedicamus patrem ⁊ filium cum
sancto spiritu. et cetera. oracio. Omnipotens sempiterne deus
qui dedisti nobis famulis tuis. 30
Ihesu crist þine ore for myne synnes þou hongedest on roode.ʹ
for þo ilch fyue woundes þat þou on erþe bleddest hele my
blody soule þat ich am wiþ ywounded þorouȝ myne fyue wittes
in þe worschipp of þine fyue woundes. ⁊ þat it mote so be fyue
Pater nostres. ⁊ fyue Auees. Omnis terra adoret te deus. et 35
M. 28) cetera. oracio. Deus qui sanctam crucem ascendisti.

17 on: *between* o *and* n *space for 2–3 letters. No traces of erasure between the
letters.* 18 miȝtty: *smudge of red ink on* m. 19 of miȝht. of wisdom,
sic for on miȝht. on wisdom. 20 of loue, *sic for* on loue. þat: *Corpus:* þah *7a: 2.* 21 o reule: *Corpus:* an almihti godd þrile *7a: 4.*
27 Pater: Pat *on erasure.* 28 Auees *on erasure.*

For þe seuene ȝiftes of þe holy gost þat vchon mote habben. and
for þe seuen tydes þat men reden ⁊ syngen in holy chirche þat
ich mote in hem slepen or waken. And for þe seue boonen in þe
Pater noster aȝein þe seuen dedlich synnes þat þou witie me wiþ
þem and wiþ alle her braunches. And ȝiue me þe seuen heienes- 5
ses þat þou haste bihoten þine chosen in þe blisse of heuene.
seuen. Pater nostres. ⁊ seuen. Auees. Emitte spiritum tuum ⁊
creabuntur. et cctcra. oracio. Deus cui omne cor patet. et cetera.
oracio. Ecclesie tue quesumus domine et cetera. oracio. Exaudi
quesumus domine supplicum preces. et cetera.   10
For þe ten hestes þat ich haue broken summe oiþer alle. and
vntreulich tiþed in bote. of þat ilche breche forto sauȝtten wiþ
þee derworþi lorde, ten pater nosters. ⁊ ten auees. versiculus.
Ego dixi domine miserere mei et cetera. oracio. Deus cui proprium est misereri. et cetera.   15
In þe worschipp of þee lorde ⁊ of þi moder Marie and Peter ⁊
Poule. ⁊ alle þine Apostles þat I mote oueral folowe her lore. ⁊
(M. 30) þorouȝ her praier haue þe twelue bouȝes þat blosmen of charite
as seint Poule writeþ derworþe lorde. twelue. Pater nostres. ⁊
twelue. Auees. Annunciauerunt opera dei et cetera. oracio. 20
Exaudi nos deus noster apostolorum et cetera.
Lorde in þe worschipp of þee ⁊ of þi moder Marie ⁊ alle þine
Halewen fyue. Pater nostres. ⁊ fyue. Aues. Letamini in domino et
cetera. oracio. Omnium sanctorum intercessorum et cetera.
For alle þe Men ⁊ wymmen þat me any harme han done oiþer 25
seide. oiþer wolde. lorde ȝif it be þi suete wille forȝiue it hem.
And for alle þat me any goode han done. oiþer seide. oiþer
wolde suete lorde helpe hem ȝif it is þi wille. And for alle þat
wirchen þe seuen werkes of Mercy. Ad te leuaui. Kyrie eleyson.
Christe eleyson. Kyrie eleyson. seue pater nostres. ⁊ seuen 30
Auees. Dispersit dedit pauperibus. Retribuere dignare.
For alle þat ben seek ⁊ sory ⁊ for alle þat ben in prisoun in
p. 375a cristendom ⁊ in heþenesse of | cristen folk. ⁊ for alle þat ben in
stronge temptacioun. ⁊ for alle þat ben in goode lyf þat god
helde hem þere inne. ⁊ þo þat ben in oþer god amende hem ȝif 35
it his wille be. fyue. pater nostres. ⁊ fyue. Auees. Leuaui oculos
meos. kyrie eleyson christe eleyson. kyrie eleyson. Conuertere
domine vsquequo. Pretende domine misericordiam.

---

1 vchon: *Corpus*: ich ham *7a: 23.*   33 *At the top of the page in Stephen
Batman's hand in black ink*: Supersticion

For alle þe soules þat ben forþ faren in þe bileeue of þe foure
godspellers þat holden vp al cristendom. ⁊ in þe heiȝenesse of þe
nyne woordes þat men clepen þe nyne ordres of aungels. nyne.
Pater nostres. and ix Auees. De profundis clamaui. Kyrie
eleyson. christe eleyson. kyrie eleyson. pater noster. Requiem 5
eternam. Fidelium deus omnium conditor.

(M. 32)　Atte Messe whan þe preest heueþ vp goddes flesch and his
bloode siggeþ þis Aue salus mundi. verbum patris. hostia vera.
viua caro. deitas integra. verus homo. and þan falleþ adoune
wiþ þise gretynges. Aue principium nostre creacionis. Tu esto 10
nostrum gaudium, Mane nobiscum domine. Gloria tibi domine.
Siquis est locus est in me quo veniat in me deus meus. quo
veniat deus aut maneat in me deus qui fecit celum ⁊ terram.
Ita ne domine est quicquam in me quod capiat te. quis michi
dabit vt venias in cor meum ⁊ inebries illud. vt bonum vinum 15
amplector te quid michi es. miserere. misere. Meserere mei
deus secundum magnam misericordiam tuam, al out þe psalme ⁊
(M. 34)　atte ende. Gloria patri. christe audi nos. twies. pater noster.
Credo. carnis resureccionem. Saluum fac populum tuum domine. doce me facere voluntatem tuam. Domine exaudi oracionem 20
meam. Et clamor meus ad te veniat.
Concede quesumus omnipotens deus vt quem enigmatice ⁊ sub
aliena specie concernimus quo sacramentaliter cibamur in
terris facie ⁊ faciem eum videamus eo securi est veraciter ⁊
realiter frui mereamur in celis. per eundem dominum nostrum. 25
et cetera. ⸿ After þe Messe kysseþ þe erþe. forȝeteþ al þe
werlde ⁊ beþ out of ȝoure seluen þere is sprinkelynge of loue
þere biclyppeþ ȝoure lemman in to ȝoure breestes boure þat is
liȝth of heuene and holdeþ hym fast forto þat ȝe haue geten of
hym al þat ȝe willen.　　　　　　　　　　　　　　　　　　30
Aboute Midday who so may þencheþ þan on goddes roode. as
mychel as he mest may. oiþer can. ⁊ on his pyne. ⁊ his passioun.
and bigynneþ þo ilch fyue gretynges þat ben wryten toforne. ⁊
also kneleþ to vchone and blisseþ ȝou as it seiþ. ⁊ beteþ ȝoure
breest and makeþ a wiselich boone.　　　　　　　　　　　35
Adoramus te christe ⁊ benedicimus tibi Tuam crucem adoramus. Salue crux sancta. O crux lignum. ⁊ ariseþ þan ⁊ bigynneþ

---

7 flesch: *upper part of* h *blotted.*　　12 Siquis est locus est, *sic for* Sed
quis est locus.　　24 ⁊¹, *sic for* ad.　　securi, *sic for* sicuti.　　29 fast:
written above line between hym *and* forto.

þe Anteme. Salua nos christe per virtutem. wiþ þe token. ⁊
(M. 36) siggeþ stondynge þis psalme. Iubilate. wiþ. Gloria patri. ⁊ þan
þe anteme euer þus. Salua nos christe. and blisseþ ȝou wiþ. qui
saluasti petrum in mari miserere nobis. and beteþ ȝoure breest.
⁊ þan falleþ doun ⁊ siggeþ. christe audi nos. Ihesu christe audi 5
p. 375b nos. kyrie eleyson. christe eleyson. | Kyrie eleyson. Pater noster.
⁊ ne nos. Protector noster aspice. ⁊ respice deus faciem christi
tui. Deus qui sanctam crucem ascendisti. And eft bigynneþ.
Adoramus. as ȝe dude bifore þe psalme. and þe orisoun ⁊ þe
anteme. and þus seiþ þise fyue psalmes. Iubilate. Ad te leuaui, 10
Qui confidunt. Domine non est exaltatum. Laudate dominum.
in sanctis eius. In vchone of þise psalmes ben fyue verses. þe
orisouns. Deus qui sanctam crucem. Adesto domine deus qui
pro nobis. Deus qui vnigeniti. Iuste iudex. wiþ. O beata trinitas.
(M. 38) And who so ne cunne þise fyue. so seie he euere on til he cunne 15
þe oþer. ⁊ ȝif hem þenche to longe. so leten hij þe psalmes, and
þus ȝe mowen saien ȝoure auees ȝif ȝe willen.
Lefdy seint Marie for þat ilch mychel blisse þat þou haddest
inwiþ þe in þat ilch tyme þat Ihesus crist goddes son took
flesch ⁊ bloode in þe ⁊ of þe after þe aungels gretynge vnderfonge 20
þise gretynges of me wiþ þat ilch. Aue, ⁊ make me to telle litel of
my selue. ⁊ of vche blisse outewiþ. and enfourme me inwiþ and
erne me þe blisse of heuene als wisse as in þilk flessche þat he
took of þe nas neuer no synne ne in þine as ich leeue clense my
soule of fleschlich synnes ⁊ bygynne þe. Aue. to. dominus 25
tecum. in stede of Anteme. ⁊ after þe psalme al out. Magnificat.
fyue siþes ȝif þat ȝe wil seiþ. ⁊ after vchone an. aue. þe anteme.
Spiritus sanctus superueniet in te. Aue maria. graciam tuam
quesumus domine mentibus nostris infunde. et cetera.
Lefdy seint Mary for þat ilch mychel blisse þat þou haddest 30
whan þou seiȝ þi blisful son borne of þi clene body to maken
hele wiþ þine holy maydenhede ⁊ moderhede. halewe me þat
am þorouȝ wille broken ⁊ þorouȝ dede. ⁊ ȝiue me grace in heuene
to see þi blisful lore and þi Maidenes worschipp. ȝif it be þi
swete sones wille. to make me worþi to be blissed in her felaw- 35

---

3 Salua nos *on erasure.*   7 *Small hole in MS. after* respice.   16 *last
minim of* m *and* e *in* psalmes *blurred.*   28 graciam: *between* g *and* r *space
for 2–3 letters.* g *unusually small. No traces of erasure.*   34 Maidenes:
last e *written above line (at end of line).*

rede Aue maria. Ad dominum cum tribularer. Aue regina
celorum aue domina angelorum. Egredietur virga de radice
Iesse. Deus qui virginalem aulam.
Lefdy seint Marie for þat ilch mychel blisse þat þou haddest
þo þou sei3 þi derworþe son after his deþ arisen to blisful lyf. 5
his body bri3tter þan þe sunne. leene me to day wiþ hym arisen.
bodilch dy3en gostlich lyuen in þi felauschipp on ende forto ben
in blisse wiþ hym in heuene. for þat ilch mychel blisse þat þou
(M. 40) haddest leuedy of his blisful arysynge. after my sorou3es þat ich
am inne lede me to blisse. Aue maria. Retribue seruo tuo. and 10
fyue Auees, al out. Gaude dei genetrix virgo inmaculata. Ecce
virgo concipiet ⁊ pariet filium. ⁊ vocabitur nomen eius emanuel.
Deus qui de beate Marie virginis vtero.
Lefdy seint Marie for þat ilch mychel blisse þat þou haddest þo
þou sei3 þi blisful son þat þe iewes þrussschen and duden to 15
p. 376a deþe. ⁊ wenden haue wrou3th wiþ | hym as wiþ anoþer man wiþ
outen hope of vp arisynge sei3 hym wurþilich ⁊ semelich
stei3e vp to þe blisse of heuene on holy þursday.· 3iue me grace
to werpe wiþ hym al þe werlde vnder foote ⁊ stei3e wiþ hym
hei3elich whan i dy3e gostlich on domesday bodilich to þe 20
heuene riche blisse, Aue maria. In conuertendo. fyue Aues.
Gaude virgo gaude dei. Ecce concipies in vtero ⁊ paries filium ⁊
vocabis nomen eius Ihesum, Deus qui salutis eterne.
Lefdy seint Mary for þat ilch mychel blis þat fulfild al þe
werlde of blis ⁊ vnderfenge þe in his vnimete blis ⁊ wiþ hise blis- 25
ful armes sett þe in þi throne ⁊ quenes croune vpon þine heued
bri3tter þan þe sunne. heuenlich quene vnderfonge þise gretynges of me here on erþe. þat i may blisfullich grete þe in heuene.
(M. 42) Aue Maria. Ad te leuaui, fyue Auees. And here saiþ forþe
3oure Auees an hundreþ oiþer fyfty. oiþer þries fyfty, Alma 30
redemptoris mater. Ecce ancilla domini. O sancta virgo virgi-
num, oiþer. O Maria piissima, 3if 3e wil 3e may saie vche
psalme fyue siþes. for þe psalmes beþ nempned after oure
leuedies name after þe fyue lettres who so nymeþ 3eme. and alle
þise fyue orisouns after hire hei3est blisses. ⁊ so it erneþ by fyue 35
And telle þe Antemes and þou schalt fynde in hem fyue gretynge

---

5 Small hole in MS. after and below son.   7 bodilch, sic for bodilich.   felauschipp: pp crammed together.   on ende, sic for on erþe.
13 vtero: small crack in parchment over r.   18 Small hole in MS.
(mentioned at p. 12 l. 7) after stei3e.   19 m expuncted and crossed out
with thin stroke after hym¹.

(M. 44) ȝif ȝe willeþ seggen hem doþe write hem. And vche man sigge as hym bereþ on hert best: for þe more þat a man dooþe þe more grace god hym ȝiueþ. Ac looke euere þat noman ydel be Ac wirche oiþer bidde. Ac looke þat he do euer sumwhatt þat god may oft awaken. þe houres of þe holy gost ȝif ȝe willeþ 5 siggen hem siggeþ vche tyde of hem bifore oure leuedies tyde. ȝoure graces siggeþ stondynge bifore Mete. ⁊ after as ȝe owe. and wiþ þe. Miserere. goþ toforne ȝoure autere and whan ȝe drynken blisseþ it. ⁊ seiþ þus, Benedicite dominus. Potum nostrum filius dei benedicat. In nomine patris ⁊ filij ⁊ spiritus 10 sancti Amen, And blisseþ ȝou afterward wiþ Adiutorium nostrum in nomine domini. Qui fecit celum ⁊ terram. Sit nomen domini benedictum. Ex hoc nunc ⁊ vsque in seculum.

whan ȝe go to bedd aniȝth oiþer in þe euenynge falleþ on knees and þencheþ what ȝe hane þat day done and trespassed aȝeins 15 oure lorde ⁊ crieþ hym ȝerne mercy and forȝiuenesse. ⁊ ȝif ȝe hane any goode dede done. þonkeþ hym of his ȝifte. for wiþ outen hym ȝe may noþing wel done ne þenchen. ⁊ siggeþ Miserere mei deus. kyrie eleyson. christe eleyson. kyrie eleyson. Pater noster. Credo. carnis resureccionem. Saluos fac seruos 20 tuos ⁊ Ancillas tuas. Deus cui proprium est et cetera. stondynge seiþ þis. Visita domine habitacionem istam. And (M. 46) after wiþ þre croices in þe forhede wiþ þe þombe. christus vincit. christus regnat. christus imperat. and þan wiþ a large croice as att. Deus in adiutorium. wiþ þis clause, Ecce crucem 25 p. 376b domini fugite partes aduerse vicit leo de tribu | Iuda. radix dauid Alleluya, And þan foure crosses wiþ þise foure clauses, crux fugiat omne malignum. Crux est reparacio rerum. Per crucis hoc signum fugiat procul omne malignum. Et per idem signum saluetur quodque benignum, And after þat. In nomine 30 patris ⁊ filij, et cetera, on ȝoure self ⁊ on ȝoure bedde. ⁊ as forþ as ȝe may ne do ȝe nouȝth bot sleepe.

Hij þat ne cunnen nouȝth her Matyns siggeþ hij her pater noster. þritty for Matyns and þritty. Auees, And after vchone.

---

2 dooþe: *second o possibly written over an original e.* *Below this line left part of page slightly worn away resulting in certain 'shine-through' of letters.* 5 oft, *sic for* of. 14 whan: *space between* w *and* h *left for coloured initial. Parchment particularly worn round* w. to: *hole in parchment* (*mentioned at 13:4*) *where* o *was written. Only upper part of letter visible.* 23 croices: *small crack between* e *and* s (*mentioned at p. 13 l. 13*). 33–4 pater noster. þritty *on erasure.*

Gloria patri. ʒif hij cunne. ⁊ an orisoun who so can. concede
nos. oiþer. Deus cui proprium. Benedicamus domino. Deo
gracias. ⁊ anime omnium fidelium defunctorum, At þe endynge
of vche tyde þat ʒe saie or what ʒe seie lateþ euere þat be þe
laste woorde ⁊. Benedicite dominus. Deus det viuis graciam. 5
defunctis veniam ⁊ requiem, etc. At euensong seiþ twenty. att
vche tyde fyftene. ⁊ att Matyns seiþ. Domine labia mea aperies.
Deus in adiutorium. And at vche tyde. Deus in adiutorium. Att
complyn. conuerte nos, byfore. Deus in adiutorium. as me
doþe at þe seruise of oure lefdy. In stede of þe seuene psalmes. 10
þritty pater nostres. and. Auees. In stede of þe fyftene psalmes.
fyftene. pater nostres. and. Auees. and euere. Gloria patri. atte
nende. Atte commendacioun þritty. pater nostres. and. Auees,
Atte. placebo. ten. atte. Dirige. twenti. pater nostres. ⁊ Auees
Who so is seek lete of half. ⁊ ʒif he is riʒth seek lete of al. and 15
take his sekenesse in þolemodenesse. ⁊ gladlich. And also herieþ
þat holy chirche redeþ and syngeþ in vche tyme as it owe to ben
yseide. And lokeþ þat ʒoure þouʒttes ne be nouʒth flyttande.
þan ʒif ʒe for ʒemeleshede forgluffeþ wordes oiþer mysnymeþ
verses. leneþ ʒou doune to þe erþe wiþ þe honde. And for 20

M. 48) mysnymynge scheweþ oft in schrift ʒoure ʒemeleshede. þis is
now þe first dale of þis booke.

V Che man fonde to keepe þe tydes. Midniʒth þe Mornynge.
Pryme. Vnderne. Midday, None. Euensonge. and complyn,
Att Midniʒth: þencheþ ⁊ haueþ in mynde. hou ihesus crist was 25
borne of his moder. And þan he took out of helle his chosen. And
att Midniʒth. he schal ʒiue þe dome, as cassiodre þe Pope seiþ.
for þat tyme in Egipt he slouʒ al þe first biʒete of Man and beste
whan he ladde forþ his folk, And in þe. Mornynge. þenk hou þe
Iewes pleied wiþ hym abobbed. and atte Morowen. he aros fram 30
deþ to lyue bitwene þe niʒth and þe day. And seint Austin seiþ
þat þan he speke first. Att Pryme. haue in mynde hou he schewed
hym to þe Maudeleyne. and he was brouʒth bifore þe Barre
tofore Pilate And how Pilate acouped hym. þis Pryme. is þe
first houre after þe sunne arisynge. whan þe day ⁊ þe niʒth beþ 35
yliche longe. þat is twelue houres in þe day and twelue in þe
p. 377a niʒth. And ʒif þat ʒe wil keepe | þise houres. waiteþ euere Somer

16 in *expuncted after* take *and crossed out with thin stroke. Another* in
written above line and marked for insertion after sekenesse.   25 þencheþ,
thin vertical stroke through þe.   37 *Several initial letters ornamented
with red between p. 15 l. 37 and p. 17 l. 15.*

and Wynter whan þe sonne is euen in þe Est ⁊ þan take to þine
houre att Prime. þe first houre after and parte so þine houres til
þou come til þi twelue houres. and make at þi twelueþ houre
complyn. as forþ as þou may gessen it. And ȝif þou haue wille to
done it.· god wil wissen þe hou þou may best queme hym. 5
And þan þe tweie houres after pryme. is cleped Vnderne.
þenche þan hou he sent wytt ⁊ wisdom in to his Apostles and
hou he was scourged atte Pyler and crouned wiþ þornes bitwene. Vnderne. and. Midday. þat is þe þridde houre after þat
men clepeþ in holy chirche þe sext houre þat is þe Middel of þe 10
day. whan þe sunne is att þe heiȝest of þe day. he henge vpon
þe roode for vs. and þat tyme he took flesche and bloode of þat
houre haueþ in mynde as mychel as ȝe may. ⁊ þencheþ opon his
passioun. and þencheþ it is þe hattest of þe day. and bitokneþ
þat his loue was hote and brennande vn to vs. and so schulde 15
oure loue be to hym ȝif we loued hym ariȝth as we auȝtten to
done. And þe þridde houre after Midday. þat is cleped. hora
nona. þe nynþe houre ihesus crist ȝaf vp his gost in to his fader
hondes and þan he bisouȝth for hem þat duden hym to þe deþ
þat ne wisten nouȝth what hij duden þat were þe symple folk. 20
for þe clerkes wisten wel in her hertes þat he was goddes son by
his wordes and by his werkes. Ac þan her hertes weren so
harded in synne þat hij hadden lorne þe knowynge of hym.
And þan an houre bifore þat þe sonne go doune in þe west þat
is þe. elleuenþe houre. þan he made his sopeere: and turned 25
þan his blissed body in to bred and his bloode in to wyne and
ȝaf it to his deciples. and þan he was taken adoune of þe roode.
þe twelueþe houre. is complyn whan þe sunne goþ adoun euen
in þe west, and þan he was buried. And þat tyme he swatt
bloode and water vpon þe Mount of Olyuete and made his 30
bisechynge to his fader. And Salamon seiþ. Sowe þi sede att
Morne and wiþdrawe nouȝth þine hande att euene for þou
noste wheþer schal sooner come vp. for ȝif þat on faileþ þat
oþer wil come vp And ȝif hij comen boþe so mychel is þe better
for þan he seiþ þou schal gadre þe more fruyt By seede is 35

1–2 þine houre: þine hou crammed together at end of line.   25 elleuenþe
houre on erasure.   26 to bred and in to wyne underlined in the black ink
that is used for the words you fayle, written on the same line between the two
columns of the page in Stephen Batman's hand.   31 Salamon. in left margin in red ink.

bitokned goddes woorde, Bidde to god in þe Mornynge. þat is
þe seede þat þou schalt sowe for þan is best tyme. and wiþdrawe
þe noȝth in þe euene tyde. for ȝif þou spede noȝth at þat on þou
schalt at þat oþer. Nou þise houres þat ich haue spoken of. vche
p. 377b man þat haþ taken cristendom owe to haue hem in mynde. | as 5
forþ as he may oiþer in þouȝth oiþer in dede. þat is be in biddynge. and wite ȝe wel who so haþ hem in mynde wiþ goode
wille. god nyl nouȝth leten þat he ne wil helpen hym att his
nede and teche hym as is best for hym boþe to lyf ⁊ to soule.
Nou to þe houres of þe day men may comen bot nouȝth to þe 10
houres of þe Planeetes. for þat tyme he was pyned. þe houres of
þe Planeetes acorden wiþ þe houres of þe day. þe Planeetes ben
þat þe dayes in þe weeke ben cleped after þat is þe sonne and þe
Mone and þe fyue sterres þat stonden lowȝer þan any oþere
sterres. Biddeþ for hym þat þis ordeinde ⁊ made for þe loue 15
of god, Here endeþ þe first Book.

OMni custodia custodi cor tuum quia ex ipso vita procedit
    ⟨ Wiþ al manere warde witeþ wel ȝoure hert for soule lyf
is in hir ȝif sche is wel ywited. þe het wardeyns ben þe fyue
wyttes. ⟨ Seiȝeynge, Spekynge, Herynge, Smellynge, and vche 20
lymes Felynge. And sumwhat we schulle speken of alle. for
who so witeþ þise wel he doþe Salamons bode. for ȝif he witeþ
wel his hert. he witeþ wel his soule hele. for þe hert is a ful
wilde beste and makeþ many wilde lepes as seint Gregori seiþ.
⟨ Nichil corde fugacius. ⟨ þat þer nys noþing þat atfleiȝeþ a man 25
so sone as his hert. Dauid goddes prophete pleyned hym sumtyme þat sche was atstirte hym: ⁊ seide. Cor meum dereliquit
me. ⟨ þat is myne hert is atstirt me. ⁊ eft he blisseþ hym and
seiþ þat sche is comen aȝein, inuenit seruus cor meum. ⟨ Lorde
he seide ich haue yfounde myne hert my seruaunt. wel were hym 30
þat myȝth so saie now whan þe holy man ⁊ so wyse and so war
lete hire atstirten. Sory may þan anoþer be for her fliȝth. And
where abrake sche fram dauid þe holy kyng and prophete: god

it wott att his ei3e þirle þat he sei3 þorou3 a biholdynge as 3e
(M. 50) schulle heren here after. Forþi my leue breþeren and sustren.
witeþ wel 3oure ei3en and cloþe 3ou to folde blak ⁊ white. þe
blak cloþ bitokneþ þe croice wiþinne and wiþ outen. þat hij ben
blak and vnworþi to þe werld and smeþe and white inwiþ þat is   5
þe soþe. Summe þat ihesus crist haþ out cooled 3ou of þe werlde
þorou3 glemes of grace. þre croices. þere ben red ⁊ blak and
white. þe rcdc croice is likned to Martirs þat scheden her bloode.
þe blak croice is likned to hem þat done her penaunce in þe
werlde for foule synnes. þe white croice longeþ to white May-   10
denhode and chastite and clennesse þat is mychel pyne forto
holden. White cloþ is likned to þe white croys for it takeþ sone
filþe. and is wers to loken to. and doþe more harme to þe ei3en
p. 378a to biholden it. þe | blak cloþ bitokneþ þe blak croice for it doþe
lesse harme to þe ei3en to biholden and is þikker a3ein þe winde   15
and wers to see þorou3 and holdeþ his hewe better. þerfore
looke 3e be cloþed to folde white wiþinne ⁊ blak wiþoute and
vnworþi to þe werlde. And scheteþ wel 3oure wyndowes and
3oure dores þat ben 3oure fyue wyttes. And now we wil speken
of þe fyrst þat is oure Ei3en, Looke þat 3e wite hem ri3th wel   20
þat þe hert atstirte nou3th as dude of Dauid þe kyng. and make
oure soule seek. For alsone as he is oute þan is oure soule seek.
þerfore ne beþ nou3th outward ne tellynge. ne lei3ynge. ne
flikerynge. for þat is a3ein kynde. For vnkyndelich it were þat
þe ded spake wiþ þe quyk. ded is vche man and womman þat   25
3iuen hem to god forto ben his spouse a3ein werldelich men and
synne. for it ne falleþ nou3th in her mouþes non swich speche
bot al to worschipp of her spouse. for werldelich men ben here
quyk þat 3iuen hem to þe werlde and to synne.

M Undus gaudebit et cetera. ⦅ Oure lorde seiþ to his deciples.   30
    3e schulle wepen and sorow3en. ⁊ þe werlde schal make
ioye and blis. and 3oure wepynge schal tourne to ioye. and her

---

3 white: h *written above line.*   3–9 *Diagonal crack in MS. on right*
side of page from line 3 *down almost to edge of margin at line* 9. *Around this*
crack and above there is certain 'shine-through' of letters.   5 werld (*at*
end of line): er *crammed together.*   6 Summe, *sic for* Sunne.   of
incomplete due to crack in MS.   7 þere: *MS. folded over* ere *at edge of*
crack.   8 likned: *MS. folded over* ed *at edge of crack.* d *incomplete due*
to crack.   12 is *written above line.* o *in* croys *blotted.*   13 *Before* and²
semicolon in red ink.   15 ei3en: *MS.* ei3em *with last minim of* m *expuncted.*
Two small stains of blue ink after ei3em.   17 folde: *traces of minims after* e.
20 Ei3en, *in red ink.*   23 tellynge: *Blot over left part of first* e.

ioye to sorouȝ and wo. þe werlde is cleped wicked cristen men
and synne þat comeþ of oure seluen. forsake þat and nouȝth þe
þing þat god haþ made for þe. For wiþ outen þi sustenaunce ne
may þou neuer wel seruen And from þe werlde we moten kepen
vs ȝif we wil queme god And bot ȝif we may amenden hem. we   5
owe to bidde for hem to god þat he amende hem ȝif it be his
wille.

(M. 52) L Eue sir wil summe saie. is it now so yuel forto loken outward
and gon to solas ȝ to games and to karoles. ȝe leue breþeren
and sustren for yuel þat þere comeþ of. For seint Austyn seiþ so 10
hij schullen karolen in helle hij þat karolen here for delytt of
body and of werldelich þinges. And so hij schullen bot hij
amenden hem here bytymes and a party Ichille telle ac al ne may
I nouȝth. And namelich to ȝonge men and wymmen and to olde
also. þat þe ȝonge ne take none ensample of hem þat hij mowen 15
weren hem by. for ȝif any man vndernymeþ hem þan hij seien
also swiþe loo:' hij done also þat þat cunnen more goode þan I
can. and better ben þan ich am. Ȝe þat willeþ do wel. ne ȝiueþ
no keep herto. for þe wise folowȝeþ wisdom and nouȝth folye.
an olde man oiþer an olde womman may better do suich þinges 20
þan a ȝonge. ac wiþ outen yuel ne may noiþer done it. nymeþ
now goode ȝeme what yuel haþ comen of loking out ward. ȝ
namelich of womman. Ac al þe wo þat euer was. ȝ ȝut is. ȝ euere
schal be. al com of siȝth ȝ þat it so be. loo here þe proue.

p. 378b Lucifer þat was þe fairest | aungel in heuene þorouȝ a biholdynge 25
þat he bihelde vpon hym self fel in to a weellate þere of and so
in to pride. and bicom of þe fairest aungel of heuene þe foulest
deuel of helle. Looke now what hym bifel for his siȝth. Eue oure
aller Moder þe first þing þat brouȝth hire to synne was her eiȝe
þirle.   30

V Idit igitur Mulier quod bonum esset lignum ad vescendum
ȝ pulchrum oculis aspectu que delectabile ȝ tulit de fructu ȝ
commedit dedit que viro suo. ⟨ þis is þus to saie. Eue bihelde
þe forboden appel and seiȝ it faire and fenge to deliten hir in þe

---

siȝth. And in þe biholdyng took her lust þerto. and name ⁊ ete
þere of. ⁊ þan took ⁊ ȝaf it hire lorde. Loo holy wrytt hou it
spekeþ openlich. and hou inwardelich it telleþ þere of. how
first siȝth bigan boþe of aungel ⁊ of man þorouȝ a womman þus
ȝede it first bifore and made þe waye to yuel lust. And comeþ 5
þe deede þere after þat al man kynde it feleþ ȝutt to þis day. and
schal do til þe day of dome. and summe wiþ outen ende. þis
appel my leeue frendes bitokneþ al þing þat lust falleþ to and
delices of synne. Whan þou man biholdest þe womman oiþer
þou womman þe man. þou art in Eues poynt þou lokest on þe 10
Appel. þat is on þi deþ. Who so hadde seide to Eue first whan
sche cast hire eiȝe vpon þe Appel. Eue þou lokest on þi deþ. ⁊
(M. 54) þerfore turne þe awayward. My leue sir sche wolde haue seide
þou haste wronge. þis Appel þat i loke vpon was forboden me to
eten. ⁊ nouȝth to biholden. þus wolde Eue oure alder Moder 15
haue ansuered. And so ich drede me ȝutt þat Eue haþ many
sones and douȝttren boþe þat wolden sigge on þis wise. wenestow þat ich lepe vpon hym þeiȝ ich looke opon hym and seie
þou haste wronge. More wonder bifel whan sche loked opon
þe Appel and tooke delytt in þe lokyng and þan ete þerof. 20

QUi viderit Mulierem adqⁱ. ⟨ Who þat seeþ a womman
forto coueiten hir. onon. he haþ forleyn hire onon in his
hert. Sche fel to þe Appel. And fro þe Appel in to þe wo of þis
werlde. And was þere inne nyne hundreþ wynter and more.
And fro þe sorouȝ of þis werlde in to þe pyne of helle. ⁊ þere 25
sche was foure þousande wynter and more and hire spouse also.
And alle þat comen of hym ⁊ of hire and ȝutt schulden haue
done to þis day ⁊ euer more for þe bytt of an Appel. ne hadd þe
grett mercy of god þat sent adoune his swete son ihesu crist
forto taken oure flesche ⁊ oure bloode and dyed vpon þe roode 30
for vs and many peynes suffred for vs er he ȝede to þe deþ.
hunger ⁊ þrust and many sorouȝes forto amende þe lust ⁊ þe
likynge þat Adam ⁊ Eue hadden. For vnderstonde ȝe wel he ne
deied for no synne bot for þat Ac his deþ was so precious þat
p. 379a it | myȝth suffise for mo werldes and synne þan may be noum- 35
bred and deliuer man of alle synnes and of alle pynes. þe

---

4 siȝth, *sic for* synne.   21 adqⁱ: cf. *Vulgate: Matt. V: 28:* Ego autem
dico vobis, quia omnis, qui viderit mulierem ad concupiscendum eam, jam
mœchatus est eam in corde suo.   22 *Accidental stroke above full
stop after first* onon.

bigynnynge and þe rote of al þis was first a liȝth siȝth of þe
eiȝe. And as men ofte seien of litel comeþ mychel. þan may
vche feble man ⁊ womman þat is borne in synne haue mychel
drede whan hij þat were þan made þorouȝ god. and clene were
wiþ outen corrupcioun Hou þat hij were bigiled and brouȝth in   5
to gret synne þat spred ouer al þe werlde.

EGressa est diua filia Iacob vt videret Mulieres alienigenas.
(A Maiden also dyne þat was Iacobes douȝtter it telleþ in
holy wrytt þat sche ȝede to biholden vncouþe men. ac it were
wymmen. and what wené ȝe þat com þere of. þorouȝ þat bihol-   10
dynge sche les her Maidenhode, and was made an hore þere
after were treuþes broken of heiȝe Patriarkes. and a mychel
burghȝ forbrent. and þe kyng and his son ysleyn. and þe
wymmen of þe burghȝ ytaken were and yladde forþ and made
hoores. her faders and her breþeren noble Princes were out-   15
lawȝed and al þis nas nouȝth by her wille ac al aȝeins hire wille
for a kyng þat was cleped Semor hadde a son þat hiȝth Sichen.
and he was of a noþer lawe þan sche was. nouȝth circumcised
caste his eiȝen vpon hire and rauisshed hire aȝeins hire wille.
sche was defouled ⁊ made an hoore. Looke now þus ȝede out hir   20
siȝth. þis and oþer goddes aungel dude wryte forto warnen
oþer wymmen of her siȝth. Also Bersabe þat was Vrries wyf
stoode att a welle and wessche her legges. And Dauid stoode in
his chaumbre and seiȝ hire. and tooke of þat siȝth swich a delytt
þat he dude þere þorouȝ þre dedlich synnes. Tresoun and   25
spouse breche. and Manslauȝth, and al þorouȝ þat first siȝth so
holy kyng as he was and goddes prophete. Now comeþ a feble
man þat holdeþ hym holy for he haþ a wide hoode and longe
sleuen. ⁊ wil seen ȝonge wymmen and seiþ þat hij mowen seen
holy men wel ynouȝ. Ȝe swich as he is for his wide hoode and   30
his longe sleeue no womman ne leue none swich. and also wymmen to desiren to seen faire men. ne desire it nouȝth. þenche on
goddes prophete and on his derlynge by whom god seide hym self.

(M. 56) to the left of line 17.

7 diua, sic for dina.   9 men. ac it on erasure.   were: ere crammed
together at end of line.   10 biholdynge: o and l connected with stroke
which makes o look like e.   12 treuþes: traces of erasure on s.   13 kyng:
traces of erasure on g.   15 faders, sic for fader.   17 was: traces of
erasure on s.   Sichen: erasure on S has caused a small hole in MS.   18 First
was: traces of erasure on s.   20 was: traces of erasure on s.   hir: erasure
between out and siȝth. Space for 4–5 letters. hir written above the erasure.
22 of oų erasure.   27 was: traces of erasure on s.

INueni virum secundum cor meum. ⟨ Ich haue founden a man seide god after myne hert Now þis man þat god hym self so mychel praised þorou3 a si3th of his ei3e castynge opon a womman. þat wesche hire self forles his hert, and for3ate hym
p. 379b self so þat he dude | þre dedlich synnes on Bersabe spousebreche 5 on Vrrie his trewe kni3th tresoun ꝛ mannes slau3th for he dude hym to dede and vche oþere. þo þat ben synful wrecches ben so foole hardy to cast 3oure ei3en vpon a womman. And þerfore ich rede vche man ꝛ womman þat desiren to ben goddes spouse þat hij þenchen here vpon. And also men oiþer wymmen þat 10 lyuen in þe werlde han gret nede to kepen hem fram suich si3thtes. 3if þat hij willen ben ysaued. For alle þe synnes þat I spake of toforne and now last alle comen of a li3th si3th. for it was gynnyng and roote of alle, And þerfore for þat wymmen
(M. 58) vnwri3en hem to men so þat hij weren gretlich ytempted and 15 synneden þere þorou3. it was comaunded in þe olde law3e in þe name of god þat 3if any pytt were. what so it were. þat it scholde ben wrei3en þat no beste fel þere inne. And 3if any vnhiled it þat a beest fel þere inne. he þat it vnhiled scholde aquyte þe beest. Now is þis a suiþe dredeful þing to womman þat sche 20 hire to mannes ei3en. for sche is bitokned by þe wrei3eynge of þe pytt. þe putt is hire faire nebbe hire white swire. hire ly3th lates. hire hondes 3if sche hondel. 3if sche holdeþ forþ in his si3th. 3utt hire wordes beþ putt. and al þat falleþ to hir þat man is ytempted of. Al oure lorde clepeþ putt. þis putt 25 he comaundeþ þat it be hiled. lest beestes fallen þere inne and drenchen in synne. Beest is þe beestlich man þat ne þencheþ nou3th on god. ne noteþ nou3th hise wyttes as a man ou3tte to done to goddes worschip and to his owen note. Ac seches forto falle in þis putt þat ich speke of 3if he it fynde 30 open. A. þe dome is wel strong to hem þat openen þe putt for hij schullen 3elden þe beest þat is fallen þere inne. for sche is gylty of his deþ bifore oure lorde And schal for his soule ansuere on domesday and 3elde þe beestes lure. ꝛ sche naþ nou3 to 3elde bot hire seluen: stronge 3elde is þis wiþ alle: ꝛ 35 goddes dome and his heste is þat sche it schal 3elde on al manere.

---

7 synful: y *probably written on top of another letter.*   17 of god þat
3if *partly on erasure.*   25 clepeþ: l *corrected from* h.   27 beestlich: l
smudged.   34 3elde: d *blotted.*   36 manere: anere *probably*
corrected. Last e *blotted.*

Vnderstonde sche wel it schal be ȝolden for sche opened
þe putt þat it adreynt inne. þou þat vnhiles þe putt. ᷠ
doos any þing whar þorouȝ þat man is any þing of þe atempted
fleschlich þere þou it wilt nouȝth drede þis dome gretlich ȝif he
is yfonded of þe so þat he synne dedlich in any manere þeiȝ it 5
ne be nouȝth wiþ þe. bot wille to þe ward, for þe fondynge aros

M. 60) first of þe þorouȝ þi dede·' be al siker of þe dome þou schalt it
ȝelde for þe pyttes openynge. And bot þou be schryuen þere of

p. 380a þou schalt | abugge be þou ful syker. For men seien a bywoorde
þe hounde wil in þere he fyndeþ open.　　　　10

PUdicus oculus inpudici cordis est inimicus et cetera. ℂ þat
þe mouþ ne may for schame þe liȝth eiȝe spekeþ it. And it is
as erande berer of þe liȝth hert. Ac now þere ben summe wymmen þat nolde for noþing do filþe wiþ man. Ac hij ne recchen
neuer þeiȝ man be tempted of hem. Ac seint Austyn seiþ. þise 15
two ben in on willynge and habbynge. wille forto ben ywilned
as wel as forto habben.

NOn solum appetere set appeti velle criminosum est. ʰᵒᵐᶜˢᵃˣᵘᵉˡⁱᵗᵘ
ℂ Knowe man oiþer haue wille to ben yknowe of man and
sechen þere after boþe it is on and dedlich synne　　　20

OCuli prima tela sunt adulterij. ℂ Eiȝen beþ arewen of þe first
Armes of leccherie·' For so as men fiȝtten wiþ þre manere of
wepen. with schetynge. wiþ spere. ᷠ wiþ sweerd Also riȝth wiþ
þat ilch wepen fiȝtteþ þe flesche aȝeins þe soule þat is wiþ liȝth
eiȝe as schote of Arewe. And wiþ spere of woundynge woorde. 25
and wiþ sweerd of dedlich hondelyng. And of þise falleþ ofte
stynkynge leccherie vpon hem þat schulden be goddes spouse.
First he scheteþ his arewen of liȝth eiȝen. for as þe Arewe is
yfeþered and fleiȝeþ liȝtlich·' so doþ þe schote of þe eiȝe and
stikeþ in þe hert. þere after he schakeþ his spere þat is schakyng 30
woord. And þe swerd of dedlich hondelynge smyteþ deþes dynt
on goddes spouse so þat he makeþ of hire þe deuels Hoore. And
it is soþ weilaway Neiȝ is it ydo wiþ hem þat comeþ so neiȝ to

M. 62) gyders. And þerfore boþe man ᷠ womman, witeþ wel ȝoure

---

8 *Two large ink-stains at right-hand corner of bottom margin.*　　11 [Au]-
gusti[nus] *in left margin in red ink. Left half of g cut off.*　　PUdicus, *sic for*
INpudicus.　　inimicus, *sic for* nuncius.　　14 do *written above line and
marked for insertion.*　　18 [Au]gusti[nus] *in left margin in red ink.*
21 [A]ugus[ti]nus *in left margin in red ink. Right minim of* u *visible before* gus.
OCuli: C *partially erased.*　　adulterij, *sic for* adultere.　　arewen: *lower part
of* a *erased.*　　22 as: s *partially erased.*

eiȝen. for al þis wo comeþ first of þe eiȝen. Nis he nouȝth a
mychel foole þat whan þe citee is biseged al aboute wiþ stronge
enemyes þat holdeþ hym openlich forþ in þe kyrnels of þe wal.
lest þat sum querel oiþer sum arewe ȝaf hym deþes dynt. Sikerlich as ich wene þe fende scheteþ mo querels to homelich wym- 5
men þan to an hundreþ leuedies in þe werlde. þe kirnels of
ȝoure castels ben ȝoure doores ⁊ ȝoure wyndowes, and þo ben
ȝoure fyue wyttes. And þerfore schete hem fast lest þe deuels
querels ne hyrtt ȝou nouȝth. For his querels beþ fondynges
boþe bodilich and gostlich. For sone so þe eiȝe is yblynded þe 10
herte is sone ouercomen. and ybrouȝth sone þorouȝ synne to
grounde.

Sicut Mors per peccatum in orbem ita per has fenestras intrat
in mentem. ⸿ As deþ comeþ first in to þe werlde þorouȝ
synne. Also þorouȝ þe eiȝe comeþ deþ in to þe soule, Lorde | 15
p. 380b crist. what vche man wolde scheten fast her wyndewes and hij
myȝtten scheten out deþ of fleschlich lyf. And a man oiþer a
womman þat schulde serue god ne wil nouȝth scheten her eiȝen
fram soule deþ. And wel hij mowen ben cleped þirles of soule
deþ. for many man ⁊ womman han ben sleyn þorouȝ hem boþe 20
gostlich and bodilich. þorouȝ al holy wrytt it is techynge and
warnynge of kepynge of eiȝen

Auerte oculos meos ne videant vanitatem. ⸿ God seiþ Dauid
wende away myne eiȝen fram þe dwele of þis werlde ⁊ his
vanitees. 25

Pepigi fedus cum oculis meis nec cogitarem de virgine. ⸿ Iob
seiþ Ich haue made forward with myne eiȝen þat i ne schal
mysþenchen. God it wot he seide ful wel. for after þe eiȝe comeþ
(M. 64) þe þouȝth. and þere after þe dede. And þat wist Ieremye þe prophete ful wel þat meued hym þus ⁊ seide. 30

Oculus meus depredatus est animam meam. ⸿ Weyleway he
seiþ myne eiȝen han robbed my soule. whan goddes prophete made swich a mone of hise eiȝen: what werestou þan may
a synful man make for his oiþer a womman. whan goddes
prophete þat was halewed in his Moders wombe and myȝth 35

---

6 to: t *partially erased.*   kirnels: kir *partially erased.*   7 ⁊ ȝoure *partially erased.*   11 ybrouȝth: *blot in red ink above* b.   15 *Blot in red ink
in bottom margin under left column.*   23 Dauid *in right margin in red ink.*
26 Iob *in right margin in red ink.*   30 meued, *sic for* meneþ.   31 Ieremias. *in right margin in red ink.*   33 werestou, *sic for* wenestou.

nouȝth synne dedlich. þe wise man askeþ in his book ȝif þat any
þing harmeþ þe man oiþer þe womman more þan her eiȝen.
OCulo quid nequius totam faciem lacrimare facit quam
vidit.⸉ Alle þe leer schal flowe þe teres for þe eiȝe siȝth.
now we haue spoken of þe eiȝen. speke we now of þe oþer 5
wyttes.
SPellyng ⁊ smecchyng ben in þe mouþe boþe. as siȝth in þe
eiȝen. Ac we schullen leten of Smecchyng And speken of
Spellyng ⁊ herynge. Spekynge ⁊ heryng comen boþe in mene to
gidres. And þerfore boþe man ⁊ womman avise hem wiþ whom 10
þat hij speken of filþe or of werldelich þinges. for þise þinges ne
fallen nouȝth to swich men to speken of ne heren, And þerfore
whan hij schulle speken wiþ man oiþer wiþ womman. makeþ
vpon ȝou þe tokne of þe holy croice. and spekeþ wiþ hem in goddes
drede, And ȝif hij schullen speken to preest hij owen to saien 15
her. Confiteor. and after Benedicite dominus, And þan hereþ
woordes þat beþ nedeful to heren. ⁊ ansuereþ hym schortelich
þere nede is. And in sobre woordes and faire. so þat whan ȝe
goþ away þat he ne cunne by ȝou goode ne qued, ne preyse ȝou
ne lak ȝou. bot euene bitwene two. Oiþer while many men ⁊ 20
wymmen whan men speken to hem to techen hem: hij willen
haue aȝein o woord two oiþer þre. And bicomen his Maister þat
is comen forto techen hem. ⁊ wolden by her tale ben yholden
wyse. And naþeles her woordes willen | techen what hij ben.
And þorouȝ þat hij wenen to be wise yholden. men vnderston- 25
den þat hij ben sottes. For hij hunten after prys. ⁊ hij cacchen
folye. for whan hij gon from hem. hij willeþ saien þis man oiþer
þis womman is of mychel speche. Eue helde longe tale wiþ þe
neddre in paradys and tolde hym al þe lesson þat god hadd forboden hem forto eten of þe Appel. And so þe neddre vnderstoode 30
þorouȝ her woordes onon riȝth her feblesse. and her brotylnesse
of fallynge. And fonde way þorouȝ her mychel speche hou he
schulde brynge hire to forlernesse.
OUre lefdy seint Mary ne dude nouȝth so. ac sche dude al
oþer wise. ne telde sche þe aungel no tale. Ac asked hym 35

p. 381a
(M. 66)

1 synne: small hole in MS. (mentioned at p. 21 l. 17) above first n.   3 unus
sapiens. in right margin in red ink.   15 owen to: thin vertical stroke before o. Traces of erasure on wen to.   16 Confiteor: Confite on erasure.   23 her tale partially effaced.   24 woordes willen partially
effaced.   29 god: MS. godd with last d expuncted.   30 And: d
expuncted by mistake by scribe. In MS. placed below godd (l. 29).

schortlich þing þat he ne couþe. And þerfore vche man ⁊
womman folowe oure lefdy and nouȝth þe kakel dame Eue.
Forþi wiþ whom þat ȝee speke holdeþ ȝou euere stille. bot ȝif
ȝee knowe hem þe better þat ȝe schulle speken to. And ne beþ
nouȝth of henne kynde. For þe henne whan sche haþ leide an 5
eye sche kakeleþ it out. ⁊ þan comeþ þe keme and bereþ away
her eiren. þat sche schulde brynge forþ quyk briddes of ȝif þat
sche helde hire stille. Riȝth also fro þe kakelande man oiþer
womman þat kakeleþ ydel speche þe deuel bereþ away fram
hem alle her goode werkes. þat schulden ȝif hij helden hem 10
stille. beren hem vp to heuene ward. þe wrech Pedder makeþ
more noise and cry of his sope. þan a riche Merceer of al his
derworþe ware. And naþeles to gostlich men spekeþ and askeþ
hem conseil. and telleþ hem tales of ȝoure spouse. And hij to
ȝou. bot kakeleþ nouȝth of non oþer þing. for ȝif ȝee do ȝee 15
breke silence. For it ne falleþ nouȝth to goddes spouse noþing to
speke bot of her lemman Ihesu crist. and þing þat falleþ to his
worschipp. And whan ȝee schullen schryue ȝou looke þat it be to
gostlich men and to none oþer. And namelich wymmen. And
biddeþ hem inwardelich for goddes loue þat hij haue ȝou in 20
mynde in her byddynges. for þe godspel seiþ.

SEt multi veniunt ad vos in vestimentis Ouium intrinsecus
autem sunt lupi rapaces. (⸿ Oure lorde seiþ. witeþ ȝou ⁊
beþ war. for many comeþ to ȝou in white cloþes as scheep. ⁊
beþ vnderneþen rauisshande wolues. And siþen þat god hym 25
seluen warneþ vs þere of.' we owen þe better to be war of hem
and kepe vs fram hem. Werldelich men leueþ lytel. ⁊ religiouse

wel lesse. Ne wilneþ nouȝth to speke wiþ hem to Michel. And

"spouse"
whan ȝe speke wiþ any suich beþ in drede lest ȝe schulle agylt

p. 381b
ȝoure spouse. Eue wiþ outen drede spake wiþ þe neddre. | And 30
oure lefdy was a dradde to speke wiþ Gabriel þe Aungel. Man
oiþer womman þat wil be goddes spouse. i rede he ne speke
nouȝth in pryuete bot ȝif he haue witnesse noiþer þat on ne þat
oþere. for þere may neuere come goode of on noiþer partye
forto be longe in talynge and often. Als wel Men owen to 35
fleiȝen it for gostlich fondynges and bodilich boþe as for
sclaundre. For þe trewe is ay mystrowed. and þe les is often
leued And re trewe bilowen for defaut of witnesse. And þe yuel

6 keme, *sic for* kene. *Cf. Corpus*: kaue *16a: 20*, *Nero*: coue *28:35*, *Titus*:
ȝeape *10:10*.   38 re, *sic for* þe.

bleþelich bileued. And þerfore schulde þe goode haue euere
witnesse aȝeins wicked ouertroweynge. And ȝif it falle so þat a   *silence*
man oiþer a womman be enclosed out of þe chirche þirle ne
holde hij no talynge wiþ noman ne no womman bot onlich wiþ
her spouse ihesu crist. And bereþ þerto reuerence for þe sacre- 5
ment. ℂ To hir seruaunt at þe hous þirle. to oþere at þe par-
loures. speke ne owe ȝe nouȝth bot att þe þirles. Silence euere
holdeþ att þe Mete. For siþen oþere Religious it holden. ȝe
owen to holden it þe better. Ȝif ȝe han dere Gestes doþe ȝoure
M. 70) seruaunt in stede of ȝou gladen hem. And forto vnsperre ȝoure 10
þirle ones or twies and makeþ signes toward hem of glad chere.
for sumtyme curteisie is yturned to yuel. in Onelich Mannes
hous oiþer wommans owe mychel to ben on vche friday holden
silence bot ȝif it be dubble fest. And þan holdeþ it sum oþer day
in þe weke. þerfore in Aduent and ymbringe dayes. Wedenys- 15
day and Friday and saterday. In þe Lenten. þre dayes in þe week
holdeþ silence. And in al þe sueiȝeng week. And on Ester Euen
to ȝoure seruaunt ȝe may speke wiþ loude woorde what ȝe
willeþ. And ȝif any o frende ȝou comeþ. hereþ his speche and
Ansuereþ hym wiþ loude woorde. And þonkeþ hym mychel. A 20
foole he were þat miȝth grynde whete and grindeþ grauel,
whete is holy speche as seint Anselme seiþ. And he gryndeþ
grauel þat chauleþ of ydel speche and werldelich þine two
cheken ben þe two gryndel stones. þe Tunge is þe clappe. And
þerfore ȝif ȝe wil be goddes spouse. Looke þat ȝoure chekes ne 25
grynde nouȝth bot soules hele And þat in alle ȝoure fyue
wyttes ne be nouȝth yfounden bot soules foode, And þan chese
ȝe þe better part as god hym self seiþ þat þe Maudeleyn dude.
Sche ne þouȝth on kyn ne on none erþelich goode bot onelich on
hym. And Martha her suster was aboute erþelich þinges. and 30
ȝaf al hire besynesse forto serue pouere men. And whan sche
blamed Marie hire suster for sche sett hire doune att Ihesu   *Mary & Martha*
p. 382a cristes feete to heren hym speke and nolde helpe hire suster
forto diȝtten her alder mete. | And Martha blamed hire. Ihesus
crist Ansuered for hire and seide. Martha. Martha þus þat sche 35
haþ chosen þe better pat and it ne schulde nouȝth be bynomen

---

12 in: *added above line and marked for insertion. i probably corrected.*
19 frende, *sic for* fremde.   29 onelich: *dot below* e,   32 blamed
partially effaced.   35 for *written above line and marked for insertion.*
þus: *dot below first minim of* u.   36 pat, *sic for* part.

hire. Now who so takeþ hym to any degre out of þe commune
Poeple forto serue god and ne doþe nouȝth as sche dude. þat is.
ȝiueþ no keep to erþelich þing bot onelich to haue al her blis
and al her foode in hym. hym were better ben in þe werld and
done as Martha dude til þat god sent hem þe grace þat hij miȝt- 5
ten come to þat oþere. And biseken fast nyȝth and day ȝif þat
it were his swete wille to sende hem þat grace þat hij myȝtten
come to þat ilche degre forto quemen hym as þe best manere
were, And þan hij schullen haue grace forto queme hym wel
better þan þat hij ȝeden to heiȝe degre by her owen wille. for 10
þe deuel is ful queynt and putteþ a man to heiȝe degre of heiȝe
lyf. forto make hym þe faster in his seruise as ȝe schulle heren
here after. And þis semeþ now in þis werlde for non dar saye
þe soþe. And þerfore ich rede þat vche man holde hym paied
wiþ his state what so it be tyl god wil sende hym bettre And þan 15
doþe he wel. I ne speke nouȝth of þe state of þe synne. for out of
þat state I rede þat he hiȝe hym als sone as god sendes hym
grace. Ac womman ne owe nouȝth to prechen bot ȝif sche be þe
ouer holyer. for seint Poule forbedeþ hem. bot man ne forbedeþ
he nouȝth. Ac he seiþ. How may a man preche bot he be sent. 20

QUomodo vero predicabunt nisi mittantur Et iterum. ecce
ego mitto vos sicut oues in medio luporum. ⸿ þat is hou
may a man preche bot he be sent of god. Loo seiþ oure lorde. I
sende ȝou as a scheep amonge wolues. And vnderstonde ȝee
wel. þat þere nys non sent of god þat is proude oiþer coueitouse 25
oiþer leccherouse. oiþer losenioure. oiþer fast holdande her
goodes. For hij ben Antecristes prophetes. And ypocrites. And
Heretikes. Ne ben her wordes neuer so goode. Hij schullen
take no stede. For hij ne lyue nouȝth after her speche Antecrist
schal speke faire woordes and make hym poppe holy. and þerwiþ 30
he schal disceyue þe folk.

QUare enarras iusticias meas ⁊ assumis testamentum meum
per os tuum. ⸿ þat is whi tellestou my riȝthwisenesse. and
takes my testament in þi mouþe. þou þat folowes þe compaignye

---

1 Now: *traces of erasure on* w. w *slightly blurred*. ow *crammed together at
end of line*.   3 onelich: *traces of erasure on* h.   h *expuncted between*
haue *and* al.   10 wille: *traces of erasure on first* l.   12 lyf: *traces
of erasure on* y.   forto: *erasure under* to, *which is partially erased*.
26 leccherouse: le *partially erased*.   29 her *written above line and marked
for insertion*.   30 *After* make *at end of line a cross in the same ink*.
32 [D]auid *in left margin in red ink*. au *on erasure*.

of Hoores and þeues. þei3 suich myster men speken goddes
woord.' men taken ensaumple att her lybbynge. and nou3th att
her woord And here þe proue þere of. þe grete clerkes and þe
Maisters þat duden ihesu on Roode. Hij weren swich mysters
men. And þerfore þe folk tooken ensample att her werkes. ⁊ 5
p. 382b nou3th att her wordes. For hij precheden | goddes woord wel to
þe poeple. Ac hij ne lyueden nou3t þere after. And þerfore þe
folk took ensample att her libbynge and nou3th att her prechynge. And þerfore hij 3eden to helle wiþ hem. and 3utt done
and schullen tyl god haue sent his grace vn to hem. for it seiþ 10
att hem bigan þe feiþ. And att hem it schal ende. ⁊ Ihesus crist
badd his deciples done as hij seiden bot nou3th as hij done
Mulieres non permittendo docere. ⟨ No womman ne preche
bot sche be þe holyer holden ne teche 3ee ne schulle
noþing swere bot nay. ⁊ 3e. sikerlich as god biddeþ in þe god- 15
spel. 3e. 3e. ⁊ nay. nay.' þat is to saie. nay wiþ þine hert. ⁊ nay
wiþ þi mouþ. And also. 3e. 3e. Naþeles techen 3e may. bot
M. 72) ri3th siker is it nou3th. Onelich man ⁊ womman ne owen to
chastise non bot her owen seruauntz For oft þorou3 swich
chastisynge ariseþ wraþþe oiþer fals loue. bitwene man and 20
womman.
AD summum vos volo esse rarilinquas. item pauciloquas. ⟨ þe
wise seiþ ichille þat 3e speke seeld and litel. For many putten
her woordes forþ att vnmy3th. And so duden iobes frendes þat
seeten stille a seuene ny3th by hym er hij bigunnen to speken. 25
ac þo hij hadden ygonne. hij couþen nou3th lynne.
CEnsura silencium nutritura est verbi. ⟨ Silence is Foster
Moder and bryngeþ forþ chanel. þat is gode speche and
nou3th worþ. and on oþer maner he seiþ.
IUge silencium cogit celestia meditari. ⟨ þat is. longe þou3ttes 30
and wille yholden bryngen þe þou3ttes toward heuene. As 3ee
seeþ by ensaumple. Att water Milnes Men stoppen þe water and
it ariseþ vpward So schulden þe woordes been seelden and wel

---

2 ensaumple: p *written over erased letter (possibly* h).   13 permittendo, *sic for* permitto.   Paulus. *in right margin in red ink.*   22 rarilinquas. item pauciloquas, *sic for* rariloquas. tuncque pauciloquas.   Seneca.
in right margin in red ink.   27 Gregorius. *in right margin in red ink.*
silencium, *sic for* silencii.   28 chanel, *sic for* chauel.   gode *on erasure.*
speche: *erasure below the word affecting lower parts of letters.*   Erasure be-
tween speche *and* and. *Space for 5–6 letters. Faint traces of strokes visible.*
29 nou3th: *MS.* mou3th *with first minim faintly written.*   30 Gregorius. *in
right margin in red ink.*   þou3ttes, *sic for* silence.   31 wille, *sic for* wel.

bisett. And þerfore stoppeþ ʒoure þouʒth from þing as ʒe willeþ
þat hij clymben vp toward heuene and nouʒth fleiʒen al to þe
(M. 74) werlde. For men saien. Mo men slen wiþ woorde þan wiþ knyf.

MOrs ⁊ vita in manibus lingue. þat is lyf and deþ is in þe
Tunge seiþ Salomon þe wise.   5

QUi custodit os suum custodit animam suam. Who þat
witeþ wel his mouþ. witeþ wel his soule.

SIcut vrbs patet ⁊ absque Murorum ambitu sic et cetera.
(⟮ þat is as þe citee þat is wiþ outen wal may sone be nomen.
riʒth so it fareþ of Mannes citee and wommannes þat ben her 10
bodyes hit may sone be ouercomen bot ʒif he keepe his mouþ.

QUi Murum silencij non habet patet inimici oculis Ciuitas
Mentis. (⟮ þat is who so holdeþ nouʒth his woordes. he is
as a burghʒ wiþ outen wal. And þe fende wiþ his felawschipp
entreþ in atte ʒate vn to þe hert and robbeþ hym of alle his 15
p. 383a goode werkes. In vitas Patrum. it telleþ | of an holy man þat
men comen to and praiseden wel a man þat lyued holy lyf vn to
hym. Ac he was of mychel speche.

BOni vtique set habitacio eorum non habet ianuam intrat ⁊
asinum soluit. (⟮ ʒe goode hij ben ac her mouþe ne haþ no 20
ʒate. for who so wil may go In and lede forþ þe asse. þat is þe
vnwise soule.

SIquis cupiens se religiosum esse ⁊ non refrenans linguam
suam set seducens cor suum. vana est religio. (⟮ þat is ʒif any
wene þat he be religious and ne bridleþ nouʒth his tunge fram 25
ydel speche his religioun is fals. Bridel ne sytteþ nouʒth one in
þe Mouþ. ac it geþ al aboute þe eren. And so it mote fare by
man. He moste bridel alle his fyue wyttes for alle hij ben in þe
heued. Ac of þe tunge is mychel doute for it slydreþ al in wete.
For oft we þenchen to speke bot litel, And after on woord glytt 30
forþ anoþer liʒthlich And so we ben brouʒth forþ in to ydel
speche er euere wite we.

IN multiloquio non deerit peccatum. (⟮ Ne may nouʒth mychel
speche be wiþ outen synne. For fram soþe it glytt in to fals. ⁊

---

4 Salomon *in right margin in red ink.*   6 Gregorius. *in right margin
in red ink.*   7 witeþ: i *almost completely erased.*   8 patet, *sic for*
patens.   Gregorius. *in right margin in red ink.*   11 hit: it *in a different
hand on erasure.*   12 patet: at *blotted.*   oculis, *sic for* iaculis.   15 entreþ: *almost the whole of* n *and parts of first* e *and* t *erased.*   16 In *on
erasure.*   17 a *expuncted after* praiseden *at end of line.*   23 cupiens,
sic for putat.   33 Salomon *in left margin in red ink.*

out of Mesure in to vnmesure. Men seeþ often of dropes wexen
a mychel floode and drenchen þe londe þere þe goode corne is
sowen. so it fareþ here on þis manere. Often þorou3 mychel
speche is þe soule adreynt and leseþ her fruytt. þat ben her
(M. 76)   goode werkes. so þat longe it is er it may comen a3ein in to þe   5
state þat it was aforne.

E T os nostrum tanto est ab eo longinqum quantum ininico
proximum. tantum que minus exauditur in prece quantum
amplius inquinatur in loqucione. ⟨ Seint Gregori in his Dialonge seiþ þis. As nere as oure mouþes ben to werldelich filþe   10
and to þinges þat ben werldelich. as fer it is fram god whan we
speke to hym. For we casten hym away. Ne wil he nou3th heren
oure steuen. for oure Mouþ stynkeþ vpon hym fouler þan any
roten dogge.

S I extenderitis manus vestras auertam oculos meos a vobis. 7   15
cum multiplicaueritis oraciones non exaudiam vos. ⟨ þat is
þei3 3e holde vp 3oure hondes and make many folde 3oure
boones ichille turne myne ei3en fram 3ou ward. And I nylle 3ou
nou3th yheren 3ee þat playen wiþ þe werlde for 3oure hondes
ben blody. By hondes in holy wrytt. is bitokned her werkes and   20
by bloode is bitokned synne.

I Niquitatem si aspexi in corde meo non exaudiet dominus.
⟨ þat is 3if I loke to wickednesse þat is consente þerto.' god ne
hereþ me no3th Ac 3if we be in neuere so grett synne: and we |
p. 383b   biseche hym þat he deliuer vs wiþ goode wille.' þat he hereþ and   25
elles nou3th. Oure lefdy seint Marie we rede in holy wrytt. þat
sche ne spake bot foure syþes and þo were woordes of gret
my3th.

A D Mariam in sempiterno verbo dei facti sumus vt ad vitam
reuocemur. responde verbum 7 suscipe verbum. 7 profer   30
verbum 7 concipe dominum. ⟨ Whan sche ansuered þe Aungel
Gabriel þe woordes were so my3tty. whan þat sche seide Ecce
ancilla domini, þat goddes son of heuene bicom man. And þe

---

1 dropes: pes *crammed together at end of line.*   wexen: en *partially era-*
sed.   5 goode: *traces of erasure on go.*   6 it: *traces of erasure on* t
7 longinqum quantum ininico, *sic for* longinquum quanto mundo.
8 tantum que, *sic for* tantoque.   quantum, *sic for* quanto.   9 Gregorius. *in left margin in red ink.*   Dialonge, *sic for* Dialouge.   15 SI, *sic*
for CUm.   20 holy: l *and lower part of* y *partially effaced.*   21 bloode:
second o *and left part of* d *partially effaced.*   22 Dauid *in left margin*
in red ink.   24 in *written above line and marked for insertion.*   29 ber-
[nardus] *in right margin in red ink.*   31 dominum *on erasure.*

lorde þat alle þat ben in heuene ⁊ in erþe ne myȝth nouȝth ouercomen. sche ouercom wiþ þat woord And bitent hym in her
Maidens wombe þat al þe werlde myȝth nouȝth at holden.
þat oþer woorde was of mychel myȝth also.

(M. 78)

VOx eius Iohannem exultare fecit in vtero matris sue. 5
❡ Whan sche com to Elizabeth and spake to hir. þe voice of
hir made seint Iohn to styren in his Moder wombe. þe þridde
woord was atte Bridale att Architryclyncs hous whan sche seide.
son hem faileþ wyne. And att þat woord he turned water to
wyne, þe fierþe woord was þan sche myssed hir son and after- 10
ward fonde hym in þe Temple þere he desputed wiþ þe Maisters
of þe lawȝe. and þan god bouȝed hym to a Smythe and a womman. Looke now how seeld speche haþ mychel strenkþe.

VIr lingosus non dirigetur in terra. ❡ Man ne womman of
fele woordes ne schullen neuere lede riȝth lyf. þat is to 15
saye of ydel speeche and of werldelich.

DIxi custodiam vias meas. vt non delinquam in lingua mea.
❡ þat is to saie. I schal keepe my wayes so þat i schal gete
my pes wiþ my tunge to comen to þe blisse of heuene.

CUstus iusticie silencium. ❡ þe tylyng of riȝthwisenesse is 20
silence. and he þat sileþ bryngeþ soule hele.

IUsticia inmortalis est. ❡ Riȝthwisenesse is vndedelich Salomon
seiþ. hope and silence beþ to gedres and in hem schal stonde
gostlich strenkþe. For who so is mychel stille ⁊ holdeþ silence
longe. he may speke sikerlich to god whan þat he biddeþ hym 25
any þing and hope þat he schal wel spede ȝif he bidde riȝthfullich. and wiselich. for þise two ben coupled to gedres. In hem
schal be al oure strengþe aȝein þe fendes fondynges and his

(M. 80) wyles. Hope is a swete spyce for it spyces þe herte inwiþ aȝein al
þe bytter þat þe body drynkeþ. Who so cheweþ spyces he holdeþ 30
his mouþ to gedre þat þe strengþe ne go nouȝth out. And ȝif
he ne do þe breþ goþ out. Riȝth so he þat openeþ his mouþ wiþ
mychel werldelich speche. spytteþ out hope. and leseþ þe

p. 384a strenkþe þat he schulde haue to god and strenkþeþ | hym to þe

---

14 psalm [ista] *in right margin in red ink. Right minim of* m *cut off at margin.*
17 psalm[ista] *in right margin in red ink.* meas: *lower part of* e *erased.*
20 CUstus, *sic for* CUltus. ysay[as] *in right margin in red ink. Traces of* a
after y *at edge.* 21 sileþ, *sic for* tileþ *due to* sil *in* silence. 22 solo-
mon *in right margin in red ink. Right minim of* m *and part of abbreviation sign
for* on *cut off at edge.* 30 spyces: *Cf. Corpus:* sweteð *20a:25, Cleopatra:* sweteð *32ʳ:23, Nero:* sweteð *34:27, Titus:* swetes *15:11.*

fende ward. what makeþ vs strong aȝein þe fende bot hope of
heiȝe mede as men seiþ. ȝif hope ne were hert to brast. A swete
Ihesu þine ore how stont hem þat ben in al wo wiþouten hope
and þe hert ne may nouȝth brest.

MOn habetis linguam vel aures prurientes et cetera. ⟨ þat 5
is ne haue ȝee noiþer tunge ne ere to werldelich speche.
þat is ydel tofore god.

COntrariorum eadem est disciplina. ⟨ Of silence and of
speche nys bot a lore for hij ben euer goande to giders
(M. 82) ⟨ Speke we now of yuel speche þat is þre folde ydel. ⁊ yuel. ⁊ 10
attry. þe first is yuel. þe oþer is wers. þe þridd alder werst. ydel
speche is al þat no good comeþ of to goddes worschipp and to
note of mannes soule ne to help of hem seluen to god ward ne to
her euen cristen.

DE omni verbo ocioso reddes racionem in die iudicij ⟨ Of 15
vche ydel woorde seiþ oure lorde þou schalt ȝelde rekenynge whi it is yseide ⁊ for what þing. Now siþen þat ȝee schulle
ȝelde rekenynge of vche ydel woord. hou wil it þan be of þe
werk þat is attry speche and foule. nouȝth onelich til hem þat
speken it Ac to hem þat heren it. And also of Leccherie and 20
Glotonye. and oþer filþe, Swich. speches ben alle schraped out
of goode mannes mouþ and wommans. Hou auȝtt it þan to ben
to Men and wymmen þat ȝiuen hem to ordre. Forsoþe mychel
auȝtten hij to sperren her fyue wyttes þerfro. Attry speche is
heresye foul. þwertouer ⁊ lesynges. bakbitynges. and Losenge- 25
rye. Alle þise ben wicked heresyes. þis ne regneþ nouȝth in
'M. 84) Engelonde. þe losengere ablyndeþ þe Man. and putteþ þe Pryk
in his eiȝe. þe bakbiter cheweþ mannes flesch opon fryday. and
pykeþ wiþ his blak byl vpon þe quyk Caroynes as þe deuel of
helle hym biddeþ. Wolde he ȝutt gon to ded flesch it were þe 30
lesse tale þerof. þat is wolde he speken of hem þat roten in
synne: þe lesse harme it were. Ac he doþe to hem þat aren quyk
in goddes seruise. He is to bolde a Rauen ⁊ to ȝyuer.

NE videatur hec Mortalitas minus dicens in Esdra quod
Melchias edificauit portam stercoris. Nomen. chorus 35

---

5 [Iero]ni[mus] *in left margin in red ink.*   MOn habetis, *sic for* NOn
habeatis.   13 mannes: *MS.* mānnes.   14 ie *in left margin in red ink. The
reference has not been identified.*   15 ele, *in left margin in red ink. The reference
has not been identified.*   19 werk, *sic for* wers.   27 *Hand drawn in left
margin, the forefinger touching* E *in* Engelonde.   34 videatur: *a corrected
from another letter.*   Mortalitas, *sic for* Moralitas.   dicens, *sic for* decens.

domino in corpore filius Reab. id est. mollis patris nam ventis
aquilo discipat pluuias ad faciens tristis linguam detrahentem.
⟨ þise two mysters Men ben þe deuels gonge fermers and fer-
men his gonge schame it is to seien. ac ȝutt it is fouler to done it.
For so he doþe als oft as he wiþ lesynge hyleþ mannes synne 5
þat stynkeþ foule vpon god. þus hij ben euere besy in her foul
myster. Her by men may knowen þe synne of hem by þat god
(M. 86)   seiþ in þe godspel. Losengeryc is þre fold. þe first is yuel. þe
p. 384b   oþer is wers | and þe þridd alderwerst.

VE illis qui ponunt pulmillos etc. Ve illis qui dicunt bonum 10
malum. ⁊ malum bonum ponentes lucem thenebras. ⁊ tene-
bras lucem. hoc. de. detractoribus ⁊ adulatoribus conuenit. ⟨ þe
first is. ȝif man is goode prayse hym bifore hym ⁊ make hym
better þan he is. And ȝif he doþe wel oiþer seiþ. heueþ hym vp
wiþ praysynge biforne hym. þis man god acurseþ, þat oþer is. 15
ȝif þat a man doþe yuel or seiþ yuel þeiȝ it be so open synne þat
he ne may it noȝth wiþ sigge. And þan bifore hym makeþ his
yuel lesse þan it is. and seiþ þat it nys nouȝth so yuel as men
seiþ of ne artou nouȝth in þis þe first. ne þou ne schalt nouȝth
be þe last. And conforteþ hym in þis synne so þat he holdeþ þe 20
lesse tale þere of. And seiþ to hym also þou haste many feren.
lete god yworþe ne gostow nouȝth al one many man doþe mychel
wers þan þou haste ydone. þe þridde is alderwerst þat forpray-
seþ þe Misdede. as he þat seiþ to a Man þat robbeþ his pouer
men. oiþer doþe harme to oþer and holdeþ wiþ hym ⁊ seiþ. Sir 25
þou dooste wel. Alle her chateux ben þine and her bodyes att
þine owen wille. It fareþ by þe Cherle as by þe wyþye. þe more
men croppen it. þe more it wexeþ And þus it is by al þing þat
men holdeþ wiþ A noþer in his yuel þat he doþe.

ADulancium lingue alligant hominem in peccatis. ⟨ þus þe 30
fykelers hilen þe stynk þat it ne may nouȝth stynken. and
þat is þe werst þing þat is. For ȝif þat hij wisten hou þat it
stank: hem wolde wlaten wiþ al. and amenden hem þan sumtyme þere of.

CLemens homicidiorum duo genera dicit esse Petrus. ⁊ 35
eorum parem esse penam voluit qui corporaliter occidit. ⁊

---

1 ventis, *sic for* ventus.   2 ad faciens, *sic for* ⁊ facies.   10 pulmillos, *sic
for* puluillos.   Ihesus *in right margin in red ink.*   30 Augustinus. *in
right margin in red ink.*   35 homicidiorum, *sic for* homicidarum.
Petrus. *in right margin in red ink.*

qui detrahit fratri. �ↄ qui videt et cetera. ⟨ Bakbiters ben two
Manere. þe first is yuel. þe latter is wers. þe first comeþ al
openlich and spekeþ yuel and seiþ out his atternysse als mychel
as he can and may. And þe latter comeþ forþ on oþer manere and
bigynneþ forto syken er hij it willeþ bigynnen and makeþ a longe 5
prolong tofore al aboute er it come forþ þat yuel þat hij þenchen
forto speken. And hij maken many ensamples forto ben yleued
þe better. And whan it schal comen forþ þan it is yuel attyr so
weylaway. He seiþ wo is me þat he haþ suich woord. Ich was
many tyme aboute forto haue stilled it. ȝif ich hadde miȝth. Ac 10
now it is so fer forþ gon. þat I ne may nouȝth and þat me sore
reweþ. And longe it is agon þat ich it wist first Ac euere ich
haue stilled it vn to now. Ac for me schulde it nouȝth haue
comen forþer. Ac now it is so ferforþ brouȝth þat i ne may it |
nouȝth wiþsaken. And þerfore me is ful wo. yuel men seiþ þat it 15
is. and ȝutt it is wel wers. wel wo is me þat ich it schal siggen.
and soþ it is. and þat is mykel sorouȝ. þise beþ neddres. Salomon spekeþ to vche Man and Womman and biddeþ hem kepe
hem wel fram hem. and ȝiue hem to her lemman Ihesu crist
þat þus faire spekeþ to ȝou and clepeþ ȝou his schewer 20

Z Elatus sum syon zelo magno. ⟨ Vnderstondeþ whas
spouse ȝe ben ȝif ȝe kepeþ ȝou ariȝth to hym. And biholdeþ
hou louelich he spekeþ to ȝou Ich am Ielous of þee syon he
seiþ. Syon þat is schewer on oure tunge. Loo ȝutt it hym þencheþ þat he seiþ nouȝth ynouȝ whan he seiþ. Ich am Ielous 25
ouer þe. bot ȝif he seie þerto wiþ mychel ielosie. zelo magno.

E Go sum deus zelotes. ⟨ Ich am þe Ielous god þat am Ielous
ouer my lemman.

A Uris zelo audit omnia. vbi amor ibi oculus. ⟨ Salomon
seiþ. þe ielous ere hereþ al þing þere as is loue. þere is his eiȝe. 30
Wyte ȝee wel ȝee þat ben his lemmans. his eiȝe is euere to ȝou
ward and biholdeþ ȝif ȝe ȝiue any louelates to any þing bot to
hym. Zelatus est syon. He is is Ielous of þe Syon. þat is his
schewer. And he seiþ to þe. ȝiue me þi louelates. ȝe. to me and
to non oþer. 35

O Stende michi faciem tuam. ⟨ þat is to saie schewe me þi
loue nebb. and seche me nouȝth outward. Ac seche me in

---

6 prolong, *sic for* proloug.   21 Zakarias, *in left margin in red ink.*
27 Exodus *in left margin in red ink.*   29 Salamon, *in left margin in red*
ink.   zelo, *sic for* zeli.   30 *Traces of erasure on* þere¹, l *in* loue, *and* eiȝe.
33 is is, *sic dittography.*   36 In canticis *in left margin in red ink.*

þine hert ȝif þou be trewe to me as spouse owe to ben. Ne
þencheþ no wonder þan. þeiȝ hij ben mychel out of þe werlde.
wiþ hert. Ich am schame fast he seiþ. I nylle nowhare clyppen
(M. 92) my lemman bot in deerne stede. and þat wyte vche man to soþe.
þe more þat ȝoure þouȝttes ben to erþlich þinges. þe lesse is þe 5
loue of ȝoure lemman inward werldelich þinges I clepe þat
synne falleþ to.

Qui exteriori oculo negligenter vtitur. iusto dei iudicio
interiori cecatur. ⸿ Who so ȝemeleslich witeþ þe vtter
eiȝen.ʹ þorouȝ goddes riȝthwise dome he ablyndeþ þe inner þat 10
he ne may see god gostlich. ne louen hym. For after þat men
louen hym þere after men felen his suetnesse. more oiþer lesse.
(M. 96) Als sone as a Man oiþer a womman hereþ any speche þat draweþ
a Man oiþer a womman fram her spouse. also smertly doþe ȝou
þennes wiþ þis vers. 15

Declinate a me Maligni.ʹ ⁊ scrutabor mandata dei mei. ⸿ Goo
away fro me þou wicked man. ⁊ I schal reherce þe comaundementz of my god.

Narrant michi fabulaciones.ʹ set non vt lex tua. ⸿ Hij tolden
me fables. bot nouȝth þi lawȝe. þan goþ to ȝoure spouse 20
wiþ. Miserere mei deus, oiþer wiþ ȝoure. Pater noster. ȝif ȝe ne
cunne it nouȝth. For þat is þe best þat ȝe may þan done. for
p. 385b þorouȝ | ansueres aȝein þere auȝtt arise sum sparkel. and þis
worde is goode to wymmen þan hij ben in swich cas. And per
auenture he wil saie. i nolde for no good þenchen yuel to þee 25
ward. Ac þeiȝ ich schulde dye leuen ich mote non is wers þan me.
forȝiue me þis and i nyl nomore. So may falle sche forȝeue it
liȝthlich for his faire speche. and spekeþ forþ wiþ hym. Ac euer
is his þouȝth in his last speche And þan whan he is gon away
M. 98) swich þouȝttes wil lasten in her hert and wexeþ more ⁊ more 30
And euere þe lenger þe wers it is. And so it fareþ of man by
womman whan sche spekeþ faire ⁊ casteþ enchesoun. and seiþ
sche ne dar nouȝth. By her tale sche wolde ȝif sche durst and
draweþ hym to hire ward wiþ loose woordes. and þat draweþ a
man on hire. And þerfore seie schortlich naye atte first and quyte 35
ȝou of hem. And I rede for any faire speche þat vche man and

4 bot: b *partially erased.*   vche: *traces of erasure on* v.   5 erþlich:
irregular sign above þ.   16 dauid. *in left margin in red ink.*   19 dauid.
in left margin in red ink.   NArrant, *sic for* NArrauerunt.   20 lawȝe
crammed together at end of line.   23 auȝtt, *sic for* miȝtt(?).   26 leuen,
sic for louen.   29 And: *lower parts of* An *blotted.*

womman be war and looke how dere ȝoure soule was bouȝth.
and sette þere on prys. And bot ȝif þat ȝe mowe haue more
þerfore þan he þat bouȝth it ȝaf þerfore.· ne selle it nouȝth so
liȝthlich to his enemy. for a lytel lykyng and ȝiueþ keep hou
ȝoure spouse clepeþ ȝou.   5

EN dilectus meus loquitur michi, surge propera amica mea.
ᴄ Looke ich here my spouse clepeþ me. ich mote gon. ȝe. goþ
swiþe to ȝoure dere spouse.

SUrge propera Amica mea. columba mea. formosa mea.
ostende michi faciem tuam. sonet vox tua in auribus meis. 10
ᴄ Come to me my lemman. my culuer. my schene spense. schewe
me þi loue nebb and þi leuesom leere. turne þe to me þou þat
wilnes speke wiþ non bot wiþ me. þi steuen is me swete and þi
þouȝth schene.

VNde ⁊ subditur vox tua dulcis et cetera. ᴄ Speke to hym 15
and haue hym to lemman þat is þousande siþes fairer þan
þe sunne. þus louelich ȝoure lemman Ihesus crist spekeþ to ȝou.

(l. 100) ᴄ Ac herkneþ now anoþer speche al awayward fram þis and al o
grym to hem þat schulden ben his lemmans.

SI ignoras te o pulchra inter Mulieres egredere ⁊ vade post 20
vestigia gregum tuorum. ⁊ pasce edos tuos iuxta thabernacula
pastorum. ᴄ Ȝif þou knowest nouȝth þi seluen þou faire wym-
man oiþer man among oþere. and noste nouȝth whas spouse
þou art and schuldest ben. þou þat art here among wymmen
and þou were amonge Aungels þan þou miȝth knowe þi seluen. 25
as þeiȝ he seide. þere schulde þi fairnesse litel be seene. And
ȝif þou art me trewe as spouse ouȝ to bene. ȝif þou haste it forȝeten: and litel letest þere of. Egredere. he seiþ o grym. goo out
he seiþ ⁊ folowe herde of gett. þat ben flesch lustes þat stynken
(p. 386a) as gett done. and vndo. | þi tyches þat ben þi fyue wittes þat ben 30
suete to god ȝif hij ben wel kepte. As Tiches ben swete flesche
tyl hij ben ȝonge. and as of a Tyche comeþ a synkande gott. so

---

5 Incan[ticis] *in right margin in red ink.*   8 incan[ticis] *in right margin
in red ink.*   10 *Traces of erased letter in red ink at edge of MS.*
11 spense, *sic for* speuse.   schewe: h *partially erased.*   14 incant-
[icis] *in right margin in red ink.*   15 *Traces of erased* I *and one more
letter (possibly* e) *in red ink at edge of MS.*   18 al²: a *corrected from* o.
19 hem: em *on erasure.*   In cant[icis] *in right margin in red ink.*   20 egredere: de *partially effaced.*   vade, *sic for* abi.   *Traces of erased* I *in red ink at
edge of MS.*   21 edos: ed *partially effaced.*   27 ouȝ: *MS.* ouȝtt *with*
tt *expuncted.*   30 done: d *partially erased.*   32 synkande, *sic for*
stynkande.

dooþ of a Lust a stynkande lykyng to god. Feede he seiþ þine
eiȝen wiþ oute totynge. þine eren wiþ oute herynge. þi Mouþ
wiþ oute spekynge þat is to seie of filþe. þine hondes wiþ outen
hondelynge. þi nose wiþ outen smellynge, And also alle þi wittes
fram filþe of synne and alle þine lymes. For riȝth as þou seest of 5
(M. 102) a ȝonge tyche comeþ a Stynkande gott. so of an eiȝe siȝth comeþ
a stynkande likyng. oiþer of an herynge. ⁊ ȝutt more of felynge.
wheþer euer any man oiþer womman hadd any swich fondynges
for any suich tokenynges þat ȝaf hem to swich tollynge and
peckande outward as a wanton Brydde in a Cage þat þe Catt com 10
and lauȝt hym in her cloches wheþer it ferde euere þus of any
onelich man oiþer womman þat pecked so outward þat þe catt
of helle þat is þe deuel of helle com and rent out her soules. out
of her bodyes and bare it vn to helle. ȝis god it wott haþ it and
þat is harme þe more. ȝutt he seiþ. Egredere, Goo out he seiþ 15
as dude iacobes douȝtter. þat is to saie leue my confort and take
þe werldes confort. for i warne þe þou ne schalt nouȝth haue
boþe my confort ⁊ þe werldes. þou þat schuldest be my spouse
schaltow folowe geett of helle þat ben fleschlich lustes.

O Sculetur osculo oris. ⟨ þat is cusse me lemman wiþ cusse of 20
þi mouþ Mouþe alder swettest. þis cusse my leue breþeren
and sustren is a swetnesse of hert and a delytt of vnmete swete
þat werldelich sauour is bitter þere aȝeins. Ac wiþ þis cusse ne
cusseþ he non þat louen any þing bot hym oiþer elles þat hij
(M. 104) louen it for hym. and in hym, For Salamon seiþ. Ȝif þe wardeyns 25
wenden out. þan is þe hous yuel yloked. Oure fyue wittes ben
oure wardeynes of oure hous þat is oure body. Now ȝe han herde
of spellyng þat falleþ to þe mouþe. ⁊ now we wil speken of
smellynge.

D E odoribus non sago nimis cum assunt non respuo. cum 30
absint non relinquo. ⟨ Of smel seiþ seint Austyn ne fynde
i bot litel ȝif it be neiȝ en goddes halue ⁊ ȝif it be fer me ne
recche.

---

19 fleschlich: *second* l *corrected from another letter.*   20 [Ia]cob[u]s *in*
left margin in red ink. Only right minim of u *visible at edge of MS.*   cusse
of written above line and marked for insertion.   22 of², *sic for* so.
24 elles: *irregular curl above first* e *connected with first* l.   30 [A]ugu-
stinus *in left margin in red ink. Traces of* A *before* u *at edge of MS.*   odoribus: *erasure below rib.*   sago, *sic for* satago.   31 absint, *sic for*
absunt.   relinquo, *sic for* requiro.   smel *on erasure.*   32 it be¹
on erasure.   ne: *faint traces of erasure on upper parts of letters.*

ERit pro suaui odore fetor. ⸿ Oure lorde seiþ Aȝein swete
smelles hij schullen haue stenches. and of þis þing beþ war.

(M. 106) þe deuel wil maken a þing to stynk for men schulden nouȝth
noten it And he wil also make swete smelles aboute hym þere he
duelleþ. for men schulde wenen and vnderstonden þat it com 5
fro god And þat he loued hem so wel and þat hij weren holy, so
p. 386b þat hij myȝtten haue a lykyng | þere inne of pryde. Ac Alle swich
Tretevales of hym ben brouȝth to nouȝth þorouȝ haly water. and
wiþ knelynge. and Crouchynge Aȝen stencheʒ þenche on god
hou he was done on þe roode vpon þe Mount of Caluarie. and 10
hefeled þe stenche þere of ded bodies þat laien þere ʒ stunken
ʒ roteden abouen erþe and stunken vpon hym so foule ʒ beþ
nouȝth squaymous. And also he was pyned in his siȝth whan þe
Iewes blyndfelden hym ʒ buffeteden hym aboute þe Chekes and
badden hym rede who smott hym. And also whan he hong on þe 15
roode he was pyned in his siȝth whan he wepe for hem þat
duden hym on þe roode and for vs wrecches þat done hym on þe
roode al day. And þe bloode and þe water comen boþe to geder
in his eiȝen and he miȝth nouȝth wipen it out. And also of his
Moders teres and of hise deciples þat he seiȝ were flowen 20
from hym. And also his frendes þat he dyed fore seiȝen þe lere
of hym þat he bouȝth so dere. And þat his deþ and his pyne þat
he suffred stoode þan in so litel stede. for þere bileeued non in
hym bot his Moder and þe þeef. For al þe pyne þat he suffred
ȝutt was þis þe most pyne þat he hadde for þat pyned hym more 25
þan al þe tourment þat þe iewes hym duden. And al þis was to
ȝiuen vs briȝth siȝth of hym. þenche no Man ne no womman
long þat wil ben his spouse þeiȝ hij ben mychel al one ʒ out of
felawschipp of þe werlde. For ȝif hij louen hym al þe solas in
þis werlde is bitter to hem. þe iewes smiten hym ʒ beten hym 30
in þe mouþ and spatten opon hym and he feled galle opon his

---

1 [domi]nus *in left margin in red ink. Traces of right part of* d *visible at
edge of MS.*   [d]icit: *written below* nus. *Traces of* d *at edge of MS.*
4 it: t *corrected from another letter* (a ?).   7 lykyng: k *looks like a correction for* b.   11 hefeled, sic *for* he feled.   15 hym[1] *written above
line and marked for insertion.*   16 whan he: *lower parts of* ha *and* he
partially effaced.   20 hise: *from this word the letters of the final words of
each line down to l.* 29 *are partially effaced.*   21 lere: *only faint traces
of* e (?) *between* l *and* r.   22 h *in second* his *corrected from another letter.*
26 was: w *and* s *partially effaced.*   28 þeiȝ: i (*above the line*) *and* ȝ *partially effaced.*   29 solas in: s *in partially effaced.*   31 spatten: s *partially erased.*

tunge. þan owe we wel to stoppen oure mouþ fram filþe. ȝif we
þenchen wel here opon. And al þis he dude forto lerne vs þat we

(M. 108) schulde nouȝth grucchen for mete ne for drynk. And ȝif a Man
oiþer a womman were bischett hij auȝtten raþer dyen in þe pyne
þan ben to gredy and to maken men to saie þat hij ben gredy. 5
Deþ me owe to flen as forþ as men may wiþ outen sclaunder. Ac
er þat he arered any sclaunder hij ouȝtten to dye Martir in her
Meseise. Nis it nouȝth gret synne þat men saien þat hij ben gredy
oiþer daungerous. ȝif hij weren in þe werlde hij mosten sumtyme ben apaied wiþ lesse. Wharto schal a man gon in to stede 10
of meseise forto sechen eyse. for ich vnderstonde þere ben
summe þat wil sechen more lordeschipp and ladyschipp þan
hij myȝtten haue hadde per auenture. ȝif þat hij hadden ben in
þe werlde. I rede vche man oiþer womman. ȝif any wil goo to
swich degree of Religioun. þenche what hij þenchen oiþer what 15
hij schulden þenchen. for riȝthfullich her lyf schulde be sorouȝ

p. 387a and wo here on erþe. ꝫ elles | ben hij nouȝth Ihesus deciples bot
ȝif hij sechen as he dude. ȝif hij sechen after eyse of body hij ben
Antecristes prophetes. for her lyf is contrarie aȝein ihesus
cristes lyf. And þerfore who so wil ȝiue hym to parfyt lyf. he 20
mote take sorouȝ ꝫ wo in pacience. ꝫ biwepe his synnes and oþer
mennes forto hane mede of her lemman. and be wiþ hym in þe
blisse of heuene. Hym seluen had here al manere stormes.
Vpbraydynges. Schemes. Teenes. and alle sorowȝes þat euer
myȝth men heren. 25

ET factus sum sicut homo non audiens: ꝫ non habens in ore
suo redarguciones. ꝭ Ich helde me stille as doumbe ꝫ deef
þat had non ansuere. þan þeiȝ man vs mysdoo oiþer myssigge.
þis is oure lemmans sawȝe þenche on me hou I was biseie for
þi loue ꝫ take ensaumple att me. 30

(M. 110) ÞE fyfte wytt is mychel nede ꝫ gret drede forto witen wel.
for it is in alle þe oþer þat is vche lymes felynge. And þerfore
oure lorde wolde be most pyned þere inne. For in þis wytt he
ne hadde nouȝth pyne in o stede. ne in two. ac in alle stedes. and
ȝutt in his sely soule he was pyned þre folde þat smott hym to þe 35
hert as a spere. His Moders pyne ꝫ sorouȝe. and þe Maries. and

---

17 *Catchwords* ben hij nouȝth Ihesus *in black ink at the bottom of right
margin. Catchwords enclosed in a rectangle with the head of a man and a leaf
as ornaments to the left.* 26 dauid. *in left margin in red ink.* 28 had,
sic for haþ.

his deciples þat ne leueden hym nomore for he ne halpe nouȝth
hym seluen att þat gret nede. And of þe forlernysse of hem þat
duden hym to þe ded. þis styked euere in his soule.

Q Uasi inquit membris flere se videtur. et cetera. (For so ful
of sorouȝ nas neuere man þat he swatt bloode. Ac his 5
Anguisch was so gret in his soule ar he com to þe pyne þat þe
swete of bloode ran adoune of his blissed body þat it stoode
vpon þe erþe as bloode dropes al abouten hym vpon þe gras.
þere he kneled. and so largelich he swatt þat it ran adoun by
hym as goutes and stremes of bloode for drede and sorouȝ þat 10
he hadde aȝein þe deþ. and þat nas no wonder. for euere þe
quycker flesche þe strenger is þe pyne. A litel prickyng in þe
eiȝe dereþ more þan a gret wounde in þe hele. Vche Mannes
flesch and wommans was as nouȝth aȝein þe tenderhede of
his flesch. for it was taken of a clene Maydens blode. and May- 15
dens flesch is tenderer þan a noþer wommans. Ensaumple þat
his flesche was quyk. a Man leteþ hym bloode vpon þe hole half
forto drawe a way þe sekenesse of þe seek half. And in al þe
werlde nas yfounde an hole half on noman forto ben yleten
bloode on for þe sekenesse þat man lay inne for his synne. bot 20
Ihesus crist oure leche þat lete hym bloode nouȝth in on stede.
Ac on fyue half. grete woundes and brode for oure fyue wyttes.
þat we haue misspended in fleschlich likynges. And werldelich
desires wiþ outen þe woundes in þe heued and þe rewful garses
þat he hadde. þus þe hole half drouȝ | þe sekenesse fram vs and 25
heled vs ȝif we wil oure seluen þat is to saye. ȝif we wil folowe
his waies and done after his techynge. And botȝ ȝif we wil. we
bileue stille in oure sekenesse. And in al þinge we mote louen
hym and dreden hym. By bloode is bitokned synne in holy wrytt.
Ac vnderstondeþ here whan a man is laten blode. he holdeþ 30
hym pryue in chaumbre. and Men bryngen hym bred and wyne
oiþer ale to conforten hym for his bloode letynge. And he þat is
lorde of alle lordes and kyng of alle kynges þat is Ihesus crist
whan he was leten bloode. was he hudd in chambre. naye it was
vpon an heiȝ hulle in þe hattest of þe day. And what ȝaf men 35
hym to mete oiþer to drynk. noiþer wyne ne ale bot a lytel
soure aysyl and stynkeande galle whan he seide me þrustes.

M. 112)

p. 387b

M. 114)

---

4 Augustinus. *in left margin in red ink.*   flere se, *sic for* fleuisse.   16 is
corrected from one or two other letters.   27 botȝ, *sic for* bot.   35 what:
t *on erasure.*   37 stynkeande: de *partially erased.*

Where was euere ȝiuen to any blode letynge so pouer pitaunce.
who so gruccheþ þan for mete oiþer drynk. he offereþ þan oure
lorde þis bitter drynk ⁊ liþer. as þe iewes duden. and he is þe
iewes make. And þe þrust þat he hadde was for oure soules to
brynge hem to his blis. And vnderstondeþ wel þat vche soure hert 5
and grucchynge is to hym bitterer þan þe galle was. ne be we
nouȝth þe iewes make god it wott ich hadde leuer were he my
broþer oiþer my suster see hym honge gyltles. þan one tyme
(M. 116) kysse so as ich wolde mene And also vche onelich man ⁊ womman
schulde vche day schrapen her putt god it wott. þat putt was 10
wel yordyned for hem. for it wil make hem harde honden.

MEmorare nouissima ⁊ ineternum non peccabis et cetera.
⟨ Haue here deþ in mynde. and þou schalt neuer synne, And
many men ⁊ wymmen hane gret gladnesse of her faire honden
(M. 118) and fallen in to lykyng of pride. Nou nys þere nouȝth bot beeþ 15
smeþe and soft inwiþ. ⁊ þolemody aȝein yuel. and scheme, and
teene. And þan ben ȝee Ihesus cristes deciples. and elles
nouȝth. þis is now þe ridd dale of ȝoure booke. Dauid spekeþ of
onelich men and wymmen þat bitter ben and waymody of hert

SImilis factus sum Pellicano solitudinis et cetera ⟨ Ich am 20
liche þe Pellicane þat is a weymode bridde and sleþ her
briddes for teene. and after smyteþ hire seluen to þe hert. ⁊
arereþ hem wiþ her bloode. þat is þe weymode man oiþer
womman þat takeþ hem to serue god þat slen her briddes. þat
ben her goode werkes þorouȝ her grette hert. For alssone as hij 25
synnen dedlich: Alle her werkes þat ben goode dyen. and þe
wykked quyken. Doo þan as þe Pellicane doþe. beþ sory and
schryueþ ȝou. and þan hij qwyken aȝein, Riȝth as a man þat is |
p. 388a blody is griselich bifore mannes siȝth.ʾ riȝth so is man þat is in
synne to goddes siȝth. And noman ne may wel iugge bloode atte 30
Barbours ar it be colde. nomore ne may a Man oiþer a womman

---

12 ineternum, *sic for* in eternum.   Sa *in right margin in red ink. Traces
of* l *at edge of MS.* m *written below* Sa. *Traces of a letter at edge. Name
intended was* Salomon.   13 neuer: ue *blotted. Possibly a correction.*
17 cristes: *second* s *on erasure.*   18 ridd, *sic for* þridd. *Erasure after* ridd.
ȝoure: re *partially effaced.*   20 Dau[id] *in right margin in red ink.*
21 liche: lic *on erasure.*   Pellicane: P *on erasure.*   and: nd *on erasure.*   22 hert: e *partially effaced.*   23 hem: *MS.* hēm.
26 werkes: es *crammed together.*   dyen: dy *on erasure.*   27 wykked:
wyk *on erasure.*   Pellicane: ne *on erasure.*   sory: s *partially effaced.*
p. 388a *Red ink is used to ornament certain initial letters on this page.*
30 may: a *corrected from* e.

iuggen hem seluen tyl þat her bloode is hott in wraþþe oiþer in
any oþer synne als longe as hij beþ in Any likyng to þe synne.
Ac whan þe hete is ypassed þan þenche on ihesu cristes passioun.
And whatt sorou3 ⁊ wo he hadd for Adams synne. for þat synne
brou3th hym to al þat pyne þat he suffred And charge þan his   5
pyne. ⁊ looke þan what þou arte. þou nart bot erþe and no goode
nast of þi seluen And 3if þou wilt þus deme þi seluen þou schalt
haue grace of god forto wiþstonde þat ilche vice þat þou haste ne
be it neuere so strong. And þou wilt folowe þere opon wiþ
biddynge 3erne. And oft þenche on seint Petre þe worde þat he   10
seide to hym þo he lay in prisoun and was so feble for hunger
þat he my3th nou3th wel speke And 3utt oure lorde com to hym
and badde hym bidde vn to hym 3erne. And so mote we do
in wel and in wo alway bidden to hym. And euere þe more
anguisch þat we haue þe faster we schulde bidden vn to hym. for 15
þan hereþ he soonest oure biddynge. For vnderstonde wel þis
poynt þo þat ben his childer he nyl nou3th delyueren hem þerof
als longe as hij mowen suffren it. For it is al for her goode. For
þe more sorou3 þat a man suffreþ here for his loue. þe nerre
hym he schal come. and þe nerre hym þat he comeþ. þe more   20
ioye he schal haue. For þere ne may non come to parfit lyf bot
3if he haue many sorou3es boþe in body and in soule. As Ihesus
crist hadd hym seluen and as hise chosen. Wene 3e þan þat a
man schal come to parfit lyf for þat he bicomeþ a man of ordre:
Nay þe hei3er þat he clymbeþ þe ferrer he is þerfro bot 3if he   25
rewle hym by wisdom and by queyntise. And þan wil god sett
hym þere as best is for hym. And 3if he goo by his owen wille
oiþer by oþer mannes techyng and nou3th by skyl. þe hei3er þat
he clymbeþ þe wers he quemeþ god. Vnderstonde þat wel vche
man whan ich speke of onelich men oiþer of Ancres. takeþ it on 30
non oþer maner þan i speke it here. For als gret myster haþ o
man come to blisse as anoþer. Whi ne haþ nou3th a lewed man
als gret myster come to god as a Clerk. Als grett. 3if he looke to
hym. for als dere bou3th god on as a noþer. Ac he ne 3iueþ
nou3th als gret grace to on as to a noþer þerfore þere he 3iueþ his 35
grace. he 3iueþ more after þe goode wille þan after þe dede.
And þat he seide vnto samuel þe prophete. whan he badde hym
enoynt Dauid to be kyng ouer his folk. He seide i ne chese

---

13 vn *written above line and marked for insertion.*

dwelling symbol

p. 388b nouȝth myne men by her strengþe | ne by her fairhede. Ac i
chese hem by her goode wille. Now vnderstondeþ þat a mannes
body is cleped in holy wrytt sumtyme an hous. and sumtyme a
Citee and sumtyme goddes temple and holy chirche. þan riȝth
as ȝee see þat an Ancre is bischett in an hous and may nouȝth 5
out. riȝth so is vche mannes soule bischett in his body as an
Ancre. And þerfore vche man lered and lewed ȝif he wil queme
god and be his deciple helde hym in his hous. Schete his dores
and his wyndowes fast þat ben his fyue wyttes. þat he take no
likyng to synne ne to werldelich þynges. and þan he is an Ancre 10
and wel better quemeþ god þan hij þat byschetten hem and
taken hem to heiȝe lyf. and ben werldelich. þat is setten her
hertes vpon werldelich þinges. for hij quemen litel god oiþer
nouȝth.

NEmo potest duobus dominis seruire et cetera. ⟨ Noman 15
seiþ oure lorde may serue two lordes to queme. þat is to
saie. Noman may serue god and Mammona. þat is richesse. Ac
do as Dauid seiþ.

DIuicie si affluant nolite cor apponere. et cetera. ⟨ Ȝif richesses fallen vpon a Man ne sette he nouȝth his hert þere 20
opon. He þat wil goo to heiȝe lyf take ensaumple att þe apostles.
And looke hou hij lyueden after þe best manere to queme god.
For hij ben foundement of al holy chirche. þat is a gaderynge of
goode folk in goddes name þat is holy chirche. ꝛ non oþere. þise
chirches þat þise men done make is cleped an hous of orisoun. 25

DOmus mea domus oracionis vocabitur. ⟨ Myne hous seiþ
oure lorde is hous of Orisoun. And þerfore vche mannes
body is cleped hous. for it schulde be fulfilde of biddynges to
hym. Now hise Apostles were proued in þe werlde. Hij nere
nouȝth bischett and duelleden amonges men in sorouȝ and in 30
wo in þis werlde. and tauȝtten þe folk and lyueden after her
techynge þat þe folk myȝth take ensample of hem forto do wel.
And ne schal a man neuer loue god parfitelich. bot ȝif he do so.
For Ihesus crist seide to Peter þries Louestow me. And Peter
seide Lorde þou wost þat i loue þe. And þan seide ihesus. fede 35
my scheep. And to iohn his derlynge he seide also. And so

p. 388b *Red ink is used to ornament certain initial letters on this page.*
15 dominus. *in right margin in red ink.* 19 dauid *in right margin in red ink.*
25 make: *irregular curl after e, possibly indicating* n. 26 dominus. *in right*
margin in red ink. 35 þan: a *corrected from* e.

schulde vche man do þat hym loued putt hym in perile forto
saue his folk. Look how þou woldest do ȝif þou were wiþ þe
kyng and louedest hym. þou woldest aunter þi lyf forto saue his
lyf and his worschipp. More auȝttestou þan forto aunter þe
forto saue ihesus cristes lyf and his worschipp. þat ȝaf his lyf for 5
þe. His lyf þou sauest whan þou helpest a man out of synne in
als mychel as in þe is. For he dyed for synne. And so he seiþ
hym self. who so doþe dedlich synne he doþe hym on þe roode. |
p. 389a And þan vndestonde wel þis. þe kyng ne may nouȝth saue þee
in bataile so fer forþe þou miȝth auntre þe for his loue. Ac þe 10
kyng of heuene ihesus crist þou ne may neuere auntre þe so fer
forþ in bataile for his loue þat he ne may wel saue þe þat non
enemy schal deren þe. And so he seide hym seluen to þe holy
prophete þat lyues man in paradys. Hely he seide wostow nouȝth
wel þat ich am wiþ þe. And als longe as ich am wiþ þe noiþer iew 15
ne sarazene ne may nouȝth deren þe. Goo aȝein þem and chese
þe oþer prophetes. also dauid seiþ.

SPerabo in deo ⁊ non timebo quid faciat michi caro. ⟨ þat is.
bileeue in god ⁊ I ne schal nouȝth drede what no flesche may
do to me. Ȝif any harme falle þe bodilich. it is for þi goode for he 20
suffred bodilich hame for þe. And he wil alowen þe it better þan
alle þe kynges of erþe willen oiþer mowen. Ac vnderstonde wel
Slee þe ne schal noman. aunter þou þe neuer so fer for his loue
til tyme be þat he wil haue þe til hym. Ȝif it so be þat þou rewle
þe by wisdom ⁊ queyntyse. Ac vche man þat schal seruen his 25
lorde owe to take hise termes in tyme as he may hym best
serue. And so do vche man to god. and haue þise verses in
hert.

Nunc stude. nunc ora nunc cum feruore labora.
Sic erit hora breuis. ⁊ labor iste leuis. 30
⟨ Now stodie. now bidde. now wirche. And so schal þe þenche
þe day schort ⁊ þe werk liȝth. Take nouȝth to mychel of oþing.
bot euere as þi wytt is scharpest. vse as þise verses seien ⁊ þan
may þou wel queme god. ⟨ Now forþ in oure matere þat we
spake of bifore of wraþþe. And on þis manere deme þi seluen 35

p. 389a *Red ink is used to ornament certain initial letters on this page.*
9 vndestonde, *sic for* vnderstonde. 16 nouȝth: uȝ *probably on erasure.*
uȝt *crammed together.* 18 dauid. *in left margin in red ink.* SPerabo: bo
written above line and marked for insertion. ⁊ *written above line.* 21 hame,
sic for harme. 29 versus *in left margin in red ink.* 29–30 *Marked
as a couplet by connecting strokes in red ink.*

wraþ

(M. 120)

p. 389b

(M. 122)

whan þe lust is ouer as men seiþ. Lete lust ouergoo ⁊ eft it wil
þe lyke, as þe versifiour seiþ.
Impedit ira animum. ne possit cernere verum. ⟨ Wraþþe ablyndeþ þe hert eiȝen þat we ne may nouȝth iugge þe sooþe.

Magna quedam est transformans naturam humanam 5
⟨ Wraþþe forschapeþ þe man and oþer synnes also in to
bestes kynde.

Homo cum in honore esset non intellexit comparatus est
iumentis insipientibus ⁊ similis factus est illis. ⟨ Man whan
he is houen vp in to worschip ne knoweþ nouȝth hym seluen he 10
is likned to a Mere. Looke whan a Man is wroþ. biholde his
semblaunt. of Mouþ. of eiȝen. and alle hise lates. and þou may
deme hym þan out of his wytt. Bedes ne may he none bidde bot
as he þat is went in to woluen kynde, Ira furor breuis est et
cetera. ⟨ Wraþþe is a wodeschip þat turneþ man in to beeste.| 15

Est enim homo animal mansuetum natura. By riȝth skyl man
schulde be Milde. for sone so he leseþ his myldeschipp he
leseþ his innocent kynde. nys þere þan noþing best bot late
reuþe falle ouer þe hert. Anoþer þenche aȝein wraþþe ȝif men
myssaien þe oiþer Misdone þe. þan þenche þat þou art erþe. 20
and to erþe þou schalt turne aȝein. And þenche þan what men
done on þe erþe. Men spytten on þe erþe. þenche þat ȝif men
duden so wiþ þe Men duden þe erþe kynde for so men done on
þe erþe. And þan ȝif þou berkest aȝein þou arte houndes kynde.
⁊ ȝif þou styngest aȝein wiþ attry woord. þan artow neddre 25
kynde and nouȝth Ihesus cristes spouse. þenche what þi spouse
dude whan men duden hym scheme and teene. how myldelich
he it suffred.

Qui tamquam ouis ad occisionem ductus est ⁊ non aperuit
os suum. ⟨ þat is whan men ladden hym to pyne and 30
duden hym tourment. nomore ne queiȝtte he þan a lombe. Ful
feble and leþi is he in goddes seruise þat þe wynde of a woord
may cast in to synne. In oþer halue he is dust and vnstable þat
doune bloweþ alsone for þe puf of a wyndes blast. and þan
heueþ it vp þat schulde be putt vnder feete. And beren vp hym 35
toward heuene. Ac it is wonder of oure gret Manschipp þat we
charge so mychel of þis werlde þat nys nouȝt bot stynkeande
tofore god. Seint Marie. seint Andrew miȝth suffren þat þe

3 versus *in left margin in red ink.*   5 MAgna, *sic for* MAga.   8 dauid *in left
margin in red ink.*   19 ȝif: *two red dots above* ȝ.   34 bloweþ *on erasure.*

roode bare hym vp toward heuene. Also oþer Martirs þat badd
wiþ folden honden for her enemyes and knelande as seint
Steuene whan men stoneden hym in þe mouþe and oueral ȝif
we couþe goode and vnderstondynge hadde ariȝth of god we
wolde þonken hem of þe gret godenysse þat hij done vn to vs. 5
for þe gret mede þat we schulle haue þerfore. we wolde þonken
hem wiþ wel goode wille. þou seest wel þat þou art endetted to
hem here þat done þe bodilich goode.' more þan owestou louen
and helpen hem þat done þe gostlich goode nyllen hij ne willen
hij, ⁊ þerfore loue hem for Ihesu cristes loue þi spouse For ȝif þou 10
loue hym þou wil loue hem þat he biddeþ þe loue ⁊ bidde for hem.

Dllige inimicos tuos et cetera. ⸿ Loue þine enemyes he seiþ
and do hem goode. and for her loue god schal ȝiue þee
gostlich mede ⁊ bodilich boþe more þan for þine frendes. For
þine frendes done for þe. and þou for hem. what mede wiltow 15
ask þere of of god

Impius velit nolit etc. ⸿ þe wicked seiþ oure lorde ȝiueþ vs
pyement nylle he ne wille he alle þat done vs harme alle is goode
to vs ȝif we willeþ taken it þolemodelich. ⁊ þenche | on þe holy
man in vitas patrum þat kissed his honden and blissed hym for 20
þat he hadd hurt hym wiþ hem. And so I rede þat we do. blisse
we hem and saie to hem. wel is me for þe gode. þat þou doos to
me. Ac me is wo for þine harme for it is game to me and ernest to
þe. þise holy men þoleden woundes for oure lordes loue. and we
lete þat we ben holy. and saie þat we louen hym. And we ne may 25
nouȝth þolen þe puffe of a wyndes blast. And þat is gret tokne
þat þere is litel charite in vs.

Quid irritaris quid in amaris aut verbi flatum qui nec
carnem wlnerat nec inquinat mentem. ⸿ þere is litel loue
of charite þat puffeþ out for a litel wynde. for noiþer it woundeþ 30
þe flessche. ne fileþ vs bot ȝif we wil oure seluen. And Men
seien often by ensample. þere þat mychel fyre is. it wexeþ wiþ
þe wynde more ⁊ more. And so schulde þe fyre of brennande loue
do þat we schulden haue to oure spouse ihesu crist wexen more ⁊
more. for suich wynde of wordes and of oþer harmes. Anoþer 35
ensample. A man þat were in prisoun for gret dett. And a Man

p. 390a
f. 124)

6–7 *Small holes indicating that a crack in MS. was stitched together before
the text was written. The crack begins after* schulle *and goes downwards to the
left in the direction of* art.   16 of of, *sic dittography.*   27 [Ber]nard
in left margin in red ink.   28 in amaris aut, *sic for* inflammaris ad.

com to hym wiþ a Bygyrdel fol of siluer. ⁊ dussched it doune
vpon hym þat he my3th be deliuered þere þorou3. þei3 it 3af
(M. 126) hym a ful yuel strok. and hurtt hym sore. for þe gladnesse þat
he schulde be deliuered þerþorou3. he wolde for3eten his hurtt.
And it nolde nou3th greue hym bot lytel. We ben alle in gret 5
dette of synnes to oure lorde. and þerfore we crie to hym 3erne
in þe. Pater noster. whan we saie. ⁊ dimitte nobis debita nostra
et cetera ⁊ in þe Godspel it seiþ. Dimittite ⁊ dimittetur vobis.
For3iueþ. ⁊ I schal for3iue 3ou wiltow better forward. þou arte
endetted to me. of many synnes and fele. 10

POnens in thesauris Abyssos. glosa crudeles quibus donat
Milites suos. ⟨ God doþe in his tresore þe yuel of þe vnwrast man, to oure biheue. to aquyten vs out of his dett.

SImilis factus sum Pellicano. et cetera. ⟨ þe Pellicane is a
Bridde þat leeue is to wonen one. and sche is a lene bridd. 15
And so schulde vche man and womman. þat schulde be goddes
spouse holde hem one bot whan tyme were. þat is holde hem
out of þe felawschipp of þe werlde. And hij schulden fasten in
Mesure forto kepe hem lene þat her flesche ne ouer3ede hem
nou3th. þat is þat hij ne fellen nou3th in to foule synnes of 20
Leccherie. oiþer of Glotonye 3if þat hij weren of hott complexioun so þat hij mi3tten nou3t wel chastisen her flesche so
þat it ne were nou3th þe soules Maister

Iudith clausa in cubiculo ieiunabat omnibus diebus vite sue. |
p. 390b ⟨ Iudith was bitent in al her lyf and lad hard lyf. Fasted. waked ⁊ 25
trauailed ⁊ so falleþ þerto vn to goddes spouse to done. and
(M. 128) nou3th putten hem in sty forto fatten as Hogges.

IX habundancia panis ⁊ superfluitate vini et cetera. Gret plente
of bred and superfluite of wyn maden Sodom ⁊ Gomorre þat
hij fellen in to synne of leccherie. And þat was þe most enche- 30
soun of her forlerenysse. Tueie manere Men and wymmen þere
ben þat gon to hei3e lyf forto serue god þat hym seluen spekeþ
of in þe passioun.

WLpes foueas habent volucres celi nidos.' filius autem
hominis non habebat vbi caput suum suum reclinet. 35

10 [Da]uid *in left margin in red ink. Traces of letter at edge of MS.*   11–13 *Crack
mentioned at p. 47 ll. 5–6 extends from after* Abyssos. *in the direction of* man, *the
thread still being in existence on this side.*   11 donat *on erasure.*   13 [Da]uid
in left margin in red ink. Traces of a letter at edge of MS.   23 were: *three
small dots in red ink on* w.   28 IX, *sic for* EX. Salamon, *in right margin
in red ink.*   35 habebat, *sic for* habet.   suum suum, *sic dittography.*

⸿ Foxes han her holes. And bryddes han her nestes. Ac mannes *fox é bird*
son ne haþ nouȝth where on he may leggen his heued. By þe
Fox is bitokned fals Men ⁊ wymmen. þat schapen hem to heiȝe
degre er þat hij ben cunnande. and bicomen þan ypocrites. and
bigilen symple Men. and hem seluen aldermest. For þise ben 5
euermore gederynge and setten her hertes in erþelich þinges.
and to vnþewes And cracchen al to hem þat hij mowen repen and
renden. þise ben likned to þe fox þat freteþ hennes and gees.
and haþ a symple semblaunt. and is þeiȝ ful of gyle. And so
done hij maken hem holy. and ne ben nouȝth. hij wenen to 10
bigilen god. as hij done symple folk. tut pur lamour de dieu
soit. Hij willeþ saien al be it for þe loue of god. ȝe swich willeþ
trauaile ful litel þerfore. And ȝif þe fox do yuel. ȝutt men sayen
wers by hym. And so done Men by hem þat ben bidande. swich
men wenden in to Hole as kyng saule dude. He went þider in 15
forto make foule þere inne. And so done hij þat taken holy lyf
forto filen it. For Saul went forto seche Dauid forto haue slayn
hym. And Dauid went in to hole forto hyden hym fram hym.
as it telleþ in Libro Regum, And so done summe maken hem
holy. for hij mowen þe bettre done her queedschippes and ful- 20
fillen her wille þan ȝif hij weren in þe werlde. For hij hopeþ þat
Men nylleþ nouȝth haue no gret suspecioun vn to hem. as men
wolden haue ȝif hij weren werldelich. Who so comeþ and goþ to
hem⸴ be hem wel war of her pryue synnes; For seint Iohn þe
Ewangelist goddes derlyng spekeþ of a Beest þat comeþ vp out 25
of þe erþe and dude make a lyknesse of anoþer Beeste. þat aros
out of þe erþe aforne hym þat was slayn and quyked aȝein. And
it was comaunded þat þere ne schulde be non noiþer litel ne

mychel þat it ne schulde haue þe Merk of þat oiþer in | þe
honde. oiþer in þe forheued. And ȝif hij nolde nouȝth take þe 30
Merk hij schulde be slayn. and ȝif he took it he ȝede to helle.
þat Beest bitokneþ Leccherie. And is seide by waie of holy
chirche aȝein antecristes comynge. þat non ne schal be avaunced
to holy chirche. bot it be þorouȝ kynred. oiþer þorouȝ seruise of
grete lordes. oiþer þorouȝ Simonye And al þis schulde goo 35
þerto more for bodilich sustenaunce and worschipp of þe

6 h *crossed out after* in.   7 cracchen: *first c on erasure.*   10 maken:
traces of erasure on m.   22 vn *written above line and marked for inser-*
tion.   25 goddes: *MS.* godddes *with second* d *expuncted.*   p. 391a
Red ink is used to ornament certain initial letters on this page.   36 þorouȝ
crossed out with faint stroke after more.

werlde. þan for any loue þat hij han to god And þe Merk in þe
honde bitokneþ þat hij scholden done her leccherie pryuelich
first. and so hij schullen forlese. þe knoweynge of god. And
þorou3 þat blyndnesse þat þe deuel haþ ablent hem hij schullen
done her leccherie openlich. And þan hij þe Merk in þe forhede. 5
And þan ne schal noman durre speke of God for hem. þat hij
ne schullen done hem to þe deþ. þise ben Heretykes and fals
prophetes. and ypocrytes seint iohn seiþ. And þise he seiþ ne
mowen nou3th ben ysaued. for þorou3 her Leccherie hij beþ
bicomen proude. ⁊ coueitouse. and Vsurers. and Marchaundes. 10
of Mennes soules. and of wymmens as god seiþ in his godspelle.
EGo sum pastor bonus ⁊ cognosco Oues meas ⁊ cognoscunt me
mee et cetera. ⟨ Ich am a goode shepehirde and knowe wel my
schepe and myne schepe knowen me. þe goode hirde 3iueþ his
soule for his scheep. þe Marchante ne 3iueþ no keep to þe 15
scheep for it ne falleþ nou3th vnto hym. Ne nomore þan done hij
For hane hij her delices here. hij ne holden no tale swich myster
men. For hij han forsaken þat streytt waie þat liþ to heuene
and taken to þe hei3e waie þat ledeþ to helle as þe Godspel seiþ.
ARta est via que ducit ad celum. ⟨ God seiþ þe weye is 20
streytt vn to heuene and litel folk goþ þere inne. And wide
vn to helle and Michel folk goþ þere inne. And vche man be war
of þis poynt. Hij þat forsaken þe werldes catel and bidden her
mete þat hij ne bicomen nou3th loseniours for hij ne schulden
glose no man ne no womman. And þan per auenture may bifalle 25
þat 3if hij seiden þe soþe 3if hij couþe.' hij ne schulden nou3th
be welcome 3if hij comen anoþer tyme. For werldelich men and
wymmen ne louen none soþe saw3es. bot al putten hem to
Mercy and noþing to ri3thfulnesse. And it were inpossible þat
þise schulden ben ysaued. For holy wrytt seiþ. 3if Man schal be 30
saued he mote vnderstonde boþe. And þat makeþ þat Men bico-
men losenioures and defautt of cunnyng and grace. for hij ne |
p. 391b   wirchen nou3th wiselich by cunnynge ⁊ by queyntise. Sapiencia
⁊ Prudencia, bot 3if hij han þise two I nolde nou3th 3iue a nedel

---

12 dominus *in left margin in red ink.*   13–21 *14 small stitch-holes in MS.*
at right edge of column.   14 wel *crossed out with black stroke touched up*
by red stroke after knowen.   15 ne *written above line and marked for*
insertion.   20 dominus *in left margin in red ink.*   29 ri3thfulnesse:
wis *crossed out after* ri3th. ful *written above and marked for insertion.*
p. 391b *Red ink is used to ornament certain initial letters on this page.*
34 nedel: el *crammed together.*

for al her werk as to come to parfit lyf forto loue god. And
serue hym ne schal neuer Man ne womman wiþouten þise two.
for nomore is þat on worþ wiþouten þat oþer. þan hope wiþouten
drede. wisdom þat is Ihesus crist. hym self. Looke þat þou
seche after his lawȝe boþe þe hard ⁊ þe nesche þat is þe riȝth-   5
wisenesse ⁊ þe Mercy. and looke what he biddeþ þe do for he
spekeþ diuerslich. And ne holde nouȝth to hard on o woord þat
he seiþ tyl þou haue þe proue þer of. riȝth wel. for he seiþ in þe
godspelle.

S I oculus tuus scandalizat te et cetera. ⟨ Ȝif þine eiȝe sclaunder   10
þe. putt it out. ȝif þou do so bodilich þou errest. Ac it is þus
vnderstonden. Ȝif þou seest a siȝth þat þou haste any likyng to
synne oiþer may haue þorouȝ þat siȝth.' wiþdrawe þine eiȝe. and
þan puttestow it out. ⁊ so do of alle þine lymes.

P Rudencia. þat is queyntise. þat is þat þou be queynt in   15
discrecioun. þat is euene bytt bente nouȝth to mychel ne to
litel in noþing þat þou schalt done. And namelich to gon to any
ordre oiþer schape to heiȝe lyf er þou haue proued þi self. And
ȝut þeiȝ þou haue proued þi self. ȝutt goo þerto in gret drede,
and bot ȝif þou do þus þou ne quemest nouȝth god And þerfore   20
ȝif þou wilt queme hym þou most taken an euene weye in Mesure
bitwixen hope and drede. Of þis wisdom and þis queyntise
telleþ Salomon. Saule. on Ebru. Abutens siue abusio. ⟨ þat is
on oure tunge note iuge. and so done hij. for hij beren fals
name. þe goode man ⁊ þe goode womman hideþ hem and done   25
goode werkes. þat is takeþ no praysynge to hem of her werkes
þat hij done. And þan fleiȝen hij vpward to þe heuene ward as þe
bridde doþe. And þat hij seche no praysynge here for her goode
dedes þat hij done. þan mowen hij seien as Iob seiþ.

R Eposita est hec spes mea in sinu meo. ⟨ þat is mannes   30
hope is hidde in his bosome, Bosome þat bitokneþ siker
stede þat is in ihesu crist Ne wille here no praysynges for nouȝth
þat þou doost and þan ben þine goode dedes hudde and ȝif þou
lokest after praysynge. Loo what god seiþ in þe godspelle.

10 Dominus *in right margin in red ink.*   15 *Irregular vertical stroke in*
black ink in right margin.   18 proued: d *partially erased. From this word to*
the bottom of the page a narrow strip of the MS. has been worn.   24 note
iuge, *sic. Cf.* Corpus: mis notunge *35b: 14,* Cleopatra: mis notunge *53ʳ: 20,*
Nero: misnotinge *57: 13,* Titus: misnotinge *36: 24.*   28 *Horizontal*
fold in MS. over praysynge *here.*   29 Iob seiþ *on erasure.*   30 Iob
in right margin in red ink. b *partially effaced.*   31 þat: a *irregularly*
compressed.

AMen dico vobis receperunt mercedem suam. ⸿ I saye ȝou
forsoþe hij han resceyued her Mede here. 3if þou doo þi
werkes openlich here þou doost mychel better þan ȝif ȝou dudest
so þat noman wist it. ȝif þou take no liking to þi seluen. bot do
it in þat entent for þat hij schulden done þe better þer þorouȝ 5
þat seen it. Seint Poule telde his goode dedes þat he | dude
openlich tofore þe folk in þat manere hou he fasted. hou he dude
penaunce And his anguische þat he hadde al he telde. Briddes
whan hij fleiȝen heiȝe. hij ne ben noþing agast Ac þeiȝ al hij
fleiȝen heiȝe ȝut hij moten come doun to þe erþe to her mete. 10
And þan hij ben agast last hij schulden be taken wiþ sumwhat.
And þerfore hij pikken o pikkyng after her mete and loken vp as
suiþe. And so scholde vche man do þat wolde seruen god. He
moste do as þe bridde doþe wiþ his sustenaunce þat he schal
haue of þe erþe. ben euer agast of þe deuels wyles lest he cacche 15
hym. And þerfore þe broode ende of þine hert is sett vpward in
þi body ⁊ þe smal dounward in tokenyng þat þou schalt ȝiue alle
þi wordes and alle þine þouȝttes vp to heueneward. And vn to þis
werlde barelich þi sustenaunce as þou may best serue god For
god ȝiueþ a man sum tyme riches forto prouen hym hou he wil 20
dispenden it. And summe ȝif hij weren pouer. hij ne schulden
nouȝth wel quemen god. And summe ȝif hij weren riche hij ne
schulden quemen hym so wel as hij done in her pouerte Ac
nymeþ ȝeme her to. þere ben in þis werlde foure manere folk.
Riche and riche. And þere ben Pouer. and pouer. þat is pouer 25
here and in helle boþe. And Riche and riche. þat is Riche here
and Riche in þe blisse of heuene boþe. And þere ben Riche and
Pouer. þat ben hij þat ben Riche here and gon to helle. And
þere ben Pouer ⁊ Riche. þat ben hij þat ben Pouere here and gon
to heuene. þis manere folk ben in þis werlde. Ac euere haueþ 30
þis in ȝoure hert þat ȝe no good done of ȝou seluen for so biddeþ
oure lorde.

1 receperunt: *second* e *slightly irregular, possibly due to correction.*   mercedem: *last* m *blotted.*   Dominus *in right margin in red ink.* s *partially effaced. Horizontal fold in MS. over* dem suam. Dominus.   2 Mede: Me
on erasure. M *corrected from another letter.*   4 *After* þou *accidental dot.*
5 schulden: en *crammed together.*   5–6 þer þorouȝ þat: þer þorouȝ þ *on
erasure.*   p. 392a *Red ink is used to ornament certain initial letters in the
paragraph ending at l. 32.*   9 fleiȝen: leiȝ *crammed together at end of
line. Traces of erasure between second* e *and* n.   10 fleiȝen: l *partially
erased.*   19 as: s *partially erased.*   22 riche hij: riche h *on erasure.*
23 hij: h *partly on erasure.*   25 ben Pouer *probably on erasure.*

(f. 130) CUm omnia benefeceritis dicite a me ⁊ invtiles serui sumus.
(f. 132) ydel. Ʒif þat ʒee wil fleiʒen heiʒe as þe bridde doþe þat haþ
litel flesche as þe Pellicane þat is a lene bridde, ⁊ nouʒth as þe
Ostryk. þat makeþ semblaunt as he schulde fleiʒe Ac euere his 5
feet ben on þe erþe. And so done werldelich men And wymmen
here. maken semblaunt forto fleiʒe heiʒe wiþ holy lyf. Ac euere
her hert is sett on bodilich delices þat maken her bodyes heuy
and fatt as god seiþ þorouʒ þe prophete.

INcrassatus est dilectus meus ⁊ recalcitrauit. ⟨ My lef is fatted 10
and wynseþ wiþ þe heles. As þou sette a fatt Mare þat is ydel.
Swich Men þeiʒ hij wenen to fleiʒen hij fallen alway doune. Ac
þe gode gostlich Man ⁊ womman setteþ heiʒe his hert in swete
þouʒttes to Ihesu crist his spouse as þe brydde þat sitteþ on
(f. 134) grene tre and syngeþ Mery. Bridd haþ nest hard outwiþ and 15
(p. 392b) scharp and smeþe and soft inwiþ. So mote vche Man and | wom-
man be hard outewiþ wiþ pynsynges of flesche in biddynge and
in wakynge. and euere laye þe wreche þat god haþ taken for synne
stille in þine hert as a ston And þat schal helde þe fram synne
and noþing better. And looke þat þou be wiþinne smeþe and 20
soft wiþ swete þouʒttes. and goode willes to ʒoure spouse Ihesu
crist And saie to hym as spouse owe to done to oþer.

FOrtitudinem meam ad te custodiam. ⟨ þat is i schal wite my
strengþe to þee lorde. þo þat ben werldelich men hij maken
her nest al framward þis. Fair ⁊ smeþe outwiþ And hard ⁊ scharp 25
inwiþ. And þise schullen late bringe forþ any goode briddes
þat ben goode werkes.

IN nidulo meo moriar ⟨ þat is ich derne my nest as done
wormen. Ac doumbe bestes lerneþ wisdom þat derneþ in his
nest a derworþe ʒymme ston. þat noþing may harme his 30
briddes. ne noþing may neiʒ þe ston. þat derworþe ʒymme ston
is Ihesus crist þat is derworþe ouer alle ʒymme stones þat non
attre of synne ne may neiʒen. he is cleped þe achate. doþe hym
in ʒoure neste þat is in ʒoure herte. þenche what pyne he hadde
(f. 136) on his flessche wiþ outen. hou swete and hou softe he was inwiþ 35

---

1 dicite: *letter erased between* i *and* c.   5 as *partially erased.*   schulde:
h *and* l *partially erased.*   11 sette: et *blotted.*   13 hert *on erasure.*
23 dauid. *in right margin in red ink.*   29 Ac, *sic for* At. *Corpus, Cleopatra, Nero and Titus read* Of.   derneþ, *sic for* earn deþ.   33 ne
written above line and marked for insertion.   35 inwiþ: *MS.* in wiþ *with
connecting stroke.*

euere whan man dude hym þat wouȝ And þou schalt dryuen
out attry synne. for be it neuere so bitter pyne þat þou þolest. he
þoled more for þe And þan schal al þi pyne þenche þe liȝth
namelich ȝif þou þenche wel þat he was gyltles and we ben
gylty. And ȝif þou haue þis ston in þi nest þat is in þi hert ne 5
þar þe noþing dreden þe attry nedder of helle who so ne may
nouȝth haue it in his hert.' haue it outwiþ. Looke opon þe
Crouche ⁊ make on þe þe tokne. and make ofte þe tokne of þe
crois opon hem. And þenche we opon þe harde peynes þat oure
spouse suffred for vs þere opon and lyue hard lyue. And þenche 10
ofte þe gret godenesse þat he haþ done vn to vs and oure trespas
toward hym And crie hym mercy and schryue vs often þat we
be Nidyf þat slouȝ Oloferne. For Nidyf on Ebru is schrift on
oure tunge þat sleþ þe deuel gostlich. For þi seien Men her.
Confiteor. and schryuen hem ofte to slen Oloferne þat is þe 15
deuel. For so seien Men it is A name stynkynge in helle secundum
nominis ethimologiam. Olofernus. id est. olens in inferno secundum interpretacionem infirmans vitulum saginatum. Olofernus is þe fende þat makeþ feble and vnstronge. And fatt
Chalf to wildeþ þat flesche sone so it euere fatteþ þorouȝ mete. 20
oiþer þorouȝ dryk. oiþer þorouȝ eise. it bicomeþ wilde as I seide

(M. 138) tofore Incrassatus est dilectus meus. et cetera. For sone so þe
flesche haþ his wille he rigoleþ aȝein þe soule as a fatt Mare and
p. 393a ydel. And | þerfore I rede þat vche man teme it ful wel so sone
it awildeþ wiþ harde discipline oiþer penance wiselich ⁊ warlich 25
for þe godspel seiþ.

Habete sal in vobis in omni sacrificio offeretis sal. ⸿ þat is.
Haueþ salt in ȝou in al sacrifise þat ȝe do to me. Lookeþ
þat þere be salt wiþ al. Salt bitokneþ wisdom. For salt saueþ
and sauoures. And so it fareþ by wisdom. Al þat euere do we to 30
god bot þere be wisdom wiþ al it ne quemeþ hym nouȝth.
Flesche wil stynke ⁊ brede wormes bot it be salt. Also al þat we
do to god. penaunce or any oþer þing wiþ outen wisdom. it
stynkeþ opon god And þerfore it seiþ toforne þou mostest haue
wisdom wiþ þe and queyntise. For þat on nys nouȝth worþ 35
wiþouten þat oþer. And þerfore it is goode þat Men ȝiue goode
keep to þis poynt for þe godspel seiþ þus.

2–10 Stitch-holes mentioned at p. 50: ll. 13–21 seen at left edge of column.
11 ofte on erasure.   13 Nidyf (twice), sic for Iudith.   15 Confiteor on
erasure.   21 dryk, sic for drynk.   27 dominus, in left margin in red ink.

QUodcumque pecieritis patrem in nomine meo dabit vobis.
℟ þat is what ȝe aske of my fader in my name ȝe schullen
it haue. biddeþ þat ȝoure ioye be fulfilde. He biddeþ hem
asken Many vnderstonden þis woorde amysse. þou moste taken
it on þis manere. Looke what Ihesus one on englisch is. it is 5
als mychel to saie as saueoure. Looke þat þou ne aske nouȝth
bot saluacioun of soule principallich first ⁊ þat þi ioye be fulfild.
and so he badde to his deciples. Biddeþ þat ȝoure ioye be fulfild. Also he seiþ in a noþer godspel whan þat is deciples bigan
to stryuen which schulde be Maister whan Ihesus was went 10
fram hem. And Ihesus tooke a childe and brouȝth amonges hem
and seide to hem. Leteþ be al þis I saie ȝou forsoþe who þat
schal comen in to þe blis of heuene he moste be as þis childe is.
And who þat ȝiueþ any þing to þis childe he ȝiueþ it me. Also
þis most be taken on þis manere. þou mostest be loþles as þe 15
childe is. and liȝthlich forȝiuen þi wraþþe And help þere þou
seest þat nede is bleþelich. And Ihesus seide to his deciples. ȝe
clepe me ȝoure Maister and ich am redy to serue ȝou alle. And
þan he tooke water ⁊ wesche her feete. ℟ Now what þing þat þou
ȝiuest to a man oiþer a womman þat in þat manere is a childe 20
þou ȝiuest to hym. And who þat doþe þat Man oiþer womman
any harme.' he toucheþ þe Peerle of cristes eiȝe. And so he seiþ
hym seluen. And þat is non bot þe parfytt Man in hym as hise
apostles weren. Anoþer Ihesus seiþ what ȝe ȝiuen þe leste of
myne ȝe ȝiuen it me. þat ben Men ⁊ wymmen vnder his lawȝe 25
þat louen hym ⁊ dreden hym. Vnderstondeþ wel þat hij lyuen
p. 393b   after | lustes of her flesche ne ben nouȝth vnder his lawȝe. Ac
vnder þe fendes lawȝe hij ben. for god haþ forboden Man
Lustes and likynges of his flesche And ȝif þou susteynes hem
þou susteynes þe fendes childer. And þerfore þou it schalt 30
abuggen. For alle þe creatures þat beþ vnresonable schullen
abuggen þat hij han sustened goddes enemyes. þe sunne. and
þe Moone. ⁊ alle þe oþer Planetes, Wenestow passe quyte þan
þou þat art a beste resonable wiþoute pyne and þou sustene
goddes enemye. Goddes enemy is vche Man þat willes ⁊ woldes 35

1 dominus *in left margin in red ink.*   2 fader: d *corrected from
another letter.*   3 *In left margin hand with forefinger pointing at line beginning*
deþ þat ȝoure.   5–14 *The instrument used for the stitch-holes mentioned at p. 50: ll. 13–21 left its mark at right edge of column. Some of these
holes are found on each leaf down to p. 87 at the corresponding places.*
15 þe *on erasure.*

liþ in synne ⁊ haþ likyng þerto. In þe þridde Godspel oure
lorde seiþ. what þat ȝe ȝiue in my name Michel schal be ȝoure
mede, And now vnderstonden summe þat to whom þat hij
ȝiuen her Almes in his name þat hij schullen hane gret mede
þerfore Ac hij vnderstonden wrong. To swich may þou ȝiue   5
þine Almes. þou schalt be pyned þerfore. Ȝif þou ȝiue a Man
any þing for his loue and he be in dedly synne ⁊ þou it wost þou
sustenest hym in his synne. And god ne may nouȝth chastisc
hym for þe. For þou makest his body so strong þat he holdeþ
his synne forþ. And god wolde chastise hym þorouȝ pouerte ⁊   10
meseise. and he ne may nouȝth for þe for þou holdest hym vp.
And þerfore þou arte coupable of þe synne þat he doþe.
COnsencientes ⁊ agentes pari pena punientur. ⸿ þe consentande ⁊ þe dede doer schullen haue o peyne. And þou ne
myȝth nouȝth excuse þe þat þou narte consentande to his synne   15
whan þat þou ȝiuest hym so þat he is þe lenger sustened in his
synne. Ac Man wil ansuere on þis wise ⁊ seie I nott nouȝth by
hym bot goode. And þeiȝ he ne wite it ⁊ his hert forȝiue hym.
þat it is so. he nylle it nouȝth witen. Vnderstondeþ wel þat he is
coupable ⁊ by þis ensaumple þou may wel see. Looke here whan   20
þou schalt bugge any þing here in þis werlde. Looke þat þou
wilt avise þe ful wel er þou paie þi siluer þat þou be nouȝth
bigyled. Nille nouȝth vche man do þus þat goode can. And bot
ȝif þou wilt looke als besilich aboute gostlich þinges. elles hold-
estou better bodilich þing þan gostlich. And so ne doþe god   25
nouȝth ne none of hise. He biddeþ þat þou schalt wiselich
ȝiue þine almes. Beþ war vche Man of þis poynt And chargeþ
it riȝth wel. For I warne ȝou wel. god it chargeþ gretlich Now
hou schaltou þan ȝiue þine Almes whan he seiþ þat þou ȝiuest
in my name as þou doost of þat oþer. Look what his name is.   30
p. 394a Saueoure. þat is to saie. Looke þat þou ȝiue þat þou ȝiuest | to
hem þat ben in waie of saluacioun and vnderstonden his lawȝe.
And ȝif þi conscience forȝiue þe þat he nys nouȝth. Fonde to
brynge hym in to þe lawȝe ȝif þou may wiþ any queyntise. And
god wil ȝelde it þe. Ac despise hym nouȝth for þou nost what   35
his wille is. For swich may his wille be. þeiȝ he be riȝth a synful
Man. god may sone amende hym, bot susteyne hym nouȝth in
his synne, And vnderstonde wel ȝif þou susteyne a wicked Man.
oiþer a womman and þou it wost. þou dooste more harme to god

24 als: s *blotted.*

þan þou susteyned oiþer iew oiþer Sarazene. For god seiþ a
wicked cristen Man schal be in more pyne þan oiþer of hem.
And siþen þat god schal ȝiue hym more pyne þan may þou wel
wite he greueþ god more. And so þou may þan wel wite þat þou
greues god more ȝif þou susteyne hym. I ne speke nouȝth of 5
synful Men. for þere nys non of vs þat we ne be synful. Ac I
speke of wicked Men ⁊ commune synners. for hij willeþ make
god a fals Man in as mychel as in hem is. þat saien ȝif it were so
as holy wrytt seiþ. noman schulde be saued Oiþer god nyl nouȝth
forlesen þat he dere bouȝth. Oiþer þat seien. God tooke alle out 10
of helle And att Domesday he schal make alle goode, And also.
Goo ich where I goo. I ne goo nouȝth al one. þise ben Men þat
wil fordo þe lawȝe. þat god haþ made and his woorde. Also hij
willeþ fordo ⁊ maken hym a leiȝer in as mychel as in hem is.
And hij schulleþ failen of her purpose. for god seiþ þis in þe 15
godspel.

CElum ⁊ terra transibunt verba autem mea non transibunt,
Heuene and erþe schullen passen ac myne woordes schullen
neuere passen. ⟨ Seint Austyn seiþ þeiȝ þe flesch be oure foo it
is comanded þat weschulle holden it vp euen bitwene two neiþer 20
to wel ne to wo done it for it is fastned wiþ þe derworþe gost
goddes owen. fourme. for we may sone þorouȝ vnwisdom sle
þat on wiþ þat oþer.

NAtura mentis humane que ad ymaginem dei creata est ⁊
sine peccato est. Augustinus deus maior et cetera. ⟨ And 25
þis is on of þe most wonder on erþe þat þe heiȝest þing after
god hym self þan is Mannes soule. as sein Austyn wytnesseþ.
It schal be fest so fast to þe flesche þat nys bot foule fen and
erþe. þat þorouȝ þat ilch fastnynge it is so fast ybounden þat it
foloweþ þe flesche forto quemen it in his foule kynde. And goþ 30
out of his owen heuenlich kynde forto payen hir ⁊ wraþþes her
schaper þat hire schoope lyche hym self þat is þe kyng of
heuene ⁊ of erþe. þis is a wonder ⁊ ouer wonder. and an hoker-

M. 140)

---

1 Sarazene: *zene partially erased.*   2 schal be: al be *partially erased*
7 synners: *first* s *blotted.*   17 nus *in left margin in red ink. Left minim
of* n *and part of abbreviation mark cut off at edge.*   18 Heuene and erþe
schullen: Heuene and erþe schull *on erasure.*   19 it *blurred.*   20 it *written
above line and marked for insertion.*   euen: *curl from unfinished letter* (b?)
above first e.   22 spouse *crossed out after* goddes. *Marks for transposition
above* spouse *and* owen.   24 [A]ugustinus *in left margin in red ink. Traces
of* A *at edge.*   27 þan, *sic for* þat.

p. 394b　lich wonder seiþ seint Austyn | Ac for þis poynt it was ⁊ is. God
wolde nouȝth þat it lepe in to pride ne wilne to clymbe as Lucifer dude þat was wiþouten charge. And þerfore he fel adoun in
to helle And god þere fortyed hym to a clott of heuy erþe as men
done a beeste þat is a rayker and wil bleþelich goo fram his　5
felawes Men tyen to a kibber oiþer schakelen it þat he ne goo
nouȝth fram his felawȝes þis is þat iob seiþ in his book

QUi fecisti ventis id est spiritubus pondus et cetera
ℂ Lorde he seiþ þo haste ymake to hem birþen to fleiȝe wiþ
soule. þat is þe heuy fleiȝe þat alway draweþ dounward vnto his　10
foule kynde. Ac þorouȝ þe heiȝschep of hir it schal bicome ful
liȝth. ȝe liȝtter þan þe wynde ⁊ briȝtter þan þe sunne. And it be
so þat hij ne folowen nouȝth þe fleiȝe to swiþe in to þe lowe
kynde. þan i rede for his loue þat sche is yliche to. ne lete
nouȝth þe fleiȝe haue of hire þe Maistrie. For sche is here in　15
vncouþ þede yputt in a Prisoun ⁊ in a qualme hous. It nys
nouȝth yseen hou heiȝ ⁊ of what dignite þat sche is in her owen
londe. ȝif þe flesche ne haue nouȝth þe Maistrie. þe flesch is here
an hame to hir as erþe þat is in erþe and as Men seien on englisch. Cok is kene on his owen dunge hylle. ⁊ þat is wel seen on　20
(M. 142)　þe fleiȝe. It haþ to mychel Maistrie se weilaway þe while And
Dauid likneþ onelich Man and womman to þe Pellicane ⁊ to þe
niȝth foule þat woneþ vnder Euesynges And name bereþ of
Ancre. For Ancre holdeþ þe schippe and kepeþ it fram stormes.
So vche Man ⁊ womman þat ȝiueþ hym to parfyt lyf ⁊ ordre　25
schulde holde vp holy chirche þat is likned to seint Peter schipp.
Hij schulden lyuen so holy lyf þat hij kepten holy chirche þat
ben cristen Men fram stronge temptaciouns of þe fende And of
þe werlde ⁊ of þe flesche And þe commune Poeple schulde
holden þem vp wiþ her Almes bodilich. So schulden hij ben　30
besy niȝth and day to holden hem vpp gostlich for þis name
Ancre crieþ euermore þus. Looke þat þou holde forward þat þou
haste taken on honde to holde hem vp gostlich as hij done þe
bodilich. þis falleþ to alle Men þat lyueþ by Mennes Almes.
Hij taken þus on honde tofore god as alle men of holy chirche　35
done. And as þe niȝth foule fleiȝeþ by nyȝth and takeþ her pray
So schulde vche Man ⁊ womman do þat desireþ forto serue god

4 þere fortyed, *sic for* þerefor tyed.　　8 iob. *in right margin in red ink.*
spiritubus, *sic for* spiritibus.　　10 fleiȝe, *sic for* flesche (*also on ll. 13, 15,
and 21*).　　11 heiȝschep: ȝs *crammed together.*　　36 And: An *on
erasure.*　　takeþ: *upper parts of* ta *on erasure.*

Flei3e by ny3th vp toward her spouse Ihesu crist forto take her
pray of hym þat is soules foode ⁊ bodilich | boþe þorou3 goode
þou3ttes of loue longynges. ⁊ in bedes biddynge. þis ny3th is
day. And ny3th whan Man oiþer womman haþ deuocioun as is
in pryue stede. as it seiþ bifore ynou3 of Pryuete.   5

Vigilaui ⁊ factus sum sicut Passer solitarius in tecto. ⟨ Ich
wake seiþ Dauid as þe sparowe þat woneþ one vnder roofe.
þe sparewe haþ þise þre propertees. sche is euere chiterande
And sche haþ þe fallande yuel. And sche bredeþ bleþelich in þe
hous euesynges. þat þe sparewe is chiterande bitokneþ vche   10
Man ⁊ womman þat desiren for to queme god schulden euermore be spekande of god. oiþer biddande oiþer þenchande on
here spouse Ihesu crist in londe and in watere. And in alle
stedes haue in mynde in al þing þat a Man doþe. þat þe sparewe
haþ þe fallande yuel bitokneþ þat. vche Man schulde be fallande 15
to god ward þat is lete litel of hym self And be meke ⁊ mylde
a3ein alle sorou3es as Ihesus crist was. Whan þe sparewe makeþ
her nest in þe euesyng sche draweþ first out o strow and siþen
a noþer and makeþ her nest and bringeþ forþ her briddes. And
3if þe Euesyng be hard sche bideþ werst aboute þe first strowe   20
er þat sche haue it out. And þan comeþ anoþer li3thlicher.
Ri3th so fareþ ihesus crist by vs þat ben in synne. He wolde
make his nest in oure hert and wonen þere and bringe forþ his
briddes. Ac for oure foule synnes he ne may nou3th. What doþe
he þan. He bynymeþ vs first oure þou3ttes first on ⁊ þan a noþer 25
þat we han to synne. And þan þe likynge. And þan þe synne.
And so litel ⁊ litel he comeþ in to oure hert And makeþ his
nest þere. and bryngeþ forþ his briddes. þat ben goode werkes.
And 3if it be so þat we ben harded in synne. he haþ þe more
trauaile. aboute vs to bringe vs out þere of. As seint augustinus 30
witnesseþ. he mi3th better make al þe werlde of nou3th. and
arere a Man fram deþ to lyue. þan bringe a Man out of þe lest
synne þat his hert is sett opon. for he haþ 3iuen man his free wille
frelich forto chese wheþer he wil þe yuel or þe goode. And he
haþ 3ouen vs knowlechyng of boþe and tokenynge. And sette in 35
oure free wille forto chese þat on oiþer þat oþer. And þerfore he

---

5 as: *small hole in MS. over* s.   6 dauid *in left margin in red ink.*
8 þise *written above line and marked for insertion.*   23 bringe: *dot*
above ri, *perhaps mistaken for* y.   30 augustinus *written between the*
columns and marked for insertion.

wil þat we bidde hym ȝerne of helpe and þan he wil helpe vs
þat we schulle chesen in þe goode. and elles nouȝth bot ȝif it be
þorouȝ oure biddynge. oiþer summe oþer þat bidden for vs þat
loueþ vs. And so he comeþ in to oure hertes and bringeþ forþ þan
goode werkes to his worschipp ⁊ to oure note þat ben his briddes. 5

Ecclesiasticus vigilaui honestas et cetera. ⟨ Noþing ne ata|meþ
wilde flesche so wel as wakynge. þan ȝif ȝoure flesche be wilde
wakeþ and biddeþ fast. as oure lorde seiþ þis þorouȝ Salomon
in his prouerbes. who þat ariseþ erlich and secheþ me. he schal
fynde me. wakynge is mychel praysed in holy writt. 10

VIgilate ⁊ orate ne intretis in temptacionem. ⟨ Wakeþ seiþ
oure lorde and biddeþ þat ȝe ne falle in no fondynge.

MEdia nocte surgebam ad confitendum tibi et cetera. ⟨ I
schal arise att Midniȝth and schryue to þe seiþ dauid to
god. Oure lorde seiþ in þe Godspel. wakeþ att Midniȝth ⁊ att 15
cok crowe and in þe Mornyng. for ȝe ne wite whan þe lorde wil
come.

BEatus quem inuenerit vigilantem. ⟨ Blissed be he þat I
fynde wakynge in þe first tyme. oiþer in þe secounde.
oiþer in þe þridde. þat is þe Mannes elde. in þe ȝouþe. oiþer in 20
þe Middel. oiþer in þe last ende. He wakeþ wel þat kepeþ hym
out of dedlich synne. þan fyndeþ oure lorde hym wakyng whan
he comeþ. whan Moyses ledde þe folk out of Egipte in to wildernesse. god fedde hym wiþ Manna. And he þat lay in his bedde
after þe sunne arisyng hadde no mete þat day. for it went þan o 25
way. And als mychel hadde he þat gadered an handful as he þat
gadered a slytful. ⁊ vche Man most gederen for hym seluen.
Oure lorde hym self tauȝtt vs to arise erlich þorouȝ his erlich
arisynge fram deþ to lyue. And also whan he went wiþ his
deciples he aros in þe Mornynge and badde his bedes to his 30
fader for vs.

PErnoctauit in oracione. ⟨ Wakeþ and biddeþ by niȝth he
biddeþ vs. And as he tauȝtt he dude hym seluen boþe in
techynge ⁊ in dede. And so schulde euerych goode techer do in

---

1 *First* helpe: el *crammed together at end of line.* 6 Ecclesiasticus: *MS.*
Eccus. vigilaui honestas, *sic for* vigilia honestatis. Noþing ne: in *and* ne
partially effaced. 9 prouerbes: b *corrected from another letter.*
10 Dominus *in right margin in red ink. Traces of erased letter below* s.
12 Daui[d] *in right margin in red ink. Part of* i *cut off. Traces of erased letter
below* i. 18 Domin[us] *in right margin in red ink. Traces of letter at
edge of MS.*

dede þat he techeþ. and namelich Men of ordre þat þe Mister
taken on honde. Ac ich am adradde it fareþ now by many of
hem as god seide to þe clerkes of Iewrie þe grete Maisters and
seide hem an ensaumple It was a Man þat badd his o son do þat.
and he seide he wolde do it. And he badde his oþer son and he 5
seide he nolde do it and dude it And he þat seide he wolde do it
dude it nouȝth. and he asked hem wheþer was better to praisen.
And þe Maisters seiden he þat dude it. And þat is bitokned by
eueryche Man þat goþ to ordre and to heiȝe lyf ꝺ doþe nouȝth as
he schulde do. ne ne bereþ hym þere after nomore þan he dude. 10
Alle we ben goddes sones lettred and lewed. And þe symple
p. 396a Man is adradd | to goo to heiȝe lyf and to ordre. Ac he doþe it
in þe dede as ferforþe as he may. þat bitokneþ þat oþer son þat
seide he nolde nouȝth done it and dude it. He is better to pray-
sen þan þe clerk þat takeþ on honde to done it and ne doþe it 15
nouȝth. Also it is bitokned by þe Iewes and by þe Sarzines. þe
Iewes token vnder honde to seruen god and ne duden it nouȝth.
and þerfore he parted hem fram hym, And þe Sarzines duden
it. ꝺ he ȝaf hem his grace. Now viij þinges þere ben þat techen
vs to wake and be waker in goddes seruise. þis schort lyf þat 20
lasteþ bot now. þe stronge waye þat we haue forto gon. And for
þe gret good þat we schulle haue þerof ȝif þat we dispenden þis
litel tyme and þis schortt here to goddes worschipp. Oure
synnes þat ben so many. Deþ þat we ben syker of and we ne
witeþ what tyme þat it wil come. And vnsyker whider þat we 25
schullen. goo wot we neuer. þe hard dome and þe stronge on
domesday and streytt and so narewe wiþ al þat we schullen
ȝelden rekenynge of euerych ydel þouȝth. What schal be þan
of wicked willes and dedes þe godspel seiþ.

DE omni verbo ocioso reddes racionem in die iudicij, Item 30
capilli de capite non peribunt. id est cogitacio non euadet
inpunita. ⸿ Of vche ydel woord we schulle ȝelde rekenynge. Ʒeꞏ
þe leste her of þine hede ne schal nouȝth ben vnpunysched þat
is to saie þe leste þouȝth þat euere þou þouȝttest

QUid facies in illa die quande exigetur a te omne tempus 35
qualiter sit a te expensum. ꝺ vsque ad minimam cogitacio-

---

16 Iewes: wes *crammed together at end of line.*   30 [Domi]nus *in left*
margin in red ink.   Item *possibly on erasure.*   31 capite: *lower half of*
i *effaced.*   34 þou: ȝ *erased after* u.   [A]nselm[us] *in left margin in red*
ink. Left minim of m *cut off at edge of MS.*   35 quande, *sic for* quando.

nem. (How schaltow do þat ilche day whan vche tyme þat þou haddest here schal be asked of þe how þou it haste dispended. ꝛeꞏ so fer forþ vn til it come to þe last þouꝛth þat euer þou þouꝛttest. þe seuenþe þing stireþ vs to waken. þe sorouꝛ of helle þere þise þinges ben in þe vnymete pynes. þe sorouꝛ of vchone 5 lasteþ wiþ outen ende. And þe vnymete bitternesse. þe viij þing is hou mychel is þe Mede in þe heuene. And who so haþ þise viij þinges often in mynde. hij willeþ schaken of hym sleep of sleuþ in stille niꝛttes whan Man ne seiþ nouꝛth þat letteþ hym. For noþing þan bereþ witnesse of god bot goddes 10 owen Aungels þat is in swich tyme ydone. for þere nys nouꝛth forlorne as by day. For þat þing þat is done in pryuete. is soule foode. And þan ben Aungels helpeande to hym more þan by day. whan þere is lettynge of many þinges.

(M. 146)

O Racio Hester placuit Regi assuro. (þe quenes boone 15 Hester plesed þe Kyng Assur. Hester on Ebru bitokneþ þe boone þat Men biddeþ on hidels. Assur on Ebru is on Englisch oure lorde.

V T quid auertis manum tuamꞏ ꞇ dexteram tuam de medio sinu tuo in finem. (þat is whi drawestow | þine honde and 20 ꝛutt þi riꝛth honde of þi bosome on ende. þat riꝛth honde bitokneþ þine goode werkes. Bosome bitokneþ pryuete. oiþer siker stede boþe. whi drawestow out ꞇ makes ende þere schulde be non. ꝛif it were hydde, þat is whi takestou praisynge of þi seluen and takes þi mede þat endeþ here. 25

p. 396b

A Men dico volis receperunt mercedem suam. (þat is þou þat schewes þi goode dede. þou has resceyued þi mede forsoþe. þat is priuete. as ich seide of bifore. Bosome is siker stede bitokneþ þat is sette þi bedd in siker stede. þat is in Ihesu crist. for sikerer stede ne wot i non. þat wilneþ nouꝛth to be 30 praised here of noþing þat we done ne takeþ non to ꝛou seluen. bot al ꝛiue hym þe Maistrie. For þeiꝛ ꝛe be schett in ꝛoure chaumbre ꝛe may resceyue ꝛoure mede here þorouꝛ ꝛoure liking And ꝛe may saie ꝛoure Bedes in þe commune. ꞇ ꝛut ꝛe may take ꝛoure mede in heuene þerfore, And ꝛe ꝛiue oþer Men 35 goode ensaumple to do wel þere ryst dubble mede and treble,

---

3 last: a *corrected from* ė.   19 [D]auid *in left margin in red ink. Left part of* a *cut off at edge of MS.*   23–4 schulde be non *on erasure. Small hole in MS.* (*mentioned at p. 59 l. 5*) *after* schulde.   26 volis, *sic for* vobis. dominus. *in right margin in red ink.*

ȝif þe fende putt any kikyng in þine hert þat þou letest wel of als
smertlich putt it to ihesu crist. and þenche ȝif þou haste any
þing wel done. it is his werk and nouȝth þine. þou wost wel it
ne falleþ nouȝth to þe for to take likyng to þe, for a werk þat
anoþer man doþe.   5

M. 148) **M**Agna verecundia est gaudia agere. ⁊ laudibus inhiare vnde
celum merere potuit nimium transitorij fauoris querit.
℄ Michel goode seiþ Gregori it is to do wel. and to do wharfore to
haue þe blisse of heuene. and þan wil sellen it for a wyndes puff
of praysynge here. And þat may be bitokned of Moyses goddes   10
prophete whan he drouȝ out his honden of his bosome as he
stode biforne oure lorde vpon þe hulle. It semed as it hadd ben of
þe spitel yuel, And þat was for he schulde take no praisyng to
hym seluen to fer forþ. And it bitokneþ þat suich biddynge and
goode dedes doynge in þat manere ben foule tofore god.   15

DEcorticauit ficum meum nudans spoliauit eam. ⁊ proiecit
alibi facti sunt Rami eius. et cetera. ℄ Oure lorde seiþ hij
han bipiled my fygere and rent away al þe rynde. and þe bowȝes
þat schulden be grene ben bicomen al drye. and white rondes
þere inne. þis is derk to vnderstonden. Ac ich it wil openen.   20

M. 150) þe fygere bitokneþ cristen Man ⁊ womman. And þan is þe
figere ypiled whan goode dedes ben yopened þorouȝ likyng. þat
is þe lyf oute. and þe deþ is þere inne. noiþer it ne bereþ fruyt
ne it ne greneþ ac bicomeþ white rondes. To noþing nys it þan
worþ bot to þe fyre. þe bowȝes whan it adedeþ. it whiteþ out-   25
wiþ and drieþ inwiþ. and kesteþ his rynde. Also goode dede

p. 397a adedeþ whan it is vnhiled. þat hileþ it. is þe rynde ⁊ holdeþ | it
in strengþe. for whiles þat is hidde. it is grene and likeworþi to
goddes eiȝen. for grene is þe colour þat is most likeworþi to þe
eiȝe. And whan it is drie it is nouȝth worþ bot to þe fyre of   30
helle. þe first pylyng of al þis nys bot a litel likynge of pride.
þat is a wellate of hym seluen. nys þis gret reuþe. ne ben hij vn
cely þat wiþ goodes of heuene geteþ hem helle. Oure lord likneþ
goode dede to gold hoord who so fyndeþ it he hideþ it.

QUem qui inuenit homo abscondit ℄ Gold hoorde is goode   35
dede and is euened to heuene for men it buggeþ wiþ al.

---

1 kikyng, *sic for* likyng.   6 verecundia, *sic for* vecordia.   gaudia
sic for grandia.   Gregorius, *in right margin in red ink.*   7 nimium,
sic for nummum.   16 meum, *sic for* meam.   Iob. *in right margin in*
red ink.   22 þat, *sic for* þan.   32–3 vn cely, *sic for* vncely.
35 dominus. *in left margin in red ink.*

DEpredari desiderat qui thesaurum publice in via portat.
℟ (þat is he þat bereþ tresore in þe waie þat is ful of þeues:
hym lyst to ben yrobbed Al þis werlde nys nouȝth bot a waie to
helle oiþer to heuene. and is bisett ful of helle Michers þat
(M. 152) robben alle þe golde hoordes þat hij mowen vnderȝeten. and 5
namelich of hem þat ȝelpen her goode dedes. þenche on þis
ensaumple. A Sooper þat bereþ soope and nedeles crieþ out on
his goode by þe stretes as he goþ. And a riche Marchaunde goþ
forþ al stille. Herkneþ what bifel of Ezeche þe kyng for þat he
schewed his celle of Aromaunce his derworþe þinges. Comen 10
þeues and robbeden hym þerof. Nys nouȝth ywriten of þe þre
kynges þat presented oure lord þe þre lawȝes.

PRocidentes adorauerunt eum ⁊ apertis thesauris suis
obtulerunt ei munera. aurum. thus ⁊ Mirram. ℟ þe þre
kynges þat hij wolden offre to oure lörde. Hij helden it euere 15
(M. 154) hidd. Loo hou goode it is to be one and yhudd boþe in þe olde
lawȝe ⁊ in þe newe it scheweþ, whan a man schal bidde his bedes
þat he ne be nouȝth yletted and þat wil ben herd of god. For
amonge folk ne scheweþ ne nouȝth bleþelich his pryuetees to
noman, ⁊ þerfore in þe olde lawȝe whan hij badden her bedes. 20
hij wenten in to þe feelde for noþing schulde letten hem. And þere
god schewed hym to hem. and graunted hem her askyng.

EGressus est ysaac in Agrum ad meditandum. quod ei fuisse
creditum consuetudinem. ℟ Ysaac þe Patriark forto þenche
onelich on god went in to þe feeld and þere he mett wiþ Reb- 25
ccha. þat is goode grace.

REbeccha. Nomen. interpretatur multum dedit. ⁊ quicquid
habet ment'. et cetera. ℟ Also Iacob þat oure lorde schewed
hym his nebbe schaft. and ȝaf his blissynge. and turned name
better. Also by Moyses and Hely goddes derworþe frendes. þat 30
p. 397b   god often schewed | hym to. hij drowen hem in to onelich stedes
whan hij badden her bedes to god. Ac hij neren nouȝth bischett
ne helden hem alway stille in on stede. hij ȝeden among þe
poeple. and tauȝtten hem hou hij schulden kepen goddes lawȝe.

(M. 156) SEt ieremias solus sedet. ℟ Ieremye satt one and telde whi 35
forre oure lorde haþ filled hym ful of his þretenynge.

---

1 Gregorius. *in left margin in red ink.*   12 lawȝes, *sic for* lokes.
13 dominus *in left margin in red* ink.   20 bedes: s *partially effaced.*
24 creditum consuetudinem, *sic for* creditur consuetudinarium.   25 Reb-
ccha, *sic for* Rebecha.   26 goode, *sic for* goddes.   27 Nomen, *sic for*
enim.   28 ment', *sic for* meriti.   30 Hely: He *on erasure.*

QUia communicacione replesti me. (Wel were hym þat
were fulfilde of his þretenynge as he was. For þere schal
neuer man wel serue god ne kepe hym out of synne. bot he be
fulfilde of his þretenynge. þat is. þat he haue þe drede of god in
his hert. And þenche opon þe wreche þat he haþ taken for 5
synne.

IEremie quis dedit michi fontem lacrimarum. (þat is who
schal ȝiue me þe welle of teres to biwepe slayn folk. Vt lugeam
in terra fil. t'. et cetera. (þe mest dale of þis werlde is slayn
þorouȝ dedlich synne. To his wepynge þe prophete biddeþ one- 10
lich stede witterlich. who þat schal biwepen his synnen and
oþer mennes he moste seche onelich stede.

SEdebit homo solitarius ⁊ tacebit ⁊ leuabit se supra se. (Who
þat wis so do he most sitten one and holde hym stille. and so
heiȝen hym self abouen hym self.   15

BOnum est sub silencio prestolari salutare dei. (Goode it is
to speken and to bisechen þe grace of god þat men may bere
goddes ȝok. fram his ȝouþe. He bereþ goddes ȝok fram his
ȝouþe þat letes his yuel and nyl do it no more. For he bicomeþ
ȝonge þorouȝ newe lyf   20

BEati qui portauerunt iugum domini ab adolescencia sua.
dabit percucienti se maxillam ⁊ saturabitur obprobrijs. (He
. 158) þat wil so do. bedeþ forþ his cheke aȝein his mysdoer as it seiþ
in þe sautere. þere ben two þewes. þolemodenesse ⁊ edmodenesse. þolemodenesse is þat man suffreþ þat men done hym 25
yuel. Edmodenesse is þat man suffreþ þat men myssiggen
hym. seint Iohn þe Baptist by whom oure lorde seide.

INter natos Muliorum non surrexit maior Iohanne Baptista.
(þat is to saie. amonge alle þat euer were borne of womman ne
aros non heiȝer þan seint iohn þe Baptist. no·' þis mote be vnder- 30
stonden on þis manere. for in þat tyme þat he was. þere nas non
better þan. for Ihesus crist seiþ also of seint iohn þe Ewangelist.

INter ceteros magis dilectus. (þat is among alle oþer he is
moste biloued. Also þat is vnderstonden by þat tyme also. for
who þat wil loue god now as hij duden. hij mowen ben heiȝed | 35
. 398a as hij ben now. þan seint John Baptist souȝth onlich stede ȝete

---

1 communicacione, *sic for* comminacione.   7 dedit, *sic for* dabit.
9 in terra fil. t'., *sic for* interfectos filie.   14 wis, *sic for* wil.   21 Iere-
[mias] *in right margin in red ink.*   28 Muliorum, *sic for* Mulierum.
Domin[us] *in right margin in red ink.*   33 Dominus *in right margin in red*
ink.   among: a *and* n *partially effaced.*

726 C 78   F

flei҃ʒ he his owen kynde þat were holy and chosen of god And
þei҃ʒ al were he þorou҃ʒ myracle bi҃ʒeten. ҃ʒutt ne durst he nou҃ʒth
dwelle amonges hem ne amonges oþere lest he schulde haue
filed his lippes þorou҃ʒ foule speche.

BE michi quia pollutus labijs ego sum et cetera. ⸿ Wo is me 5
he seide for ich am amonges men þat hane foule lippes.

QUia in medio populi polluta habentis labia ego sum vel
habito. ⸿ þat is ich am amonges folk þat foulen her lyppes
(M. 160) wiþ foule speche forsoþe take Metal. golde oiþer siluer: yrne
oiþer steel and laye it by a þing þat is rusty. and it schal drawe 10
rust þere of ҃ʒif hij liggen to geder longe. and so doþe vche
goode Man ⁊ womman takeþ rust of synne ҃ʒif þat hij ben in
feble compaignye þat is leef forto speke foule speche. ⁊ ҃ʒutt þe
deede is wers. Forþi flei҃ʒ seint Iohn in to wildernesse ⁊ þere he
bi҃ʒate þre hei҃ʒenesses. On þat he fulled oure lorde. and he 15
schewed hym þe holy Trinite. þe fader in his steuene. þe holy
gost in Culuer wise. And þe son in his honde þere. And þerfore
he hadde þise pryueleges of prechoure. Merytt of Martirdom.
And Maydens mede. Crovne opon crovne Ac for þis point ne
schal noman bischete hym þat he ne come nou҃ʒth among þe 20
folk. for he ne dude nou҃ʒth so. he ҃ʒede aboute and preched þe
comynge of ihesu crist for he was chosen þrto. And also þere
ne were bot þre prechoures þat ben cleped roote of prechynge
Iohn þe Baptist he preched of penaunce and he dude it in dede.
for in gestes it telleþ. who þat ordeyned a law҃ʒe hym self schulde 25
stonde þerto. and do do it in dede ҃ʒif þat cas fel. And so dude
seint Iohn. He was ordeyned of god to be his forgoer and preche
of penaunce. and þerfore he dude it in dede. And so schulde
vche prechoure do þat he seide do in dede. And Ihesus crist was
anoþer prechoure and he preched of Mercy and he dude it in 30
dede. Who þat asked hym of help he halp hem. and sou҃ʒth
where þat Men wolde haue Mercy. forto ҃ʒiue it hem, so hym
was leef for to do mercy. And atte last he ҃ʒaf his lyf forto saue
oure soules. And so he biddeþ þat we schullen done forto saue
oure broþer. He is þi nei҃ʒbur and þi broþer þat helpeþ þe out of 35
synne. And þat ҃ʒiueþ þe ensampl jn wel lybbynge þat þou
schuldest do also. He nys nou҃ʒth þi nei҃ʒbur þat lyueþ in yuel

---

5 [Ys]aias *in left margin in red ink. Traces of letter at edge of MS.* BE, *sic*
for VE.   22 þrto, *sic.*   26 do do: *dittography.*

lyf. ne þou ne schalt hym: nou3th loue bot forto helpe hym out
of synne 3if þou may. And 3if þou ne may. Kepe þe out of his
compaignye. and ne helpe hym noþing to bodilich sustenaunce
wharþorou3 þat þou be | susteyner of synne.

E Gestas ⁊ ignominia ei qui deserit disciplinam. et cetera, 5
(⟨ In þat chapitre þou schalt fynde þis. 3if a wise Man goo
amonge þe compaignie of foles he makeþ hem wers þan hij
weren. 3if he be lecchour oiþer lei3er. oiþer what fole þat he be.
he is þe bolder þorou3 hym. and hardeþ hym þe more in his
synne, And þerfore he seiþ he is liche to hem and to her damp- 10
nacioun bot 3if it be forto amende hem. ac for noþing ne drawe
nou3th to Michel to hem. lest þou appaire þi seluen.

C Un sancto sanctus eris.' ⁊ cum viro innocente innocens eris.
⁊ cum electo electus eris. ⁊ cum peruerso peruerteris. (⟨ Be
wiþ holy þou schalt be holy. and be wiþ innocent þou schalt be 15
innocent. Be wiþ chosen þou schalt be chosen. and be wiþ
schrewes þou schalt ben a schrewe. of þis þing ich rede vche
Man be war lest þat he ne take no synne on þis manere.

A Ttendite a falsis prophetis et cetera. (⟨ Oure lorde seiþ.
kepe 3ou from fals prophetes. by her wordes and by her 20
werkes 3e schulle knowen hem, seint Iohn þe ewangelist seiþ þat
alle commune lecchoures. and alle proude Men. and coueitouse
Men. And Loseniours. alle ben fals prophetes. And namelich
Men of Ordre bot hij ben chosen. And Salomon clepeþ þise
wycked Men for þise wolde envenym al a cuntre on of hem. 25
Poule was þe þridde prechoure. And preched of loue and charite.
⁊ he seiþ þis woord.

M Ichi autem absit gloriari nisi in cruce domini nostri Ihesu
christi (⟨ þat is. Blis be done away from me. bot onelich in
Ihesu cristes roode. He loued so god and his euene cristene þat 30
he 3ede among þe Sarzines and spake goddes word And hij
beten hym wiþ 3erdes. And þe Iewes beten hym wiþ Staues.
And 3utt he nolde nou3th leten. And þe Clerkes wolden haue
done hym sworne opon þe Book. þat he ne scholde nou3th haue
spoken of Ihesu crist and hij acurseden hym ⁊ alle Ihesus 35
deciples. and putten hem out of her synagoge þat is to saye out

---

1 nou3th: no *on erasure.* 4 *In the middle of the bottom margin of p. 398*
a hand in black ink with forefinger pointing upwards. 5 Salomon. *in right*
margin in red ink. 8 oiþer²: i *written above line and marked for insertion.*
13 CUn, *sic for* CUm. dauid. *in right margin in red ink.* 19 dominus.
in right margin in red ink. 28 Paulus. *in right margin in red ink.*

of þe commune poeple þat is now cleped holy chirche a gaderynge of Cristen folk. and flemeden hem, 3e schullen fynden it in
þis Godspelle.

CUm venerit paraclitus quem ego mittam vobis. et cetera,
þere 3e schullen fynde þat Ihesus crist warned hem þere 5
of er he dyed vpon þe roode. And he seide hem what Clerkes
schulden done hem. He warned hem bifore þere of for hij ne
schulden nou3th ben abaischt whan it come. Now after þise
p. 399a Men it were best forto done. For þe foundement of | oure law3e
al is sett in þise þre poyntz. Mercy. penaunce. and loue. whar- 10
for a Man mote done after alle þise þre prechoures. And nou3th
charge þat on al one. Now ich vnderstonde þat 3if a Man wil
looke after þe libbynge to come to þe blis of heuene þorou3. þe
best ensample were after Ihesu crist hym seluen þat ich vnderstonde þat was Peter ⁊ Poule for hij ben princes of alle þe 15
Apostles. Now was þis Peteres lyf. Peter wrou3th for his Mete
and preched þe folk. ⁊ he seide hym seluen. Haue ich a kirtel ⁊
a Mantel I kepe nomore. And bred he seide ich haue ynou3.
and sumtyme wortes. And Poule preched also and seiþ þat he
ne ete neuere Mannes mete bot 3if it were his vnþonkes þat he 20
ne hadde no space forto ernen it. And ich vnderstonde þat hij
were Men of holy chirche. þis i saye for þat Men sayen now. It
ne falleþ nou3th a Man of holy chirche to wirche for his Mete
and erne his Mete wiþ his honden. In on Manere hij seien soþe.
hij ne au3tten nou3th to taken her sustenaunce of anoþer Man 25
and erne her sustenaunce neuer þe latter. bot 3if he 3af it for þe
loue of god and took scarslich his sustenaunce þerof. And by
goddes ordinaunce and by hise Apostles ⁊ by þe lyf þat hij lyueden he ne schulde take of a Man ri3th nou3th bot scarslich her
sustenaunce and 3iue þat oþer forþ. and 3ut hym were better 30
erne it þan take it. for he schal see þis þat vche Man schal be
besy forto ansuere for hym seluen. And 3if he take oþer mennes
charge opon hym. and neuere latter mede forto bidde for hem.
bot 3if he be þe warrer he may li3thlich falle in Rirage whan he
comeþ to acounte bot 3if his acounte be þe better arayed Seint 35
Siluester þe Pope þre hundreþ 3ere after þat ihesus crist died on

---

4 dominus. *in right margin in red ink.*   5 Ihesus: us *blotted.*   6 Clerkes: 1 *corrected from* h.   12 *wil*: MS. wel *with* e *expuncted and* i
written above.   34 *From* Rirage *to bottom of column certain initial letters
ornamented in red ink.*   w *expuncted before* whan.

þe Roode he was þe first Man þat resceyued londes ⁊ Rentes.
And þan seide a voice abouen þat hij alle herden þat weren in
þe chirche of Rome whan þe Pope Siluester was at his seruise.
Now is venym pult in holy chirche ⁊ þerfore ich wot wel þat god
ordeyned it neuere. Ac he suffred it forto ben ordeyned And 5
Siluester it ordeyned þan. For þan Men of holy chirche weren
wedded Men als wel as oþer. Seint Mark made a cobler a
Bisschop þat hadde a wyf ⁊ childer of Alisaunder And þan Siluester ordeinde ȝif þat hij wolden haue þe Londes ⁊ þe Rentes
þat Men wolden ȝiuen hem. þat hij schulden ben chaste, And 10
ȝif þat hij wolden holden her wyues.' hij ne schulden haue none
londes ne Rentes and hij chesen forto ben chaste for gret charge |
of wyf ⁊ of Childer An he graunted hem þan and sett swich a
payn þere opon þat ȝif a preest lay by a sengle wenche. he
schulde haue ten ȝere penaunce. and vche ȝere of þe ten ȝere.' 15
þre Moneþes faste bred ⁊ watere. bot þe seuendaies. ⁊ þe heiȝe
feste dayes ⁊ þan hij schulden eten a porcioun of fysch. In þe
canoun in Decree. hij þat willen looke þere after hij schullen
fynden it. And þis he ordeyned for a symple preest. And ȝif he
be of heiȝer dignite þe more penaunce. And me þenche þat it 20
were better þat hij hadden wyues hem seluen þan þat hij tooken
oþer mennes wyues oiþer lemmans for god haþ forboden vs
boþe þise horedom ⁊ spousebreche boþe in þe elde lawȝe ⁊ in þe
newe. lawe. Vche Man þat hereþ þis laye his honde on his hert
ȝif he be ordred and looke how he feleþ hym i warne hem wel 25
goddes woord schal stonde on what manere so hij it turnen it
schal stonden as he þouȝth.

TOta die verba mea execrabantur. (⁋ þat is al day hij turneden
myne wordes aȝeinward and alle her þouȝttes weren in
yuel. þise Men Peter ⁊ Poule wrouȝtten for her mete. Hij maden 30
basketes and Pauylounes. And fram Morn vnto vnderne hij
wrouȝtten. And so dude oure lefdy after þat hire son was went
vp fyftene ȝere, And fram vndrun to noone hij precheden þat
we clepe now myd ouer noone þat is þe nynþe houre of þe day.
For at þat houre Ihesus crist died. And þan hij ȝeden ⁊ bad- 35
den her herberewe to pouere men. And on niȝth hij weren in

---

1 Rentes: *second* e *by correction.* 17 feste: *MS.* festes *with second* s
expuncted. 20 dignite *on erasure.* 28 Daui[d] *in right margin in*
red ink. Only left part of i *visible at edge of MS.* 34 clepe: c *by correction.*
noone: oo *crammed together at end of line.*

biddynge bot whan hij mosten nedes slepe. And after hem were
good to take ensample who þat miȝth þise Men hadden þe
riȝth rewle of holy chirch naþeles by heryng as men seiþ and by
wordes. ȝ by werkes. men forsaken mychel þis chirche. and
namelich þe lered. And drawen fast to anoþer chirche þat schal 5
comen þat Antecrist schal be Maister of. þat is of alle proude
Men ȝ of coueitouse Men. ȝ Leccherous Men þat ben commune-
lich here in dauid seiþ he hated þis chirche and so schulde vche
Man þat wolde be goddes deciple.

O Diui ecclesiam malignancium ȝ cum impijs non sedebo. 10
Ʂ þat is I hated þe forwaried chirches. And I ne satt nouȝth
wiþ þe wicked, Oure lefdy was mychel one þe aungel fonde hire
al one.

I Ngressus Angelus ad eam dixit Aue Mariaria gracia plena
dominus tecum. Ʂ þe Aungel com in to hir it seiþ þan sche 15
was mychel one. In holy wrytt we ne fynde þat sche spake bot |
foure siþes. Naþeles sche tauȝt many holy Man and spak to hem
often. Ac þise foure siþes þat sche spake beren gret charge and
weren of mychel myȝth. ȝ þerfore Men redeþ of hem in holy
wrytt. God hym seluen he was one ȝ went in to wildernesse 20
forto do penaunce. And þere þe fende tempted hym. And þat
was in þe last endynge of hys lyf þre ȝere ȝ more er he dyed to
ȝiue vs ensample þat we ne schulden nouȝth schape vs to hastilich to heiȝe degre of ordre er þat we were wel proued in þe
werlde þorouȝ temptacions more and more. and þat we were 25
stronge þorouȝ goode werkes. to we be worþi to come to heiȝer
degree in lyue in goode lyf and fonde forto do as we hadden taken
þe ordre and heiȝe lyf. and þan wolde god putt his honde þerto
and help vs. Ac now many gon to ordre er þat hij ben proued.
And þat is wel seen now in þis werlde by her berynge for god 30
letteþ hem þerfore go after þe fyndynges of her hert.

E T dimisi eos secundum desideria cordis eorum ibunt in
adinuencionibus suis. Ʂ I lete hem go after þe desires of her
hert hij schullen gon in her fyndynges.

p. 400a

---

3 men: n *blotted and possibly corrected.* 4 wordes: r *partially effaced at
end of line.* 10 daui[d] *in right margin in red ink.* 14 Mariaria, sic
for Maria. dominus *in right margin in red ink.* 28 wolde: de
crammed together at end of line. 32 [D]auid *in left margin in red ink.
Left part of a cut off at edge of MS.*

INnocens omni verbo credit et cetera. ℂ þe Innocent leueþ
vche woord and in þat he is a foole seiþ Salomon for holy
wrytt defendeþ it

KArissiMi nolite omni verbo credere et cetera. ℂ Myne
frendes ne leueþ nouȝth alle woordes. þe queynt and þe 5
wyse lokeþ his waie toforne er he goo. for he dredeþ pyne.
Wysdom wil þat þou avise þe what spiryt spekeþ to þe Quo
spiritu quisque loquatur.

DEclina A malo ⁊ fac bonum. ℂ Wiþdrawe þe fram yuel ⁊ do
þe goode. Yuel wircheþ þe Man oiþer þe womman þat 10
wircheþ wiþ hasty wille, For he þat nys nouȝth abidande doþe
a pert folie Man of yuel queyntise þat is ypocrisye þat feiȝeneþ
hym symple. Swich ben forto haten. for god warieþ hem in þe
godspel. and seiþ þus.

VE vobis ypocrite. ℂ Hij þat ben of lytel witt speken folie ⁊ 15
heresie. Ac þe wise vnderstondeþ wysdom in al þat he
schal do and aviseþ hym ful wel er he agynne any þing And
þencheþ what wil come of þe endyng. Now nys non so gret
folie as Man to putt hym to heiȝe degree er þat he be proued.
for he mon sone repent hym bot ȝif he wirche wiselich. Oure 20
lord seide þis ensample to þe Maisters of þe iewes þat tauȝtten
his lawȝe. It was a Man and bad his o son done þat. ⁊ he seide
he wolde done it. And he bad his oþer son ⁊ he seide he nolde
noȝth done it. And he þat seide he nolde nouȝth done | it dude
it And he þat seide he wolde done it dude it nouȝth. And he 25
asked hem which was þe better to praisen and hij seiden he þat
dude it, And þat he seide by hem þis may be vnderstonden in
þis manere. þe Iewes token vnderhonde to seruen god and hij ne
duden it nouȝth, And þe Sarzines seiden hij nolden. and hij serueden hym. Also it may be seide by cristen Men þat now ben. by Men 30
of ordre þat han taken vnder honde to done goddes comaundement ⁊ techen þe commune poeple. and hij ne done it nouȝth.
Ac þe symple Men þat louen god ⁊ dreden hym. hij nyllen
nouȝth gon to þat ordre for drede of þe heiȝenesse þerof. Ac

p. 400b

---

1 [S]alamon *in left margin in red ink. Left part of a cut off at edge of MS.*
mon *below* ala. *Only right minim of* m *visible at edge of MS.* 4 [S]ala-
mon *in left margin in red ink. Left part of a cut off at edge of MS.* mon *below*
ala. *Left minim of* m *cut off at edge of MS.* 9 [D]auid *in left margin*
in red ink. 16 vnderstondeþ: *from* deþ *at beginning of line to bottom*
of column, the first few words of each line are partially effaced, particularly
tauȝtten *21,* o son done *22 and* th *in* noȝth[1] *24.*

hij seruen hym als wel as hij mowen and done it in dede after
her power as hij hadden taken þat ordre. þise Men quemen god
And þe oþer ne quemen hym nouȝth. for hij ne done nouȝth
þat hij han taken on honde to do. Anoþer ensaumple he seiþ.
ȝif þou come to a Bridale ne sette þe nouȝth in þe heiȝest stede 5
an Auntre ȝif þere come anoþer better þan þou.' for þan worþ-
estow putt adoune and þan wil þi nebbe rede. Al þis is seide by
hem þat setten hem seluen in heiȝe degre of ordre er hij ben
proued And to alle oþer þat to any manere degre gon out of þe
commune poeple. Whan hij han cauȝtt a coope hij wenen þat 10
hij ben abouen And many of hem ben wers þan hij weren whan
þat hij weren in þe werlde. For in many poyntes hij trespassen
þat hij nyten nouȝth of. ne willen nouȝth vnderstonden it. for
hij gon reccheleslich þerto. And for þat hij mowen liȝthlich
haue her sustenaunce so. and wiþ more eyse þan hij trauaileden 15
in þe werld And þerfore god leteþ hem worþe. ⁊ ne helpeþ hem
nouȝth. þat is. ne sendeþ hem nouȝth his grace of riȝth knoweynge. Als sone as it comeþ in his hert. nay he seiþ it is good to
serue god, Loo he seiþ þe Maudeleyn ches þe better part and
nott neuere how sche chees. ne what sche dude. And so he goþ 20
forþ to heiȝe lyf. And he nott neuere where he schal bigynne
forto serue god. And þerfore hij bicomen loseniours. And
losengen Men for her sustenaunce. and bigylen boþe hem ⁊ hem
seluen aldermest. For Men synnen vpon hem and wenen þat hij
ben goode Men and mychel good cunnen of þe lawȝe of god. 25
And þan hij cunnen wel lesse þan hij. For ȝif hij couþen good
hij nolden nouȝth done so as hij done. hij wolden erne her Mete
and seruen god so. tyl þat god wolde sette hem as hij weren
worþi. for he wott best þat vche Man auȝtt to trauaile for her
sustenaunce and | nouȝth bidde it bot ȝif he ne myȝth erne it for 30
sekenesse oiþer for elde oiþer croked. and bot ȝif he were prechoure and trauailed fram toun to toun and preched. And ȝutt
it were for hem bettere þat hij erned it þan þat hij badden it ȝif
hij miȝth þeiȝ he were a preest. Neren nouȝth Peter ⁊ Poule
Prestes. ȝis forsoþe Als gode i trowe as any were siþen. þan 35
miȝth a noþer Preest wirche. It schulde kepe hym out of
slauþe. For ydelnesse and Este. And Ese. ben þe deuels Baners.

p. 401a

---

1 in *written above line and marked for insertion.*   12 þat *written above
line.*   p. 401a *Red ink is used to ornament certain initial letters in this
column.*   31 croked: d *on erasure.*   36 of of: *dittography.*

And what man oiþer womman þat he fyndeþ any of þise Merkes
inne: he may wende in and out as he wil. For þorouȝ þise þre
hij bicomen fals prophetes. And Heretikes and ypocrites And
losenioures. And þise ben þe werst manere folk þat þere ben.
for god hym self in þe godspel acurseþ hem as ȝe han wryten   5
toforne in þis book Now also Ihesus crist hym seluen suffred
hunger and þrust to ȝiue vs ensample þat we schulde teme oure
bodyes ȝif hij weren to fatt. þat we miȝth haue hunger and þrust
after his blis as he hadd forto bringe vs þerto.—

B Eati qui esuriunt ⁊ siciunt Iusticiam. et cetera. ℂ Blissed   10
ben hij þat han hungere and þrust after riȝthwisenesse. Also
whan he schulde bidde his bedes. he went vp vnto hilles fram
his Apostles. By Hille is bitokned heiȝe Mannes lyf. þat is þenche
heiȝe and lyue lowelich and þolemodelich. For to swiche Men
haþ þe deuel envie. And þere is god next and stondeþ biside   15
hem. and ȝiueþ hem bodilich strengþe and gostlich boþe. And
swiche Men may done wiþ god al þat hij willen þat ordeynen
her lyf by wysdom and queyntise

M. 162) Q Uociens inter homines fui minor homo recessi. ℂ þe ofter i
was amonges Men þe lesse Man i was whan i went fram hem.   20
Hou miȝth he seie þis woorde skilfullich for he was more heiȝed
tofore god and þe bettere loued þan he schulde haue ben and he
ne hadde nouȝ comen amonge hem. and ben one for he tauȝtte
þe folk. For þis skyl it may be seide þat vche Man þenche whan
þat he haþ best done þat he is ydel as he dude whan he hadd   25
tauȝtt þe folk. þan he quemed god best and þan he þouȝth þat
he was ydel, Man ne owe take no wel late to hym seluen as oure
lord seiþ.

C Um omnia benefeceritis discite a me ⁊ invtiles serui sumus.
ℂ þat is whan ȝe han wel done saie ȝe ben ydel. þat is   30
knowe þat we be nouȝth parfit to god als longe as we ben
Pilgrymes in þis werlde and þat we ben vnsuffisaunt to affye vs
in oure werkes. |

p. 401b E Cclesiasticus. nec oblecteris in turbis assidua est enim com-
missio. ℂ þat is. a Man schal neuere þenche good among   35
folk. for þere is euere synne. þe Steuene of heuene seide vn to vs
areseine.

---

10 dominus *in left margin in red ink.*   19 Ieremias *in left margin in*
red ink.   21 heiȝed: *second* e *written above line in red ink and marked for*
insertion by caret in the same ink.   34 nec, *sic for* ne.

FVge homines ⁊ saluaberis. ⁅ þat is fleiȝe Men and þou schalt
be saued. and eft þat voice seide. fuge. tace. quiesce. fleiȝe. ⁊
be stille. and wone stille in o stede stedfastlich out of Men. Now
ȝe han forbise boþe of þe elde lawe and of þe newe how good
(M. 164) it is to ben one. Al þis Onynge nys nouȝth elles bot fleiȝe 5
þe compaignye of wicked Men ⁊ wicked wymmen, þat
god in þe godspel haþ forboden þe And kepe þe in good compaignye. And þan miȝttow lerne good ⁊ do good. Eot resouns
þere ben whi vche Man auȝtte to nyme ȝeme þe better to hym
seluen. I saie hem schortlich. nymeþ þe better ȝeme to hem. 10
And þere I speke schortlich þere stodie ȝe lengest. For þat
stodiynge schal bringe ȝou in to vnderstondynge better þan
forto rede forþ aþing hastilich. And anoþer ȝif i schulde write þe
al. it were longe er i schulde come to þe ende. Ȝif a wilde Lyoun
com rennande in þe stretes. nolde nouȝth vche Man schete his 15
dores ⁊ his wyndowes fast.

SObrij estote ⁊ vigilate in oracionibus quia aduersarius vester
diabolus tamquam Leo rugiens circuit querens quem deuorat
cui resistite fortes in fide. ⁅ Beþ sober and wakeþ in biddynge
for ȝoure aduersari þe fende goþ abouten in þe stretes for to 20
loken wham he may deuouren aȝein wham stondeþ ȝe stronge in
feiþ. Anoþer resoun þe apostle seiþ.

HAbemus thesaurum istum in vasis fictilibus ⁅ Who so
bereþ haliway in a brotil vessel as glas in gret þronge it
may liȝthlich breken. ⁊ so done we. we bere halyway in a brotyl 25
vessel. wel brotiler þan þe glas þat is maydenhode oiþer chastite
in oure brotile fle aboute. For maydenhode may neuere ben
ybett and it be ones ybroken nomore þan þe glas. Ac ȝut it
brekeþ wiþ wel lesse þan þe glas. For glas ne brekeþ nouȝth bot
ȝif it be wiþ sumwhat. and þat brekeþ wiþ a stynkande wille. ac 30
þat may be made hole aȝein ȝif it laste nouȝth longe. þe proue
here of. Iohn þe good ` godspeller þouȝt haue broken his
(M. 166) Maidenhode whan þat he was wedded and afterward was
mayden.

---

17 Aug[ustinus] *in right margin in red ink.* 18 deuorat,
sic for deuoret. 21 stondeþ ȝe: *written together with thin*
vertical stroke after þ. þ *was possibly inserted subsequently.* 23 apostolus
in right margin in red ink. 25 ⁊ *written above line.* 27 fle, sic
for flesch. 34 mayden *partially effaced at end of line.*

Virginem virgini commendauit. ⟨ Maiden was bytauȝtt maiden
seiþ oure lord

IN mundo pressuram in me autem pacem habetis. ⟨ In þe
werlde is þrong seiþ oure lorde ⁊ in me ȝe schulle fynde pes.
þe þridde. heuene is heiȝe ⁊ hem is litel ynouȝ to werpen al þe 5
werlde vnder | foote þat clymben schal so heiȝe.

VIdi Mulierem Amictam sole ⁊ lunam sub pedibus eius.
⟨ Seint Iohn seiþ in þe Apocalips he seiȝ a womman cloþed
in þe sunne ⁊ þe Mone vnder her fete. By þe sunne is bitokned
þat vche riȝthwise Man owe to ben ycloþed in soþe. Sunne þat 10
is ihesus crist he is sunne of riȝthwisenesse. Looke we þan þat
þe sunne be nouȝth derk in vs þorouȝ no dedlich synne. By þe
Mone is bitokned þe richesse of þis werlde þat waneþ ⁊ wexeþ
as doþe þe Mone. And ȝif we clymben heiȝe we moten haue
hem vnder fote. þat is ne setten nouȝth oure hertes vpon hem. 15
and ne take nomore of hem þan nede is vche Man after þat his
state askeþ. þis word is feþered. nyme ȝeme vche man what his
state ouȝth forto ben I ne speke nouȝth þat a Man ne may haue
good ynouȝ and queme god ful wel ȝif he wil. Bot he þat wil be
in state as he ouȝtte to ben Look to goddes holy Halewen ⁊ take 20
ensample att hem. For alle þe worschipes of þis werlde hij setten
att nouȝth and alle þe richesses. And att lesse þan nouȝth. For
hij bringen a Man to nouȝth. þat is to synne and after to pyne
wiþ outen ende bot ȝif hij ȝiuen þe bettere kepe to her honde
and gon þe wiselicher. þe fierþe resoun is. Riȝth gentil Men ne 25
schulden wiþ riȝt bere none purses ne bagges for it falleþ to
begenyldes to beren hem. And goddes spouse is gentil sche ne
schal bere noþing bot as a gentil man auȝtt to do. It falleþ to
burgeys to bere purs þat is to saie, her hertes ne auȝtten nouȝth
to be sett in no werldelich þinges. A Man þat can ⁊ haþ grace 30
may haue good ⁊ mychel rychesse þeiȝ he ne sette nouȝth
his herte gretlich þere vpon. þe fyft resoun is. Riche Men
maken large lyueree and good Men ⁊ wymmen maken large
relyf.

---

1 was bytauȝtt: was by *partially effaced at end of line.*   dominus *in*
right margin in red ink.   3 habetis, *sic for* habebitis.   dominus *in*
right margin in red ink. Right part of s *cut off at edge of MS.*   7 [Io]
hannes *in left margin in red ink.*   *Traces of letter at edge of MS.*
17 state: te *on erasure.*   19 we *crossed out after* ȝif.   26 riȝt: ȝt
crammed together at end of line.

p. 402a (left margin, line 6)
M. 168) (left margin, line 27)

ECce relinquimus omnia ⁊ secuti sumus te. Lord seide seint
Peter we han forsaken alle þinges ad folowen þe. What
forsook Peter bot an olde nett. nay it nys nouȝth al so in þe
forsakynge of werldelich good. For hij wrouȝtten for her Mete
in þe werlde. Ac þus it is. We schulle forsaken alle Manere 5
vices and folowen þe lorde boþe here and in heuene as none ne
may bot Maidens one.

HIi secuntur agnum quocumque ierit vtroque pede id est.
integritate cordis ⁊ corporis. ⦅ þat is non ne may folowe
hym in hert ⁊ in body ⁊ in soule bot Maydens. þe sexte resoun 10
is, to be pryuee wiþ god oure lorde.

DUcam te in solitudinem ⁊ ibi loquar ad cor tuum. ⦅ Ichille
p. 402b   lede þe seiþ oure lorde in to priue | stede. and þere ichille
louelich ⁊ bleþelich speken vn to þe for me is loþ prees
(M 170).   EGo dominus in ciuitate non egredior. ⦅ þe seuent resoun is 15
forto be briȝth in heuene. þe eiȝtted resoun is forto haue
quyk bonen. Lokeþ þerfore þat ȝe ben Ester. Ester on ynglisch
is als mychel to sayne as hydd. sche was assurs quene And assur
on ynglisch is as myȝtty. sche red al hire folk fram þe deþ
þorouȝ her bone. for þe kyng hereþ her bone and graunteþ hir 20
what sche wil habbe. þat bytokneþ Men ⁊ wymmen þat ben in
clene lyf. for Michel folk beþ ysaued þorouȝ swich mennes
biddynges. Hester was Maradoches douȝtter, Maradoche
spelleþ. Amare conterens inprudentem, þat is totreden þe
schemeful. Schemeful ben hij þat any þing speken to swich Men 25
oiþer wymmen bot good. ȝif þere doþe any so. hij beþ þan
Maradoches douȝttere. þat is bitterlich vndernymeþ hem and
seiþ þis vers, Narrant michi iniqui fabulaciones.' set non vt lex
tua, Lorde hij tellen to me fables and nouȝth þe lawȝe, oiþer þer
þis vers.   30

DEclinate A me maligni ⁊ scrutabor mandata dei mei. ⦅ þat
is goþ fro me ȝe wicked and i schal reherce þe comaundementz of my god And seiþ þis vers þat hij mowen heren ⁊

---

1 [P]etri *in left margin in red ink. Traces of letter* (P) *at edge of MS.*
relinquimus, *sic for* reliquimus.   2 ad, *sic for* and.   12 [d]o-
minus *in left margin in red ink. Traces of* d *visible at edge of MS.*
17 bonen: e *with macron subsequently crammed in after first* n.   21 Men:
MS. Mem *with last minim of* m *expuncted.*   28 dauid *in right*
margin in red ink.   29 fables: *above a irregular curl, possibly belonging*
to an unfinished b.   oiþer þer: *probably dittography.*   31 dauid *in*
right margin in red ink.

wendeþ away fram hem. Semeþ hadde deþ aserued and he
M. 172) cried mercy. And salamon forȝaf it hym vpon a forward þat
he helde hym att home in ierusalem. And he brake forward for he
went out after his þralles ⁊ he was sone biwraied vnto Salamon
And he was done to þe deþ. þis Semeþ bitokneþ Man oiþer 5
womman þat haþ trespassed aȝeins god. Salamon is oure lorde.
keep ȝou wel in ȝoure hous þat is Ierusalem ȝoure body scheteþ
wel ȝoure fyue wyttes ⁊ ȝe schulle lyuen. For Salamon oure
lorde ȝiueþ sone Mercy att swiche a forward þat ȝe ne trespas
nomore. For ȝif þe fyue wyttes gon out þat schulden ben att 10
home and ȝeme as wel þat þere were inne þerfore ȝif hij gon
out þe hous is yuel ykept. þerfore ne leteþ hem nouȝth out for
M. 174) ȝemeleshede so þat hij ne ben nouȝth ytempted to þe deþ. Holde
ȝou in as þeues þat ben flowen to holy chirche. for ȝif hij gon
M. 176) out þere nys nouȝth bot honge. þe sparowe haþ þe fallande 15
yuel. So moten we haue fleschlich fondynges and gostlich boþe
forto harden vs ⁊ maken vs stronge. for we schulden elles leten
to wel of oure seluen. and bicomen to wilde. And þerfore it is
god þat we fallen dounward ⁊ be lowe of herte. For ȝif god lete
vs haue alle oure wille: we ne schuld nouȝth knowen oure seluen. 20
M. 178) Aȝein alle temptaciouns here is remedie good. Ne wene non of
heiȝe lyf þat he ne schal bene ytempted. For þe heiȝer of lyf |
p. 403a and þe better þat god loueþ hem þe more hij moten ben
ytempted ⁊ þe strenger more þan þe leþi. And here ensample.
þe heiȝer þat þe hule is þe mo wyndes ben þere on. By hylle 25
in holy wrytt. is bitokned heiȝe lyf þe heiȝer man of lyf þe mo
puffes of fondynges ben vpon hym ⁊ þe stronger.

T Unc maxime inpungnaris tunc te inpungnari non sentis.
(Seke man haþ two states þat ben riȝth dredeful. as seint
Gregori seiþ þat on is whan he feleþ nouȝt his owen sekenesse 30
And for þi ne secheþ he nouȝth þe leche ne þe lechecraft ne ne
askeþ no mannes red ne no conseil and so asterueþ he ferelich
er he it wene. þis is he þat ne feleþ no fondynges as þe aungel
seiþ in þe Apocalips

D Icis quia diues sum ⁊ nullius egeo ⁊ nescis quia miser es ⁊ 35
pauper ⁊ secus. (þus þou seist þe nys no nede medicine.

22 *Catchwords* and þe better *in black ink at the bottom of right margin. Catch-*
words enclosed in a rectangle with two heads (*each with a leaf in the mouth*)
as ornaments pointing left and right. 26 is: *traces of erasure on* s.
28 Gregorius. *in left margin in red ink.* tunc, *sic for* cum. 33 as: s
partially erased.

Ac þou art blynde in herte and ne seest nouȝth þat þou art
, pouer ⁊ naked of alle goode þewes. ⁊ of holynes ⁊ of gostlich
werkes. þat oþer dredeful astate is þat seke man haþ ⁊ is al
froward þis oþer. þat is þat he feleþ so mychel anguissch þat he
ne may þole þat men hondle his sore ne come þere neiȝ forto 5
helen it þis is he þat feleþ so many fondynges. ⁊ is so adrad þat
god ne loueþ hym nouȝth þat no gostlich confort ne may hym
gladen ne make hym to vnderstonden þat he may for hem þe
better ben yholpen. Ne telleþ it in þe godspelle þat an Aungel
ledd oure lorde Ihesu crist in to wildernesse forto ben ytempted 10
of þe fende.

D Uctus est ihesus in desertum a spiritu vt temptaretur a diabolo. ⟨ Ac his temptacioun þat he ne miȝth nouȝth synnen
(M. 180) was onelich wiþ outen. Vnderstondeþ alderfirst þat two maner
temptaciouns þere ben ⁊ two maner fondynges þe vtter ⁊ þe 15
inner And boþe ben of many manere. þe vtter fondynge is þat
þe likyng comeþ of. oiþer myslikynge. as of sekenesse myseise
scheme and vnhappe and vche yuel þat þe flessche feleþ. wiþinnen hert sore greme oiþer tene oiþer wraþþe for þat he is pyned
in his body. wiþouten ben þise fondynges his hele of body Mete 20
drynk oiþer cloþinge. oiþer ȝif a man is yloued more þan anoþer
⁊ more holden by ⁊ done good more þan anoþer. oiþer forto ben
yworschiped of man oiþer of womman. þise ben fals fondynges
inwiþ þat comen of lykynge and þis dele is þe inner temptacioun
and is wers þan þe vtter and swikeler þan þe oþer half ⁊ soner 25
bigileþ Men and wymmen and boþe ben o temptacioun ⁊ oiþer
p. 403b is | wiþinnen ⁊ wiþouten for þat on is liknge ⁊ þat oþer is myslik-
ynge. and boþe þise ben of two dalen ac hij ben cleped þe vtter
for hij bigynnen euer wiþ outen and entren wiþ innen. for þe
vtter þing is þe fondyng. þise fondynges comen oiþer while of 30
god as of sekenesse ⁊ of frendes deþ. and oiþer while it comeþ
hem seluen. pouerte. myshappe ⁊ oþer swich myslikyng of woord
oiþer of dede oiþer of þe oiþer of þine. þis is al myslikyng. ⁊
þise comen of god sumtyme. hele also and eise of man praysynge oiþer ygoded of sum man. þise comen also of god ac 35
nouȝth as done þe oþer wiþ outen. ac wiþ alle þise he fondeþ
man. hou þat he dredeþ hym ⁊ loueþ hym. þe inner fondynges
ben of myslikynge vnþewes oiþer to hem ward. oiþer swikel
þouȝttes to hem ward þat men þenchen þat hij ben good for it is

24 temptacioun: te *blotted by red ink.*   27 liknge, *sic for* likynge.

to her likynge. And þise inner fondynges comen of þe fende. of
þe werlde ⁊ of oure flessche oiþer while. To þe vtter temptaciouns is nede pacience þat is þolemodenesse. ⁊ to þe inner is
nede wisdom ⁊ gostlich strengþe. We schullen now speken of þe
vtter ⁊ techen ⁊ techen hem þat han hem how þat hij mowen 5
þorou3 goddes grace finde remedie.

M. 182) **B**Eatus vir qui suffert temptacionem quoniam cum probatus
fuerit accipiet coronam vite quam repromisit deus diligentibus se. ⟨ Blissed ⁊ celi he is þat haþ in temptacioun þolemodenesse. for whan he is yproued it seiþ he schal ben ycrouned 10
wiþ þe crowne of lif þat god haþ bihoten to his lef ychose. For also
proueþ god his lemman as þe goldesmythþe doþe þe golde in þe
fyre. þat fals golde goþ to nou3th. ⁊ þe good golde comeþ out
trier ⁊ bri3tter þan it was toforne sekenesse is apyne ⁊ a brennynge
to þolien ac noþing ne clenseþ fire þe gold ac sekenesse doþe 15
þe soule. 3e sekenesse i saie þat god sendes nou3t sekenesse þat
summe han. for many maken hem seek for her fole hardischippes
and þorou3 vncunnynge. and swiche sekenesse ne quemeþ
nou3t god. Now how schaltou knowe þise two maneres of
sekenesses. sekenesse þat god sendes ⁊ sekenesse þat comeþ of 20
oure seluen. Sekenesse þat god sendeþ is þis þat comeþ opon þe
sodeynlich ⁊ nou3th þorou3 þine owen makyng. for to make hem
seke for greme oiþer wraþþe þat hij taken to hem oiþer þorou3
to mychel mete oiþer drynk oiþer þorou3 to gret fastynge oiþer
þorou3 3emeleshede þat hij gon in to sum stede ⁊ cacchen sum 25
hyrt þorou3 her owen defaut ⁊ myskepynge ⁊ þis is al for defaut
of wisdom ⁊ queyntise ⁊ on many oþer maneres it comeþ to

p. 404a man ⁊ to womman. ⁊ 3if it come on any manere þat hij ne | hane
nou3th kepte hem as hij au3tten to done. swich manere sekenesse ne quemeþ nou3th god oiþer to longe wakynge oiþer slepe 30
to longe and wexeþ heuy þerfore. Now remedie a3ein sekenesse
þat god sent is þolemodenesse and be pacient þere inne and þonke
god 3erne þat he wolde so visite þe and proue þe And of þe seke-
nisse þat comeþ of þi seluen crie hym 3erne mercie and for3iue-
nesse of þat þou haste þorou3 þine owen defaut so anientisscht 35
þi body þat þou ne may nou3th serue hym as þou au3tte to done.

5 ⁊ techen ⁊ techen: *dittography.*   8 *Erasure before* repromisit.
14 apyne, *sic for* a pyne.   15 ac², *sic for* as.   16 sendes: es *par-*
tially effaced.   nou3t: 3t *crammed together at end of line.*   19 nou3t:
3t *crammed together at end of line and blurred by ink.*   28 womman:
lower parts of wom *effaced.*   35 of: *written above line.*

Biseke hym þat he forȝiue it þe ⁊ ȝiue þe grace þat þou may
amende it aȝeins hym. ȝif it be his wille. ⁊ be þan þolemode for
þe mede is mychel þat liþ to þe þolemode Man oiþer womman.
for he is euened to Martir. þus is sekenesse soule Hele ⁊ salue
of her woundes and kepeþ þat hij ne cacchen nomo as god 5
seiþ þat hij schulden ȝif sekenesse ne letted it. Sekenesse makeþ
man to vnderstonde what þat he is ⁊ to knowen hym seluen.
And he is good maister þat beteþ man forto lerne hou miȝtti is
god. and hou brotel man is. ⁊ þe blis of þis wrecched werlde
Sekenesse is þi golde smyþþe þat in þe blisse of heuene ouer 10
gildeþ þi coroune. for þe more þat þi sekenesse is þe besier is þi
golde smyþþe. and þe lenger þat it lasteþ þe briȝtter it waxeþ to
Martirs euenynge þorouȝ a wo þat þou haste here and takes it
wiþ good wille. what is more grace to þe þat haddest deserued ⁊
of erned þe pyne of helle werlde wiþ outen ende ⁊ may passe 15
þat þorouȝ a litel wo here. Nolden men tellen hym alder man
(M. 184) maddest þat forsoke a buffet for a speres wounde. A nedel
prickyng for a byheuedynge. A betynge for an hongynge opon þe
galewe trees of helle. god it wott alle þe wo of þis werlde nys
bot as a schadewe to þe leste pyne of helle. Al nys nouȝth so 20
mychel as a litel dewes drope aȝein al þe grete see. þat goþ al
aboute þis werelde. and alle þe waters þerto. He þat may þan
atstirten þat ilche griselich wo and þat hetelich pyne þorouȝ a
litel sekenesse here sely may he saie þat he is.

O N oþer half lerneþ here many folde froueren aȝein þe 25
vtter fondynge þat comeþ of mannes yuel for þise oþer ben
of goddes sonde. Who þat euer mysseiþ þe oiþer mysdoþe þe
nyme ȝeme and vnderstonde þat he is þe file þat þise Lorymers
han þat hij filen þe yrne wiþ and maken it briȝth. so done hij.
hij ben þe file þat fileþ away al þe rust of þi soule þat is synne 30
and briȝtten þi soule and freten hem seluen allas þat while as þe
file doþe

p. 404b A Noþer þenche who so euere any wo doþe þe scheme. grame.
oiþer teene. he is goddes ȝerde | ⁊ god beteþ þe wiþ hem ⁊
chastises as þe fader doþe his leue childe wiþ þe ȝerde for he 35
seiþ þat he doþe so þorouȝ seint iones mouþe in þapocalips

E Go quos amo arguo ⁊ castigo ⟨ Hem he seiþ þat i loue hem i
wil nymen ⁊ chastise. I warne ȝou fore he ne beteþ none

31 briȝtten: *second t partially effaced.*   37 in apocalipsi, *in right mar-*
gin in red ink.

here bot hem þat he loueþ nomore þan þou woldest beten a
fremde childe þei3 al it agylte. Ac nou3th ne leteþ he wel of þis
þat is cleped goddes 3erd. for as þe fader whan he haþ beten þe
childe wiþ þe 3erde werpeþ it away so doþe oure lorde werpeþ
þe vnwrast man oiþer womman þat he haþ beten wiþ his dere 5
lef childe doune in to þe pyne of helle.
Virga furoris mei assur et cetera. ⟨ For þi elles where.

186)   Michi vindictam ꝝ ego retribuam ⟨ þat is. myne is þe wreche
ꝝ i it schal 3elde. As þei3 he seide ne wreke nou3th þi
seluen ne guccheþ nou3th. ne warieþ nou3th whan a man gilteþ 10
3ou ac þencheþ þat he is 3oure faders3erde ꝝ þat he wil 3elde
hym 3erdes seruise. þat is caste hem in to þe pyne of helle bot
3if hij amenden hem here. as þe fader þroweþ a way þe 3erde
whan he has beten his dere child And ne beþ nou3th þan as
vntau3t children and froward þat cracchen a3ein ꝝ biten opon þe 15
3erd. Ac doþe as þe deboner childe doþe 3if þe fader beteþ hym
wiþ þe 3erde he kisseþ it ꝝ so do 3e. For so biddeþ 3oure fader
þat 3e ne kisse nou3th wiþ mouþ one ac wiþ loue of hert hem
þat he beteþ 3ou wiþ.

Diligite inimicos vestros. benefacite hijs qui oderunt vos ꝝ 20
orate pro persequentibus vos ꝝ calumpniantibus vos. ⟨ þis
is goddes biddyng þat hym is wel leuer þat 3e dude þan 3e eten
harde brede ꝝ dranke water or wered þe hard haire oiþer 3utt
any oþer penaunce. for of alle penaunces þat is þe most. Loueþ
3oure foomen, he seiþ. ꝝ doþe hem good þat wereþ vpe 3ou ꝝ 25
3if 3e elles ne mowen. biddeþ fast for hem þat 3ou any yuel done
oiþer myssaien doþe as þe apostle lerneþ. Ne 3elde 3e nou3th
yuel a3ein yuel ac 3eldeþ euer good a3ein yuel, as dude oure
lorde hym self ꝝ alle his holy halewen ꝝ 3if 3e holden þus goddes
heste þan ben 3e his dere children þat kissen þe 3erd þat he 30
haþ 3ou wiþ ibeten. Now saien oiþer while summe. his soule
oiþer hir ichille wel louen ac his body in none wise. ꝝ þat nys
nou3th to siggen þe soule ꝝ þe body nys bot o man ꝝ boþe hem
tyt o dome. wiltou þan delen a two þat god haþ ysamened he
forbedeþ it ꝝ seiþ.   35

405a   Quod deus coniunxit homo non separet. ⟨ Ne worþe | noman
so wode þat he to dele a two þat god haþ yfastned to gedres.

---

8 dominus. *in right margin in red ink.*   10 guccheþ, *sic for* gruccheþ.
20 dominus, *in right margin in red ink.*   36 dominus *in right margin in*
red ink.   Ne worþe *crammed together at end of line.*

726 C 73   G

Inposuisti homines super capita nostra. ¶ þou haste ysett men abouen oure heuedes lorde. þat is to saie þou haste sett men vpon vs to done vs harme and tene forto prouen vs.

Transibimus per ignem ⁊ aquam. ¶ We schullen passen by fire and by water. þat is to saie þorou3 fire of fondynges. ⁊ 5 þorou3 water of anguissch ⁊ sorou3es. þenche 3utt on þis wise. þat childe 3if it spurneþ on sum þing oiþer hirteþ it men beten þat þing þat it hirteþ opon. ⁊ þe childe is paied and for3eteþ al his hirtt ⁊ stilleþ his teres. for þi frouer 3oure seluen

M. 188) Letabitur iustus cum viderit vindictam ¶ For god schal done 10 on domes day as þei3 he seide þus. dou3tter hirte þis þe. dude he þe spurnen in wraþþe oiþer in herte sore. in scheme oiþer in any tene. Looke dou3tter hou he it schal abiggen. And þere 3e schulle seen þe deuels so beten hem wiþ her baterels þat wo beþ hem. and 3e schulle ben ypayed. þis leueþ and 3e 15 schull ben ypaied þer of. For 3oure wille and goddes wille schulle ben so bounden to gider þat 3e schulle wil as he wil, and he as 3e wil. And ouer alle oþer þou3ttes þencheþ euere on goddes pyne and in al 3oure anguissch þat he þat made al þe werlde of nou3th ⁊ weldeþ it att his wille. wolde for his þralles þolen 20 swich schenschipes. hokers. buffetes and spatelynges. blinde-fellinge. þornen corounynge. þat sete so in þe heued þat þe bloode stremed adoune. And his swete body bounden naked to a piler and beten so. þat þe derworþe blood ran adoune on vche halue. þat attry drynk þat men hym 3euen þo hym þristed opon 25 þe rode her heuedes schakende opon hym on hoker and gradden so loude. Lo here he þat heleþ oþer men ⁊ may nou3th helen hym seluen. turneþ þere vp. whan ich speke hou þat he was pyned in alle his fyue wyttes. And 3e schulle seen hou litel þat it recheþ to his wo. Al oure wo. sekenesse ⁊ oþerwhat of worde 30 oiþer of werk and al þat Man may þolien a3ein þat þat he þoled And 3e schul seen hou litel it is þerto. and namelich 3if 3e þenche þat he was loþles and al þat he suffred nas nou3th for hym seluen bot for vs. For he ne agylte neuere And 3if we

---

1 dauid *in left margin in red ink.*   4 dauid *in left margin in red ink.* Transibimus, *sic for* Transiuimus.   10 propheta, *in left margin in red ink.*   viderit: e *partially erased. Traces of red ink down to* s *in* domes below.   11 domes: s *partially erased.*   þis: *traces of erasure on* s. 30 al *crossed over and expuncted after* to.   oþerwhat: hat *crammed together at end of line.* a *written above.* hat *blotted.*   31 þoled: *traces of erasure on* d.   32 schul: *traces of erasure on* l.

þolen wo. we haue wers deserued. ꝛ al þat we þolyen it is for
oure seluen.

Goþ now gladlicher by stronge waie ꝛ by swynkeful toward
þe heiȝe feste of heuene þere as oure glad frende oure
(l. 190) come kepeþ. þise besie werldelich Men gon by þe grene waye 5
toward þe galewes ꝛ þe deþ of helle. better is to goo to heuen
p. 405b þan to helle. better is to goo to myrþe wiþ me|seise þan to wo
wiþ eise. nouȝth for þan wrecched werldelich men biggen
derrer helle þan goode men done heuene.

VIa impiorum conplantata lapidibus. id est. duris affliccion- 10
ibus. ⸿ þe waye of þe wicked is sette ful of stones þat is
many hard trauailes ꝛ þouȝttes hij han for þe goodes þat hij
gaderen here. O þing to soþe wite ȝe A mys worde þat ȝe þolieþ.
A daies longynge. a sekenesse of a stounde. þeiȝ man cheped of
ȝou on of þise atte day of dome þat is þe mede þat ariseþ þere of. 15
Ȝe nolden it sellen for an hundreþ þousande werldes of gold for
þat schal be ȝoure songe

LEtati sumus pro diebus quibus nos humiliasti annis quibus
vidimus mala. þat is. wel is vs my lorde for þo ilche ȝeres
þat we were seke inne ꝛ hadden sore ꝛ sorouȝe Vche werldelich wo 20
is goddes sondes Man. And heiȝe Mannes messangere Men
owen heiȝelich to vnderfongen ꝛ maken hym gladd chere ꝛ
namelich ȝif he is pryue wiþ his lorde. And who was pryue wiþ
þe kyng of heuene while þat he woned here in erþe· þan was þis
sondes Man. sorouȝ. ꝛ wo. þat is þe wo of þis werlde it ne com 25
neuer fram hym here vntil his lyues ende. þis Messagere what
telleþ he vs. He spekeþ to vs on þis wise, God as he loued me
sent me to his lef frende. Mi come and my wonynge þeiȝ ȝou it
þenche attry and hard it is good and heleande. Nere þat þing
griselich in it self whiche þat men ne miȝth nouȝth wel biholden 30
þe schadewe were so kene and so hote þat ȝe ne miȝth nouȝth

---

1 þolen: *irregular curl above* n, *originally part of another letter.*   3 gladlicher: *traces of erasure on first* l.   4 frende: *traces of erasure on*
n.   5 þise: þ *partially erased.*   werldelich: werl *crammed together at*
end of line. Traces of erasure on d.   6 toward: t *partially erased.*
9 Salam[on] *in right margin in red ink. Only left minim of* m *visible at edge of*
MS.   10 lapidibus: *erasure above* p. *Faint traces of letter visible.*
17 dau[id] *in right margin in red ink.*   23 And: An *partially erased.*
Erasure extends diagonally down to the left towards vntil 26. *Traces of*
red ink on erasure.   24 while: hile *partially erased.*   25 sondes:
nd *partially erased.*   þis: s *partially erased.*   26 vntil: v *blotted.*
t *partially erased.*

with outen hirt it þolien.' what wolde ȝe þan segge of þat eiȝeful þing þat þe schadewe com of. I saie ȝou forsoþe al þe wo of þis werlde þat euere was or euere schal be til þe day of dome þeiȝ it were al in on. ȝutt ne were it bot a schadewe to þe lest pyne of helle. Ich am þe schadewer seiþ þe Messagere þat is werldelich 5 wo. Nedelich he seiþ ȝe mote vnderfonge me oiþer þat grise-lich wo. þat ich am of schadewe For who so vnderfongeþ me

(M. 192) gladlich ꝛ makeþ me gladd chere.' my lorde sendeþ hym worde þat he is quite of þat ilche wo þat ich am of schadewe. þus spekeþ goddes Messagere to vs. for þi seiþ seint iame.   10

O Mne gaudium existimate cum in temptaciones varias incideritis. ⸿ Al blisse holdeþ it breþeren to fallen in diuers fondynges þat is in þe vtter and in þe inner

O Mnis disciplina in presenti videtur non esse gaudij set meroris postmodum fructum et cetera. ⸿ Alle þe fondynges 15 þat we ben now wiþ yfonded þat vs þenchen wepe ꝛ nouȝth

p. 406a   wynne: afterward it turneþ | to wele and to blisse. My leue
(M. 194) frendes ȝiueþ good kepe herto for þis is a þing þat doþe mychel harme and reueþ a man grete mede.

P opule meus qui te beatificant illi te decipiunt ⸿ þis is goddes 20 word þorouȝ ysaie. who þat praiseþ ȝou tofore ȝou and seiþ wel is þe moder þat þe bare and to goderhele were þou borne in þis werlde. þise ben þine traytours seiþ oure lorde.

Q uoniam deus dissipauit ossa eorum qui hominibus placent confusi sunt quoniam deus spreuit eos. ⸿ Whi þe lord 25 brake her bones for hij pleseden to men. hij ben confounded god haþ forsaken hem

V E vobis cum omnibus hominibus benedixeritis. v.s.h. et cetera. ⸿ Acursed be ȝe þat alle Men blis for þorouȝ þat blissynge hij maken ȝou fals prophetes as her faders weren. on 30

---

1 eiȝeful: *MS.* heiȝeful *with* h *expuncted.*   5 schadewer, *sic for* schadewe.   is *on erasure.*   9 of[2] *partly effaced.*   11 OMne: M *changed from* m.   Ia[cobus] *in right margin in red ink partially effaced.* 12 breþeren: þ *partially effaced.*   to: t *partially erased.*   13 vtter: v *nearly completely erased.*   14 paulus *in right margin in red ink.* pa *and* us *partially effaced.*   16 þat vs: t vs *partially effaced.*   20 [Ysa]ias. *in left margin in red ink.*   beatificant: *cf. Isaiah III: 12:* beatum dicunt. þis is: s is *on erasure.*   23 þise: i *written above the line.*   24 [Da]uid *in left margin in red ink.*   28 *Upper part of letter in red ink erased in left margin.* ngs(?) *below in* red ink.   VE vobis ... etc.: *cf. Luke IV: 26:* Væ cum benedixerint vobis homines: secundum hæc enim faciebant pseudoprophetis patres eorum.   29 o *below* n *in red ink, partly cut off at edge of MS.*

þis manere ȝe moten vnderstonden þis. Who þat loueþ þe more
⁊ blisseþ for þi catel for hij hopen to haue sum goode of þe þe
more þorouȝ her Losengerie þan ȝif hij seiden þe þe soþe. And
ȝif hij hadden þi catel hij maden litel fors of þi soule oiþer of þi
body. þise ben þine traytours. And þat blissinge þat þou takest 5
of hem. bringeþ þe to deceyt ⁊ putteþ þe in to a pryde þorouȝ a
wel late þat þou latest of þi seluen for þat þou arte so praised.
And to bodilich harme boþe. for hij bigilen þe of þi catel. For
þorouȝ her praysynge þou ȝiuest hem þe gladlicher of þi good.
⁊ þat þou losest for hij ben ypocrites and fals prophetes. And ȝif 10
þou wost þat hij ben swiche. þou schalt be pyned þerfore þou
susteynest hem in her synne þat is in her ypocrisie. ⁊ arte coupable forto be dampned þorouȝ hem. Now beþ war of alle
swiche I rede. for gregori seiþ þat swiche men ⁊ wymmen
þorouȝ her faire speche leden þe folk in a grene waye toward 15
helle. For grene waie is soft ⁊ fair ⁊ so ben her wordes. And
þerfore seiþ ieremye þe prophete. saye þe folk her soþes. þat
is saie hem boþe þe hard ⁊ þe nesche þat is speke boþe of þe
merci of god ⁊ of his riȝthwisenesse to geder. And þan may he
þat hereþ it take which waie þat he wil. wheþer he wil go to 20
helle oiþer to heuene it is in his fre wille, for god haþ ȝouen hym
leue to chese ⁊ haþ warned hym of his harme. wharþorouȝ hym
þar wite non bot his fre wille ȝif þat he wil alway take þe brode
way þat liþ to helle and leten þe narouȝ waye þat liþ to heuene
as alle þise werldelich men done. And ȝif a man speke þus of god 25
þan puttes he hym seluen out of perile tofore god.

NOw þe inner fondynge is to fold als wel as þe vtter in
aduersite ⁊ prosperite. þat is in wele ⁊ in wo. ⁊ boþe þise

p. 406b kyndelen þe | inner fondynge. Aduersite is myslikynge. And
prosperite is likyng þat likeneþ to synne. þis i saie for þis poynt. 30
for þere is likynge þat Men fongen mychel mede fore. as likynge
in god ⁊ in þat þat falleþ to hym. þe inner fondyng is two folde
fleschlich ⁊ gostlich. Fleschelich as of leccherie ⁊ glotonie oiþer
slouþe. Gostlich as pride. onde. wraþþe coueitise. þise ben þe
inner fondynges þe seuene heued synnes and her foule kyndles 35
fleschlich fondynges may ben euened to fote wounde. And

---

10 ypocrites: es *on erasure.*   15 toward: ward *on erasure.*   18 hem:
e *partially erased.*   29 *At the left of lower margin, hand with forefinger
pointing towards left column.*   30 likeneþ: ne *written above line after* like
and marked for insertion.

gostlich fondynges þat is more drede of for þe peril may ben
cleped breest wounde. Ac vs þencheþ gretter fleschlich temptaciouns for þat we fele hem and þe oþer þei3 þat we hane hem
we ne fele hem nou3th. ⁊ ben þei3 grete and griselich in goddes
ei3en, and ben for þi mychel to dreden þe more. for þe oþer þat 5
Men felen willen schewe leche ⁊ salue. Ac þe gostlich hurtes ne
(M. 196) þenchen vs nou3th sore and þerfore we ne sechen no salue of
schrift ⁊ drawen to þe deþ er men lest wcnc. Now willen summe
saie on þis manere. 3e⸳ ich am vncunnande. I graunte wel þis
bot o þing I chille aske þe. hou ⁊ on what manere is a man cun- 10
nande. I chille segge þe go we first to werldelich cunnynge. 3if
þo schalt lerne any werldelich þinges þou moste haue þise þre
poyntes. þou moste haue wille ⁊ loue to lerne it ⁊ þan 3iue besilich þi stody þerto oiþer elles ne schaltow neuer cunne it. And
þei3 þe þenche hard atte first tyme. þorou3 wille and loue þat 15
þou haste forto lerne it. þou entres In litel and litel. And atte
last þe þencheþ it li3th ynow3. And ri3th on þis manere it
fareþ by goddes law3e. 3if þou wilt cunne it and lerne hou þou
may saue þi soule. þou mostest haue þise þre. Wille ⁊ loue to god.
⁊ þan stodye 3erne abouten what þing þat he haþ forboden þe. ⁊ 20
what he haþ bidden þe do. And þan he schal sende þe cunnyng
ynou3. þat al cunnynge comeþ of. þat is to saie 3if þou be in
good wille for after þi wille to hym ward he sendeþ þe grace and
cunnynge. Now 3if þou wilt nou3th 3iue þi stody forto brynge
boþe þi body ⁊ þi soule to blisse as þou doost to bodilich sus- 25
tenaunce þat schal faile⸳ þis Man oiþer womman ne may
nou3th saie skilfullich þat hij ne louen þe werld more þan god
And þan þei3 he reue þe þe þing þat þine herte falleþ to most ne
blame hym nou3th. 3if þi wille falle to þe werld þou mostest þan
haue þe blis of þis werlde. and þe pyne wiþ outen ende. Oiþer 30
p. 407a þou | moste haue wo ⁊ sorou3 here ⁊ blis wiþ outen ende. For ich
warne 3ou forsoþe ne may noman haue. þat is al his wille here
and elles whare For god seiþ. noman ne may serue two lordes to
queme þat is þe werlde and god. Now may vche man wel seen
þat man mote do þat in hym is. For vche man ⁊ womman whan 35
hij comen in to þis werlde and ben of age hane yer fyue wyttes
and knoweyng of yuel and of good and wille and skile forto reule
hem by. ⁊ mowen 3iuen hem þan to wheþer þat hij willen. to

---

1 of for þe peril may ben *on erasure.*   17 li3th: *traces of erasure on* h.
19 þre: e *blurred.*   20 me *crossed out after* forboden.

good oiþer to qued. Now ȝe þat ne cunnen nouȝth ne ne willen
nouȝth lerne hou ȝe mowen serue god ⁊ quemen hym. ȝe ne
schullen nouȝth onelich be taken for vncunnandnisse ac ȝe
schullen be taken for men þat despisen god. For wel wott vche
man ȝif þat he hadde a seruaunt þat couþe nouȝth serue hym ne 5
wolde nouȝth lerne. he wolde saye þat he hadde despytt of hym
and putte hym a way fram hym. Now do we þan to god as we
wolde þat god dude to vs. ⁊ make we hym no wers þan oure
seluen. And ȝutt he wil sauen vs þan and helpen vs. And skyl it
wolde þat we maden hym better Ac wolde we make hym so 10
good as oure seluen I ne can fynde noman ne neuere ne couþe.
and he schulde haue a seruaunt þat he proue hym er he made
hym pryue wiþ hym ȝif he were goode ⁊ trewe ⁊ profitable to
hym And ȝif he seiȝ þat he were nouȝth. he wolde putt hym
away. and take anoþer. Ne blame noman god þan þeiȝ he do so. 15
for he seiþ he wil assaye his seruauntz er þat he ȝiue hem au-
auncement.

ARgentum igne examinatum probatum terre purgatum
septuplum. ⸿ þat is siluer ytried wiþ fyre proued þre siþes
seuen fold oiþer here oiþer in purgatorie. And al þis gret pure- 20
geyng is in a mannes wille. for swiche wille may a man haue
here to god þat he wil purge hym here wiþ sekenesse ⁊ trauaile ⁊
many oþer harmes. so þat he schal haue a gladnesse gostlich
in þe pyne þat he þoles here so þat hij ne schullen nouȝth deren
hym. ⁊ so he haþ done wiþ many and ȝutt doþe vche day ⁊ 25
draweþ hem softlich vn to hym and al wiþ lyst. for þe goode wille
þat hij han to hym. ⁊ þat was seen by þe maudeleyne whan þat
hire broþer was ded. sche com to hym ⁊ wepe. ⁊ for he seiȝ hir
wepe. he wepe wiþ hir ⁊ arered hire broþer als smertlich.
Nomore ne may he suffre now þat we sorowe. ⁊ we han goode 30
wille vn to hym as sche hadde bot ȝif he alegge it alsone. And
ȝif we gon to | purgatori we schullen be pyned wiþ outen any
solas nylle we ne wil we. And many seyen wel were me miȝth ich
come þider þat my soule miȝth be pyned þere. Wostow Man
what þi soule is. þi soule is þi lyf whan þe soule is oute of body. 35
what pyne feleþ a mannes body þan. þi body nys bot a cloþing
to þi soule as cloþing is here a cloþing to þi body. And more
harme it wolde do þe to be beten on þi naked body þan whan

10 better: b *blotted.*   18 dauid, *in left margin in red ink.*   31 hadde:
dde *crammed together at end of line.*   38 wolde: w *blotted.*

þou art cloþed Men seþ whan þe fader wil do þe moder bete hir
childe sche wil bidde þe childe crie ⁊ bete it on þe cloþes. þan
may we say þat god loueþ vs as þe moder doþe þe childe þat
beteþ on his cloþes whan he beteþ vs here vpon oure bodyes ⁊
nouȝth opon oure naked soule. take we þan his betynge louelich. 5
Holy Men ⁊ wymmen of alle fondynges weren strongest yfonded
⁊ hem to goderhele for in þe fiȝth aȝein hij biȝeten þe blisful
kempen coroune.Loo þeiȝ hou he meneþ hym in Ieremie.

PErsecutores nostri velociores aquilis celi super montes perse-
cuti sunt nos in deserto subsidiati sunt nobis. ⟨ þat is oure 10
wiþerwynnes ben swifter þan ernes opon þe hilles. hij clymben
after vs ⁊ þere hij fiȝtten wiþ vs and ȝutt in þe wildernesse hij
spyen vs to slen. Oure wiþerwynnes ben þise þre. þe fende þe
werld. oure flesche as ich er seide. Liȝthlich ne may nouȝth a
man witen oiþer while which of þise vs werreþ for vche one 15
helpeþ oþer. þeiȝ þe fende egge vs to pride. to wraþþe. oiþer
onde. ⁊ to her attri kyndels þat ben here after ynempned. þe
flessche putteþ þerto swetnesse ⁊ softnesse. ⁊ ese. þe werlde
biddeþ man wisshen werldelich wele and oþer swich vayn
glories þat bi duelleþ caniouns to louien ⁊ so hij don. þise fon 20
he seiþ folowen vs on hilles ⁊ waiten vs hou þat hij mowen vs
harmen. Hulle þat is holy lyf bitokned þere þe deuel ensautes
oft ben strengest. By wildernesse is bitokned onelich lyf. For
also as in þe wildernesse ben wilde bestes ⁊ willen nouȝth þolen
mannes anoþing ac flen whan þat hij hem heren. riȝth so schul- 25
den onelich Men ⁊ wymmen ben wilde on þis wise. ⁊ þan hij
ben swete ⁊ lef to oure lorde. ⁊ swete hym þencheþ hem. for
wilde flesch is swetter þan oþer flesch. In þis wildernesse went
oure lordes folk as Exode telleþ toward þe blisful londe of
ierusalem þat he hem hadd bihoten. and of alle þat wenten out 30
of Egipte ne comen bot two to Ierusalem. Iosue ⁊ Calaphe þat
god ne slouȝ hem for her synne. of sex hundreþ þousande of
Men wiþ outen wymmen ⁊ children. ⁊ seruauntz. so hard | þe
deuel tempted hem in wildernesse. And þere it was bot fourti
dayes iourne hij weren fourty wynter in goynge and al for her 35
synne and her grucching þerfore beþ war who þat secheþ onelich lyf er he be proued for he may liȝthlich myskarien for þe

3 childe: c blotted.   9 Ie[remias] in right margin in red ink.   10 subsidiati,
sic for insidiati.   18 swetnesse: swet partially effaced.   19 man
partially effaced.   22 bitokned, sic.   31 Calaphe, sic for Caleb.

deuels assautes ben hard þere ⁊ queynt. And alle goddes childer

M. 198) taken þe waye toward þe heiȝe blis of ierusalem abouen. þat is
þe kyngdom of heuen þat he haþ bihoten his chosen. I rede þat
we go wel warlich. for in þis waie þat nys bot wildernesse ben
yuel bestes many. þe Lyoun of pride. þe Neddre of attri onde. 5
þe Vnicorne of wraþþe. þe Bere of heuy slouþe. Fox of wissh-
ynge. Sowe of ȝeuernesse. Scorpioun wiþ þe tail of styngynge
leccherie. þise ben þe seuen hede synnes.

þE Lyoun of pride haþ fele whelpes Vana gloria. vayn glorie.
þat is a Man þat leteþ wel of hym seluen ⁊ of þing þat he 10
deþe and wold ben yprased þere of wiþ word oiþer wiþ aqueyn-
taunce. oiþer þorouȝ Maistrie þat he can do more þan anoþer.
⁊ þis draweþ mychel to religioun And þere bicomeþ als wel as
who so putt agold ringe in a swynes nose. for nomore bicomeþ it
vn to hem be wel ypaied ȝif men praise hem yuel ypaied ȝif Men 15
mysprased hym ⁊ saie nouȝth al his wille, Indignacioun is anoþer
whelp. þat is þat hym þencheþ scorne of any þing þat he seeþ
by oþer oiþer hereþ and ne kepeþ nouȝth be chastised of lower
þan he is. Ypocrisie is anoþer whelp þat makeþ hym better þan
he is. Presumpcioun anoþer. þat is nymeþ more on honde þan 20
he may do. oiþer is to ouer trosty of goddes mercy oiþer to
bolde toward hym. oiþer to trosti opon hym seluen. oiþer enter-
meteþ hym of þing þat ne falleþ nouȝth to hym. In þis poynt
han þise clerkes sett hem hij þat seien þat noman schulde preche
of god bot ȝif he were ordred Ac hij ne loken nouȝth þere what 25
her ordre is For i saie hem forsoþe þeiȝ þat he be a Pope. oiþer
Bisschope. Monk. oiþer Frere. ⁊ he be in dedlich synne. he is
out of ordre. ⁊ ferrer fram þe grace of god þan a lewed Man þat
non ordre haþ taken of holy chirche bot his cristendom ⁊ is in
clene lyf And i saie ȝou forsoþe god holdeþ better by þe foulest 30
myster Man þat lewed is ⁊ kepeþ hym out of dedlich synne ⁊
loueþ god ⁊ dredeþ hym. þan of alle Men þat haue taken ordre ⁊
dignite and lyuen after her fleschlich likynges. for hem ne
loueþ he riȝth nouȝth. for hij ben his enemyes ⁊ werren. aȝeins
hym als longe as hij han þat wille. ⁊ alle þat susteynen hem 35
schulle it abuggen. And god vouches better saf þat swich a lewed

p. 408b Man speke of hym. þan any of hem as ȝe | han in þis boke tofore

9 [su]perbia *in left margin in black ink by different scribe.*   haþ: a
partially erased.   37 as: a *partially effaced.*

þat he wil reprocen hem whi þat hij speken of hym, and seint
Austin seiþ þat we clerkes lerne for to go to þe pyne of helle.
and lewed folk lerne to go to þe ioye of heuene.

Effusa est contencio super principes ⁊ errare fecit eos et
cetera. ⦗ Strif and wraþþe is ȝoten opon þe princes ⁊ made 5
hem forto erren out of þe riȝth waie. þat is to saie hij ȝauen hem
to delices of her bodies and god lete hem han her wille and after
kast hem to helle.

ET adiuuit pauperem de inopia. ⦗ And he halp þe pouere out
of her mesaise and summe wil saie where lered he of diui- 10
nite. hou bicomeþ hym forto speken of god her to liþ gode
answere. where lerned Peter ⁊ Poule diuinite. Ierome ⁊ Ambrose
and Gregori. of whom lerned þise Men. wheþer comen hij to
her wytt þorouȝ þe holy gost. oiþer þorouȝ stody of gret
clergie. I saie þat hij hadden it of god ⁊ nouȝth þorouȝ her 15
stody ne þorouȝ her lernynge. ⁊ ich vnderstonde þat þise were
good Men. for by hem is holy chirche yreuled now. And ich
vnderstonde ⁊ wott wel þat god is now als redy for to helpe
lewed men as he was þan þat hym wil loue ⁊ serue And wite ȝe
wel þat it is now als mychel nede as it was þan þat hastise þe 20
clerkes wiþ þe lewed Men forto schewe his myth as he haþ
alway done her toforne. for holy wrytt is ful þerof þat seiþ whan
synne miȝth nouȝth be chastised wiþ man. god it chastised And
loke now ȝif synne may be chastised wiþ Man. nay it is meyn-
tened by hem þat schulden ben heuedes and chastisen it. so þat 25
it is þe more for summe þat holden mennes wyues ⁊ lemmans
⁊ hij han siluer for to ȝiuen. hij han leue for to serue þe deuel al
att her wille. And summe seyn þat hij han ben atte holy chapiter
⁊ made her pes þat hij mowen holden her lemman ⁊ lyuen in þe
deuels seruise att her lykynge. And þerfore i may saie hardilich 30
⁊ vche man þat knoweynge haþ of god þat he it wil chastise. for
bigunnen he haþ. For þis londe is departed in þre. in wynners ⁊
defendours. ⁊ in assaillours. þe wynners þo ben þe commune
poeple ⁊ hij han ben chastised wiþ hunger. þe defendoures þat
ben þise grete Lordes þat schulden defende þe commune 35
poeple. hij han ben chastised wiþ hongeynge. ⁊ draweynge.
here is proue of ynouȝ alle Men it witen wel. þe assailours þat
is þe clergie þat schulde teche boþe þat on ⁊ þat oþer þe lawȝe of

---

4 psalmista, *in right margin in red ink.*　9 Psalmista, *in right margin*
in red ink.　　20 hastise, *sic for* chastise.

god ⁊ chastise hem ȝif þat hij duden amysse. And as by siȝth in
p. 409a þe werlde hij þat | schulden ben chastisoures ben meyntenoures
of synne and hij ben vnchastised ȝutt. Bot drede hem nouȝth
þere of god ne haþ nouȝth forȝeten hem. he wil þenche opon
hem whan he seþ his tyme. Ac ȝif ihesus hadde a trewe prelate 5
he wolde raþer be honged ⁊ drawen þerfore þan he suffred his
lord be so reuiled as he is. And ich am riȝth siker he ne
schulde nouȝth repenten hym þeiȝ he ȝede to þe deþ þerfore
nomore þan oþer holy Men han toforn hym. Now go we aȝein to *obedience*
oure matier. Inobedience þat is he þat nyl nouȝth be tauȝtt of 10
his Ouerling ne of his vnderlyng. ne ben buxum to his prelate
ne parischen to his preest ȝif hij ben of good maners And ȝif he
ne be ȝiue worschipe to þe ordre ⁊ nouȝth vn to hym for god
forbedeþ þe his compaignye bot in hope for to amenden hym.
Man be buxum to his Maister þe Maiden to hir dame. þe lower 15
to þe heiȝer. Loquacitate, þat is he þat is of mychel speche.
Ȝelpeþ. demeþ. liȝeþ oiþerwhile. vpbraideþ. chideþ. stireþ
leiȝtter. Blasfemie, þat is he þat swereþ grete oþes. þat bitterlich curseþ oiþer mysseiþ by god oiþer by any of his Halewen
for any þing þat he seþ oiþer hereþ. þoleþ oiþer redeþ. Inpacient 20
þat is he þat nys nouȝth þolemode aȝein all sorouȝes ⁊ alle
yuels. Contumacie þat is þing þat a man haþ in hert for to done
be it good be it qued þat no wiser red may hym out brynge of
þat riot. Contencion, þat is stryf to ouercomene þat on þencheþ
whan he haþ ouercomen ⁊ þat oþer is crauant. ⁊ he Maister of 25
þe ple. ⁊ crieþ as champioun þat he haþ ygeten þe place. And
siþen vpbraideþ al þat yuel þat he may on þat oþer biþenchen.
⁊ euere þe more hij seien þe better it likeþ hem þeiȝ it be of
þing þat was biforn honde amended fele ȝeres. Her amonge ne
riseþ nouȝth one bitter wordes ac ben ful stynkeand. schemeles 30
⁊ schendeful. ⁊ sum tyme wiþ grete oþes many ⁊ proude. Here
to falleþ euening of hem seluen of her commune sawȝe. Hij
þat gon to schrift wiþ swich mouþ. hij ne han no will to herie
god wiþ song oiþer biddynge to hym of any bone. for her mouþ

---

2 meyntenoures: n² *and* s *blotted. Vertical fold in MS. from upper margin
down between columns about one fourth of the page touching the final letter of
6 lines.*   18 oþes: *MS.* hoþes *with* h *crossed out.*   25 Maister:
from ter *at the beginning of line the first few words of each line are rather worn
to the bottom of the column.*   27 yuel: y *corrected from* q.   may: y *by
correction.*   30 stynkeand: *above first* n *a loop as if a* k *had been started
by mistake.*

stinkeþ fouler tofore god þan any roten dogge. Semblaunce is
anoþer whelp. þat is wiþ signes. bereande heiʒe þe heued.
crenge wiþ þe swire. Loken on side. Biholden on hoker. wynk
wiþ þat on eiʒe. bende wiþ þe mouþ. maken mowe. scornen
oþer wiþ honde oiþer wiþ heued. Suetelich syngen. werpen 5
legge ouer oþer sittand. gon styf as hij weren stichen. oiþer gon
stoupeande for pride. loue lokyng opon Man oiþer Man opon

p. 409b womman. spckcn as Innocent. whlispen for þe no|nes Alle þise
ᴢ many mo cleþed to ouer girt as meninge. oiþer heiʒeinge. in
pinchinge. in girdels girdynge of damoisels. wise nebbes depeyn- 10
tynge wiþ synneres claustringe oiþer foule flitterynge. teyn-
toure of here beiʒes. liteinge. browes whinering oiþer benchen
hem vp ward wiþ wete strikynges Many þere ben þat comen

(M. 200) from þe welle of pride. of heiʒe lyf. of heiʒe kynde. of fair cloþ.
of wytt. of strengþe. of holy þewes comeþ pride Ac þere i goo 15
.swiþe. stody ʒe longe. for i go liʒth and do bot nempne hem.
And of o word ʒe may fynde ten oiþer twelue. Ac who so haþ
any of þise þat ich haue ynempned hij han pride hou so her kirtel
is ischaped. ʒe. þeiʒ hij maken sleues of þe side gores and feden
þe lyoun whelpes in her breest þat is in her hert 20

ÞE neddre of attri onde haþ þise kyndlen. Ingratitudo, þat is
he þat nys nouʒth yknowen of goode dede þat men done
hym oiþer leteþ litel þere of oþer forʒeteþ it wiþ alle I ne segge
nouʒth one. þat men done hym. ac þat god doþe hym oiþer haþ
ydone hym vnderstondeþ ʒif a man were wel beþouʒth men 25
nymeþ here of litel ʒeme of þis vnþewe and is þeiʒ loþest to god
ᴢ most aʒein his grace. Rancor sine odio, þat is hatynge of gret
hert and bereþ it in hert. Al is attri to god þat hij euere wirchen.
þe þridd is ofþenchinge of oþers goode. þe fierþe is gladschipp
of oþers harmes liʒend oiþer gabbende opon hym ʒif hym 30
mystyde. þe fyft is wrayynge. þe sext is bakbitynge. vpbraidynge. oiþer scornynge

ÞE vnicorne of wraþþe þat haþ þe horne in þe heued þat he
sleþ wiþ þat he may come by. haþ þise whelpes. þe first is

---

1 Semblaunce: S *on erasure.*   10 girdels: dels *crammed together at
end of line.*   nebbes: s *blotted.*   12 beiʒes: b *blotted.*   liteinge: li *corrected from* b.   19 *Water-stains at various places in this column from side
and* feden *19 towards the bottom of column.*   26 vnþewe: n *and* e² *partially
effaced.*   loþest: est *on erasure. Small hole in MS. below* t.   27 sine
odio: ne od *on erasure.*   28 þat: þa *partially erased.*   31 þe seuenþ
omitted before vpbraidynge.   33 Ira *in right margin in black ink by the
scribe who wrote* [su]perbia *at* 89:9.

cheste. þat oþer stryf. Anoþer wodeschipp. biholde þe eiȝe ȝ
þe nebbe whan he is wroþ. biholde þe contenaunce opon his
lates oiþer on hir. biholde hou þe mouþ geþ ȝ þou may iugge
þat hij ben wode ȝ chaunged out of mannes kynde in to bestes
kynde. For kynde of man auȝtt to ben mylde. þe fyft whelp is 5
strokes. þe sext is wil þat yuel bitidd on hem oiþer opon her
frendes. oiþer on her godes. and do for wraþþe amysse. ȝ leten
forto done wel. forgon mete oiþer drynk wreken hem wiþ teres
ȝif hij elles ne mowen. ȝ wiþ wariynges to teren her here for
tene. oiþer on oþer manere harmen hem in soule ȝ in body. þise 10
ben omicides ȝ murþerers of hem seluen.

PE bere of slouþ haþ þise whelpes Torpor. is þe first þat is wo.
þat haþ wleche hert þat schulde brennen al in þe loue of
god. þat oþer is. Pusillanimitas þa is to pouere hert ȝ to arowȝe
wiþ alle any þing to vndernymen in hope | of goddes help. ȝ in 15
trust of his suete grace ȝ nouȝth of her strengþe. þe þridde is.
cordis grauitas, þat is while he wircheþ good wiþ heuy hert ȝ
grucchyng þe fierþe is ded sorowe for losse of any werldelich
þing oiþer of frendes. oiþer of þenchinge bot for synne þe fift is
ȝemelesschip to siggen oiþer to done. oiþer mysbisene. oiþer 20
þenchen. oiþer myswiten þing þat he haþ to ȝeme, þe sext is
wanhope of goddes mercy and of his help. ȝ þis is werst of alle.
For it to freteþ god. ȝ tocheweþ his mercy ȝ his grace.

PE fox of wisschinge haþ þise whelpes. Treccherie ȝ Gile.
þise gon wide ȝ her strengþe fals witnesse. oþer þat doþ 25
Symonye. Gouel. Oker. Fastschipp Pinching. Synnyng of her
goodes. oȝeueninge oiþer laueninge. mansauȝt. oiþer while þise
vnþewes is to þe Fox yeuened for many resones. to wil we siggen
mychel. gyle is in þe fox and so is in þe wisschinge of werldelich
goodes, to biȝeten hem. þe fox astrangleþ al a flok þeiȝ he ne 30
may bot on souken. And also a wisscher askeþ þat many þou-
sandes myȝtten be filled of Ac þeiȝ his hert to brest he ne may

---

1 þat oþer, *sic for* oiþer. þat *and* oþer *connected at end of line.*　　2 contenaunce: aunce *crammed in at end of line.*　　11 accidia *in right margin
in black ink by the scribe who wrote* [su]perbia *at 89: 9 and* Ira *at 92: 33.*
13 hert: e *partially effaced.*　　14 Pusillanimitas: as *by correction.*　　þa,
sic for þat.　　25 oþer þat doþ, *sic for* oiþer oþ.　　26 Pinching: *cf.
Corpus:* prinschipe *54b: 19.*　　27 oȝeueninge oiþer laueninge: *cf. Corpus:*
of ȝeoue oðer of lane *54b: 19.*　　*The water-stains mentioned at 92:19
have affected this side of the page at places from* oȝeueninge *downwards.*
mansauȝt, *sic for* manslauȝt.　　31 wisscher: *MS.* whisscher *with
first* h *expuncted.*　　32 filled: *MS.* fillend *with* n *expuncted.*

brynge on hym seluen bot o mannes dele. Al þat a man oiþer
a womman wilneþ more þan he may scarslich leden þe lyf by

vchone after his state. is bigynnyng ⁊ roote of dedlich synne.
þat is riȝth religioun þat vchone after his state borowe of þis
wrecched werd als litel as he leste may of Mete. drynk. oiþer 5
cloþ. And alle oþer þinges. Noteþ þat i sigge vchon after his
state for þat worde is feþered ȝe may þat wyte ȝe wel fynde in
many wordes mychel strengþe and vnderstondyng. For ȝif I
schul writen al longe it were er ich com to þe ende.

ÞE sowe of ȝiuernesse is glotonye þat haþ many pigges. ⁊ þus 10
hij ben ycleped þe first ete to erlich anoþer to late. þe þrid
to hastilich. þe fierþe to fleschlich. þe fyft to mychel. þe sext to
often. ⁊ in drynk more þan in mete. Of þise I speke schortlich.
for vche man may vnderstonde in his owen wytt þat it is a spice
of dedlich synne. and ȝif he be custumable þerto it is dedlich. 15

ÞE scorpion of stynkande Leccherie nyl ich nouȝth nempny.
for þe foule filþe of þe foule name for it miȝth done harme
in to clene hertes. Ac þise þat ben commune whiche þat men
knoweþ wel þe more harme is to many. horedam and spousebreche. gederinge bitwixen sibbe fleschlich oiþer gostlich þat is 20
in many manere dedlich. þat is to han wille to þat filleþ wiþ
skilles ȝetinge þat is whan þe skil ⁊ þe wille acorden ⁊ þe hert ne

wiþseiþ | it nouȝth bot wilneþ it ⁊ ȝerneþ it þat þe flesche prikeþ
and hunteþ þere after wiþ woweynge wiþ lokynge. wiþ tollynge.
wiþ gydy lauȝtter. wiþ hore eiȝe. wiþ many liȝth lates wiþ ȝift. 25

wiþ collyng. wiþ loue speche. wiþ cusse wiþ gropynge. sett
stede ⁊ tyme for to comen þis is al dedlich synne of þise men.
hij moten wiþdrawen hem þat nyllen nouȝth in þat foule filþe
fallen as seint Austyn seiþ

DImissis occasibus que solent aditum aperire peccatis potest 30
consciencia esse incolumis. (þat is. who þat wil his inwitt
witen al clene fer he most fleiȝe þat fetles þat is wone oft to ben
yopened. þat ingonge þat leteþ in synne I ne dar nouȝth for
drede speke þere of ne writen. lest oþer ben ytempted þere of.

---

3 after: *below* a *hole mentioned at* 92:26.   5 werd, *sic for* werld.
13 more: r *corrected from* þ.   mete: te *blurred.*   speke: *traces of erasure*
on s. p *blurred.*   20 gostlich: ch *partially effaced.*   22 þe²: e
partially erased.   23 wiþseiþ: *MS.* wiþ seiþ *with connecting stroke.*
26 collyng, *sic for* tollyng. *Cf.* l. 24.   30 DImissis occasibus, *sic for* OMissis
occasionibus. Augustinus. *in right margin in red ink.*   32 fetles, *sic. Cf.*
Corpus: foreridles 55b: 5.

Sexual immorality (margin note)

Ac ich warne ȝou of her gidilich kyndels and gidilich liȝtters
For hou so it euer is yqueynt it is dedlich synne ȝif it be wakeand
and willes wiþ fleschlich likyng bot ȝif it be in wedlok. And bot
hij it tellen openlich in schryft as hij it deden þat felen hem
gilted. elles hij ben ydampned to þe pyne of helle forto echen 5
þat fyre. Nou it is to witen whi ich haue ynempned pride to
Lyoun and alle þise oþer diuers bestes wiþ outen þis latter. whi
Leccherie is likned to þe scorpioun Loo here þe skille. þe scorpioun is a worme þat haþ sumdel þe heued likned to womman.
and nedder it is bihynden and makeþ fair semblaunt ⁊ fikeleþ 10
wiþ þe heued and styngeþ wiþ þe tayl

QUi apprehendit mulierem est quasi qui apprehendit
scorpionem. ⟨ Who so takeþ a womman on honde he
takeþ as he toke a scorpioun þat wolde styngen hym. ⟨ þis
leccherie is þat deuels best. þat he ledeþ to chepynge ⁊ to vche 15
gaderynge ⁊ he chepeþ it to sellen and biswikeþ many forwhi
þat hij ne biholden nouȝth bot þe fair heued þat heued is þe
(M. 208) gynnyng of al galnesse of synne ⁊ þe likyng while it lasteþ þat
hem þencheþ swiþe swete. þe tayl is þe ende þere of þat is sore
ofþenchyng ⁊ styngeþ þerwiþ attre of bitter byrewynge ⁊ of 20
dede. bot sikerlich hij mowen siggen þat þe tayl swich yfyndeþ
er þat attre a geþ Ac ȝif it ne smert hem nouȝth þe tayl ⁊ þat
attry ende. þan is it forto eche wiþ þe pyne of helle And nys he
nouȝth a foule chapman whan he wil buggen an Ox. oiþer an
hors. ȝif he nyl nouȝth bihelden bot þe heued one. And forþi 25
whan þe deuel bedeþ forþ his beste ⁊ chepeþ it to sellen. he
hideþ euere þe tayl ⁊ scheweþ forþ þe heued. Ac go ȝe al abouten
⁊ lokeþ toward þat ende. ⁊ to þe gynnyng ⁊ hou þe tayl styngeþ. |
p. 411á And swiþe fleiȝe þerframward þat ȝe ne be nouȝth yattred.

MI leue childer þere we gon in wildernesse with goddes folk 30
toward Ierusalem þat is toward þe holy londe þat is þe
heiȝeriche of heuene. in þe waie þiderward ben þillech bestes ⁊
þillich wormes. ne wot ich no synne þat it ne may leide to on of
þise seuene oiþer to her strenes. Vnstedfast bileue aȝein holy
lore nys it of pride. Inobedience ne falleþ it to sigaldrie fals tak- 35
ynges leuynges o fals sweuenes ⁊ alle wichcraftes nymynge of
housel in any heued synne. oiþer in any oþer sacrement. nys

---

12 Salamon, *in right margin in red ink.*   apprehendit[1]: *second* e *partially
erased.*   15 chepynge: c *partially effaced.*   33 ben *omitted after*
may.   37 nys: y *probably corrected.*

it a spice of pride þat Men clepen. Presumpcio, ȝif Man wot
what synne it is. ⁊ ȝif a man wot it nouȝth. þan is it ȝemeles
vnder þe synne of slouþe. He is slow þat nyl nouht seke remedie
to hym seluen. oiþer helpe oþer ȝif he may oiþer can of her yuel
⁊ of her lere of soule. þis Man oiþer womman is sleyn for defaut 5
of ȝemynge. typing. amys ne comeþ it of onde. oiþer atholde
fyndels lant amys nys it coueitise oiþer þift. And atholde oþers
hure nis it stronge rifcling. ȝif Man ȝemeleslich make any þing
wers þat is lent oiþer tauȝt to witen þan hij wenen þat owen it
nys oiþer treccherie. oiþer ȝemeles slauȝtt. Also reccheles hest 10
oiþer ypliȝth folilich trewþ. longe ben vnbisschoped. falslich go
(M. 210) to schrift oiþer to longe abiden. ne teche þe pater noster ⁊ þe
crede to god childe. þise ⁊ þellich oþer ben ylaide to sleuþ þat is
þe fierþe Moder of þe seuen synnes þat fordoþe childe wiþ
drynche. oiþer fordoþe þat no childe may on hir ben ystrened. 15
þise ben mansleers vnder þo þat ben ywriten And here a Man
may ȝif he wil of alle maner synnes take ensample by þise seuen
bestes.

PRoude Men ben þe deuel Beemers ⁊ drawen wynde inward
⁊ outward of werldelich worschipes þat gadreþ it inward and 20
puffeþ it outward as bemer doþe makeþ noise ⁊ loude drem to
maken her gle. Ac ȝif hij wel biþouȝtten hem on goddes beemers atte day of dome of aungels þat schullen comen on foure
half þe werlde and seien. ariseþ ȝee dede ⁊ comeþ to þe dome
þat ȝee mowen sore adreden forto ben ydampned þere no 25
proude Bemer ne schal ben ysaued ȝif hij wel biþouȝtten hem
on þis hij nolden nouȝth blowen in þe deuels dymme beme. of
þise bemers spekeþ Ieremie.

ONager salitarius in desiderio anime sue attraxuit ventum
amoris sui. ⟮ Of þe wynde draweynge in for þe loue of 30
p. 411b werldelich ernynge. | summe þere ben iogeloures þat cunne
(M. 212) seruen of non oþer gle bot make cherres ⁊ wrenchen wiþ mouþ
mys stulleli wiþ þe eiȝen. of þis myster þan serueþ þe ondeful
vnseli in þe deuels court to bryngen on lauȝtter her ondeful

2 ⁊ *written above line and marked for insertion.*   wot: *MS.* whot *with* h
expuncted.   7 lant: nt *on erasure.*   8 nis: ni *irregular or corrected*
at end of line.   10 it *omitted after* nys.   15 fordoþe, *sic for* doþe.
20 werldelich: er *crammed together before* l *at end of line.*   29 Ieremias,
in left margin in red ink.   salitarius, *sic for* solitarius.   attraxuit, *sic for* attraxit.
32 gle bot: gle bo *on erasure.*   33 stulleli: *cf. Corpus:* schulen *57a: 17,*
Cleopatra: Schulen *90ʳ: 21. Nero:* schulen *94: 10, Titus:* schuldi *68: 34.*

lorde Biholde nou of þise hou hij faren whan þat hij heren þe
good hij wrenchen away and stoppen her eren þat hij ne heren
it nouȝth. ac þe loue aȝein þat yuel is euere yopened redy þan
he wrencheþ þe mouþ whan he turneþ þe good vn to yuel. And
ȝif it is sumdel yuel makeþ it wers. þise ben forquiders her owen 5
prophetes. þise boden toforne hou þe deuelen schullen rapelich
glutten hem þorouȝ her grennyng. ꝛ hou hij schullen hem seluen
grennen ꝛ maken loþly semblaunt for þe mychel anguisch in þe
pyne of helle. Ac hij ben þe lesse to witen for þat biforne honde
hij leten her myster to maken grym chere.   10

ꝥE wraþþeful bifore þe fende skirmeþ wiþ swerd ꝛ wiþ knyf.
Hij ben his knyf werpers ꝛ plaiers wiþ swerdes and beren
hem by þe scharp ordes vpon þe tunges. Swerd ꝛ knyf oiþer
beþ keruande. worde þat hij werpeþ fram hem ꝛ kerueþ toward
oþer. And hij beden hou þe deuel schullen playe wiþ hem wiþ 15
her scharpe cloches. and crokes. ꝛ skirmen wiþ hem al abouten
ꝛ dunchen hem as pilche cloutes vche vntoward oþer. ꝛ wiþ
helle swerdes smyten hem þorouȝ out þat ben þe keruande
pynes of helle.

SLeuþe liþ and slepeþ on þe deuels barme as his dere derlyng. 20
ꝛ þe deuel laiþ his totel toward his ere ꝛ toteleþ hym al þat he
wil. For so it is sikerlich who so is ydel of good werkes þe deuel
toteleþ hym ȝerne ꝛ þe ydel vnderfongeþ louelich his lore. Ydel
ꝛ ȝemeles þis is þe deuels barme slepe. ac hij schulle on domesday arisen grymmelich ꝛ abrayen wiþ þe dredeful drem of þe 25
aungels bemen. ꝛ in helle wonderlich awaken.

SVrgite Mortui qui iacetis in sepulchris. surgite ꝛ venite ad
iudicium saluatoris. ℂ þe coueitouse Man haþ swich a bay
þat he liþ euere in þe askes ꝛ askes al abouten hym ꝛ bisilich
stireþ hem to rokely hem to hepes ꝛ bloweþ þere inne ꝛ blyndeþ 30
hym seluen. poþereþ ꝛ makeþ þereinne figures of augryme to
rekenen And þis is al þe conions blis. And þe fende biholdeþ
þis gamen and leiȝeþ þat he brestes. Wel may vche wise Man
wite þat gold ꝛ siluer nys askes. ꝛ ablente vche Man þat hem
inne blowen ꝛ bolneþ hym þorouȝ hem in hert pride And al 35
þat he rokeleþ ꝛ gadereþ to geders ꝛ atholdeþ of any þing nys
bot askes, | more þan it nedeþ to hym. ꝛ it schal in helle worþen

. 214)

. 412a

---

10 chere: he *partially erased.*   15 beden: d *by correction.*   deuel, *sic for* deuels.
24 barme: *cf. Corpus:* bearnes *57b:21.*   28 haþ swich a bay: *cf. Corpus:*
is his eskibah *57b: 23.*   34 bot *omitted after* nys.   hem: em *on erasure.*

to frouden ⁊ nedders. ⁊ be as ysaye þe prophete seiþ his couer-
ture ⁊ his whittel schullen ben of wormes

SVbter te sternetur tinea ⁊ operimentum tuum vermis. ⟨ þe
gloton is þe fendes Maunciple he stykeþ euer in þe seler.
oiþer in þe kychin his hert is in þe disches. his þouȝth is in þe 5
nappes. his lyf is in þe tunne. his soule is in þe crokke. He
comeþ bifore his lorde bismoked ⁊ bismered. A dische in his on
hondc a schale in his oþer. ⁊ biholdeþ his gret wombe ⁊ þe
fende leiȝeþ. þus precheþ vs god þorouȝ ysaye.

SErui mei comedent ⁊ vos esurietis. Myne Men schullen eten 10
⁊ ȝoure schullen haue hungere and ȝe schullen ben þe fendes
fode werlde wiþ outen ende.

QVantum se glorificauit ⁊ in delicijs fuit tantum date illi
tormentum ⁊ luctum in apocalipsi contra vnum poculum
quod miscuit miscite ei duo. ⟨ Ion þe ewangelist seiþ ȝiue þe 15
gloton þe coppe he þat wil euere drynk. Cobbe in glotonye
ȝiue hym wellande bras to drinken ⁊ ȝeteþ it in his wide þrote
þat he swelt inwiþ on ȝiue hym to þillich is goddes dome in þe
Apocalips.

ÞE Lechoures in þe deuels Court han riȝth her owen name 20
for in þise grete Courtes þat Men clepen Lecchoures þat
han forlorne schame þat sechen hou hij mowen most Leccherie
done

DE continentibus dicitur. Hij sunt qui cum Mulieribus non
sunt coinquinati. ⟨ þe lecchours in þe deuels court defoul- 25
eþ hem seluen foulelich. ⁊ her felawes alle styken of þat filþe ⁊
payeþ wel his lorde wiþ þat stynkyng breþ better þan he schulde
wiþ any recles. It paieþ wel þe deuel þat hij ben strongelich
pyned. ⁊ þat is wonder for her pyne is þe more for hem. And
þerfore þe deuels haten hem. ⁊ han gret envie to hem. And þe 30
more pyne þat þe soules han þe bettere it likeþ þe deuels. And
þeiȝ her pynes schal pynen hem. Hou þise lecchours stynken.
In vitas patrum it telleþ þat þe Aungel schewed it vn to an holy
man þat helde his nose for þe proude lecchour þat com ridand
þere ⁊ nouȝth for þe roten cors þat he halpe þe Ermyte to beryen. 35

(M. 216)

---

3 [Ys]aias *in left margin in red ink. Traces of a loop at edge of MS.*
10 [Ys]aias *in left margin in red ink.*   11 ȝoure, *sic.*   12 h *with
cross-bar in left margin in red ink.*   13 apostolus *in left margin in red ink.
Left part of a cut off at edge of MS.*   18 *Between* inwiþ *and* on *space
for 6–7 letters.*   20 Lechoures: *blot on* h.   26 styken, *sic for* stynken.
34 ridand: dand *crammed together at end of line.*

Ouer alle oþer þan han þise þe stynkeandest pyne in helle þat so *husband &*
baþen hem in Leccherie. for þe deuel schal pyne hem wiþ þat   *wyf metaphor*
218) stynk. Summe Man oiþer womman wene þat hij schulle in þe
first 3ere. whan þat hij bigynnen to serue god ben hardest
ytempted.· nay it nys nou3th so. noiþer in þe first ne in þe   5
secounde. ⁊ also whan hij han serued god fele 3eres. ⁊ her temptacions ben awaye. hij ben adradde þat god haþ for3eten hem.
412b ⁊ ne loueþ hem nou3th. ⁊ haþ forsa|ken hem. Nay in þe first 3ere
ne in þat oþer nys it bot bal play. ac nymeþ 3eme hou it fareþ
by a forbisen whan a Man weddeþ his wyf ⁊ holdeþ hir al softe- 10
lich þat þei3 sche trespas he ne takeþ no 3eme þere of Ac fondeþ
to drawe her loue to hym so þat sche loue hym inwardlich in
hert. And whan he vnderstondeþ þat sche loueþ hym wel þan
whan sche mysdoþe he schal reprouen hire ⁊ chastise hir louelich. ⁊ sett sum ey3e to hir ⁊ chastise hire so. And sche ne loueþ 15
hym neuer þe lesse þei3 þat he do hir duresse ⁊ bynyme hir her
vnþewes. And þat he doþe hire duresse he doþe forto turnen
her loue fram hymward and turneþ to þe grym toþe. And he
seeþ þan þat sche ne loueþ hym neuer þe lesse ⁊ þat he vnderstondeþ for wel ne for wo þat sche nyl nou3th chaungen her 20
loue ac euere doþe better and better. þan wott he wel þat sche
loueþ hym faiþlich. And þan le leteþ of al his reddure ⁊ turneþ
al þe wo to wel ⁊ to wynne al her lyf tyme. So doþe Ihesus crist
oure spouse draweþ vs first wiþ loue tyl þat he se þat we loue
hym wel. ⁊ forbereþ vs þat we ne be nou3th yfonded to oft. Ac 25
afterward he wiþdraweþ hym ⁊ leteþ vs ben yfonded forto loke
3if oure loue be stedfast And whan he wott ⁊ seeþ þat it is
stedfast. þan he 3iueþ vs pes al oure lyf As whan he lesse his
folk from Pharaon out of Egipt londe he dude for hem al þat
220) hij wolden ⁊ ledde þem þorou3 þe rede cee drie fote by xij 30
waies. ⁊ bitwixen vche waye stode þe cee vp as a wal for vche
kynde of þe xij kyndes hadde a waie by hym one. And Pharaon
com after and his folk ⁊ adreynt vchone and her vitaile ⁊ her
armure com al vp to his folk And whan hij comen in to wildernesse he 3af hem hunger ⁊ þrust ⁊ many werres and on ende he 35
3af hem eise ⁊ rest. ⁊ wele ⁊ wynne to hem þat were pacient. ⁊ al
her hert wille til þat hij kepten his comaundementz And hij þat

---

16 ⁊ *by correction.*   21 bett *in* better¹ *crammed together at end of*
line.   22 le, *sic for* he.   *line.* 28 oure *and* lyf *connected at end of line.*
yf *partially effaced.*

gruccheden ⁊ wrabbeden aȝein he slouȝ hem, þus oure lorde
draweþ þe feble ⁊ þe meseyse ⁊ þe ȝonge out of þis werlde softlich ⁊ al wiþ lyst, ⁊ sone so he seeþ hem harded he leteþ werre
awaken ⁊ techeþ hem to fiȝtten ⁊ wo þolyen ⁊ after longe swynk
he ȝiueþ hem swete reste. ȝe here I sigge in þis werlde er hij 5
comen to heuene. And þan hem þencheþ so goode þe rest after
þe swynk. þe eise after þe myseise hem þencheþ þan so good ⁊
so swete.

NOu ben in þe sautere after þe temptaciouns þe vtter ⁊ þe
inner þat temeþ alle þe oþer foure dalen ⁊ þus to deleþ hem. 10
fondynges liȝth ⁊ derne. fondynge liȝth ⁊ openlich. ⁊ al is vnder-
p. 413a stonden | here inne.

NOn timebis a timore nocturno a sagitta volante in die a
negocio perambulante in tenebris ab incursu. ⁊ demonio
meridiano. ⟨ Of fondynges liȝth ⁊ derne seiþ Iob þis word. 15

LApides excauent aque ⁊ allimone paulata terra consumitur.
⟨ Liȝth dropen þirlen þe flynt þat ofte fallen þere on. ⁊ so
liȝth derne fondynges offallen a trewe hert oft Liȝth fondynges ⁊
open he seiþ also. Lucebit enim post semita. nys noȝt so mychel
doute of. 20

VEnit malum super te ⁊ nescis ortum eius. ⟨ Ysaye seiþ. yuel
come vpe þe ⁊ þou wost nouȝth his wexinge. stronge temptaciouns ⁊ derne is ek þat Iob meneþ hym of.

INsidiati sunt ⁊ preualerunt ⁊ non erat qui ferret auxilium.
⟨ þat is myne fon wayten me wiþ trecherie ⁊ gyle ⁊ tresoun ⁊ 25
(M. 222) strengþen in vpe me as þe wal were to broken ⁊ þe ȝate open.
þe first ⁊ þe þridde fondynge of þise foure ben almost vnder þe
inner. And þe secounde ⁊ þe fierþe ben vnder þe vtter ⁊ beþ
almost bodilich ⁊ eþe forto felen. þe oþer two ben gostlich ⁊ þe
more forto dreden. forþi many þat hij ne wenen nouȝth beren 30
in her hert þe lyouns whelpes ⁊ þe nedders kyndels þat forfreten
þe soule as Salamon seiþ

TRaxerunt me ⁊ ego non dolui. wlnerauerunt me ⁊ ego non
sentiui. ⟨ Hij drowen me ⁊ i ne made no sorowȝe hij
woundeden me ⁊ i ne feled it nouȝth Osee seiþ. 35

---

13 dauid. *in left margin in red ink.*   16 Iob. *in left margin in red ink.*
allimone, *sic for* alluuione.   paulata, *sic for* paulatim.   19 Iob. *in left*
margin in red ink.   21 ysayas. *in left margin in red ink.*   VEnit, *sic for*
VEniet.   nescis, *sic for* nescies.   23 Iob. *in left margin in red ink.*
27 fondynge *written above line and marked for insertion.*   29 þe *written*
above line.   33 Salamon. *in left margin in red ink.*

ALieni commederunt robur eius ⁊ ipse nesciuit. ⟨ þat is
vnhelþe forfreete þe strengþe of his soule and he nyst it
nouȝth. And ȝut is most drede of whan þe fende of helle eggeþ
a Man to þing þat is swiþe goode wiþ alle ⁊ his soule help ⁊ þeiȝ
it turneþ dedlich. ⁊ so he doþe als oft as he ne may opon Man 5
wiþ yuel kyþe þis strengþe. Nay he seiþ I ne may bringe hym
to synne oiþer hir þorouȝ glotonye ne leccherie. Ac Ichille do as
þe wresteler wrenchen hem þiderward as hij mest drawen, ⁊
werpen hem on þat on half. ⁊ brayde hem ferlich adoune ar hij
it arst wenen. And eggeþ hem to so mychel abstinence þat hij 10
ben þe vnstronger in goddes seruise. ⁊ leden so hard lyue ⁊
pynen so þe lykham. þat þe soule asterueþ. He biholdeþ anoþer
þat haþ a rewful hert ⁊ a sorouȝful ⁊ haþ forsaken þe werlde þat
is synne.' ȝe he seiþ ichille maken hem to rewful. ⁊ hij sen pouere
Men hane gret defaut. A seynt Marie seiþ he oiþer sche nyl 15
noman helpen þis man. Men wolden me ⁊ ich badde hem. ⁊
bringeþ hem on to gedren so þat hij leten goddes seruise ⁊
wexen werldelich so mychel þat hij schullen ȝiuen hem to
worldes aghȝt ⁊ þenchen þe lesse on god | ⁊ maken feste god it
wott. Ac swich feste makeþ summe þe deuels hoore ⁊ forschepeþ 20
of her soules þat was goddes spouse þe deuels housbonde oiþer
his wyf of helle. þerfore vche Man susteyne hem seluen as hij
mowen best serue god ⁊ ne caren nouȝth to mychel for non oþer
so þat hij gederen þe more þerfore. As summe willen saye. hadde
I þat oþer hane. þan wolde I serue god wel. ⁊ whan hij comen 25
þerto þan seruen hij hym wers þan hij duden aforne. Ac ȝif þou
see Men oiþer wymmen in defautt. haue wille forto helpen hem.
ȝif þou ne may ⁊ bidde fast for hem þat god sende hem grace to
suffre her penaunce in þolemodenesse to goddes worschip ⁊ to
note of her soules þou dooste þan wel better þan þou madest þe 30
forto gadre ⁊ gyue for þe loue of god ⁊ þenche what Ihesus crist
seide to Martha for sche was an houswyf ⁊ gedred forto ȝiuen.

MArtha martha. Maria optimam partem elegit. ⟨ Marie haþ
chosen þe better part ⁊ it ne schal nouȝth be bynomen hir.
Lokeþ þat none erþelich þinges ne lette ȝou forto seruen god att 35
tyme ⁊ att termes þat þou haste sett as þine hert forȝiueþ þe þat

413b

---

1 Osee, *in left margin in red ink.*   10 to so: *MS.* so to *with transposition*
marks.   11 in *written above line and marked for insertion.* to *crossed out and*
expuncted below.   18 ȝiuen: en *partially effaced.*   19 *On 413b the upper*
parts of some letters in the first line of right column cut off.   26 þe *crossed*
out and expuncted after hym.   32 dominus *in right margin in red ink.*

þou may best hym serue. ⁊ seche after wisdome ⁊ queyntise. for
þat on nys nouȝth wiþ outen þat oþer. Swich gadering makeþ
(M. 224) hem to vnderstonde flaterers ⁊ herieþ hem ⁊ heueþ vp her almes.
⁊ hij leten good þere of ⁊ fallen in to filþe of synne þere þorouȝ.
And summe seien on scorne þat swich Men ⁊ wymmen gadren 5
hoord, ne leueþ nouȝth þat fende. Dauid clepeþ hym. Demonio
meridiano. þat is briȝth schynande deuel. ⁊ poule clepeþ hym
aungel of liȝth. For swich ofte he makeþ hym ⁊ scheweþ hym
to many ⁊ bigileþ hem. Ne siȝth þat ȝe sen in sweuene ne telleþ
it for nouȝth for it nys nouȝth bot his gyle. bot ȝif it be þe better 10
Man oiþer womman þat al her hert han ȝouen to god. ⁊ wirchen
al þat hij done by wisdom and queyntise. Hem ne schal ne
neuer bigile, Bot loke þat non ne trost opon her holynesse. For
he haþ ofte bigiled Men of holy lyf ⁊ brouȝth hem to helle for
hij foloweden her owen wille. and rewled hem nouȝth by wis- 15
dom ⁊ queyntise as hij schulden haue done ⁊ þerfore hij ne
quemeden nouȝth god. forþi. ⁊ hij hadden quemed hym. hij ne
schulden nouȝth so han ben lorne. In vitis patrum it telleþ þat
a Man was in wildernesse ⁊ lyued holy lyf. ⁊ a Man com to hym
⁊ wepe as mysaise vpon hym ⁊ bysouȝth hym herberewe. And 20
þe good Man wende he hadd ben a goode aungel ⁊ herberewed
hym ⁊ by his fader he wyst þat it was þe deuel for he made hym
p. 414a forto slen his. Anoþer Man þat lived holy | lyf he made hym to
ȝiuen alle his fader good for þe loue of god to pouere men. ⁊ atte
last made hym to done a dedlich synne by a womman ⁊ brouȝth 25
hym in to wanhope ⁊ dyed in þat foule synne for he hadd so oft
seide hym soþ toforne honde of many þinges ⁊ al to biswiken
hym on ende

Ereþ now how ȝe schulle witen ȝou wiþ his wrenches. to
summe he comeþ on þis wise ⁊ losangeþ. ⁊ þolemodelich 30
spekeþ to hem ⁊ meueþ her nede of charite. ⁊ is more aboute to
quenchen charite. ⁊ summe womman he is abouten to don hir
fleiȝe help of Man, þat sche falleþ in to dedlich sore. þat is
slauȝtt. oiþer in to summe oþer synne. And so he wil do Man

---

4 of[1] *connected with* þere *at end of line.* o *partially effaced.* 6 fende:
de *partially effaced.* Dauid: uid *partially effaced.* 6-7 Demonio meridiano, *sic for* Demonium meridianum. 7 briȝth: r, ȝ, *and* t *partially effaced.*
9 Ne, *sic for* No. 19 wildernesse: l *by correction.* 21 he: h *by
correction.* 22 deuel: l *by correction.* e *in* he[2] *nearly effaced.*
23 *Piece of MM. cut off at right-hand corner of bottom margin.* 31 meueþ,
sic for meneþ.

fleiȝe þe felauschip of womman to done hym do wers oiþer
bring hym in to dedlich þouȝttes þat hij ne ȝiue no ȝeme þerto.
And summe he doþe so haty synne þat hij han ouer gret þouȝth
of oþer Men þat falleþ in synne Man schulde wepe for hem ⁊
saie as þe holy man seide.   5

(M. 226) ILle hodie.' ego cras. ⸿ It was telde hym of þe fal of his broþer
þat dude a dedlich synne by a womman. Weilaway he seide.
strongelich was he tempted ar he fel. He fel to day Ich may to
morne. þat is to saie als vnstrong am ich as he was ȝif god ne
kepe me þe better   10

NOw of many temptacions haue ich yspoken. nouȝth
forþi. þat Men schulle fallen þere inne. Ac þat alle þat Men
wiþ ytempted ne may ich nouȝth nempny hem. Ac of þise þat
ich haue ynempned fewe þere ben now in þis werlde þat hij ne
ben wiþ þise ytempted. For he haþ so many boistes ful of his   15
letewarye þe liþer leche of helle he þat forsakeþ on he bedeþ
hym forþ anoþer. þe þridde. þe fierþe. ⁊ so alway forþ forto he
come to on þat he vnderfongeþ ⁊ þer wiþ he bigileþ hym.
þencheþ here on þe tale of þe Ampoiles þat seint Austyn telleþ
he mett a deuel and bare a gret book. att his rugge. ⁊ he hadde 20
many Ampoils abouten hym. And seint Austin asked hym what
he was and whider he scholde gon. And he seide he was a deuel
⁊ schulde go to þe Abbey forto ȝiuen þe Monkes of his drynk.
What is þat book þat þou berest he seide. And he seide þe
names of which þat he tempteþ ⁊ falleþ þorouȝ hym. And he   25
asked hym ȝif he were ouȝt in his book. ⁊ he seide ich hope wel
þat þou be. And seint Austin loked ⁊ he fonde hym þere inne
for he hadde forȝeten his complyn on atyme vnseide And
seint Anstin badde hym go þider þat he schulde go ⁊ come
aȝein by hym. ⁊ he dude so. ⁊ seint Austyn ȝede ⁊ seide his   30

p. 414b com|plyn. and þe fende com aȝein to hym. And Austyn asked
hym what he hadde done. And he seide hij weren so stedfast in
goddes seruise þat he ne miȝth nouȝth done to hem. And
Austyn took his book ⁊ fonde þat he was oute. owe seide þe
fende hastow þus bigiled me ⁊ went hym away as an olde   35
schrewe.

---

4 þat *written above line.*   12 ben *omitted after* Men².   17 forþ¹
written above line and marked for insertion.   25 of *written above line and*
marked for insertion.   28 atyme, *sic for* a tyme.   29 Anstin, *sic*
for Austin. s *corrected from* t.

(M. 228) ON oþer half owe to confort vche Man ⁊ wommam whan hij ben ytempted. ȝee witeþ wel whan a toure is ywonnen. Men owen nouȝth þan forto ȝiuen a sauȝt þerto ne to þe cite⸱ nomore þe helle werrour assaileþ wiþ fondynges hem þat he haþ ac doþe hem þat he ne haþ nouȝth. For whi. who þat nys 5 nouȝth yfonded sore. he may be adradde þat he is wonnen.

ÞE þridde confort is þat oure lorde hym self seiþ in þe pater noster ⁊ techeþ vs bidden ⁊ nc nos inducas in temptacionem, þat is lorde ne suffre nouȝth þat þe fende lede vs a long in to temptacioun. Lookeþ nymeþ ȝeme. he nyl nouȝth þat we bidden 10 hym þat we be nouȝth ytempted for þat is oure purgatorie ⁊ oure clensynge fyre ac þat we ne be nouȝth a longe brouȝth þere inne wiþ consent of hert ⁊ wiþ skilles ȝetyinge.—

ÞE fierþe is þe sekernesse of goddes help in þe fiȝttyng aȝein as seint poule seiþ Fidelis est deus qui noluit nos temptari 15 vltra quam possumus et cetera. (God he seiþ is trewe for he nylle neuer þat deuel tempte vs ouerþat he seeþ þat we mowe sufferen ac in þe temptacioun he haþ sett a footemerk as þeiȝ he seide tempte hym so fer ⁊ no ferrer. ⁊ so fer he ȝiueþ vs strengþe to wiþstonde. ⁊ þe fende may no ferrer prike þan þe merk 20 Gregori seiþ.

(M. 230) Diabolus licet afflicciones iustorum semper appetat cum ⁊ a deo potestatem non accipiat ad temptacionis articulum non conualescit. formidari igitur non qui nichil nisi permissus agere valet. (þe fift confort is þat þe fende ne may do noþing 25 to vs bot by goddes leue ⁊ þat was wel yschewed as þe godspel seiþ whan þe deuelen þat oure lorde cast out of a Man. a legion. sex þousande. ⁊ sex hundreþ. ⁊ sexti and sex crieden ⁊ seiden to oure lord.

SI eicis nos hinc mitte nos in porcos. (Siþen þou dryuest vs 30 hennes lorde do vs in to þise swyne ⁊ he graunted hem. Looke hou þat hij ne miȝtten nouȝth wiþ outen his leue gon in p. 415a to þe swyne. ⁊ þe | swyne onon riȝth runnen in to þe cee ⁊

9 a long, *sic for* along (?). *Cf. Corpus:* allunge 62a: 2.   12 a longe, *sic for* alonge (?). a *by correction. Cf. Corpus:* allunge 62a: 4.   14 sekernesse: r *written above line and marked for insertion. in red ink.* noluit, *sic for* non sinit.   15 paulus *in right margin in red ink.* noluit, *sic for* non sinit.   16 possumus etc. *traces of erasure on* ssumus et. ss *touched up in black ink.*   17 þat¹: t *partially erased.* ouerþat, *sic for* ouer þat. uer *partially erased.*   22 Gregorius. *in right margin in red ink.* afflicciones, *sic for* afflicciomem.   26 leue: u *by correction.* yschewed: che *on erasure.*   28 ⁊¹ *and* ⁊² *written above line and marked for insertion.*

adreynt hem seluen. seint Marie so hij stonken on þe swyne þat
hem was leuer to drenchen hem seluen þan to beren hem
abouten. and an vnsely synful man bare hem in his breest ⁊
name neuer ʒeme of hem. Al þat he dude to Iob. euer he name
leue þere of toforne at oure lord þat tale þat is in þe dialoge   5
look þat ʒe cunnen hou þe holy Man seide to þe deuels nedder.
SI licenciam accepisti ego non prohibeo. ⟨ Ʒif þou hast leue
to stynge. stynge on fast and bede forþ his cheke. ⁊ þan
hadde he no myʒth bot one forto enticen hym þerto. Nomore ne
haþ he on vs bot ʒif oure bileue crook and whan god ʒaf hym   10
leue of his dere frende whi is it bot for her mychel goode. þeiʒ
al it greue hem sore.
Þe sext confort is whan þat oure lord þoleþ þat we ben ytempted he playeþ wiþ vs as þe moder doþe wiþ her ʒong derlyng
þat fleiʒeþ fram hym ⁊ leteþ hym sytt al one. And whan þe   15
childe ne seeþ hire nouʒth it clepeþ dame. dame. ⁊ lokeþ ʒerne
abouten ⁊ wepeþ a while. ⁊ þan his moder comeþ to hym wiþ
sprad armes ⁊ wipeþ his eiʒen. and kisseþ hym. ⁊ clyppeþ hym.
Also oure lorde leteþ vs yworþe oiþer while ⁊ wiþ draweþ his
232) grace fram vs ⁊ his confort and we ben þan al one ⁊ felen no   20
suetenysse in noþing þat we wele do ne sauoure of hert. And
þeiʒ in þat ilche poynt ne loueþ he vs neuer þe lesse. Ac he it
doþe for mychel loue þat vnderstonde we wel þat dauid seiþ.—
NOn me derelinquas vsquequaque. ⟨ Lorde seiþ dauid ne
lete me nouʒth a longe. Loo whan he wolde he lete dauid   25
ac nouʒth a long. sex enchesons þere beþ whi god leteþ vs one ⁊
wiþdraweþ his grace fram vs, þat on is þat we ne proude
nouʒth. for ʒif his grace were alwaþ wiþ vs we myʒth liʒthlich
fallen þorouʒ a wellate of oure seluen, Anoþer enchesoun is þat
we may knowe oure owen feblesse ⁊ oure mychel vnstrengþe   30
Gregori seiþ
MAgna perfeccio est sue inperfeccionis cognicio. ⟨ þat is
mychel godenysse is to knowe wel oure waykenesse and
oure owen vnstrengþe

---

16 childe: e *nearly effaced.*   18 clyppeþ: y *by correction.*   21 suetenysse: eᴵ *resembles* o.   *Small hole in MS. after* hert.   24 dauid. *in
left margin in red ink.*   me *and* derelinquas *connected in MS.*   25–6 a
longe *and* a long: *see 104: 9, 12.*   26 sex: se *partially erased.*   þere:
traces of erasure on abbreviation mark.   27 is: s *by correction.*   28 alwaþ, *sic for* alway.   32 gregorius. *in left margin in red ink.*

ECclesiasticus intemptatus qualis sit. ⦗ þat is. vnfonded nott
neuer where þat he is. ne in what state. for he ne knoweþ
p. 415b nouȝth | hym seluen Austyn seiþ.

MElior est animus cuius est infirmitas nota quam cui
scrutatur celorum fastigia ⁊ terrarum fundamenta. ⦗ þat 5
is better is a Man to seche his owen feblesse. ⁊ his owen vnstrengþe. þan forto meten hou heiȝe is þe heuene. ⁊ hou depe is
þe erþe. for whan two beren a birden to gider þan wot neuere
þat on hou heuy it is. Ac whan þat on it leteþ þan wot he þat it
bereþ how heuy it wexeþ. Also whan god bereþ wiþ vs oure 10
temptacioun þan witen we neuere hou heuy it weiȝeþ ne what
it is. And forþi he leteþ vs one þat we mowe witen what we
beren for þat we schullen þe ȝerner clepen after hym. ⁊ crien
loude opon hym til þat he come to vs. ȝif he is longe helde it
wel vp þerwhiles. For who so is siker of good helpe ⁊ ȝeldeþ 15
þeiȝ vp þe Caste to his wiþerwynes.' swiþe mychel he is to
blamen. It telleþ it was an holy Man ⁊ he seiȝ in þe west so
many ferdes of deuelen aȝeins hem to fiȝtten wiþ hem. whan
he he was in his temptacioun þat he les his strengþe of his
bileue. and his felawe seide vn to hym. Look by esten ⁊ þou 20
schalt seen we hane more on oure half þan hij ben forto helpen
vs

(M. 234) Plures nobis quam cum illis. ⦗ þe þridde þing is þat we ne ben
neuere alto siker. for sikernesse serueþ ȝemeles. ⁊ by þis
strengþe inobedience super epistolam ad Romanos. 25

COntentum nutrit resoluta securitas. ⦗ þe fierþe is þat oure
lorde hideþ hym fram vs þat we seche hym þe ȝernelicher.
⁊ clepe. ⁊ wepe after hym as þe childe doþe after þe dame. ⦗ þe
fyft is þat we aȝeins his aȝeincome vnderfonde hym þe gladlicher ⁊ make þe more ioye of his comynge. ⦗ þe sext is þat whan 30
we hane ycauȝt hym þe ȝernelicher ⁊ þe willicher witen hym. ⁊
saien to hym. tenui te nec dimittam, I schal holde þe my lef ⁊
i ne schal nouȝth lete þe. þise sex enchesons schullen holden vs

---

1 ECclesiasticus: *MS.* ECce.   qualis sit, *sic for* qualia scit.   4 cuius,
sic for cui propria. Augustinus. *in right margin in red ink.*   7 ⁊ *written
above line and marked for insertion.*   16 Caste, *sic for* Castel. wiþerwynes: *irregular stroke connecting* n *and* e.   18 hem[1]: e *on erasure.*
Both hem[1] *and* hem[2] *probably for* him.   19 he he: *dittography.* w
and 2 *more letters imperfectly erased after first* he.   les: s *blotted.*
29 is *written above line and marked for insertion.*   vnderfonde, *sic for*
vnderfonge.   33 enchesons: *second* s *blotted.*

vp aʒeins alle fondynges wiþ confortes toforne. ⸿ þe seuent
confort is. hou þise holy men of holy lyf weren ytempted now
to seint peter þe heiʒest

ECce sathan expetiuit vos ut cribraret sicut triticum. ⸿ Loo
seide oure lorde to seint Peter. Sathan is ʒerne aboute to 5
tille þe out of myne ychosen. Ac ich haue bisouʒth for þe þat þi
bileue ne crook nouʒth along. þat is þat þou ne faile nouʒth in
bileue. ⸿ Poule hadde flessche prickyng of leccherie ⁊ of pride
in his soule. ⁊ he bede god deliuere hym þere of. |

p. 416a DAtus est michi stimulus carnis mee. ⸿ And he bad oure 10
lorde deliuer hym and he seide þat he nolde ⁊ seide.
Sufficit tibi gracia mea nam virtus in infirmitate perficitur. ⸿ þat
is my grace schal kepe þe þat þou be nouʒth strong in vnstrengþe. Seint sare was tempted þrittene ʒere of hire flesche Ac for þe
gret anguish aros þe mykel mede nolde sche neuere bidden 15
ones deliuer hir þere of Ac bad oure lorde ʒiue hire strengþe to
wiþstonde þat gret anguissch.

M. 236) DA michi domine virtutem resistendi. ⸿ And atte þrittene
ʒeres ende com þe fende vnto hir in a bloo Mannes liknes
⁊ seide to hir. Sare þou haste ouercomen me. And sche answered 20
hastilich aʒein ⁊ seide þou lixt foule þef Ac haþ Ihesus my
lorde. Looke now þere he wolde haue putt hire in to pride
forto haue hadde a litel wel late of her seluen. ⁊ þat was al þat
Ihesus crist tauʒt his deciple whan he dude wonders for hem.
þat hij ne schulden haue no gladnesse in hert þer of. bot hij 25
schulden ben gladd þat hij weren chosen to þe blis of heuene.
þis he tauʒtte and preched hem often. Ac do we as seint Sare
dude in al þing þat we do oiþer þat he doþe for vs ʒiue we þe
strengþe ⁊ þe Maistrie to swete ihesu of heuene. Antoyne and
alle þise oþer hou weren hij ytempted. Ac for þe gret mede 30
þat aros in þe fondynge aʒein. hij it suffreden louelich. ⁊ þer-
þorouʒ weren hij proued trewe champiouns. ⁊ so of serueden
coroune op Coroune as þe Goldsmyth purgeþ þe gold in þe fyre
also doþe god hise ychose in þe fire of fondynges

---

4 domin[us] *in right margin in red ink. Left part of letter* (s) *at edge of
MS.*   6 bisouʒth: *red blot below* u.   10 DAtus: *upper part of* DA
cut off.   11 [Domi]nus, *in left margin in red ink. Left minim of* n
cut off at edge of MS.   13 strong: tr *partly covered by thick downstroke of*
þ *in* þat *12.*   24 tauʒt: uʒt *crammed together at end of line. First minim
of* u *almost completely effaced.*   33 coroune op Coroune: *cf.* Corpus:
kempene crune *64a: 2.*

ÞE nynþe confort is. ȝif þe fende greueþ þe þou greuest hym
wel more ⁊ sorer for þre resonns þat as Origine telleþ he
leseþ his powere. For to vche synne he doþe al his power forto
tempten. þat oþer he echeþ his pyne. þe þridde he forfreteþ
his hert of sore greme þat he is ouercomen. Whan he is ouer-   5
comen he leseþ his strengþe ⁊ is sore aschamed and agremed
þat he has so liȝthlich lorne al his trauaile and is ouercomen ⁊
braydeþ þe corowne of blis nouȝth on ne two. Ac doþe as oft
as þou ouercomest hym als fele corounes þou haste. þat is als
fele worschipes in þe blisse of heuene seint Bernard seiþ.   10

QVociens vincis tociens coronaberis ⟨ þe tale In vitis
patrum. it witnesseþ þat an holy Man tauȝt his deciple ⁊
as he tauȝtt hym he fel on slepe ⁊ his deciple stode bifore hym
and sumtyme he þouȝth to hane waked hym. and sumtyme he
þouȝth to haue gon to his bedd. ⁊ atte last he sette hym adoune. 15
⁊ his Maister a wooke att mydniȝth ⁊ bad his grome go slepe. | ⁊
he dude so. and his Maister fel on slepe also. And alsone hym
þouȝth þat he was brouȝth in to a faire grene place. ⁊ þere he
seiȝ an aungel brynge achayer. and seuene faire Corounes þere
opon. ⁊ þan seide þe aungel vn to hym. þise haþ þi deciple   20
erned while þat þou slepe. And he awoke ⁊ cleped his grome
and asked hym what he dude whiles þat he slepe and whi þat he
satt whan þat aros. ⁊ stode whan he leide hym. And his grome
seide I þouȝt to hane waked þe. and for þou slepe so swete I ne
miȝth nouȝth for rewþe. ⁊ þan I þouȝth to haue gon to my   25
bedde. ⁊ I nolde nouȝth bot sett me doune by þe. þan asked
his maister hym hou ofte he ouercom his þouȝth. ⁊ he seide
seuen siþes. And þan wist his maister wel þat þo were þe seuen
Corounes þat his deciple hadde erned while þat he slepe for
þat he ouercom hym seluen and wiþstode þe fende. Al þus in   30
þe temptacioun ariseþ oure mede Poule seiþ.

NEmo coronabitur nisi legitime certauerit. Ne schal none
ben ycorouned bot ȝif he stronglich ⁊ trewlich fiȝth aȝein.

p. 416b (left margin, line 16)

(M. 238) (left margin, line 20)

---

2 resonns, *sic for* resouns.   3 al *written above line and marked for
insertion.*   4 *From* þridde *to the bottom of the column a number of letters are partially effaced at the beginning of each line, particularly* his trauaile
7, corowne 8, as þou 9, blisse 10, holy Man tauȝt 12, he fel 13, *first and
second* and sumtyme 14, ⁊ atte last 15, *and* a wooke att 16.   11 [Ber-
n]ardus *in left margin in red ink.*   16 a wooke, *sic for* awooke.
19 achayer, *sic for* a chayer.   23 he *omitted before* aros.   32 paulus
in right margin in red ink.   33 ycorouned: *first* o *written above line and
marked for insertion.*

his flessche. þe fende. and þe werlde. who þat fiȝtteþ treulich
aȝein þise þre ⁊ namelich aȝein þe flessch ⁊ wiþsigge þe graunt
þere of. ne prikk it neuer so hard. þan ben hij ihesus cristes
frendes and done as he dude hongen on þe roode.

CVm gustasset acetum noluit bibere. He smelled þe bitter 5
drynk. ⁊ nolde it nouȝth drynken þeiȝ h a þrist were. þeiȝ
a Man oiþer a womman þrest in þe lust and þe fende bedeþ
hym his halyway. þenche þat þere is galle vnder. and better it
is to ben ofþrest þat to ben yattred. Lete lust ouer go ⁊ eft it
wil þe like. While ȝechinge lasteþ it is gode to rudden. ac after 10
it smerteþ. weleway þat while. Many ben so sore ofrest and
drinkeþ hastilich ⁊ ne felen it nouȝth. so hij glutten it in ȝerne-
lich. And after felen þe smert ⁊ gynnen þan to sorowe ⁊ maken
reulich chere. ac þan is to late. Ac nouȝth for þan better is late
þan neuere. After yuel þan is goode penaunce spewe out þat 15
venym to þe preest ar it wilde. for ȝif it wildeþ it wil brede þe deþ.

AȜein alle temptaciouns ⁊ namelich aȝein fleschlich beþ vnder
goddes grace holy meditaciouns. goode felawschippes. ⁊
biddinge ⁊ hardy bileue. fastyng. wakynge. Alle þise ben armes
in þis fiȝth. ⁊ bodilich swynches. ⁊ also speke to sum oþer 20
þerwhiles þat þe temptacioun lasteþ. Lowenesse ⁊ alle gode
þewes ben armes in þis fiȝth. Ac who þat werpeþ away his
wepen þat he schulde fiȝth wiþ. | hy lyst ben ywounded. Holy
meditaciouns þat is þenche in goddes passioun ⁊ in oþer goode
þouȝttes 25

MOrs tua mors domini nota culpe gaudia celi·' iudicij terror
figantum mente fideli ⟨ þenche on þine synnes. on þe
ioyes of heuene. on þe pynes of helle. on þi deþ. on goddes deþ
on þe rode. ⁊ on þe pyne þat he suffred for þe on domesday.
opon þis fals werlde. What it is. ⁊ what is his mede. ⁊ what þou 30
owest god for his gode dede. What he haþ done for þe. how
vnkynde þou haste ben aȝeins hym. Vche one of þise wolde
haue a longe poyntynge. Ac whan we þenchen on þe ioyes of
heuen god wold schewe hem to vs here in sum wise to men. ⁊
of þe pynes of helle ⁊ schewed hem to vs here as schadewe. for 35
alle werldlich ioyes þat euer wore. ⁊ now ben. ⁊ euer schulle ben

---

6 h, *sic for* he.   7 and: d *partially erased. Small hole on loop of* d
mentioned at 105: 21.   11 ofrest, *sic for* ofþrest.   23 hy, *sic for* hym.
26 terror: *last* r *on erasure.*   27 figantum, *sic for* figantur.   34 wold:
d *written above line and marked for insertion.*

M. 240) *(left margin, line 11)*
p. 417a *(left margin, line 23)*
(M. 242) *(left margin, line 31)*

vntil domesday. nys bot a schadewe to þe lest ioye of heuene.
Ne alle þe werldelich pynes ne ben bot a schadewe to þe lest
pyne of helle. We ben here in þe see of þis werlde ⁊ stonden on
þe brynk of þis see. Be we nouȝth eschu of þe schadewe. þe hors
þat stondeþ opon þe brynk ⁊ is eschu for þe schadewe may 5
liȝthlich falle in to þe pytt. And so mowen we ȝif we ben
adradde of þe wo of þis werlde þat is bot a schadewe liȝthlich
fallen in to þat wo þat al þe wo of þis werld nys bot a schadewe
to. as Iob seiþ. he þat douteþ þe hore frost þe snowe schal falle
opon hym þat he seiþ here by hem þat ben adradde of þe wo of 10
þis werlde. þe wo of helle schal falle opon hem. A gret fole is he
þat fleiȝeþ þe peyntyng on a wal for þe griselichhede þereof Al
þe wel of þis werlde nys bot a schadewe to þe lest blis of heuene.
⁊ also al þe wo to þe lest pyne of helle. Nouȝth onely holy
meditaciouns of oure lorde ⁊ of oure lefdy his moder Mary ⁊ of 15
hise holy halewen ac done holy þouȝttes sum while helpen in
foure manere aȝein fleschlich temptaciouns. dredeful, wonderful. gladful ⁊ sorouȝful. þise a Man schal arere oiþer whhile in
his hert. or nede come þenche what wolde done ȝif þat we
seiȝen openlich deþ stonde toforn vs. ⁊ þe deuel of helle as he 20
doþe dernelich in þe fondynge. ⁊ ȝif oure hous brent ouer vs.
þise ben dredeful þouȝttes. Wonderful as þeiȝ þou seiȝ Ihesu
stonde bifore þe ⁊ asked þe what þe were leuest after þi saluacioun. ⁊ badde þe chesen wiþ þi þat þou wiþstonde þi temptacioun. And ȝif þou seiȝ witterlich alle þat in heuene weren ⁊ in 25
helle. Gladful as ȝif þe com bode þat þe best frende þat þou
haste were ychosen pope þorouȝ Steuene of heuene. | Sorouȝful
as ȝif þou herdest saye þat. þat man þat þou louedest most
were feerlich ded. adreint oiþer murþered. oiþer anhonged.
oiþer brent. Swich þouȝttes oiþer while wreken out fleschlich 30
temptaciouns. Holy bedes of goode Men oiþer of wymmen þe
fende douteþ swiþe mychel hem. for hij bynden hym ⁊ brennen
hym In vitas patrum it telleþ þat an holy Man Puplinus lay in
his bedes. ⁊ þe fende com þere forþ ouer hym fleiȝeande by
Iulius heste Cesar. And þis Mannes bedes as hij steiȝen 35

(M. 244)

p. 417b

---

14 to *written above line and marked for insertion.*   15 first ⁊ *written
above line and marked for insertion.*   20 of helle as: *probably on erasure.*
21 ofte *expuncted after* doþe.   þe *written above line.*   30 Swich:
S *blotted.*   33 Puplinus, *sic for* Puplius.   35 þis: *faint traces of
erased* e *after* s.

vptoward god bounden hym so þat ten dayes hij helden hym
þere stille þat he ne miȝth nouȝth away. Seint Margarete bonde
Ruffyn as men reden in her lyf þat was Barabub broþer. to
Seint Bertlemew as he lay in his bedes þe deuel seide þine bedes
brennen me ʒ bynden me   5

INcendunt me oraciones tue ⟨ And who þat may wiþ bedes
haue teres. he may haue of god al þat he wil. ȝif he bidde
riȝthfullich. And it owe to ben ygraunted and þerfore secheþ
afterwisdom þat ȝe ne bidde hym noþing bot ȝif it be wiselich
ybeden. for ȝif he graunted it. he were a more fole þan anoþer   10
Man. ȝe ne seþ no wise Man þat wil graunt any þing þat Me
asken hym bot ȝif he se þat it may wel be done. And elles he
were a fole ȝif he graunted it. Ȝe· a more fole þan he þat bereþ
a Babyl. þerfore in ȝoure biddynge biddeþ so þat ȝe ne be
nouȝth aboute to make god a fole For ȝif ȝe do it wil fallen opon 15
ȝoure seluen. For he ne wil graunt noþing bot his riȝthwisenesse ʒ his mercy mowen acorden þere inne. Ac euere he
heldeþ more here to þe mercy þan to þe riȝthwisenesse. ʒ
þerfore vche Man bidde wiselich i rede ʒ soule hele for holy
wrytt seiþ   20

ORacio lenit lacrima cogit. ⟨ þe good bede softeþ god ʒ
makeþ hym mylde to vs. as man þat haþ a sore ʒ is anoynt.
it softeþ hym. ac oure teres pricken hym. and leten hym neuer
haue rest til þat he haue ȝiuen vs al þat we asken ȝif it be skylful.
COnturbasti capita draconis in aquis Whan þe deuel assaileþ   25
ȝou. casteþ out scoldyng water opon hym as men done att
Castels opon her enemyes. For þere þat water comeþ. þe fende
fleiȝeþ sikerlich. lest his heued schulde ben yscolded Castel is
vche mannes body. And ȝif ȝoure castel be wel kirnelde. ʒ wel
warnyst wiþinne þat is wiþ good werkes. ʒ depe diched al aboute   30
þe walle. þat is þolemodenesse. þan is ȝoure Castel careles. þe
fende may longe assaile ȝou ʒ lese alle his assautes as men seþ
often. a litel rayn felleþ a gret wynde. so | done bedes and teres
wiþ al fellen þe deuels blastes and þan comeþ þe sunne and
schineþ after and makeþ al fair ʒ drye. And so doþe þe soþ   35
sunne Ihesus crist ȝiueþ liȝth ʒ suetnesse to þe soule

M. 246)

p. 418a

---

1 vptoward, *sic for* vp toward. to *written above line and marked for insertion.*
3 to *written above line and marked for insertion.*   8 ygraunted: e *touched*
up.   9 afterwisdom, *sic for* after wisdom.   25 COnturbasti, *sic for*
COntribulasti.   26 opon: *MS.* opon *with macron above second* o.   32 longe:
ge *partially effaced.* seþ, *sic for* seiþ.   33 litel: t *corrected from* l (?).

Oracio humilitatis penetrat nubes et cetera. ⸿ þe bone of þe
symple Man ⁊ womman þat is lowe of hert perceþ heuen.

Magna virtus pure oracionis que ad deum intrat ⁊ mandata
peragit vbi caro pernenire nequit. ⸿ Michel is þe miȝth of
þe schire bone þat fleiȝeþ vp tofore god and doþe þat erande so   5
wel þere þat þe flesche may nouȝth comen. þat almiȝtty god
haþ writen al þat he seiþ in þe booke of lyf as seint Bernarde
witnesseþ and sendeþ adoun his aungel to done al þat he wil.

(M. 248)   Resistite diabolo ⁊ fugiet a vobis. ⸿ Stondeþ aȝein þe deue
and he fleiȝeþ fram ȝou. stondeþ hou. Resistite in fide.   10
⸿ Stondeþ aȝein strongelich in þe bileue. beþ hardy of goddes
help ⁊ þencheþ hou leþi he is þat no strengþe ne haþ bot of hym
seluen. He ne may do no more bot putte forþ his aped ware ⁊
þreten vs to biggen þerof. Leiȝeþ hym þan to scorne stondeþ
aȝein stiflich in þe bileue and he holdeþ hym as schent   15

Sancti per fidem vicerunt regna. ⸿ þise holy halewen ouercomen þorouȝ bileue þat hij hadden Alle his wiles of synne.
for he ne comeþ nouȝth bot þorouȝ synne

We holdeþ hym mychel of pride whan he biholdeþ to
grete god hou litel he made hym in a pouere Maidens   20
wombe. ⁊ nouȝth for his goode ac for oure good dede ⁊ seide and
þoled pyne ⁊ wo for vs. þe chynche ne kept þat non ne hadde of
his good bot al hym seluen wolde it haue. so ne dude oure lorde
nouȝth. For ȝutt whan he hadd parted wiþ vs here of his good
After he liȝth adoune in to helle to þe free prisoun and delt hem   25
þere of his good. We fynde in holy Mennes lyues þat an ancre
had almest lorne þe eiȝe of hir bileue for a quayer þat on of hire
susters wolde haue borowed at hir and sche nolde nouȝth lene
it hir, And þerfore beþ war ȝe þat wil ben gostlich Men ⁊
wymmen ȝe þat desiren forto ben goddes childer beþ war þat ne   30
holde no gostlich þing fro noman þat may do anoþer Man good
als wel as ȝou þat ȝe ne be redy at helpe hym wiþ al at his nede

---

1 [S]alamon *in left margin in red ink.* mon *below* ala. *Left minim of* m *cut
off at edge of MS. Traces of* S *at edge of MS. First* a *on erasure. Traces
of erasure of* O *in* Oracio.   humilitatis, *sic for* humiliantis.   3 [A]ugustinus
in left margin in red ink.   4 pernenire, *sic for* peruenire.   7 [I]acobus
in left margin in red ink.   9 *Erasure in left margin below* acobus.
deue, *sic for* deuel.   11 [P]etrus *in left margin in red ink.*   14 þreten:
þret *on erasure.*   16 [P]aulus *in left margin in red ink. Traces of letter*
(P) *at edge of MS. Erasure above* P.   al *crossed out and expuncted after*
halewen.   18 þorouȝ: o¹ *partially effaced.*   19 hym: hy *partially
effaced.*   to *partially effaced.*   30 ȝe *omitted before* ne.

wytt oiþer any oþer þing for Salamon seiþ þou ne schalt nouȝth
sellen þi wytt for god it ȝiueþ þe. ⁊ leneþ forto parten wiþ oþer.

p. 418b ȝif þou can more þan anoþer | ne ȝutt of bodilich þing þat þou
haste more þan þe nede bihoueþ. þou art adetted þerto. For
god haþ made þe his reue and his spenser for þou scholdest 5
dispenden it to his worschipp and to note of þi soule. for þou
ne haste nouȝth here a ferþing worþ of good þattow ne schalt
ȝelde rekenyng þere of straitlicher þan any reue schal hou it is
dispended And of þine fyue wyttes hou þou haste dispended
hem in ydelnesse oiþer in goddes worschipp and to þine owen 10
note. do þan as þe reue doþe. Ȝelde owen of owen i rede as god
biddeþ in þe gospel make ȝou frendes wiþ mammona. þat is
riches ȝiue it as it comeþ ⁊ holdeþ nomore þan nedeþ.

f. 250) WHo may þan oiþer dar holde wraþþe in his hert. þat
biholdeþ hou þe gret god com adoun in to erþe to make 15
þrefold sauȝtnesse. bitwene god ⁊ man. bitwene Man ⁊ aungel.
and bituene Man ⁊ man. And after his arisyng fram deþ to lyue
whan he com to his deciples þis was his gretynge Pax vobis.
þat is pes ⁊ sauȝtnisse bitwene ȝou. And nymeþ ȝeme whan þat
lef frendes departen vche fram oþer. þat last word þat hij 20
seyen. þat Men best athold. And oure lorde left his leue frende
here in erþe in vncouþe þede. and þe last word þat he seide vn
to hem whan he went fram hem he seide þis worde vn to hem.
Pacem relinquo vobis. pacem meam do vobis. ⸿ þat is. sauȝtnisse i do amonges ȝou. and my pes i leue wiþ ȝou. 25
IN hoc cognoscetis si discipuli mei sitis si dileccionem
adinuicem habueritis. ⸿ By þat ȝe schulle knowe ȝif ȝe ben my
deciples. ȝif þat ȝe loue to gider. þis was his druery ⁊ his merk
þat he sett opon hem. for Ihesus crist is al pes. ⁊ liȝth. ⁊ loue
þere is his wonyng stede. 30
IN pace factus est locus eius. ibi confregit potencias arcum
gladium scutum ⁊ bellum. ⸿ Pes ⁊ sauȝtnes is godes stede. and
where so þis pes is. it bryngeþ to nouȝth alle þe deuels wiles ⁊
his wrenches. and al his strengþe·′ it brekeþ his bowe þat ben
his derne fondynges. ⁊ his swerde. þat ben temptacions keruynge 35
⁊ neiȝe of kynne. Ne wot ȝe nouȝ wel þere men fiȝtteþ in

---

11 owen of owen, *sic.*   26 dominus·′ *in right margin in red ink.*
28 druery: e *above line and marked for insertion.*   32 godes: d *above
line and marked for insertion.* o *and* e *crammed together. Lower parts of* e
irregular. Traces of erasure on es.   35 his¹ *above line and marked for
insertion.*

stronge ferdes als longe as hij holden hem to giders hij ne
(M. 252) mowen nouȝth ben ouercomen. Also it fareþ gostlich for al þe
deuels entent ꝯ his bisinesse is abouten forto departen mennes
hertes ꝯ wymmens ꝯ cast wraþþe þere sauȝtnesse schulde be
amonges goddes childer. For he ne haþ none envie bot to hem. 5
p. 419a ꝯ sone after his wraþþe amonges hem. he doþe | hym bitwene
onon riȝth and sleleþ on vche half adoune riȝth. Forþi att
doumbe beste lerneþ wisdom for hij han þis worschipp whan
hij schullen ben assailed of lyoun oiþer of bere. hij gaderen hem
to gyder ꝯ maken schelde of hem seluen. ꝯ þerwhiles hij ben alle 10
syker. And ȝif any be so vnsely þat he wende out he is yschent
onon riȝth. also ȝif men gon in a slider waye ꝯ vche holde oþers
honde hij mowen gon þe sikerlicher.

CVm nos vobis per oracionem opem coniungimus per lubri-
cum quas adinuicem manus tenemus vt tanta quisque 15
amplius roboretur quanto alteri vnitur. (Also in stronge
wyndes ꝯ swift wateres þat Men Moten euer waden. ȝif many
holden to geders her honden and on falle he is sone holpen vp.
ꝯ ȝif he be one he geþ sone away.

VE soly quia cum ceciderit non habet subleuantem. (Wo is 20
hym he seiþ þat falleþ ꝯ is al one for he ne haþ who hym
arereþ. Ac he nys noȝth one þat haþ god to fere. Aforbisen
(M. 254) takeþ. Grut cleueþ to geder. take dust ꝯ rowe it. it altobloweþ.
An hondeful of ȝerdes while hij ben to giders hij nyllen nouȝth
breken. A tree þat wil falle men vndersetten it wiþ anoþer. ꝯ 25
ȝif Men twynnen hem hij fallen. Ac many Men and wymmen
þat schulden ben in loue to geders in compaignye hij ben sampsones foxes þat weren tyed to geders by þe tailes ꝯ in vche
tayl a blasme brennande whan þe Philistiens ꝯ he weren wroþe.
He tooke alle þe foxes þat he miȝt and knytt hem to geder by þe 30
tailes ꝯ bonde a blasme of fyre in vche tayl ꝯ drof hem þorouȝ

---

1 ong in stronge *crammed together at end of line.* 6 doþe: do *partially effaced.* Catchwords hym bitwene *in black ink at the bottom
of right margin. Catchwords enclosed in a rectangle with two heads as ornaments pointing left and right.* 7 sleleþ, *sic for* sleþ. *First* l *written above
line and marked for insertion.* adoune: MS. adoune *with macron above* u.
14 Gregorius. *in left margin in red ink.* vobis, *sic for* nobis. oracionem,
sic for oracionis. 15 quas, *sic for* incedentes quasi. tenemus, *sic for*
teneamus. tanta, *sic for* tanto. 16 vnitur, *sic for* innititur.
17 euer waden, *sic for* ouerwaden. 20 Salamon *in left margin in red
ink.* 22 Aforbisen, *sic for* A forbisen. 31 þorouȝ: *first* o *partially
effaced.*

her feldes and so brent vp alle her cornes. ⁊ her vynes. nymeþ
goode ȝeme what þis be to siggen. Men turnen oft þe nebbe to
þing þat Men louen. ⁊ awayward fro þing þat Men haten. Tayl
bitokneþ ende. who so wil þan be tyed to gider as his foxes
were for non wolde þiderward þat oþer wolde bot al froward, ⁊ 5
ysett þan fire in þe ende þat is wraþþe. þat is þe fyre of helle.
Al þis is ywriten here for þat vchon schulde loue to geder as
goddes deciples duden. ⁊ namelich þere it owe to ben. þat is in
wedlok. ⁊ in ordre ⁊ in religioun. For þere is þe deuel most
aboute to sundren it. ⁊ þere schulde Man ⁊ womman fastest 10
cleuen to gedres in god and biseke hym þat he helde hem to
gedre ⁊ þan hij mowen ben syker þat he schal helpen hem ȝif
hij wil bidden hym of helpe þere of ⁊ elles nouȝth. ⁊ beþ nouȝth
as Sampsones foxes. non ne wolde as oþer wolde. ⁊ ȝif ȝe holde
ȝou to gedres as holy wrytt seiþ.   15

419b   M Vltitudinis credencium erat cor vnum ⁊ anima vna. | ℂ þat
          is mychel stedfast bileue schal be in on hert ⁊ in o soule.
For þerwhiles þat Men holden to giders ne may þe fende
256) noþing done ⁊ þat he wott ful wel. And þerfore whan any
frende schal sende vn to oþer. Loke þat þe sondes Man be wel 20
syker and recorde it often er he go. for a litel clout may make
a foule spott. And ȝif any frende blame oþer for her mys
berynge. oiþer for lackes þat hij han warneþ hem for hij ne seen
it noȝth hem seluen. þonkeþ hem ȝerne wiþ þis psalme.

      C Orripiet me iustus in misericordia ⁊ increpabit me oleum 25
        autem peccatoris non inpugnet caput meum. ℂ He þat
blameþ me forto amende me hym ich owe to louen ⁊ cunne hym
þonke more þan þe synner þat seiþ me softe wordes after my wille.

      M Eliora sunt wlnera corripientis quam oscula blandientis.
        ℂ Bettere ben þe blameande wordes þat ben seide forto 30
amenden me.ʼ þan cusse þat is fykel. þat is to saie þan he þat
foloweþ al my wille. And þerfore seiþ Salamon. chastise þe
wise Man ⁊ he wil loue þe afterward þe bettere ne be non so
bolde ne so fole hardy forto resceyue goddes flesche ⁊ his blode
in wraþþe ne ȝutt in non oþer synne. ne loke toward hym þat 35
com adoun to make þre fold sauȝtnesse.

1 cornes: rn *partially effaced.*   2 þis: s *blotted.*   5 þat oþer: t
partly covered by stain. o *partially effaced.*   17 hert: *upper part of* h *cut
off by upper edge.*   21 er: *irregular curl above* e.   24 dauid *in right
margin in red ink.*   26 dau[id] *in red ink almost completely erased in right
margin.*   inpugnet, *sic for* inpinguet.

(M. 258) BEati pacifici quoniam filij dei vocabuntur. ⟨ Blissed ben þe
peisible of hert for hij schullen ben cleped goddes sones.
And who þat may do þis poynt. he þat naþ nouȝth agylt drawe
þe gylt toward hym forto make hym þat haþ agilt come to
amendement ⁊ to loue þere he nolde nouȝth toforne. ⁊ so be 5
aknowen his owen gylt. þat is an heiȝe staire to god ward ⁊
mychel mede liþ þerfore. And for þe gret mede þat falleþ
þerfore. a Man oiþer a womman owe to strengþe hem þe more
þerto forto done it
who so be slow ⁊ slumbry þat seeþ hou besy oure swete lorde 10
was ihesus crist here on erþe for oure note

EXultauit vt gigas ad currendam viam pertransiuit bene
faciendo. ⟨ And after al þe oþer swynk þat he swank in þe
last endynge of his lyf. oþer Men han rest whan hij ben laten
blode and holden hem pryuelich in chambre ⁊ comen bot litel 15
in þe liȝth. And he was laten bloode opon þe Mount of Caluarie.
þider he went on heiȝ whan he wolde be leten blode. ⁊ ȝutt in
þe hattest of þe day. forto schewe to vs hou hot his loue was to
vs ⁊ hou brennande. ⁊ þere he was laten bloode on fyue stedes
brode woundes ⁊ depe wiþ outen alle þe rewful garses. here was 20
a gret swynk. And aȝein sluggers ⁊ slepers is his erlich arisinge
fram ded to lyue. and also whan he went wiþ hise deciples. he
p. 420a ros vp erlich ⁊ went fram hem. | ⁊ made his prayers to his fader
for vs. wel auȝtte we þan forto trauaile for oure seluen, and
arisen erlich forto seruen hym for it is al oure owen profit. 25

AȜein coueitise is his mychel pouerte on erþe here þat wex
opon oure lorde euere lengere more and more. For þo he
was borne so michel place ne hadde he nouȝth þat his litel swete
body miȝth lye opon. so narowe was þe stede þere he was
borne, þat vnneþe Ioseph ⁊ his moder seten þere opon and 30
(M. 260) laiden hym in a cracche wiþ cloutes þe godspel telleþ.

PAnnis eum inuoluit. ⟨ þus he was cloþed þat cloþeþ þe
sunne. þere after pouerlich fedde wiþ þe mylk of a maiden
and ȝutte wite ȝee þat Maidens han lesse Milk þan oþer wymmen han. and after in litel stede leide in a credel. ⁊ ȝutt siþen 35

---

10 *Space for 7–8 letters at beginning of line.*   may *omitted after* so?
15 holden: hol *crammed together at end of line.*   17 heiȝ: *MS.* heiȝe
with second e *expuncted.*   22 lyue: ue *probably by correction. Faint traces*
of letter above e.   32 [Domi]nus *in left margin in red ink.*   33 sunne
on erasure.   of a maiden: of a mai *on erasure.*   34 han lesse: han
les *on erasure.*

he meneþ hym þat he ne hadde nouȝt so mychel where opon he
miȝth leggen his hede.

Filius hominis non habebat vbi caput suum reclinet. ⟨ þus
pouer he was of In. ⁊ of cloþing. And of mete nedeful þat
opon palme sonenday al day he stode ⁊ preched in ierusalem in 5
þe temple. And at euen wha he hadde done he stode and loked
longelich aboute hym And non ne wolde bidde hym to mete ne
to herberewe. and þeiȝ hij hadden wolde hij ne durst nouȝth
for þe clerkes and þe Maisters of þe lawȝe. And þan he ȝede to
Bethanye ⁊ his deciples wiþ hym vn to Marthaes hous and his 10
deciples breken þe eres as hij ȝeden by þe waye for hungere
And ȝutt hij weren chalanged of þe Clerkes þat hij hadden
broken þe lawȝe for þat hij gedreden her mete opon þe sabate
day. And ȝutt alþermeste pouerte com after þan whan he henge
naked opon þe rode and mened hym of þryst ⁊ he þat al made of 15
nouȝth ne hadde bot a fote of erþe to dyen opon as by mannes
wene. ⁊ þat was more to his pyne. whan þe kyng þat al þis werlde
may welde ⁊ heuene ⁊ helle att his wille nadde nomore goode in þis
werlde vn bileued is he þat mychel wisscheþ of werldelich wele.

Aȝein glotonye is his pouer pitaunce on þe roode. Tuo 20
manere Men han nede to eten wel ⁊ drynken. Swynkeande
262) Men. ⁊ bloode leten Men. Look þat day þat he was sore trauailed
⁊ leten blode. Look what men ȝaf hym to drynk oiþer to mete.
Men ȝaf hym bot a litel galle in a spounge. Look þan who wil
grucchen ȝif he þenche wel þere opon of vnsauoure metes ⁊ 25
drynkes.

Aȝein leccherie is his beryng on erþe of a clene mayden. ⁊ al
was clene þat he ledde wiþ hym. And his hard betynge atte
420b pyler þat so he was beten ⁊ forwounded. þat fram his hede | to
his fote nas nouȝth als mychel skyn hole opon hym as Men 30
seien. þat men miȝth sett on a nedel poynt þat it nas to broken.
and summe of þise holy men seien þat he hadde a Legion of
woundes. sex þousand. ⁊ sex hundreþ. ⁊ sexti and sex. Who þan
þat is tempted of leccherie. sett þis wel att his hert and it wil
drawe out þe likynge of leccherie. Aȝein alle dedlich synnes þat 35
werreþ vs seint Peter seiþ.

---

1 hadde: a *written above line and marked for insertion.*   3 [Domi]-
nus *in left margin in red ink. Left part of* nu *cut off at edge of MS.*   habebat, *sic for* habet.   6 wha, *sic for* whan.   10 Bethanye: n *by
correction.*   12 And: An *partially erased.*   16 to *written above line
and marked for insertion.*

CHristo in carne ꝫ vos eadem cogitacione armemini.
((Armeþ ȝou seiþ seint peter wiþ þouȝt of ihesu crist
þat in oure flesch was so ypyned

Recogitate qualem apud semetipsum sustinuit contradic-
cionem vt non fatiget. ((þencheþ whan ȝe gon ꝫ fiȝtten 5
aȝein þe deuel. hou oure lorde wiþseide his wille of his flesche.

Non dum enim vsque ad sanguinem restitistis ((Ȝut ne han
ȝe nouȝth wiþstonden tyl schedyng of ȝoure blode. as he
dude for vs. wil we clepe hym to help he is euer redy biforne vs
atte Messe and scheweþ hym as þeiȝ he seide. Loo me here in 10
present. Telle to me what þou wilt. ichille ȝiue þe strengþe to
wiþstonde. þe fende and alle his wiles. ꝫ in what stede þat we
clepe to hym he is euere redy.

(M. 264) Metati sumus castra iuxta lapidem adiutorij petro philistim
venerunt. ((Lorde seie i ȝiue my strengþe to þe. þou þat 15
art ston of help. toure of treuþe. castel of strengþe. þere þe
fende ne may nouȝth do wiþ h sautes. þis is taken out of Regum.
þere þe folk of israel loged hem. by þe ston of help. And þe
Philistiens comen þat ben vnwiȝttes. afeþ on ebru. is new wodeschipp. and it telleþ þat israel went sone þe rygge. ꝫ foure 20
þousande in þe fiȝth weren sarrelich ynomen and þat was for
hij were flecchande. And þerfore in ȝoure anguisch stondeþ
stiflich aȝein wiþ gode iosephath þat sent sondes many to þe
kyng of heuenen after socoures.

IN nobis quidem non est tanta fortitudo vt possimus huic 25
multitudini resistere que irruit super nos set cum ignoramus
quid agere debeamus. hoc solum habemus residui. vt oculos
nostros dirigamus ad te. sequitur hec dicit dominus nobis
nolite timere ꝫ ne paueatis hanc multitudinem. non enim vestra
pungna set dei tantum modo confidenter state ꝫ videbitis 30
auxilium domini super vos credite in domino deo vestro ꝫ
securi eritis. ((In vs nys nouȝth derworþe lorde þat we mowe
wiþstonde þe deuels ferde ac whan we be so bistad þis one we
mowe done heuen vp oure eiȝen toward þe mylsful lorde. þou

---

1 Petrus. *in right margin in red ink.*   carne: ne *on erasure.*   5 fatiget, *sic for* fatigemini.   6 wiþseide: þ *written above line.*   7 paulus.
in right margin in red ink.   sanguinem: *second* n *by correction.*   14 petro,
sic for porro.   17 h, *sic for* his.   19 afeþ, *sic for* afech.   26 que:
e *by correction.*   28 dirigamus: *first* i *written above line and marked for
insertion.*   nobis, *sic for* vobis.   34 to *crossed out and expuncted after*
eiȝen.

M. 266)   sende vs socoures. ȝif he ne hereþ vs nouȝth crie we Ludder. ⁊

p. 421a   þrete | þat we wil ȝelde vp þe castel bot ȝif heiȝe þe swiþer wiþ
his helpe. Ac hou ansuered he þan þe goode Iosephaþ: nolite
timere, ne be ȝe nouȝt aferde. ne drede ȝe ȝou nouȝth. þe fiȝth
is myne ⁊ nouȝth ȝoures. stondeþ sikerlich with stedfast bileue 5
and ȝe ben alle syker. for þe fende ne may noþing done to vs als
long as we stonde. þis is þe fendes woord þorouȝ ysaye.

INcuruare vt transeamus. ⟨ Stoupe he seiþ ⁊ lete me ride. I
nyl nouȝth ride longe. þou may schouue me adoune he seiþ
wiþ schrift. þus wil þe fende seie ne leueþ hym nouȝth he is a 10
liȝer seiþ seint Bernard

NOn wlt transire set residere. ⟨ Nille he nouȝt wenden
ouer ac he wil sytte wel fast þere was a womman þat leued
hym so. and bowed adoune ⁊ lete hym lepe vp ⁊ þouȝth to haue
schriuen hir on þe Morne. ⁊ sche dude it eft ⁊ sche fel in fulle 15
wone. ⁊ he rode opon hire twenty wynter. And ne hadde ben a
miracle þat sche seiȝ he schulde haue riden hire so þat he

(M. 268)   schulde haue torpled adoune wiþ hire in to helle pytt And
þerfore holde we vs vp stedfastlich in þe bileue for it bringeþ
to nouȝth alle þe deuels wiles. Haue stedfast bileue as holy 20
chirche bileueþ and lete away alle wicche craftes alle tiliynges.
alle sweuens. ⁊ alle fals siȝttes þat holy men dreden. For þe

(M. 270)   fende haþ many bigiled þere þorouȝ. for þere nys non þat in his
sotile temptacions may atstonde bot one in þe bileue. And
þerfore we most fast biseche god þat he strengþe oure bileue as 25
his apostles beden hym. for ȝif þe fende may vnderstonde þat
oure bileue faileþ þan wexeþ his miȝth. We rede in Regum þat
Isbosett made a womman his ȝateward þat wyndeweþ whete.
and sche fel on slepe ⁊ Isboset was wiþ inne. And þan com
recasbesones ⁊ wen in ⁊ slouȝ Isboset. Isboset on ebru is þe 30
bymased Man to saie on english þat a myddes his wiþerwynnes
leide hym to slepen. womman ȝateward is his wittskil þat
schulde departen þe whete fram þe chaf. þe whete is his goode

(M. 272)   werkes. chaf is ydel þouȝttes ⁊ speches. þis skil þat schulde be
strong as Man and whan he vnstrengþed þan he is womman 35

2 he *omitted after* ȝif.   8 ysaya. *in left margin in red ink.*   12 Bernardus *in left margin in red ink.*   18 in *written above line and marked for
insertion.*   30 recasbesones, *sic for* recabes sones.   wen, *sic.*
34 þouȝttes: tt *and* s *blotted.*   35 Man: *small hole above* a *owing to
erasure on other side of leaf.*   vnstrengþed, *sic for* vnstrengeþ.   womman:
holes above wo *and* n *due to erasure on other side of leaf.*

þat is þe bileue faileþ. þis ȝateward þan slepeþ sone whan he
gynneþ consenten to synne þan þe lust goþ inward and þe delit
wexeþ. þan recabesones þat ben þe deuels barnes of helle gon

p. 421b   in ⁊ slen | dounriȝth þat vnseli bymased soule gregori seiþ.

IGniuie ferie est vitam carnis dileccionis perforare. ⸿ þe fende   5
þorouȝ stikeþ þe cher whan þe delit smiteþ to þe hert and þat
is þorouȝ ȝemelesschipp. gregori seiþ.

ANtiqus hostis mox vt mentem occisam inuenit ad eam in
quibusdam occasionibus loquturus venit. ⁊ quedam ei de
gestis preteritis ad memoriam reducit. audita quadam verba   10
indecenter resonat. putrauerunt. ⁊ deteriorate sunt citatrices
mee. cicatrix ergo quippe figura. figura est wlneris. Cicatrix
ergo ad putritudinem redit quando peccati wlnus quod per
penitenciam sanatum est ad dileccionem sui animum concutit.
⸿ þat is whan þe olde vnskil listneþ toward oure þouȝttes and   15
hereþ hem speken of fleschlich þinges. ⁊ spekeþ þus þe olde
swike toward þe hert of wordes þat he haþ byforne oiþer
siȝttes þat he haþ seen bifore oiþer of her owen synnes þat is
sumtyme wrouȝt al þis he putteþ forþ to þe doted soule so þat
þe synnes þat bifore weren bett ben opened and ymade newe.   20

(M. 274)   þat he may wepe ⁊ sorouȝe ynouȝ ⁊ seie wiþ þis psalme

PVtruerunt ⁊ corrupte sunt cicatrices mee. Weilaway myne
woundes þat weren faire heled ben gedred newe þorouȝ
synne. ⁊ gynneþ to roten. þat is whan þe elde synnes comen in
mynde. ⁊ þat is þorouȝ slouþe þat he falleþ in ydel þouȝttes.   25

ISboset inopinata mortem nequaquam subcumberet nisi ad
ingressum mentis Mulierem custodiam deputasset. ⸿ And al
þis vnhap comeþ þorouȝ þe ȝateward slepe þat is wommanlich
⁊ schulde be manlich. ⁊ þat is for defaut of bileue þat ouercasteþ
boþe Man ⁊ womman. ⁊ namelich aȝein þe fondynges þat   30
Isbosett died Inne. þat is ȝemeleshede. Look hou oure enemy

---

3 recabesones, *sic for* recabes sones.   5 IGniuie ferie, *sic for* IN in-
guine ferire.   dileccionis, *sic for* deleccacione.   G[regorious] *in right
margin in red ink.*   6 g[regorius] *in right margin in red ink. Traces of
letter at edge of MS.*   7 *Traces of letter in red ink at edge of MS.*
8 occisam, *sic for* occiosam.   inuenit, *sic for* inuenerit.   g[regorius] *in
right margin in red ink.*   10 quadam, *sic for* quedam.   11 putrauerunt, *sic for* putruerunt.   citatrices, *sic for* cicatrices.
13 putritudinem, *sic for* putredinem.   14 dileccionem, *sic for* dilecca-
cionem.   21 dau[id] *in right margin in red ink.*   24 is: s *blotted.*
26 inopinata mortem, *sic for* inopinate morti.   29 *Traces of erasure
after* ⁊¹.

is wayk ⁊ leþi. nys h nouȝt an vnhardy campion þat smiteþ
toward þe fote of his enemy. For flesche lust is cleped foote
wounde. For as oure fete beren vs whider þat we wil gon. so
done oure flesche lustes. Ac ne drede we vs nouȝth ful sore bot
ȝif þat þe delit smyte toward þe he hert and gynne to wexen 5
more ⁊ more. Ac þan drynk of þe atter. þat is þenche on þe
passioun of Ihesu crist. ⁊ do penaunce ⁊ dryue out þat attri
swellyng fram þe hert. þat is. þenche on attry pyne þat Ihesus
drank opon þe rode for oure synnes. pride. onde. wraþþe. hert
sore for werldelich þinges. drery for loue longyng wisschynge 10
ɔ. 422a of Catel. þise ben hert wounden, | þise ȝiuen deþes dynt onon
whan þe foote smyt þiderward þan it is to dreden. þat is þe lust
oiþer þe loue.

ſ. 276) REmedie aȝein pride is lowenesse. ⁊ onde salue is felauȝ-
schipp. wraþþe salue is loue. ⁊ suffre þat Man misdo þe. 15
Aȝein slouþe is redynge. spekynge of god ⁊ of gostlich werkes.
aȝein coueitise is free of hert. aȝein glotonye fastynge. aȝein
leccherie fleiȝe out of þe feble compaignye þere it may be done.
⁊ bidde fast to god niȝth ⁊ day þat he sende þe grace to wiþstonden it. 20

WHo so wil be lowe aȝein pride þenche hou mychel hym
faileþ of holynesse ⁊ of gostlich þewes. ȝutt þenche what
þou hast of þi seluen þou art of two dele of body ⁊ of soule. ⁊ in
oiþer ben two þinges þat mowen michel meken þe ȝif þou
ȝiuest good kepe vn to hem. In þi body is filþe ⁊ vnstrengþe. 25
Look in þe fairest stede of al þi body þat is þi neb. what comeþ
out þere of bereþ it wyn beryen oiþer smel of Aromance. þe
breren beren rosen. þi flessche what bereþ it. out of þi nose ne
comeþ nouȝth bot slyme. ne artow nouȝth bot wormes mete.
Sperua fluiudum. vas stercorum. esca vermium. ⟨ Now a 30
fleiȝe may dere þe ⁊ make þe to blenche wel owe þou to be
proude. Biholde to þise holy Men hou hij fasteden. ⁊ woken. ⁊
in which trauail þat hij weren. ⁊ so may þou knowe þine owen
vnstrengþe. Ac þat awildeþ vs þat we be cloumben heiȝe ⁊
þerfore biholde dounward ⁊ þou schalt see what þou art seiþ 35
seint austin.

---

1 h, sic for he.   2 his: i *written above line and marked for insertion.*
5 he hert, sic for hert.   15 loue *written above line and marked for in-*
sertion.   28 flesshe: e¹ *corrected from another letter.* le *blotted.*   30 Sperua
fluiudum, sic for Sperma es fluidum.

INcencium est eleccionis respectus inferioris sit cautela que
humilitatis consideracio superioris. ⟨ þat is biholde vn to
(M. 278) þise holy men þat ben of heiȝe lyf ⁊ þou may loke þan hou lowe
þou standes forbi hij done. Faste a seuen niȝth brede ⁊ water.
wake þre niȝth. what wil it vnstrengþe þi body þan may þou   5
wel see þat in þi flesche is filþe and vnstrengþe. And in þi soule
ben oþer two þinges. forȝeting ⁊ vncunnyng. ⁊ liȝth forto casten
in to synne. And þerforc biholdc to þinc synnes. drede þi feble
kynde and seie wiþ þe holy Man þat men telde hym þe fal of
his felawe.   10

ILle hodie ego cras. ⟨ Als vnstrong am ich as he was. he fel to
day ⁊ i may to morowen ⁊ biwepen his vnhappe. ⁊ dreden þat
so miȝth bitiden hym ȝif god ne helde hym vp wiþ his grace
Bernard seiþ.

SVperbia est appetitus proprie excellencie humilitatis con-   15
temptus eiusdem. ⟨ Also as pride is willyng of worschipp ⁊
heiȝenesse. riȝth so is lowonesse willing of lowenesse ⁊ to be
p. 422b litel holden. ⁊ as pride is rote ⁊ hede of alle vices⸴ so is | lowe-
nisse rote ⁊ heued of alle vertues.

QVi sine humilitate virtutes congregat est quasi qui in   20
vento puluerem portat. ⟨ þat is who þat bereþ vertues in
hym wiþouten lowenesse it fareþ by hym as who bare dust in
þe wynde. for þis lowenesse no gnare ne may ne may it atholde
þat is non of þe deuels wiles ne may hym deren. Seint antoyne
it witnesseþ þat god schewed al þe werlde vnto. ⁊ þan he seiȝ it   25
sett al ful of deuels gnares. ⁊ þan he seide vn to oure lorde. A
lorde he seide hou miȝth euere any passen alle þise and witen
hym fram hem. ⁊ oure lord seide to hym. þe þolemode Man.
For þe lowe Man of hert is so litel þat no gnare may atholde
(M. 280) hym. ⁊ þerto eke he is so strong þat al gostlich strengþe comeþ   30
þerof cassiodre seiþ.

OMnis fortitudo ex humilitate et cetera. ⟨ Al gostlich
strengþe comeþ of lowenisse.

VBi humilitas. ibi sapiencia. ⟨ þere lowenesse is þere is
wisdom. ⁊ þere þat is wisdom þere is þe faders strengþe.   35
Hou doþe þe wresteler he nymeþ ȝeme what turne þat his

---

1 INcencium est eleccionis: cf. Corpus: Sicut incentiuum est elationis 75b:
24.   sit cautela que, sic for sic cautela est.   4 hij on erasure.
15 humilitatis, sic for humilitas.   17 lowonesse, sic.   20 gregorius, in
right margin in red ink.   23 ne may ne may: dittography.   32 cassiodorus
in right margin in red ink.   34 Salamon. in right margin in red ink.

felawe can nou3th. ᴢ þerwiþ he casteþ hy. Also oure lorde sei3e
hou þe fende cast alle to helle þorou3 þe pride þat was in adam.
And þan seide oure lorde I schal werpen hym wiþ a turne þat
he neuer ne knew ne neuer schal. And oure lorde strei3tte hym
so lowe by þe erþe þat þe fende ne knew hym nou3th ᴢ þat is 5
cleped þe fallande turne. ᴢ þerwiþ he bigiled hym and cast hym
ᴢ ouercome hym. ᴢ alle his wiles er he wist. And 3utt vche day
he is bigiled wiþ þat ilch turne of þe þolemode Man ᴢ womman

OMne sublime vident oculi eius. ⟨ Holy Men þat holden
hem lowe ᴢ litel of hem seluen ᴢ 3iuen hem nou3th vnto þe 10
werlde. þe wilde bore ne may nou3th come vnto hem. Hij ben
(M. 282) careles of his tosshes. ᴢ þerfore vche man bihelde his blak. ᴢ
nou3th his white. þe white wil bygile þe ei3e oure lord seiþ.

DIscite a me quia mitis sum ᴢ humilis corde. ⟨ Lerneþ of
me to be mylde. for ich am meke ᴢ mylde. For in þise Men 15
þat ben mylde he ne heldeþ nou3th drope meel of his grace ac
foloweand he heldeþ in hem his grace.

QVi emittis fontes in conuallibus etc ⟨ þou makest welle
lorde in þe valeie. ᴢ hert bolnen ᴢ heuen as hil. take me a
bledder and blowe it and it wil fleten pricke þer inne wiþ a 20
nedel ᴢ it goþ al out ᴢ sinkeþ. And so it fareþ by pryde. als
longe as a Man leteþ wel of hym seluen þan he is blowen as
p. 423a bledder Ac lete hym loke witterlich what he is ᴢ his tayl | wil
falle

PRide salue is þis. Felawschipes ᴢ loue oþer Mennes goode 25
ᴢ it is þine owen. ᴢ wille hem goode þere my3th faileþ. For
so mychel strengþe haþ loue þat it makeþ oþers good his gode.
Loue oþere Mennes gode ᴢ it turneþ to þe. Lord what many ben
in þis werlde as ich vnderstonde wolde wel loue þat þing here
on erþe þat al þing were his þat it touched 30

ALia bona si diligis tua facis. 3if þou hast onde of oþers
goode þou attres þe wiþ halyway. ᴢ woundes þe wiþ salue.
þi salue it is 3if þou it loues. ᴢ þi strengþe a3ein þe fende. 3if
þou loue witterlich nomore schal fleschlich fondynges dere þe
þan gostlich. Looke þat we wil þat vche man ᴢ womman þat 35

1 hy, *sic for* hym.   17 foloweand, *sic for* floweand.   18 dauid. *in right
margin in red ink.*   19 bolnen: 1 *smudged by blue ink.*   20–1 *From*
and¹ *to* goþ *all words on erasure. Small hole above* n *in* and¹, *holes above* in
in inne *and* wiþ (*mentioned at* 119: 35).   25 PRide, *sic for* ONde.
28 gode: o *connected with* d *by stroke at foot of letter.*   31 ALia, *sic for*
ALiena.

(M. 284) loueþ vs. loued hem. Helpe oþer forto haue defaut þerof þi
seluen. An Ancre was almest dampned for þat sche nolde nouȝth
lenen a quayer fram fer to loken on.

Wraþþe salue is þolemodenesse þat men owen to han aȝein
yuel. þre staires þer bien þat longen to wraþþe. ȝif þou be   5
þolemode aȝein wraþþe an heiȝe staire it is ȝif þou þole þolemodelich harme þat men done þe. wel heiȝer it is. ⁊ more mede
liþ þerfore ȝif þou ne haue nouȝth agylt. And alder heiȝest ȝif
þou it þole for þi good dede. Ac many wil saye i made neuere
fors and ich hadde agylt. Ac for i ne haue nouȝth deserued it. it   10
doþe me þe more harme. þou þat so seist·ᴶ chese on of þise two.
wheþer þat þe is leuere to be iudas felawe. oiþer ihesus cristis
felawe Iudas was honged for his gylt. ⁊ ihesus crist giltles. He
þat mysseiþ þe oiþer misdoþe þe he is þi file. for þe file fileþ
away al þe rust of þe soule. For al þis word is goddes smiþe to   15
smiþe wiþ his chosen. ⁊ his belys þat he bloweþ wiþ þat ben his
wicked Men ⁊ wymmen þat clensen his childer and briȝtten
hem whi schulle we be waryand hem þat done vs good. ȝif we
weren wel avised we auȝtten to blissen hem ⁊ bidden for hem
fast for þe good þat hij done vs. wolde þe yrne ȝif it couþe   20
speken warien þe fyle þat it clensed nay bot it were a gret fole.

ARgentum probatum vocauit eos. ⫶ He clepeþ hise siluer
proued ȝif þat we wil come to oure spouse. we mote ben
yproued as þe siluer is in þe fyre. so we mote ben yproued in
þe fyre of fondynges.   25

QVid gloriatur impius si de ipso facit flagellatum pater
(M. 286)   vester ⫶ þenche on þis ensample, on domesday is day sett
p. 423b   forto ȝelde vche Man | after þat he haþ deserued. doþe he þe
þan wrong þat demes þe or þat day come. for þan is riȝth sett
vn to alle Men. for two þinges god haþ holden to hym seluen   30
worschipe ⁊ wreche.

Mchi vindictam ego retribuam. ⫶ Myne is þe wreche. I it
schal ȝelde.

GLoriam meam alteri non dabo. ⫶ My blis and my glorie I ne
schal ȝiue to Man Now þise Men þat wraþþen hem here of   35
harmes þat men done hem and of wronges and þise men also

10 ne haue *written above line and marked for insertion.*   12 cristis:
is² *written above line and marked for insertion.*   19 auȝt (*at end of line*):
ȝ *crammed in.*   22 probatum vocauit, *sic for* reprobum vocate.   26–7 facit
flagellatum pater vester: *cf. Corpus*: flagellum fatiat pater meus *78a: 2.*
32 Mchi vindictam, *sic for* Michi vindicta.   36 hem: m *by correction.*

þat desiren forto haue Lordeschippes ouere oþer ⁊ haue alle Men
vnder foote for her ryches. þat on wil bynyme god þe wreche
þat falleþ to hym. ⁊ þat oþer his glorie þat is his blis. And so
wolde Lucifer haue done. And þerfore þe harme fel opon hym
seluen. he bicom of þe fairest aungel of heuene þe foulest deuel 5
of helle. and so schulle alle done þat hym folowen bot ȝif hij
amenden hem here whiles þat hij lyuen. for alle swich Men wil
bynymen god wiþ strengþe al þat falleþ vn to hym dauid seiþ.

LAcum aperuit ⁊ effodit eum ⁊ incidit in foueam quam fecit.
⟨ Hij maden a graue and dalf it. and fel hem seluen in þe diche, 10
þat hij maden. ⁊ so it schal fare by vche wicked Man ⁊ womman.
þe harme þat hij wolde done to oþer. it schal falle to hem seluen
here oiþer elles where. For atte day of dome þou schalt seen hou
þe deuels of helle schullen beten hem þo þat ben þine enemyes
⁊ han done þe harme here ȝif þat þou ȝiue þe wreche in to his 15
honde. for we schulle wil as god wil. and he schal wil as we wil.

SLouþe salue is þis gostlich gladnesse þorouȝ hope of gret
mede þat we schulle haue þorouȝ redyng. þorouȝ holy þouȝttes. oiþer of mannes mouþe to here Men schulle ofte lete biddynges forto heren and forto reden. for þorouȝ heryng ⁊ redyng 20
comeþ þe deuocioun. and ȝiueþ good kep to þise verses.
Nunc stude. nunc ora. nunc cum feruore labora;
Sic erit hora breuis ⁊ labor iste leuis.
⟨ þat is now stodye. now biseche now wirche euere as þi wytt is
scharpest and so schal þe þenche þe day schort ⁊ þe werk liȝth. 25
SEmper in manu tua sacra sit leccio tenenti librum sompnus
subripiat ⁊ cadentem faciem sancta suscipiat. ⟨ Holy redynge

p. 424a   euere be in þine honde þat þi nebbe falle sleping | opon þe þe
holy pagyn. Ac euere as a man may do best and best wille haþ
so holde hym. þat is to saie in biddyng oiþer in heryng oiþer in 30
redyng oiþer in spekyng oiþer in þouȝth of goddes passioun.

SAlue aȝein coueitise is largesse frenesse of hert. naþeles a
(M. 288)   Man may be to fre as seint Gregori seiþ. Mete and drynk
blyndes þre tymes liȝth þouȝttes liȝth wordes. and seching of
lustes ac vnderstondeþ þere ben þre degrees of fleschlich 35
fondynges on is cogitacio. anoþer affectus. þe þridd consensus,

cogitacio. þat ben liȝth þouȝttes þat ne hirten nouȝth þe soule
bot hij bispatten it as fleiȝes done confiteor serueþ þere of
crouchynge ⁊ knelyng ⁊ culpyng atte breest done hem away
affectus. þat is whan þe þouȝth goþ inward and þe delytt wexeþ
and þe lust þan wexeþ wounde and depeþ inward in to þe soule   5
⁊ þat is after þat þe lust goþ. þan is nede to crie Sane me domine
hele me lorde for ich am wounded in to my soule.

R Vben primogenitus meus non crescat ruben. ⟨ Rede þouȝth
þou blody delytt ne wexe þou neuere consente, þat is ne
consente þou neuere þerto. ne drawe non vnlust vpe þe as þing   10
þat were amased. and liþe adoun and leteþ hym vp ⁊ seiþ
crauant. þan he bicomeþ neer þat aforne stode fer and biteþ
deþe bytte þat stode arst fer fro ȝou dauid seiþ.

(M. 290)   E Rue a framea deus animam meam ⁊ de manu canis vnicam
meam. ⟨ Whan þe dogge of helle comeþ als smertlich stonde   15
aȝein ne loke nouȝth what he what he wil do ac nyme onon þe
roode staf in þine honde ⁊ in þi mouþe. þat is make on þe þe
merk of þe croice arise vp smertlich ⁊ stir þi seluen holde vp
þine eiȝen ⁊ þine honden after socours wiþ Deus in adiutorium.
Veni creator spiritus. Exurgat deus ⁊ dissipentur. Saluum me   20
fac. Domine quid multiplicati, Ad te leuaui oculos meos.
Saieþ þise Psalmes. ⁊ ȝif ȝou ne come nouȝth sone help crieþ
ludder wiþ good hert. Vsquequo domine obliuisceris me. pater
noster. Credo. Aue maria, And smertlich falleþ. a doune to þe
erþe and braideþ vp þe roode staf casteþ hym a furwe half þe   25
helle dogg þat nys nouȝth elles bot blisse al aboute þe and
spytte hym amydde þe berd ⁊ scorne hym þat he wolde wiþ so
litel hire þi soule goddes spouse. bihode what he payed deme
opon hir prys and be euere þe derere for þat sche coste dere ne
selle hir nouȝth for so litel to his fo. þat he paied so mychel fore   30
his owen hert blood ⁊ make hir nouȝth þe deuels hore. to litel
hij mowen do þat ne mowen nouȝth heuen vp her þre fyngers
(M. 292) ⁊ nempne goddes passioun his derworþe bloode ⁊ crepe in to
p. 424b his | woundes as þe prophete seiþ.

6 Sane, *sic for* Sana.   8 crescat, *sic for* crescas.   11 hym *written
above line and marked for insertion.*   14 animam: *traces of erasure on
first* a.   16 what he what he: *dittography.*   20 Exurgat: *traces of
erasure between* u *and* r.   25 furwe, *sic. Cf. Corpus:* fowr 79a: 22.
28 goddes *crammed together at end of line.*   bihode, *sic for* biholde.
29 hir: r *blotted.*   sche *written above line and marked for insertion.*
33 passioun: pass *partially erased.*

INgredere petram absconde fosse humo ⟨ Go in to þe ston
and in to þe doluen erþe.

FOderunt manus meas ⁊ pedes meos dinumerauerunt omnia
ossa mea. ⟨ Hij doluen myne feet ⁊ myne honden ⁊ rekened
myne bones. 3e þe nayles weren ragged biforen for hij weren of 5
a wommanes makyng ⁊ baren þorou3 in to þe tree skyn. ⁊
flesch. ⁊ bon. al þat hij stoden on. ⁊ þerfore þe prophete biddeþ
þe crepe in to þe doluen erþe.

COlumba mea in funeribus petre ⁊ cauernis macerie
⟨ Michel loued he þat culuer þat he made swich hidels to 10
hir. þo þat he clepeþ culuer looke þat hij han culuer kynde wiþ
outen galle. þat is wiþouten bitternesse of hert ⁊ filþe of synne.
come þan boldelich to hym ⁊ make schelde of his passioun.
oiþer 3utt in wille to leten her synne als sone as god sendeþ
hem his grace whan þat hij han bisou3th þere after 15

DAbis scutum cordis laborem tuum. ⟨ Lord þou schalt
3iue me hert a schelde a3ein þe fende wiþ his swynkful

(f. 294)   pyne. He schewed it to vs witterlich ynou3 þat he is oure
schelde, þe fi3t þerof makeþ hym agast ⁊ bryngeþ hym att
fli3th. ⁊ 3if 3oure temptacioun go so ferforþ takeþ seint Benett 20
salue nou3th so mychel as he dude. for he tooke so mychel þat
rigge ⁊ wombe brusten on blode. ac wiþ a smert discipline oþer
to drawe out of likyng 3if þou werest þe slepeande he wil come
vpe þe for delytt is dedlich wiþ outen dede so ferforþ it may go
and last. 25

NVmquam enim iudicando est dileccio esse mordia racio
recluditur ⁊ negat assensum. ⟨ Whan þe skyl fi3tteþ no
lenger a3ein þan it is dedlich For in þe ginnyng trede þe nedder
on þe hede er þat he were to bolde þe prophete seiþ.

BEatus qui tenebit ⁊ allidet paruulos suos ad petram. 30
⟨ Blissed be he seiþ þe prophete þat brekeþ to þe ston atte
first skirminge.

IN canticis capte vobis wlpes paruulas quidam. enim. ⟨ þe
first prickyng sleþ þe vyne þat ben oure soules þat moten han

1 in *omitted after* INgredere.   absconde fosse, *sic for* abscondere in fossa.
propheta *in right margin in red ink.*   3 dauid *in right margin in red ink.*
9 funeribus, *sic for* foraminibus.   19 fi3t, *sic for* si3t.   22 discipline: *second i written above line and marked for insertion.*   26 iudicando,
sic for iudicanda.   dileccio, *sic for* delectacio.   mordia, *sic for* morosa.
27 recluditur, *sic for* reluctatur.   skyl: k *blotted.*   30 dauid. *in right
margin in red ink.*   32 skirminge: *cf. Corpus:* sturunges *80b: 8.*
33 capte, *sic for* capite. in canticis.   *in right margin in red ink.*

mychel tilying as þe vine of alle trees it most haue mooste cost
and it ne may nouȝth beren hym seluen. nomore ne may a man
beren hym seluen, ne kepen hym bot þorouȝ þe grace of god.
And wel more keping ⁊ tilying it mote haue þan þe vine and
liȝthlich þou may sle þe vine. ⁊ ȝut wel liȝthlicher may þe soule 5

(M. 296)
be sleyn. And þerfore ⁊ for many oþer enchesons man is likned
p. 425a
to þe vine. þe fende is bere kynde bihynde. ⁊ | asse bifore. þat
is leþi bifore ⁊ stronge bihinde. ⁊ þerfore smyte hym opon þe
schulders for he is þing pruddest ⁊ hym is schame loþest. þat
is atte first whan he tempteþ stonde stiflich aȝein wiþ gods 10
passioun ⁊ he fleiȝeþ als swiþe. ⁊ of þat synne he ne schal
nomore tempte þe. Ac anoþer may for þere ben fele of hem. A
lefdi seide a spark brouȝth al hir hous on brennyng ⁊ so it fareþ
ofte of litel comeþ mychel. þerfore vche Man ⁊ womman beþ
war of þe deuel, he is redy to blowen it ⁊ kyndleþ it more and 15
more. ⁊ þerfore quencheþ it onon riȝth wiþ ihesus cristes bloode
for it is goddes riȝthful dome a man þat nyl nouȝth whan he
may he ne schal nouȝth whan he wold Also aȝein coueitise
þenche hou pouer ihesus crist was att his bereynge he ne hadde
none hous to be borne inne ne no cloþing forto ben ywounden 20
inne and pouerlich was sustened afterward and afterward his
moder susteined hym wiþ her rok for sche span þat tyme And
after more pouerte whan he henge on þe rode naked.

AȜain leccherie þenche opon his betynge wiþ scourges
knotted ⁊ take þe a discipline oiþer two. ⁊ þat wil drawe þe 25
likyng fram þine hert And bidde fast to ihesu crist ⁊ he schal
deliuer þe ⁊ þou bidde wiþ good wille, er þou lest wene for þat
synne ne may noman wiþstonde wiþouten his grace bot hij þat
ben chaste of kynde. oiþer þorouȝ art þat is to vnderstonde by
art þat hij deliten hem in oþer þinges ⁊ þerfore hij ne han no 30
wille þerto. oiþer usen letewaries to fordone her kynde.

AȜein glotonye beþ sober. fasteþ gretelich for þat is þe best
medicine þere aȝeins ⁊ þencheþ opon þe meþfulnesse of
Ihesu crist whan he henge opon þe rode And he asked a drynk
⁊ hij ne ȝeuen bot a litel galle ⁊ eysil ⁊ myrre menged to gedre. ⁊ 35
he wiþdrouȝ hym ⁊ nolde nouȝth drynk it þeiȝ al he were of
þrust.

(M. 298)
NOw we schulle telle of schrift two þinges nymeþ ȝeme of
schrift. þe first of which miȝth it is. þat oþer what it schulde

2 hym: ym *on erasure.*

be. Now ichille dele þis on sextene partyes as men breken bred
to childer þat bot ȝif þe bred were broken to hem hij miȝtten
dyen for hunger, Schrift haþ many miȝttes. Ac ichil tellen bot
of sex þre to þe fende ⁊ þre to oure seluen schrift schendeþ þe
fende ⁊ toheweþ of his heued ⁊ to dreueþ al his feerd. And oure 5
seluen it wassheþ of al oure filþe. ⁊ ȝeldeþ vs þat we hadde
lorne ⁊ makeþ vs goddes childer. Iudyf is schrift on oure tunge

p. 425b þat | is þe fende whan Men schewen her synnes to þe preest ⁊
ben sori þerfore þan schenden hij þe fende whan a Man is in
wille to done his synnes nomore þat raþer he wolde dyen ⁊ 10
draweþ out al þe rote of þe likyng þan is his heued of.

COmpuncte sciencie in cubiculo abscidit caput. ⟨ Ac ȝutt he
nys nouȝth al fullich slayn.

1. 300) VAga o vna mulier ebria. id est. Iudif fecit in domo regis
nabugodonosor. ⟨ þat is erþe mouþe do out al þat heued al 15
þe gynnyng ⁊ al as it was þan he fleiȝeþ ⁊ alle his wrenches ⁊ alle
his wiles as Iudif dude Oloferne Also iudas Machabeus who
stoode aȝeins hym also þe folk in. Iudicum asked whan iosue
was dede who schulde ben her leder

QVis erit dux nostrum Iudas ascendit et cetera. ⟨ Oure 20
lorde seide late Iudas go bifore ȝou and i schal take ȝoure
enemyes in to ȝoure handes what is þis to saie. Iosue spelleþ
hele and Iudas schrift as Iudif doþe þan is Iosue ded whan þe
soule is slayn þorouȝ synne ⁊ is quyked aȝein þorouȝ schrift.
For schrift is baneoure ⁊ bereþ þe baner bifore goddes ferde ⁊ 25
bynymeþ þe fende his londe. Iudas to drof al þe londe of
Chanaan bodilich and so doþe schrift gostlich

OMnia in confessione lauantur glosa confitebimur tibi deus
confitebimur. ⟨ þis was bytokned þat Iudif wesche ⁊
despoiled hir of widewen schrude þat bitokneþ synne ⁊ cloþed 30
hir in haliday weden

M. 302) LAuit corpus suum ⁊ exuit se vestimentis viduitatis. iohel
seiþ.

REddam vobis annos quos commedit locusta ⁊ brucus.
rubigo ⁊ erugo. ⟨ Schrift ȝeldeþ vs al oure lorne. þis was 35

---

7 Iudyf, *sic for* Iudyþ.   8 *In left part of bottom margin hand in black*
ink with forefinger pointing upwards.   12 sciencie, *sic for* consciencie.
14 VAga o, *sic.*   Iudif, *sic for* Iudiþ.   15 erþe, *sic for* er þe.
17 Iudif, *sic for* Iudiþ.   20 nostrum, *sic for* noster.   ascendit, *sic for*
ascendet.   23 Iudif, *sic for* Iudiþ.   29 Iudif, *sic for* Iudiþ.

bitokned þat iudif schredd hir wiþ haliday weden ovrnementz
bitokneþ blis as oure lorde seiþ.

ERunt sicut fuerunt ⁊ proieceram. et cetera. (⸿ Schrift schal
make þe Man swich as he was er he synned. þe þridde þing
endeþ hem boþe for it makeþ vs goddes childer. Iudas biȝate 5
beniamyn of iacob his fader to ben his riȝth honde sone þat is
of þe eritage of heuen. now ichil tellen hou ȝe schullen go to
schrift

(M. 304) SCrift schal be wrayful. þou schalt biwraie þi seluen ⁊ non
oþer as summe wil saien þus ich it dude þorouȝ oþer oiþer 10
þe fende it maked me done. þus Adam and Eue wered hem.
Adam wytt his synne opon Eue and Eue opon þe nedder þe
fende ne may strengþe non to synne þeiȝ þat he egge hem
þerto ac wel wele he leteþ þere of whan men seien o fore he is
p. 426a proude, | for hij ȝiuen hym strengþe þat naþ non bot onlich 15
þorouȝ oure seluen. ȝif þou witest þi synne on þine vnstrengþe
þou puttest þi synne on þe fader þat made þe. ȝif þou seist
þou ne haste no cunnyng þou puttest þi synne on þe son þat
bouȝth þe. ȝif þou seist þou ne haste no grace þou puttest þi
synne on þe holy gost ⁊ on alle þise þre þou gabbest for ȝif þou 20
wilt bidde hem. hij ben redy to ȝiuen þe strengþe witt ⁊ grace,
ȝif þou bidde wiþ good wille ⁊ folowe it in dede als forþe as þou
may. for at domesday þou schalt fynde alle þise þre aȝeins þe
ȝif þou woldest excusen þe in þis manere. Nay þou schalt saie
þus by myne vnwraist wille i beiȝe to þe fende ⁊ to his wrenches 25
poule seiþ

SI nosmet ipsos diiudicaremur non vtique iudicamur. (⸿ Ȝif
we wraie vs here ⁊ deme wel oure seluen we schulle be quyte
atte mychel dome þere seint anselme seiþ þise wordes.

HInc erunt accusancia terrens supra iratus iudex. subtra 30
patrinus horrendum chaos inferni intus vrens consciencia.
foris ardens mundus peccator sic deprehensus in quam partem
se premet. (⸿ On domesday schal þe deuel of helle stonde on þi
riȝth half þine blake synnes on þi left half ⁊ biclepe þe of þi

---

1 iudif, *sic for* iudiþ. 12 Eue and *on erasure.* 18 þou¹:
o *by correction.* 19 grace *on erasure.* 23 þou schalt: *words connected in MS.* aȝeins: aȝe *crammed in at end of line.* 26 [P]aulus
in left margin in red ink. Left part of a cut off at edge of MS. 27 diiudicaremur, *sic for* diiudicaremus. 29 [A]nselmus *in left margin in red
ink. Traces of A at edge of MS.* mus *below* nsel *in red ink. Two minims of*
m *cut off at edge of MS.* 30 subtra, *sic for* subtus. 31 patrinus,
sic for patens. horrendum, *sic for* horridum.

soule murþer and riʒthwisenesse þere al redi þat no reuþe nys
wiþ forto biwraie þe abouen þe. þe erþe demer dredeful to
biholde ⁊ storne. for als soft as he is here. als sterne he is þere.
þe prophete seiþ here.

AGnus dei qui tollis. ⟨ Here he is lombe ⁊ þere lyoun for he 5
wot alle oure gyltes Bineþen vs þe wide þrote of helle redy
(I. 306) to swelewe vs. And oure conscience þat is oure inwit brennande wiþinnen vs ⁊ al þe werlde on fyre abouten vs. þe synful
þus bisett to which of þise may he turnen hym: nys here bo
berne ⁊ here þat wo Word þat griselich word þat sorouʒful 10
word þat god schal seye.

ITe maledicti in ignem eternum qui preparatus est diabolo ⁊
angelis eius. ⟨ Goþ ʒe awaried out of myne eiʒen siʒth in to
þe fyre þat euer schal last þat was made for þe deuel ⁊ for his
aungels for ʒe fordude my dome þat i demed man to þat was to 15
lyuen in sorouʒ and wo here in þis werlde and after come to my
blis. þerfore ʒe schulle now haue þe deuels dome to brenne wiþ
hym wiþouten ende. þan schullen þe synful crien swich a cry
þat heuen and erþe may agrisen of þat ilch cry. |

(p. 426b) Ascendit homo tribunal mentis sue si illud cogitet quod 20
oportet eum exhiberi ante tribunal christi. assit accusatrix
cogitacio testis consciencia carnis timor. ⟨ þat is þenche man
on domesday Austin seiþ. For skylle sitteþ þere on dome settel
comeþ þere after his þouʒth ⁊ accuseþ hym ⁊ seiþ þus þou dedest
þere ⁊ þere ⁊ on þis wise. His witt biknoweþ al soþ it is ⁊ mychel 25
more. After þat þan schal drede come ⁊ bynde hem þorouʒ
hest of domes Man, ʒutt nys he nouʒth ypayed þeiʒ hij ben
ybounden ac biddeþ pyne ⁊ sorouʒ wirche in hem al þat he can
(I. 308) ⁊ may. pyne wiþ outen ⁊ sorouʒ wiþ innen. who so demeþ þus
hym seluen here salþ he is for þe prophete seiþ. 30

NOn iudicabit deus in idipsum. ⟨ God nyl nouʒth þat a Man
for o synne be twies yiugged

SI accusat deus excusat in vite viam. ⟨ ʒif þou biwraye þe
here god wil were þe þere.

2 erþe: cf. Corpus: eorre 83a: 8.   3 prophecia in left margin in red
ink.   9–10 bo berne ⁊, sic for buten.   10 dominus in left margin in red
ink.   12 eternum: traces of erasure on n.   18 wiþouten: en partially
erased.   19 ilch written above line and marked for insertion.   20 Augustinus. in right margin in red ink.   Ascendit, sic for Ascendat.   cogitet, sic
for cogitat.   22 carnis, sic for carnifex.   29 wiþinnen struck out after
þus.   30 salþ, sic for seli.   31 propheta. in right margin in red ink.
33 accusat, sic for tu accusas.

SChrift schal be bitter aȝein þat þe synne was swete. Iudyf
þat spelleþ schrift was Marachies douȝtter. And iudas þat
spelleþ schrift also wedded Othomar. Bitter and sorouȝ in
schrift þat on comeþ wiþ þat oþer. þat on wiþ þat oþer nys
nouȝth worþe. Iudif and Marachie boþe ben sauen in fiȝth 5
Phares and zarim nymeþ here foure þinges to stire ȝou to make
sorouȝe. ȝif a Man hadde lorne fader ⁊ Moder. wyf ⁊ childe ⁊
broþer suster ⁊ alle his frendes. and alle in on tyme nolde he
nouȝth be sory. God wott he may be wel sorier þat haþ lorne
god his fader ⁊ Marie his moder and holy chirche his spouse. 10
þat he ne haþ no good of nouȝth þat hij done þere inne. Alle þe
aungels of heuene þat weren his frendes toforne. Alle halewen

(M. 310) his breþeren ⁊ his sustren. Alle hij ben to hym als fremde ⁊
dede as in hym. he haþ sleyn hem and lyueþ in loþ of hem alle
OMnes amici eius spreuerunt eum ⁊ facti sunt ei inimici. 15
⸿ Alle þat weren his frendes alle spyen opon hym. his children dyen þat ben his good werkes al clene, and ȝutt opon al þis
hym seluen þat was goddes childe ⁊ lyche to hym. makeþ hym
þe deuels barne of helle ⁊ bicomeþ liche hym.
VOs ex patre diabolo estis. ⸿ Ȝe ben þe deuels childer of 20
helle ⁊ he is ȝoure fader seiþ oure lorde in þe godspelle.
LVctum vnigenitum fac tibi planctum amarum. ⸿ Make bitter
Man as womman doþe for hir child þat seeþ it dye to-

p. 427a forne hir. Now by þis worde. | bot ȝif a Man wepe als mychel
for his synnes as þe wyf doþe for hir childe for sche leteþ teres 25
wiþouten mesure and bot ȝif a Man dude so for his synnes he
nere nouȝth verray repentaunt. Nay it nys nouȝth so. Ac þou
schalt wil make sorouȝ ⁊ haue doel ⁊ ioye þe in god as þe prophete seiþ.
GAudete in domino semper ⁊ delectare in deo ⁊ ipse dabit 30
tibi peticiones cordis tui. ⸿ þat is ioye þe in þe lorde ⁊
delite þe in god ⁊ he schal ȝiue þe þe askyng of þine hert Now
here beþ tway contraries, glade þe in god ⁊ sorouȝe for þine

---

1 Iudyf, *sic for* Iudyþ.   2 Marachies, *sic for* Meraries.   3 in, *sic*
for and.   4 wiþ², *sic for* wiþuten.   5 Iudif, *sic for* Iudiþ.
Marachie, *sic for* Merari.   14 dede: *dot below second e, probably*
not to indicate expunction.   15 eum, *sic for* eam.   ieremias, *in*
right margin in red ink.   20 dominus. *in right margin in red ink.*
22 Ieremias *in right margin in red ink.*   vnigenitum, *sic for* vnigeniti.
30 propheta *in left margin in red ink.*   31 *After* is *two vertical parallel*
lines in red ink.

synnes. ᚪ a Man may nouȝth haue boþ att ones. and boþe we
moten haue at ones on þis manere. wil be sori for þi synne ᚪ
glade þe alway in god þat is haue hym alway in þine hert ᚪ in
þi mynde in al þat þou doost. ℂ Anoþer enchesoun forto maken
sorouȝ. A Man þat were dampned for a murdre forto ben 5
ybrent oiþer anhonged. þou þat doost a dedlich synne þou
murþerest goddes spouse þat is þi soule. þou art dampned to
ben ybrent ᚪ anhonged opon þe galewes of helle for þou chaff-
ares þan wiþ þe fende as ysaye seiþ.

Pᴇpigimus cum morte ᚪ cum inferno ruimus pactum. ℂ þat 10
is þou haste treuþe pliȝth ᚪ made dede forþward wiþ þe fende.
he ȝiueþ þe synne ᚪ þou hym þi soule. For synne is his chaffare
þat he chaffareþ wiþ. al, þe þridde enchesoun. a Man þat hadde
al þe werlde in welde ᚪ forlese it al att o tyme for his quedschipp
hou wolde his hert att stonde. Nou vche man þat liþ in dedlich 15
synne he haþ forlorne þe kyngdom of heuen. ᚪ oure lorde ihesu
crist þat is þousande hundreþ fairer þan heuene ᚪ erþe and al
þe werlde. þe fierþe encheson is whi a man miȝth make sorowe.

(ᴵ. 312) Qᵛem enim christi ad bellum conuencio et cetera. ℂ þe
kyng of þe londe haþ bitauȝtte his dere childe a kniȝth 20
forto wyten ᚪ ȝemen and his enemy comeþ ᚪ ledeþ hym awai
and to werray opon his fader. nys nouȝth þis kniȝth sory. So it
fareþ here þe fader of heuene haþ bitauȝtt vchon of his childer
an aungel forto witen ᚪ warden ᚪ elles yuel vs schulde bistonden.
Ac we putten hym away þorouȝ synne ᚪ maken hym fol sori 25
in als mychel as in vs is. And oure eueryich to swich a gentil
wardeyn ȝiueþ to litel reuerence ᚪ cunneþ hym to litel þank for
427b his seruise. I rede þat we do vs in his warde | ᚪ be ful tender ouer
hym to helden hym wiþ vs. swich enchesons þere ben ᚪ many
oþer whi þat a man auȝtte to wepen for his synnes. For god doþe 30
wiþ vs as a Man þat haþ an yuel dettour takeþ often Oten for
whete. so doþe oure lorde of vs. wiþ riȝth wc schulde ȝelde hym
blode for blode. and þeiȝ oure blode aȝein his blode may be
sette at aliȝth prys. Ac he doþe as þe yuel dettour doþe takeþ
oure teres for his blood. ᚪ ȝutt he is ful wel ypayed. he wepe opon 35
þe rode. on lazar. on Ierusalem. for oþer Mennes synnes. wepe

---

10 ysayas, *in left margin in red ink.*   fedus *omitted after* morte.   ruimus,
sic for iniuimus.   15 att *crammed together at end of line. First* t *blotted.*
19 bellum, *sic for* belial.   30 auȝtte: auȝ *by correction.*   34 *Erasure*
above sette.   aliȝth, *sic for* a liȝth.

we for oure owen. In vitis patrum it telleþ an holy man preched
ꝥ seide wepe we for oure synnes lest þat oure teres ne seþen vs
in helle.

(M. 314) SChrift schal ben hole þat is al holelich made al to o Man.
Þat is whan ȝe come toforne hym þat schal schryue ȝou. ȝe 5
schulle telle hym al holelich þat comeþ þan to ȝoure mynde ꝥ
nouȝth wiþholde sum ꝥ telle sum. þe pouer womman whan
sche makeþ fair hir hous sche doþe out al þe grettest first ꝥ after
þe smaller ꝥ þan þe dust arist to swiþe sche flasscheþ on water
so do ȝe whan ȝe swepe ȝoure hous þat is ȝoure bodies þat is 10
goddes temple putteþ out first þe grete ꝥ þan þe oþer ꝥ after þe
dust of liȝth þouȝttes. ȝif hij passen forþ to swiþe flassheþ þere
opon teres þat ȝe ne ablynde nouȝth þe hert eiȝen. þe Man þat
haþ many dedlich woundes ꝥ doþe hele hem alle bot on ꝥ dieþ
for þat ilch on als wel he myȝth dye on alle. A schipp wiþ many 15
holes stoppe alle bot on ꝥ it synkeþ for þat ilche on als wel it
myȝth drenchen on alle. Men tellen of an holy Man þat lay on his
deþ bedd ꝥ his Abbot com to hym. ꝥ asked ȝif þat he were clene
schriuen ꝥ he seide ȝe bot a synne he dude in his childehede.
þe Abbot badde hym tellen it ꝥ he seide nay it nas no fors 20
þereof. ꝥ algate his abbot gate it out of hym ꝥ þan he dyed and
a niȝth he com to þe abbot ꝥ seide ne hadde he nouȝth tolde
hym þat synne he hadde gon to helle ꝥ also anoþer for he had o
noþer tyme neded a Man forto drynken. ꝥ a leuedy also for þat
sche lent a pouer womman her cloþing on opon an halyday was 25
nere dampned to þe pyne of helle

(M. 316) SI consciencia desit pena satisfacit ⟨ ȝif þi conscience forȝiue
þe þat þou nart in no peril of soule þan is wel. so þat þere ne
p. 428a be no ȝemeleshede. þat is þat þou haste souȝth | als ferforþe as
þou canst and may. 30

SChrift schal be naked þat is nouȝth be saumpled fair ꝥ
hendelich Ac saie þe wordes after þe werkes for þat is
tokne of hatynge. ȝif þou hatest þi synne whi spekestow good
þere of saie out þi filþ astow wilt schende þe fende. sir ich haue
yhadd a lemman oiþer ich haue ben a womman foule of my 35
seluen. þis nys nouȝth naked schrift. ne bicloute it nouȝth ac

---

15 on²: dot under n, *probably not indicating expunction.*   19 ȝe *written
above line and marked for insertion.*   31 be saumpled, *sic for* besaumpled.
33 tokne of: *words connected at end o* line.   36 bicloute it: *words connected at end of line.*

saie sir goddes mercy ⁊ þine ich am a foule hore oiþer a foule
lecchoure a stronge þeue aȝeines my lorde þeiȝ to foule Men
may saie ac holde þe for swich in hert for ynouȝ it is to saye so
þat þi schrift fader vnderstonde what þou woldest menen. Sex
þinges fallen to schrift. þat men clepen circumstaunce. þat ben 5
tagges on ynglissch i ne can none oþer ynglisch þere of. ⟨ On is
þis þe persone þat þou doost þe synne wiþ al oiþer who it dude
ȝif it be a womman. saye þus ich am a womman ⁊ schulde wiþ
riȝth be more schameful þan a man. Ich haue spoken. done as i
dude for þi my synne is þe more þan of a Man. for it bicomeþ 10

. 318) wers in my mouþe. a Maiden. a wyf. a Nunne. an Ancre. A
womman þat Man leueþ so wel ⁊ han ben arst ybrent ⁊ auȝtten
ben þe better ywar. sir it was swiche a Man. Monk. Frere
Preest clerk wedded Man nouȝth nempny þe name bot swich
ordre for þe heiȝer degre þe more is þe synne. Stede. sir ich 15
dude in suich stede in chirche bihelde hym atte auter. i bihelde
wrastelynges fole gamens ⁊ ydel oiþer spoken bifore Religious
þere men schulde neiȝen holy þing hondled hym. ⟨ þe tyme
ich was of swich elde þat ich auȝtte þe wiselicher haue ywited
me. ich it dude in lenten ⁊ on halyday whan oþer Men weren 20
atte chirche ich was sone ouercomen ⁊ þe synne is þe more þan
ich hadde ben cast wiþ strengþe I biþouȝth me wel hou yuel it
was to done. and dude it neuer þe latter. þe manere. sir on þis
wise þus i lered first ⁊ vsed it forþ on þus fele wise þus foullich

. 320) schamelich. i souȝth delytt hou ich miȝth best paie my lust. Tale 25
is anoþer. tellen hou oft þus oft yspoken yseide les. þouȝth þus
fele þouȝtte. forȝemed þing þat myȝth haue holpen man oiþer
forȝeten þing. lauȝen eten dronken lesse oiþer more þan hij
hadden nede to þus ofte in wraþþe siþþen i was last schriuen.

. 428b C̶Ause whi þou dedest it oiþer yholpe þerto þorouȝ wham it 30
bigan. Ich it dude for | delite of yuel loue. for biȝete. for
drede. for flaterynge. Ich it dude for yuel þeiȝ þere com non of.
Mi liȝth lates tolled hym vpe me oiþer loose ansueres. for
wraþþe ich it dude forwhi þe yuel lasteþ ȝutt. þus leþi was myne
hert seie þus vchon after oþer Ieremie seiþ.   35

---

4 vnderstonde: der *crammed together at end of line.*   5 circumstaunce:
i *written above line and marked for insertion.*   14 name: n *blotted.*   bot:
t *by correction. Blot after* t.   20 oþer: þ *blotted.*   21 is þe: *words connected at end of line. Separated by thin vertical stroke.*   28 lauȝen: *MS.*
lauȝtten *with* tt *expuncted.*   29 siþþen: *second* þ *lacks its loop.*

Effunde sicut aqua cor tuum. ℂ As water schede out þine hert
whi biddeþ he as water. for oyle whan it is schadde þe licour
leueþ þereinne. ⁊ of wyne þe smel, ⁊ of Milk þe hew ac water
geþ out al clene ⁊ ȝif þou ne doost nouȝth so loo hou god þrete-
neþ þe.

ECce ego ad te dicit dominus ostendam gentibus nuditatem
tuam regnis tuam ignominiam ⁊ proiciam super to Abhom-
(M. 322) inaciones tuas. ℂ þou noldest nouȝth vnwrie þi self ⁊ þerfore I
schal schewe alle þine quedschippes to alle kyngdomes on erþe
⁊ of heuen ⁊ to helle and trusse al in þi nekk as a þef ⁊ cast þe
adoun in to helle wiþ al to geder.

QVid confusionis qui ignominie erunt quando dissipatis
folijs ⁊ dispersis vniuersa nudabitur turpitudo fames
apparebit et cetera. ℂ What schame schal be þere ⁊ what
schendelik whan al schal ben vnwrien nouȝth onlich of dede ac
of word ⁊ of þouȝth ⁊ wrongen out al þe ruse.

OMne tempus inpensum requiretur qualiter sit expensum.
ℂ þe schal vche tyde ⁊ vche tyme ben yrekened hou it is
dispended quando dissipatis folijs. He loked hou Adam ⁊ Eue
gedreden leues to hile wiþ her kykeham. þus done Men now
after hem hiden her filþe.

DEclinantes cor suum in verba malice ad excusandas
excusaciones in peccatis. ℂ Hij bowen her hertes vnto
wordes of wickednisse forto hile hem in her synnes ⁊ so done
men now. þeiȝ he wot his neiȝbur in synne ⁊ he miȝth techen
hym ⁊ couþe hou he miȝth techen hym ⁊ couþe hou he miȝth
amenden hym. ȝe. he seiþ god amende alle. alle ben we synful.
And he seiþ soþ per auenture þeiȝ þat oþer lye in synne ⁊ hym
þencheþ wel þat he nys nouȝth in þat synne for he haþ þat happe
þat he kepeþ hym out þere of þorouȝ cunnyng þat he haþ. ȝif
þat oþer couþe þat he can he schulde kepe hym bettere þan he
doþe. And he is in gretter synne þan he is ⁊ vnderstondeþ it
nouȝth for he is out of loue ⁊ charite For god biddeþ þat he

---

1 aqua, *sic for* aquam.   ieremias. *in right margin in red ink.*   2 biddeþ:
thin stroke connecting first d *with dot below, probably not intended for expunction.*   6 dominus, *in right margin in red ink.*   7 to, *sic for* te.
12 qui, *sic for* quid.   erunt, *sic for* erit.   .Bernardus, *in right margin in
red ink.*   13 fames, *sic for* sanies.   16 ruse: *cf. Corpus:* wursum
87b: 16.   17 .Anselmus, *in right margin in red ink.*   20 kykeham, *sic
for* lyke ham.   22 .dauid. *in right margin in red ink.*   malice, *sic for*
malicie.

schal helpe his broþer in al þat he can and may And he seþ his
broþer lye in synne ⁊ couþe helpe hym ⁊ conseil hym ⁊ nyl
nouȝth in þat he is in more synne þan he. for þat is þe grettest |

p. 429a synne þat is. For do i neuer so many good dedes ⁊ i be out of
charite ⁊ of loue al nys nouȝth as to saluacioun per auenture þe 5
lesse pyne he may haue Look þan what it is forto go reccheleslich
forþ and miȝth teche his broþer ⁊ nyl nouȝth I rede þat vche
Man charge þis poynt. Schrift schal be oft ymaked ⁊ þerfore
seiþ dauid in þe sautere.

COnfitebimur tibi deus confitebimur. ⸿ We schulle schryue 10
to þe lorde we schulle schryue to þe lorde twies he it seiþ for
we schulle ofte go to schryft. and oure lord seide hym seluen to
his deciples.

EAmus iterum in iudeam ⸿ Go we efte seide oure lorde in to
iude. Iude spelleþ schrift and Galibe wel forto lerne. And so 15
he ȝede ofte þerfore out of Galile in to Iude. For after bapteme
it is þe sacrement þat þe fende hateþ ⁊ so haþ hym seluen ben
aknowen ȝif it be done as it auȝtt forto be to holy Men often For

M. 324) sum schrift quemeþ hym. þou wilt wassche þine honden twies
on a day. and wilt nouȝth wasche þi soule þat is goddes spouse 20
ones in a week to goddes clene clippynge. Confiteor Crouchynge
Culpynge atte breest al is helpyng ⁊ doþe awai venial synnes.
Ac euer is schrift þe hede of alle.

SChrift schal be on hast ymaked, ȝif it come by niȝth in þe
mornynge. ȝif it come by day schryue hym er þan he go to 25
slepe what Man durst slepe whan he seþ his dedlich fo holde a
swerd ouer hym forto slen hym. Oure dedlich fo is þe fende ⁊ he
stont ouer vs euer more redy whan we ben in dedlich synne to
smyten vs adoun in to helle nere þe gret mercy of god þat holdeþ
vs vp to loke ȝif þat we wil amenden vs. And many þat slepeþ 30
so in her synne ⁊ nappeþ on helle brynk torpleþ in ar hij last
wene. Is þere any Man now þat fel in a diche þat wolde aske red
whan he schulde arise Men wolde holde hym for a fole and
more þan wode. A womman þat haþ forlorne her nedel secheþ

---

3 þe: þ *by correction.*   8 *After* poynt. *two vertical parallel strokes
in red ink.*   10 dauid. *in left margin in red ink.*   11 schulle *written above
line and marked for insertion.*   14 dominus, *in left margin in red ink.*
15 Galibe, *sic for* Galile.   31 in[1] *written above line and marked for insertion.*   torpleþ: t *blotted.*   *Traces of strokes in red ink under* in[2].
34 A *by correction on erasure.*   secheþ: *traces of erasure on* che.
echeþ *crammed together at end of line.*

it onon ri3th ⁊ turneþ vp vche straw in þe hous til sche haue it
founden. A souter þat haþ forlorne his al he secheþ it onon ri3th.
Bot god almi3tty schal ligge seuen dayes er he be sou3th þis nys
nou3th wel done.

Cliircumdederunt me canes multi. ⹋ Many houndes seiþ 5
dauid han bisett me. whan gredy houndes comen nys it
nou3th nede of 3erd to smyten hem away hij wolden elles bynymen a Man al þat he hadde. Als ofte as þe hound of helle comeþ
to 3ou smyte hym on þe snoute þat he ne bynyme 3ou nou3th
3oure good werkes. for þorou3 3oure good werkes 3e schulle be 10
p. 429b fed of god more oiþer lesse after þat hij ben. Smyte | hym þan
on þe snoute wiþ þe 3erde of 3oure tunge þat is telle al þat he
can for þat is hym dynt loþest. An hounde þat freteþ leþer men
beten hym onon ri3th for mychel fole he is þat abideþ til a
morewen for þan he haþ for3eten it ⁊ doþe it efte þe soner. 15
þerfore atte first tyme beteþ þe hounde of helle ⁊ þan he wil be
(M. 326) þe sorer adradd to comen a3ein to þe. Nyne resouns þere ben
whi a Man au3t go sone to schrift. On is þe pyne þat okereþ for
synne is þe deuels gouel þat he 3iueþ to oker. he 3iueþ vs synne
⁊ we hym oure soules. þe lengere we lyen þere inne þe more we 20
fallen in Oker a3eins hym þat is to ben ypyned here. oiþer in
purgatorie. oiþer in helle.

EX vsuris ⁊ iniquitate redimet et cetera. ⹋ Anoþer þe mychel
lere þat we lesen for alle oure goode dedes ben lorne þat we
done as forto haue any mede fore in þe blis of heuene. 25

ALieni commederunt meum robur et cetera. ⹋ Straunge han
eten my strengþe for noþing þat i do is likeworþi to god ne
hym ne quemeþ. ⹋ þe þridde deþ þat is vnsiker for he nott 3if he
schal þat day lyuen vn to euen

ECclesiasticus filij ne tardas qui ad dominum vest' et cetera. 30
⹋ þe fierþe þat is sekenesse. for þan may a Man nou3th
þenchen bot one on his yuel more þan on his synnes

3 almi3tty: *traces of erasure on* t¹, *which is touched up partly covering* 3.   4 wel:
l *partially erased.*   6 dauid. *in left margin in red ink.*   10–11 be
fed: *words connected at end of line.*   15 *Circular cut in MS. at edge.*
19 deuels: *irregular mark above* u.   23 dauid *in right margin in red ink.*
25 Ieremias *in right margin in red ink.*   26 meum robur, *sic for* robur
eius.   Straunge: *traces of erasure on* s.   30 ECclesiasticus: *MS.*
ECtus. *Cf. Ecclus. V: 8:* Non tardes conuerti ad Dominum, & ne differas
de die in diem.

ECclesiasticus sanus confiteberis vt viu'. et cetera. ⟨ þe fifte
after fal. schame is to ligge longe ⁊ namelich in stynche. Now
nys þere noþing þat stynkeþ so foule as synne

SVrge qui dormis. ⟨ Arise ȝe þat slepen, þe sext is þat þe
wounde wexeþ euer more and more and wers to helen.   5

PRincipi constalere medicina paratur. ⟨ þe seuenþ is. þat is
yuel wone. ⁊ bitokener Lazar þat stank in þe byriels to
schewe þat it is strong to brynge a Man out of yuel wone. Oure
lord dude foure þinges er he arered hym. he kneled and helde.
vp his honden. ⁊ wepe. ⁊ cried loude to his fader to schewe hou   10
yuel it is to come out of longe liggeyng in synne.

M. 328)   IVam difficile surgit quem moles male consuetudinis premit.
⟨ þat is hou arewelich he ariseþ þat vnder wone of synne liþ so
longe ⟨ þe eiȝtted resoun is. þat synne nys nouȝth sone ybett
draweþ anoþer ⁊ þe þridde ⁊ þe fierþe. ⁊ so þe last is wers þan   15
þe first for þe depper a Man wadeþ in þe fendes seruise. þe
latter he comeþ vp. gregori seiþ.

Peccatum quod per penitenciam non diluitur mox suo pondere
ad aliud trahit. ⟨ þe nynþe resoun þe heiȝer ⁊ þe soner a
Man bigynneþ to done his penaunce. þe lesse he haþ to beten in   20
p. 430a   pyne of purga|torie and þe more heiȝeþ his ioye in heuene.
þise ben þe ix resons whi a Man auȝtte þe soner arise out of his
synne.

SChrift owe to be done edomlich þat is lowelich lete litel of
hym seluen as þe puplicane dude þat com in to þe Temple ⁊   25
leide hym adoune on þe erþe ⁊ lete þat he nas nouȝth worþi to
loken vpward to heuene so gretlich hym þouȝth þat he hadde
agylt god. And noȝt as þe Phariseu þat com in to þe Temple ⁊
seide lorde i þanke þe. I faste twies in þe wek. ⁊ I ȝiue myne
tiþes of al þat me neweþ by þe ȝere I ne am nouȝth swich as   30
ȝone Puplicane ȝonder And oure lord seiþ þat he ȝede out
synful ⁊ þe Puplican synnes were forȝouen hym. þe Phariseu
was a man of Religioun ⁊ clerk ⁊ þe Puplican was a commune

---

1 ECclesiasticus: *MS*. ECtus. *Cf. Ecclus. XVII: 27*: Confiteberis viuens,
viuus & sanus confiteberis . . .   4 Arise: *traces of erasure on* A.
7 bitokener, *probably for* bitokeneþ.   11 augustinus *in right margin in*
red ink.   12 IVam, *sic for* QUam.   18 gregorius *in right margin*
in red ink. Traces of letter in red ink at edge below us.   24 edomlich, *sic.*
25 *Circular cut at edge (mentioned at 138: 15).*   30 ȝere: ere *crammed*
together at end of line.   33–140: 1 *MS.* a Man of þe commune poeple
with marks of transposition above a *and* commune.

Man of þe poeple. and lyued by his chaffare. Men seen þise
herlotes ⁊ þise beggers done opon hem ragges ⁊ hiden her good
cloþes ȝif þat hij han any. ⁊ crien fast opon þe riche men after
(M. 330) good ⁊ so geten good of hem þus þe lowe Man of hert bigileþ
god al day and geteþ of his goode þat is putteþ forþ his sore ⁊ 5
hailseþ hym by his deþ on þe rode. by his derwore blode. by
his moder teres. by þe mylk þat he souke of her swete tates. by
hir sorouȝes þat sche hadde for hym. by his dere spouse þat is
clene soule. by alle his aungels. by alle his halewen þat he help
hem for her loue ȝe seen also þere a Man ȝiueþ gladlich. alle 10
beggers gederen to hym. Now nys þere noman so large ne so
leef to ȝiuen as hym is. for he secheþ oueral where þat he may
ȝiuen his gode For hym is an hundreþ so leef to ȝiuen as vs is
for to asken hym. Naþeles Man schal nouȝth al way halsy hym
as ich haue yseide bot in nede þan halse hym als mychel as þou 15
may to kepe þe out of synne. And eueryche day þou may charge
hym þus ⁊ saie þus ȝif it be his swete wille nouȝth so straitlich as
whan þou art ytempted hard. Ac so as þou biddest þine bedes
saye it vche day ⁊ þan may þou say it redilicher whan þou haste
nede ⁊ it wil queme hym ful wel. For þe more þattow art aboute 20
forto ouercomen þe fende. þi flesche ⁊ þe werlde wiþ wisdom ⁊
queyntise ⁊ strengþe. þe better it likeþ hym ⁊ þe more he wil
helpen þe ȝif it be so þattow ȝiue al þi strengþe vn to hym. ⁊ lete
alway þat þou may do no good dede of þi seluen bot þorouȝ his
grace And þan ne schaltow neuer ben ouercomen. And many 25
wil saien her holynesse forto ben ypraised ⁊ þan it is yuel Ac þou
may saie what þou doost to þi pryue frendes in hope þat hij
p. 430b schulle | do þe better ⁊ to oþer also in þat ilch manere ⁊ do more
note ⁊ queme god better þan þou heled it ⁊ nolde it nouȝth
siggen. Ac in none oþer manere Poule telde alle his goode dedes 30
in prechynge as he preched for so he seiþ in his pistles
SChrift schal be schameful ⁊ bitokneþ þat þe folk of israel went
þorouȝ þe rede cee. þat we moten þorouȝ rudy scheme ⁊
penance passen to þe blis of heuene Goode riȝth is þat we ben

---

3 men *written above line and marked for insertion.*   6 derwore, *sic for*
derworþe.   10 hem, *sic for* hym.   10–11 alle beggers: *words connected*
at end of line.   13–14 is for *written above line and marked for insertion.*
22 he *written above line.* it *crossed out and expuncted below.*   28 *In*
the middle of bottom margin hand in black ink with forefinger pointing towards
right column.   33 scheme: m *by correction.* e¹ *and* m *probably connected*
afterwards.

aschamed tofore Man þat forʒeten þe schame þat we duden
bifore goddes eiʒen poule seiþ.

NAm omnia nudata sunt ⁊ aperta oculis eius ad quem nobis
et cetera. ⟨ For al þing is naked toforn his eiʒen þat we
schulle rekenen wiþ al. of al oure penaunce sche is þe mest deel. 5
Austin seiþ.

VErecundia pars est maxima penitencie. et cetera. ⟨ Seint
Bernard seiþ þere nys no ʒimme ston so likeworþi to
mannes eiʒen as þe nebbe þat is rody ⁊ rede for his synnes tofor
goddes eiʒen. for it likeþ god almiʒtten so wel þat alle þat ben 10
in heuene han gladnesse þere of. Schrift is a sacrement þat haþ
þe liknesse outwiþ þat it scheweþ inwiþ. for þe soule þat nas
bot dede. haþ ycauʒtt quyk rode ⁊ fair hewe. Schrift schal be
dredeful as ieremie seiþ.

QVociens confessus sum videor michi non esse confessus. 15
⟨ þat is als ofte as i was schryuen i helde me vnschryuen.
for euer ich was adradd þat som what ich hadde forʒeten
Austin seiþ.

VE laudabiles hominum vite non remota misericordia dis-
cucias eam. ⟨ þe best Man þat euer liued here on erþe. wo 20
schulde hym wore and he schulde ben yiugged after goddes
riʒthwisenesse.

SEt misericordia superexaltat iudicium. þat is þe mercy
weiʒeþ euer more to vs ward ⁊ ouer doþ alle his iuggementz
als longe as we ben here in þis lyue. trespas we neuer so gretlich 25
we may haue merci ⁊ we willen.

SChrift schal be sorouʒful. who so seiþ as he can and doþe as
he may. god ne bit nomore. Ac hope ⁊ drede schullen euer be
ylymed to gedre ⁊ þerfore in þe olde lawe it was comaunded þat
two gryndel stones noman schuld departen hem asundre. þe 30

M. 332)

neþer ston þat liþ stille ⁊ bereþ heuy charge bitokneþ þe drede of
god þat schulde euermore be stille in mannes hert. for þat schal
teiȝen hem fram synne as a bonde dogge þat is tiȝed. And þe
ouer ston þat goþ aboute bitokneþ þe mercy to ȝiuen a Man
ensaumple to stiren hym in goode werkes. ⁊ hope to haue gret 5
mede þerfore ⁊ þat we schul suffre here hard to be quite of
harder. þise two noman ne parte hem asundre hope ⁊ drede. |

p. 431a For þat on wiþ outen þat oþer nys nouȝth worþ to vs.

S Pes sine timore luxuriat in presumpcione. Timor sine spe
generat in presumpcione. ⟨ Drede wiþ outen hope makeþ 10
man vntrusten. ⁊ hope wiþouten drede makeþ Man ouer
trusten, ⁊ vntrust ⁊ ouertrust þise ben þe deuels trystes. astow

(M. 334) seest an hunter whan he schal hunte ⁊ setteþ his nettes ⁊ his
gnares. And þan hunteþ aboute for to dryue þe cely bestes
þiderward. for ȝif hij comen þider he is siker of hem. So it fareþ 15
by þe fende whan hope ⁊ ouerhope þise ben his tristes. For may
he brynge a Man in to wanhope þat he hope þat he nys nouȝth
worþi to haue þe mercy of god. þe fende biddeþ no better. he is
þan siker of hym. Oiþer ȝif he may brynge hym in to ouerhope.
so þat he lye in his synne ⁊ haue it in vsage, And þan he seiþ 20
þise wordes god is merciable. he nyl forlese non þat he dere
bouȝth. He bouȝth alle cristen folk. ⁊ he seiþ soþ. ⁊ he is disceyued
in þat ilche seggeyng. He bouȝth alle cristen Men. bot fals
cristen Men ne bouȝth he nouȝth. for whi hij ben out of his
lawȝe. ⁊ non ne schal be saued bot hij þat ben founden vnder þe 25
lawȝe of god þat he haþ ordeyned. And summe seien also. go i
where i go i ne schal nouȝth go al one. And he seiþ soþ God is
boþe lord of helle as þe kyng of Engelonde is lord in his owen
londe boþe of yuel Men ⁊ of goode. þe good he saueþ after his
power ⁊ þe wicked he doþe in his prisoun tyl tyme þat hij 30
schullen ben anhonged oiþer to drawen. And so doþe oure lord
þo þat ben founden vnder his lawȝe hij schul comen to hym vn
to his blis. wiþ outen ende And hij þat ben founden out of þe
lawȝe þat he haþ ordeyned in holy chirche he schal cast hem in
to þe prisoun þat is þe pyne of helle wiþ outen ende. And an 35
holy man seiþ. ȝif he schulde go to helle. he wolde þere com

---

3 þe: *traces of erased abbreviation mark above* þ.   4 a Man *partially*
effaced.   9 gregorius, *in left margin in red ink.*   presumpcione, *sic*
for presumpcionem.   10 generat, *sic for* degenerat.   presumpcione,
sic for desperacionem.

non bot he. For euerich soule þat þere comeþ schal be as a
brennande bronde. And þe mo brondes þat ben on þe fyre þe
hatter is þe fyre. þere ben ȝutt anoþer manere of Men þat saien
were it so as holy writt seiþ noman schulde ben ysaued. and
here hij leiȝen. For alle Men schulle ben ysaued. For hij þat ben 5
taken in dedlich synne hij ne ben none Men for hij chaungen
hem in to bestes kynde.

HOmo cum in honore esset et cetera. ⸿ Man whan he is in
worschipp ⁊ vnderstondeþ hym nouȝth he is likned to a
Mere for he doþe aȝeins kynde in als mychel as he synneþ. And 10
p. 431b summe | seien Leccherie is kyndelich synne ⁊ hij leiȝen apertе-
lich. for þat synne ⁊ vche synne is vnkyndelich ⁊ here þe proue.
God is kynde ⁊ Man is liche hym ⁊ god nys nouȝth chaungeable
þat he haþ made ben chaungeable, þan Man in his owen kynde
is liche god þat is kynde. and whan he doþe a dedlich synne he 15
makeþ hym liche þe deuel ⁊ in þat he makeþ hym vnkyndelich.
Also Men seien it is a synne þat schal sonest be forȝouen. Ac
god ne forȝaf neuer. o. synne by it one for whan he forȝiueþ on
he forȝiueþ alle. for who þat is gilty in on he is gylty in alle for
he is out of loue ⁊ charite. ⁊ god ne toke neuere so mychel wreche 20
in erþe as for leccherie,

QVi offendit in vno reus est in omnibus. ⸿ And god seiþ also
þat heuene ⁊ erþe schal passe ⁊ his word schal stonde. I
rede þat hij ȝiuen gode kepe to þis word þat seien ȝif holy writt
were soþe noman schulde be saued. And here hij willeþ make 25
god fals in als mychel as in hem is. For he seiþ noman may
noumbre þe folk þat schal be saued bot he al one. I warne ȝou
wele þise ben wicked Men ⁊ god ne vouches nouȝth saue þat
his word be spoken to hem þe prophete seiþ.

ADherere faciam linguam tuam palato tuo quia domus 30
exasperans est. ⸿ I schal seiþ oure lorde felten þi tunge to
þi palate of þi mouþ for þe hous is schrewed To swich Men ȝif
þat hij schulde ben yholpen. it most be þorouȝ queyntise oiþer
þorouȝ miracle. For þorouȝ holy writt telle hem neuere so

---

8 dauid. *in left margin in red ink.*   9 hym *written above line and*
marked for insertion.   11 *Upper parts of letters cut off on first line.*
22 QVi offendit . . . omnibus: *cf. James II: 10:* Quicumque autem totam
legem seruaerit, offendat autem in vno, factus est omnium reus.   And: d
on erasure.   31 tunge: u *by correction.*   32 þi¹, *sic for* þe.   34 þor-
ouȝ², *sic for* þeiȝ.

mychel þerof an auntre it is gret ȝif euere schulle hij done þe
better. Ac nouȝth for þan i ne saie nouȝth þat hij ne mowen wel
ben ysaued ȝif þat hij willeþ hem seluen. And þerfore i rede þat
vche Man ⁊ womman payne hem þerto þat hij mowen ben
ysaued ⁊ swiche Men ⁊ wymmen en egre god forto take wreche   5
of hem.

SEcundum multitudinem ire sue non queret. ⟨ God he seiþ
nyl nouȝth sechen after þe michelhede of his wraþþe.

PRopter quid irritauit impius deum dixit enim in corde suo
non requiret. ⟨ þe wicked he seiþ whi an egreþ he god. for   10
he seiþ in his hert he nyl nouȝth eft sechen ne so straitlich as
men seiþ þise two vnþewes robben god to gretlich. for þat on
reueþ god his riȝth dome. ⁊ þat oþer altocheweþ his mercy ⁊
slen hym in als mychel as in hem is. Ȝif þou holdest god to
nesche biholde vn to his aungels þe fairest þat were in heuene   15
p. 432a bicomen þe foulest deuels of helle for he hadde a litel ly|kyng
þat he was fair. And he desired for to be euen wiþ god and he ne
dude it neuer in dede bot he wolde haue done it ȝif þat he hadde
myȝth And here may ȝe see þe proue þan a Man may be lorne
als wel þorouȝ a wille as þoroȝ a dede. wenestow þat he wil more   20
spare me oiþer þe þan he dude his aungels. Also look to Adam
⁊ to Eue for þe bytt of an Appel lyued here. nyne hundreþ
wynter ⁊ two ⁊ þritty. in sorouȝ ⁊ in wo ⁊ neuere lowȝe leiȝtter.
and foure þousande wynter ⁊ sex hundreþ ⁊ foure was in helle
⁊ þere schulde haue ben wiþouten ende ne hadde Ihesus crist   25
dyed for hym opon þe rode. And also look to Noes flod, nere
of al þis wide werlde saued bot viij soules foure men ⁊ foure
(M. 336) wymmen. Also his folk þat he ladde out of Egipte alle were slayn
for her synne. Daton ⁊ his kynde þe erþe opened ⁊ hij fellen
adoun in to helle And Abiron ⁊ his kynde brend wiþ þe fyre þat   30
com of her rechels. Fatt his broþer hij helden aȝein Moyses.
Also Moyses dude honge twenti hundreþ ⁊ mo for þat hij layen
by commune wymmen. ⁊ on slouȝ a Man ⁊ a womman. as hij
layen to gedre. And Moyses blissed hym ⁊ al his kynde vn to þe
nynþe kne. þorouȝ goddes comaundement Laieþ þise in ȝoure   35

---

1 done: *traces of erasure on* e.   5 en egre, *sic for* enegre.   7 dauid
in right margin in red ink. a *on erasure. Traces of letter above.*   9 dauid *in
right margin in red ink. Right part of* d *cut off at edge of MS.*   18 he¹
written above line and marked for insertion.   29 Daton, *sic for* Datan.
31 rechels. Fatt, *sic for* rechels-fatt.   34 Moyses *partially effaced.*
34-5 þe nynþe: e nynþ *partially effaced.*

hertes ⁊ þat schal kepen ʒou fram synne. ʒif þou art in wanhope
of his mercy. loke to Peter þat forsoke hym þries in on niʒth. ⁊
þe þef also þat henge on his riʒth side. also to dauid. to þe
mavdeleyn þat hadd in hir seuen maisters deuels. and vche a
deuel hadde a Legioun as summe of þise clerkes seien sex 5
þousande ⁊ sex hundreþ ⁊ sexti ⁊ sex. ⁊ here a Man may fynde
mercy ⁊ in many stedes in holy wrytt.

SChrift schal be wise ⁊ to wise Man ymaked. nouʒth to olde
sott ne to ʒong prest nouʒth to ʒonge of wytt i mene ne
velaious ⁊ þat he cunne kepe hym seluen, in clene lyf. For hou 10
schal he techen anoþer þat can nouʒth techen hym seluen.
Bygynne att pride ⁊ go so dounward. ⁊ þe spices ⁊ þan þe ten
hestes ⁊ þan þine fyue wittes.

SChrift schal be soþ ne leiʒe nouʒth on þi seluen. QVi
causa humilitatis mentitur fit quod prius nonfuit. id est. 15
peccator. ⟨ þat is he þat leiʒeþ opon hym seluen for mychel
lowenesse makeþ hym synful þeiʒ he arst nere.

BOnorum meritum est culpam cognoscere vbi culpa non
est. ⟨ Goode it is to ben aknowen of þe lowe Man of hert
p. 432b. gylt þere non is. for often we agylt þat we ne wot nouʒth of | and 20
wenen to done a litel synne ⁊ we done a gret synne ⁊ weiʒen it
lesse þan we schulde ⁊ þat is als yuel oiþer wers seie we þan as
ſ. 338) Anselme seiþ.

ECiam bonum vestrum ita est alio modo corruptum vt possit
non placere aut certe displices deo. ⟨ In vs nys no gode 25
dede for oure good is goddes. ⁊ oure synnes ben oure owen And
whan i do þe gode þat god haþ sent me sum yuel of myne is
euere menged þere among and forfreteþ it. for oiþer ich it do
vngladlich oiþer to late. oiþer to raþe. oiþer to litel. oiþer to
mychel. oiþer i lete wel þere of þeiʒ i wolde þat non it wist. 30
oiþer ich wolde þat Men it wist oiþer i do it schemeleslich oiþer
vnwiselich. ⁊ þus euermore sum yuel of myne is menged wiþ
þe good þat god haþ sent me þat litel i may praise my seluen

---

10 velaious, sic for velainous.   he, sic for ne.   14 [A]ugustinus
in left margin in red ink. Left part of first u cut off at edge of MS.
15 nonfuit, sic for non fuit.   18 BOnorum meritum, sic for BOnarum men-
tium. cognoscere, sic for agnoscere.   20 is: s by correction.   24 ,Anr-
selm[us] in right margin in red ink. Traces of stroke in red ink above comma.
vestrum, sic for nostrum. alio, sic for aliquo.   25 displices, sic for dis-
plicere.   31 schemeleslich, sic for ʒemeleslich.   32 þus: s
blotted. sum: s blotted.

oiþer nouȝth seint marie whan swich holy men seiden þus by
hem seluen what may we wrecchen þan saye Poule seiþ.

Cio non est in me hoc est in carne mea bonum. ⟨ In me seiþ
seint Poule nys no good dede þat is in my flesche Nou þan
þere nys non oþer bot take an euen waye of mesure euer bitwene 5
hope ⁊ drede. nouȝth drede hym to mychel. ne hope to mychel
in his mercy þat we ligge þe lenger in oure synnes for hope of
his mercy, bot haue swich drede to hym as þe good wyſ haþ to
hir housbonde, þat is a loue drede for loue þat sche haþ to hym.
sche dredeþ hir to agilten hym. and þeiȝ sche agilt hym sche 10
nyl nouȝth fleiȝ fram hym nomore wil god þat we do. For
agylte we hym neuer so mychel ȝut he wil þat we come to hym
and þe more þat we han agylt hym. þe gladder he is of oure
come aȝein to hym and turne oure hertes to hym for he seiþ hym
seluen in þe godspel. He is gladder of o synful Man þat comeþ 15
to hym and doþe hs penauce here. þan of an hundreþ alle bot
on riȝthful þat neuer duden penaunce. It mote ben vnderstond-
en in þis manere. childer þat dyen er þan hij ben cristened hij
ne done no gode werkes naþeles hij ben riȝthful þorouȝ her
cristendom. also Men þat lyen in her synne til þe last endynge ⁊ 20
þan han grace of repentaunce ac hij ne han done no gode werkes
here whare of hij owen to resceyuen any mede of in heuene bot
þorouȝ her repentaunce and after her repentaunce here wheþer
it be litel oiþer | mychel. for so sory may a man be oiþer a
womman þat hij han agylt her lorde þat he wil ȝiue hem ful 25
heiȝe mede in blis ac god seiþ þis worde.

Etribuet vnicuique iuxta opera sua. ⟨ þat is he schal ȝelde
vche man after his werkes and þerfore i rede þat vche Man
be aboute to do good werkes als many as he mai hym seluen. ⁊ ne
trust nouȝth to gretlich to oþer mennes werkes ⁊ fonde forto 30
wite which ben þe sex werkes of mercy ⁊ do hem for þere of
schal he be chalenged. þat is fede þe hungri ⁊ cloþe þe naked ⁊
ȝif þe þrusti a drynk and herberewe þe herbereweles. ⁊ visite þe
seke ⁊ þe prisouns and seint austin setteþ þerto þe seuenþe
berie þe dede þise þat haue nede. ⁊ ȝiue nouȝth hem þat han 35

p. 433a

---

3 Paulus, *in right margin in red ink.* seiþ: þ *blotted.*   4 good: d *blotted.* dede:
first d *blotted.*   7 for: f *by correction on erasure.*   14 hym²: y *by correction.*
16 hs, *sic for* his.   penauce, *sic for* penaunce.   18 cristened: i *written*
above line.   19 werkes *partially effaced.*   24 it *on erasure.* oiþer¹:
iþer *partially erased.*   25 hij: h *blotted.*   26 seiþ: i *written above*
line and marked for insertion.   27 dauid, *in left margin in red ink.*

ynou3 for of hem gete 3e bot litel mede. And 3if any is þe cras-
ker for wel fare forto done synne þorou3 þat þou 3iuest hym.
þou may li3thlich gete þe pyne for hym ⁊ no good for þou sus-
tenes hym in his synne for wel fare he ne may nou3th tempre
hym seluen. ⁊ also ne troste nou3th to gretlich in her biddynges 5
so þattow do þi seluen þe lesse I rede Of swich men he is more
ioyful þat is þe Man þat forsakeþ his synnes ⁊ doþe here good
werkes mo þan he dude yuel werkes. as poule dude.

SChrift owe to ben willes ⁊ weldes ⁊ nou3th drawen of þe
þattow canst saye Men ne schulle nou3th asken bot in nede 10
one for yuel þat may come þere of bot 3if it be þe wiselicher
asked. Ac his schrift fader owe forto aske hym 3if he wot which
ben þe dedlich synnes ⁊ þe ten comaundementz. and þe twelue
Articles of þe feiþ þat ben in his crede. And 3if he ne can hem
nou3th he is endetted forto techen hem hym. ⁊ his pater noster 15
namelich for his bileue is comprehended in þe pater noster. of
alle bedes it is þe best And his fyue wittes he owe forto reherce
hem hym 3if he vnderstonde þat he ne can hem nou3th. for oft
men seien on olde Englisch. he þat wil nou3th whan he may.
he schal nou3th whan he wolde. ne more foly ne mai be þan 20
sett god terme for þe terme is in goddes honde. And þerfore
recheþ þerto whan he bedeþ it redy And elles þou may loke eft
þere after a good while er it come ⁊ Poule seiþ whan he bedeþ
þe his grace reche þerto wiþ boþe þine handes 3if þou wenest
wel to do austin seiþ.   25

p. 433b
(f. 340)

Coacta confessio deo non placet. ⟨ Schrift yneded | ne
quemeþ nou3th god Ac bettere is late þan neuer Austin
seiþ.

NVmquam sera penitencia si tamen vera. ⟨ Nis nou3th to
late schrift þat is soþlich ymaked Ac better is as dauid 30
seiþ.

REfloruit caro mea ⁊ ex voluntate mea confitebor ei. ⟨ þat is
i schal florie my flesch and wiþ my goode wille schryue me.

FLores apparuerunt in terra nostra. ⟨ þat is floures schewed
faire in oure londe. þat is to saye gode werkes han schewed 35

---

14 Articles: *irregular stroke on left part of* e, *perhaps for correction.*   26 con-
fessio, *sic for* seruicia.   Schrift, *sic for* Seruises.   29 aug[ustinus] *in right
margin in red ink. Parts of abbreviation sign for* ustinus *seen at edge of MS.*
32 dauid *in right margin in red ink.*   35 In cant[icis] *in right margin
in red ink.*   oure *written above line and marked for insertion.*   her *crossed
out below.*

hem in oure londe þat is oure bodies. He þat goþ wiþ good
wille to schrift he doþe a way his foule cloþing þat is synne and
cloþes hym newe þat is in goode werkes. he takeþ god vn to
hym for his delices he seiþ is to wone wiþ Man.

IN libro sapiencie ⁊ delicie me esse cum filijs hominis ⟨ Schrift 5
owe to be owen. noman ne schal biwraie oþer. Ac many
cunnen nouȝth elles schryuen hem bot hij nempny oþer. Ac by
name ne schulle hij nouȝth nempny hem. Robert ne William.
Ac hij schullen saye what ordre he is of Monk oiþer Frere.
Bisschopp oiþer Clerk. Wedded Man oiþer womman for þe 10
heiȝer ordre or dignite þe more is þe synne

SChrift schal be stedfast wille to lete þe synne ⁊ holde þe
penaunce. ynouȝ is þat he seie to þe preest ich am in wille to
lete my synne þorouȝ goddes grace, ⁊ ȝif i falle to come aȝein

(M. 342)   VAde ⁊ noli amplius peccare. ⟨ Loo askeþ god nomore siker- 15
nesse bot goo ⁊ wil synne nomore.

SChrift owe to be biþouȝth bifore longe of fyue þinges.
gadereþ ȝoure synnes of alle ȝoure eldes and so vpward þan
þe stede and in vche elde. and bigynne att childehode ⁊ so
vpward. and þere after þine fyue wittes ⁊ by alle þine lymes sun- 20
drilich. tymen ⁊ stedes. nou ȝe han þe sextene stiches þat ben þe
sextene dolen þat ich bihiȝtte ȝou to tellen ȝou schrift. þis þat
ich haue now seide is bihouelich to alle Men ⁊ is þe fift dele of
þis book

NOw to Men ⁊ wymmen þat willen ben parfytt in goddes 25
seruise oiþer sechen after þat lyf. pride. gret hert. onde.
oiþer wraþþe slouþe. ȝemeleshede of ydel speche ⁊ ydel þouȝttes. and ydel hereynges. fals gladynges. heuy mournynges.

(M. 344)   ypocrisie. mete. drynk to litel oiþer to mychel. grucchynge. ⁊
grym chere. silence breken. siȝth to longe to any þing bot to 30
god. ⁊ to his worschipes. houres ⁊ bedes mysseide wiþ outen

p. 434a   ȝeme of hert oiþer in vntyme sum fals | word of play. of leiȝtter.
schedyng of crummes Lete þinges moulen. cloþes vnwasshen.
⁊ vnsewed. broken nappe. oiþer. dische. oiþer spone. ȝemeles
witen any þing þat Men wiþ faren. keruynge for ȝemeleshede. 35
of þellich þinges schriueþ ȝou. for þer nys non so litel þing þat

---

5 ⁊ delicie ... hominis: cf. *Prov. VIII: 31*: & deliciae meae esse, cum filij
hominum.   15 dominus *in right margin in red ink.*   20 *Under* alle *a*
thin stroke in red ink.   22 of *omitted before* schrift.   27 ȝemeleshede:
3 *partially erased.*

þe deuel ne abreueþ it on his book. nouȝth þe lest drepe of ale
oiþer of ani lykour þat may man to helpe. Ac schrift ⁊ orouȝ of
hert it schrapeþ a way al clene, þan ich rede þat vche man oiþer
womman ȝiue hym als litel to writen as he lest may. And wymmen beþ war whan ȝe gon to schrift of fleschlich fondynges 5
goþ to non bot ȝif ȝe wot wel þat he be gostlich man. bot it be
in doute of deþ. ⁊ ȝe ne may haue non oþer þus ȝe may þan saie
Fleschlich fondynges gon to fer vpe me, þat ich hadde oiþer ich
haue my feblesse goþ to swiþe vpe me for myne foule ȝoutes as
þeiȝ ich hunted þere after, ȝif ich were wyse it ne schulde nouȝth 10
so ich am a ferde þe delit in þouȝth lasteþ to longe ⁊ so ofte þat
it comeþ to skilles ȝetinge ne dar ich bidde ȝou non oþerewise
do to none ȝonge prestes ne to olde. bot ȝif þat hij ben þe bettere,
Ac whan ȝe come to a good gostlich Man telleþ out þan þat
foule filþe so openlich þat ȝou þenche þat ȝe hyrt his eren. 15
Liȝth giltes ben forȝouen ȝou onon riȝth. Alsone as ȝe aper-
sceyuen it falleþ adoun to þe erþe ⁊ seggeþ ich haue agylt lorde
⁊ seiþ, mea culpa, lorde ich crie þe mercy þe preest ne þar
nouȝth legge opon ȝou no penaunce bot litel for swich giltes a.
pater noster. oiþer a psalme. Ac in þe Absolucioun he schal saie 20
þus Al þat ȝe euer don mote stonde ȝou in remissioun of ȝoure
synnes ⁊ haueþ done.

NOw vche man of þe commune poeple ne can nouȝth saye
al þis þat is writen in þis book ne on þis manere. þerfore
hij moten done þus whan hij gon to schrift. hij mosten biþen- 25
chen hem bifore longe bisilich ⁊ gaderen to gedre as hij mowen
⁊ cunnen ⁊ tellen þe seuene dedlich synnes. þe ten comaundementz her fyue wittes hou hij han dispended hem. ȝif hij
cunnen hem nouȝth her schrift fader mote techen hem ⁊ he is
endetted þerto ⁊ ȝe asken hym hem. ⁊ ȝoure bileue he owe to 30
teche ȝou also. ⁊ ȝif ȝe ne aske nouȝth. ne he ne techeþ ȝou
nouȝth þan schal it falle as god seiþ in þe gosspelle. whan þe
blinde ledeþ þe blinde. boþe fallen in þe diche. And so schullen
hij falle in to þe dyche þat is in to þe pyne of helle for ȝemeleshede þat ȝe no wolden nouȝth sechen þat god haþ forboden 35

---

1 drepe, *sic for* drope.　　　2 ani *written above line and marked for inser-*
tion.　　man: a *corrected from* e.　　　5 fleschlich: *second* ch *partially*
erased.　　9 ȝoutes, *sic for* þouȝtes.　　13 prestes: *first* s *by correction.*
20 *After* in *erasure between columns.*　　23 commune: u *by correction.*
29 techen: h *blotted.*　　　34 ȝemeleshede *originally intended to be two*
words. Subsequently connected by thin stroke.

p. 434b ȝou to done. ȝef þe preest seþ þat ȝe beþ vncunnand | ⁊ nyl
nouȝth teche ȝou. boþe ȝe schullen gon o waye I saie ȝou
forsoþe ⁊ who þat seiþ ȝou oþer he leiȝeþ apertelich ⁊ desceyueþ
ȝou boþe in body ⁊ in soule for boþe schulle ben on wiþ outen
ende. For als wel schal þe body be pyned atte day of dome as þe   5
soule as hij ben here ⁊ in þat ilch elde þat Ihesus crist was whan
he died in þe state of þritti wyntere schal vche Man ⁊ womman
arise Man in his lyknesse ⁊ womman in her liknesse. Ac al is
cleped Man in holy wrytt for al comen of Man. And whan ȝe han
telde als mychel as ȝe can. þan haueþ a drede in ȝoure hert þat   10
ȝe ne can nouȝth telle alle ȝoure defautes. ⁊ sorouȝeþ. ⁊ a wille to
leten ȝoure trespas for euer als forþe as ȝe may, so þat ȝe wolde
raþer suffre ded þan do it any more þorouȝ þe grace of god ⁊
þan haueþ a stedfast bileue þerwiþ al þat god wil forȝiue ȝou
alle ȝoure trespas ȝif ȝe be in þat wille þat ich haue iseide to   15
forne ⁊ elles nouȝth. ⁊ here ensample ⁊ proue gode ynouȝ. Ȝe
wot wel ȝif a Man haue stiked ȝou ⁊ comeþ ⁊ askeþ ȝou forȝeuenesse. als longe as ȝe seeþ þat he is in wille forto stike ȝou eft ȝe
ne wil nouȝth forȝiuen it hym þeiȝ he ask ȝou forȝiuenisse And
ȝif ȝe dude me þenche þat ȝe were more þan a fole. Now wiþ   20
euerych dedlich synne þat a Man doþe he doþe god on þe rode
in als mychel as in hym is for he dyed for synne. ⁊ he wot þi
þouȝth ⁊ þi wille þat þou wilt done hym eft on rode. he were a
more fole þan þou by als mychel as he is wiser þan þou ȝif he
forȝaf it þe And þerfore ne þenche noman of forȝeuenesse of   25
synne of god als longe as he ne haþ wille to leten his synne ne no
sorouȝ þerfore for he mote haue boþe oiþer elles it nys nouȝth
worþ þat he doþe. Now on þis manere is þe schortest schrift þat
is i saie ȝou forsoþe Ac a Man may go oft to schrift þat liþe in
his synne forto aske conseil hou he may wiþstonde synne he   30
(M. 348) may haue þe soner grace to leten his synne, After schrift falleþ
to speken of penaunce þat dude bote ⁊ þis is þe sext dele of oure
book.

---

1 *In top right-hand corner of p. 434b off-set of red ink caused by capitals
and ornaments on p. 435a. Certain letters at the end of the first 5 lines are
partially effaced.*   2 ȝe *by correction on erasure.*   gon o: on o *partially effaced.*   3 ȝou: ȝ *partially effaced.*   6 ben *partially effaced.*
12 ȝoure: ȝ *by correction.*   forþe: o *blotted.*   so *blotted.*   25 forȝeuenesse: *second e in the shape of o.*   27 sorouȝ: u *by correction.*

Al þat Men done here of goode werkes to kepen hem fram synne al is strong penaunce ⁊ martirdom to hem þat kepen hem out of dedlich synne for hij hongen wiþ ihesu crist on þe rode as Poule seiþ. |

ɔ. 435a Si compatimur conregnabimus ⟨ þat is to saie, ȝif we scotti 5 wiþ hym here of his pyne on erþe we schulle scotti wiþ hym of his blis in heuene for þi seiþ seint Poule.

Michi autem absit gloriari nisi in cruce domini nostri ihesu christi. ⟨ And al holi chirche it seiþ.

Nos autem gloriari oportet in cruce domini nostri Ihesu 10 christi. ⟨ Al oure blis ⁊ al oure gladnesse mote be in Ihesu cristes rode. þis woord likneþ to alle Men ⁊ namelich þat gon to ordre ⁊ parfytt lyf whas blis auȝtte al to ben in goddes rode holelich. Now Ichil tellen of þre manere of goddes ycorne. þat on ben likned to good Pilgrimes. þat oþer to dede Men. þe 15 þridde to hongen on rode wiþ her goode wille wiþ Ihesu crist. þe first ben good. þe oþer ben better. þe þridd ben al þer best. to þe first seiþ seint Peter.

Obsecro vos tamquam aduenas ⁊ peregrinos vt abstineatis vos a carnalibus desiderijs que militant aduersus animam. 20 ⟨ Ich halsi ȝou he seiþ as good Pilgrymes þat ȝe wiþholde ȝou fram flessches lustes þat arisen aȝein þe soule. þe good Pilgryme holdeþ euere forþ his riȝth waye. þeiȝ he se oiþer here ydel gamens ⁊ wonders by þe waye he ne wiþstondeþ noȝt as foles
ɪ. 350) done ac holdeþ forþ his waie ⁊ heiȝeþ toward his gyst. he ne 25 bereþ nouȝth wiþ hym bot scarslich his spendynge, ne cloþing bot þat hym nedeþ als liȝthlich as he may. þise ben þise holy Men þat ben in þe werlde hij ben þere as Pilgrymes ⁊ wiþ good lyf ledynge here gon to þe blisse of heuen as poule seiþ.

Non habemus hic manentem Ciuitatem set futuram inquiri- 30 mus. ⟨ Here haue we no wonying ac we sechen anoþer þat is to comen ⁊ libben by þe lest þat hij mowen libben here þeiȝ

---

2 strong (*at end of line*): o *written above line representing* ro.   4 *Catch-words* Si compatimur *in red ink at the bottom of right margin. Catchwords enclosed in a rectangle with two heads as ornaments pointing left and right. Hand with forefinger in black ink at middle of bottom margin pointing towards right column.*   5 paulus. *in left margin in red ink.*   8 paulus *in left marginin red ink*   19 petrus *in left margin in red ink.*   23 wo *crossed out after* euere. here *written above line and marked for insertion.*   24 gamens: a *by correction.*   26 scarslich: *erasure above* a.   30 paulus *in left margin in red ink.*   32 by *omitted after* libben[2].

hij ben in þe werlde bot done as þe Pilgryme. For Pilgrime goþ
wiþ mychel trauaile to seche good halewen as seint Iame ⁊ oþer ⁊
ne haþ no þouȝth bot þat he were þere. So done gode men in þe
werlde han no þouȝth bot al vp toward heuene ⁊ hou þat hij
mowen queme god to come þider forto finden god hym self ⁊ his   5
moder Marie ⁊ alle his holy halewen to lyue wiþ hem wiþ outen
ende. þise Men finden seint Iulianes herberewe þat way ferand
Men clepen to. þise ben good ac ȝutt ben oþer bettere. for þeiȝ al
ben hij Pilgrimes ⁊ gon forþ in þe werlde hij bicomen burchmen.
for of sum þing þat hij seen in þe werlde hij leten good þerof   10
and atstonde sum del. ⁊ many þing falleþ to hem þorouȝ which
hij ben yletted so þat more harme is hij comen late hom ⁊

summe neuer, | who is þan more out of þis werlde þan þe goode
Pilgrime þat haþ þis werldes good vnder honde ⁊ loueþ it nouȝth
ac ȝiueþ it as it comeþ ⁊ goþ vntrussed liȝthlich as Pilgrim.   15
þise ben good ac þise ben better þat þe apostle spekeþ of ⁊ seiþ.

Mortui estis ⁊ vita vestra abscondita est cum christo in deo

⁊ cum apparuerit vita vestra tunc vos apparebitis cum eo
in gloria. ⟨ Ȝe ben dede ȝoure lyf is yhudde wiþ crist in god ⁊
schal springen after þe daweyng after niȝttes þesternes And   20
wiþ hym ȝe schul springen clerer ⁊ briȝtter þan þe sunne in his
blis. þo þat ben þus ded. her lyf is heiȝer þan þe Pilgrym. for he
haþ many lettynges þat þe dede ne haþ noȝth For þe dede ne
holdeþ no tale þeiȝ he lye vnberied ⁊ rote abouen erþe praise
hym oiþer lak hym do hym schame al hym is yliche leef. þis is a   25
sely deþ þat makeþ quyk Man. And sikerlich who so is þus ded
in þis werlde þat is þat he ne holdeþ no tale þeiȝ Men mysdone
hym oiþer myssayen hym. haue he sorouȝ. haue he wo. he goþ
euermore forþ ⁊ ȝiueþ no tale þere of In þis Man oiþer womman
liueþ god as seint poule seiþ.   30

Viuo ego iam non ego. viuit autem in me christus, Ich liue
nouȝth ich ac crist liueþ in me as þeiȝ he seide werldelich
speches ⁊ werldelich þouȝttes ⁊ alle werldelich þinges alle I

---

1 *Hole in left margin.*   goþ: þ *corrected from* s.   5 self *crammed*
together at end of line.   6 holy: *traces of erasure on* ol.   7 ferand:
d *partially erased. Erasure between columns touches last letter of certain lines*
from ferand *to* hem *11.*   10 þing: g *partially erased.*   þerof: f
partially erased.   11 atstonde: t *written above line.*   hem: h
partially erased.   þorouȝ: þor *partially effaced.*   12 harme: ar *partially*
effaced.   17 apostolus *in right margin in red ink.*   31 paulus *in right*
margin in red ink.

finde ded in me for alle myne wittes ich haue ʒouen to crist hym
forto seruen ⁊ herien ⁊ louen þus is euereych Religioun ʒif hij
liuen ariʒth as Religious auʒtt to done. þus hij ben ded to þe
werlde ⁊ quyk in crist. þis is an heiʒ staire Ac ʒut þere is an
heiʒer. Ac who stood euere þere inne god it wott þat is he þat 5
seide þus.

M Ichi autem absit gloriari nisi in cruce domini nostri Ihesu
christi per quem michi mundus crucifixus est ⁊ ego mundo.
ℂ þat is he þat seide þus crist me schilde forto haue any blis in
þis werlde bot onelich in Ihesu cristes rode my lorde þorouʒ 10
whom þe werlde is me vnworþi here as þef þat is honged a lord
hel ʒe stode he þat spak on þis wise. þise ben þat no gladnesse han
here in her hert bot whan hij han sorouʒ ⁊ wo for ihesu cristes loue.
þese stonden heiʒest ⁊ þise ben þe good Men þat speken fast of
her lorde ⁊ many scornes ⁊ many schames han þerfore. ⁊ þat is al 15
þair gladnesse ⁊ þerfore hij nyllen nouʒth leten it for non
harme þat man may don hem þeiʒ hij deden hem to þe deþ
þerfore. þis staire is þe heiʒest staire of alle þe oþer ⁊ þis a Man
may haue þat liueþ in þe werlde ⁊ trauaileþ for his mete as
Poule ⁊ Petere duden ʒif hij willeþ. for hij nere in non oþer | 20

p. 436a   Religioun bot lyueden among þe commune pople ⁊ wrouʒtten
for her mete ⁊ ʒeden aboute ⁊ tauʒtten þe commune poeple. þe
pilgrim þat is in þe werlde many tyme he is yletted to gon his
iourne to heuene ⁊ þat is for non oþer þing þat he is letted bot
for he ne setteþ nouʒth al his wille ⁊ al his loue in ihesu crist. Ac 25
þe dede ne ʒiueþ no tale of no schame ne of no worschipe. ne of
hard ne of nesch ne of wele ne of wynne bot suffreþ al in pacience. Ac he þat hongeþ þat is he þat is glad of swich schames ⁊

M. 354)   secheþ þere after al forto do his lordes worschipp þise han hyre
ouer hyre. for hij ne ben neuere gladd bot whan hij han sorouʒ. 30
⁊ wo for cristes loue her lorde, hou schal it ben of hem. þat han
her blis here summe in likyng of flesche. summe in werldes
duele summe in oþer wickednesse. bot ʒif hij amende hem in
þis lyf hij ne mowen neuere come to blis bot ʒif hij forsaken it
entierlich forsoþe by no worde þat men may finde in holy writt. 35
for who so wil go wiþ Ihesu crist he most folowe his wayes. for

---

3 done: ne *corrected from* m.   4 ⁊ *partially effaced.*   6 *Stop after*
þus *in red ink.*   8 quem, *sic for* quam.   12 hel ʒe, *sic for* heiʒe.
14 Men: e *blotted.*   18 þis: þ *smudged.* s *blotted.*   30 whan
crammed together at end of line.   34 it *written above line and marked
for insertion.*

he it seiþ who þat wil come wiþ me take þe croice opon his bak ⁊ folowe me. þat is suffre sorou3 ⁊ wo þolemodelich ⁊ be pacient þere inne. Many seien hij wolden bleþelich þolen flesches hardeschips ac schame ⁊ tene ne mowen hij in none manere þolen. Ac þise ne ben bot half honged on goddes rode bot 3if þat hij ben di3th forto þolen boþe.

VTilitas ⁊ asperitas. ¶ Schame ⁊ tene þise two seiþ seint Bernard ben two ledder steles þat gon vp toward heuen als euen as hij mowen. bitwene þise two ben alle good þewes sette as stakes in þe ledder þat Men gon vp by. And dauid hadde þise two schame ⁊ tene. þei3 al were he kyng he clombe vpward by þise two ⁊ seide bodilich to oure lorde

VIde humilitatem meam ⁊ laborem meum et cetera. ¶ Biholde lord quoþ he ⁊ se my lowenesse ⁊ my swynk ⁊ for3iue me alle myne synnes. Noteþ wel þise two wordes þat (M. 356) dauid seiþ. Se my swynk ⁊ my pyne ⁊ my sore ⁊ my sorou3 ⁊ my lowenesse a3ein wou3 ⁊ scheme. boþe þise biholde in me quoþ dauid goddes derlyng. I haue þise two ledder steles.

DImitte vniuersa delicta mea. ¶ Leue byhynde me quoþ he ⁊ werpe away alle my synnes ⁊ alle my gyltes þat ich be li3tted of al her heuynesse þat ich may li3thlich stei3e vp to heuene by þis ledder. þise two schame ⁊ tene were Elyes wheles p. 436b þat he went vp by brennande vn to paradys. Fire is | hote ⁊ rede. by þe hete is euerych wo vnderstonden þat þe flesche feleþ ⁊ by þe red schame Ac þise two faren as wheles don turnen euere abouten. ⁊ ne stonden nou3th stille. so done þise two gon ⁊ comen sone. ⁊ ne lasten none while þis is also bitokned bi cherubyns swerd þat is bifore paradis 3ates þat is al brennand ⁊ wheleand abouten. ⁊ non ne comeþ vn to paradys bot þorou3 sorou3 ⁊ scheme þat ouerturneþ li3tlich as þe whe doþe ⁊ ne lasteþ no while. And nas goddes rode yrudded ⁊ yreded wiþ his derworþe blode forto schewen on hym seluen þat pyne ⁊ sorou3 ⁊ wo schulden ben yfastned wiþ scheme. nys it writen by hym seluen.

FActus est obediens patri vsque ad mortem mortem autem crucis. ¶ þat is he was buxom to his fader nou3th one to þe

5 half honged: *cf. Corpus:* halflunge *96a: 5* 6 [B]ernard[u]s *in left margin in red ink.* 7 *Left part of* s *cut off at edge of MS. below* ernard. VTilitas, *sic for* VIlitas. 12 bodilich, *sic for* boldelich. 22 ⁊ tene: ⁊ t *partially effaced.* 29 to: o *stained by white substance.* 30 þat: at *tained by the same substance.* whe *sic for* whele. 35 FActus: s *blotted.*

deþ ac to þe deþ on þe rode. By þat he seiþ first deþ is pyne
vnderstonden. ⁊ by þat he seiþ deþ on rode is scheme bitokned
for swich was goddes deþ on rode pyneful ⁊ schemeful. ouer alle
oþer. who so euere dieþ in god ⁊ on goddes rode þise two he
most þolien scheme for hym ⁊ pyne. scheme i clepe to be holden 5
vnworþi ⁊ litel holden by ⁊ suffre many daungers of hem þat per
auenture miȝth haue ben vnder hem ⁊ serued hem. in þise two

M. 358) þinges is al penaunce. ⁊ aȝein þise two ben gladnesse ⁊ blis
ordeynde. aȝein scheme worschipp aȝein pyne delytt in ioye. ⁊
blis ⁊ rest wiþ outen ende ysaye seiþ.   10

IN terra inquit sua dupplicia possidebunt ⟨ Hij schullen seiþ
ysaye in her owen londe welden tofolde blis, aȝeins two fold
wo. þat hij dreiȝen here.

IAcobi. mali nichil habent in celo boni vero nichil in terra.
⟨ For as þe yuel ne han no lott in heuene. nomore ne han þe 15
good no lott in erþe ne þenche noman longe þeiȝ he suffre wo ⁊
scheme ⁊ tene in vncouþ þede ⁊ in vncouþ londe for so haþ many
gentil Man ⁊ womman þat ben in vncouþ þede done. whan hij
han comen in to vncouþ londes ⁊ han no spendynge hij neren
noþing aschamed to done what Men wold bidden hem done. 20
And so mote vche Man swynk oute ⁊ at home rest. Nis he
nouȝth a feble kniȝth þat secheþ rest in þe fiȝth ⁊ ese in þe
place.

MIlicia est vita hominis super terram. ⟨ Al þis lyf is a
kniȝthschip þat fiȝtteþ here on erþe as Iob witnesseþ ac 25
after þis fiȝth ȝif we wel fiȝtten eise ⁊ rest abiden vs at home in

p. 437a oure | owen londe þat is heuen riche. Lokeþ now hou witterlich
oure lorde hym self witnesseþ.

CVm sederit filius hominis in sede magestatis sue sedebitis
⁊ vos iudicantes. Beda. in sedibus qui es in perturbata in 30
iudicio honoris eminencia commendatur. ⟨ Whan i sitte forto
demen seiþ oure lorde ȝe schulle sitten wiþ me in dome ⁊ deme
wiþ me al þe werlde þat schullen ben ydempt kynges kaisers.
kniȝttes ⁊ clerkes. In sete is eise ⁊ rest ⁊ bitokneþ þe swynk þat

5 hym: hy *by correction.*   be: e *by correction.*   11 ysayas,
in right margin in red ink.   inquit: t *on erasure.*   iacobi. *in right margin*
in red ink. i¹ *partially effaced.*   14 *Hole in right margin (mentioned at*
152: 1).   24 Iob. *in right margin in red ink.*   29 dominus, *in left*
margin in red ink.   30 Beda, *sic for* Bernardus.   qui es, *sic for* quies.
in perturbata, *sic for* inperturbata.   33 ben: *originally* bem *with last*
minim of m *erased.*   34 kniȝttes: i *written above line.*   sete: *second* e
stained by white substance.

is here. In þe worschip of þe dome þat hij schullen demen bitokneþ heiȝeschipp ⁊ worschipful ouer alle. Vnderstondeþ aȝein
pyne þat hij suffren here ⁊ scheme for goddes loue myldefullich
⁊ þolemodelich hij schullen haue heiȝeschipp ⁊ worschipp. Nis
þere nouȝth þan bot þolen gladlich ⁊ louelich for bi god hym 5
self is writen.

Qvod per penam ignominiose passionis venit ad gloriam
resureccionis. ⸿ þat is þorouȝ schemeful pyne he com to
blisful arist. nys no wonder þan þeiȝ we wrecche synful suffren
here pyne ȝif we wil on domesday blisfullich arisen ⁊ so we 10
mowen þorouȝ his grace ȝif we wil biseen oure seluen.

Quoniam si complantati simus similitudini mortis eius simul
⁊ resureccionis erimus. ⸿ þat is. ȝif we ben y ymped to þe
liknesse of goddes deþ we schulle ben lyche to his blisful arist.
þat is to saie. ȝif we lyue in schame ⁊ in pyne for his loue. in 15
which two þat he died. þan schullen we ben yliche to his blisful
arist. oure bodies briȝth as is werlde wiþouten ende as seint
poule witnesseþ.

Saluatorem exspectamus qui reformabit corpus humilitatis
nostre configuratum corpori claritatis sue. ⸿ Lete oþer 20
asemini her bodyes toforne honde abide we oure hele and þat
schal asemy oure bodyes after his owen.

Si compatimur conregnabimus. ⸿ ȝif we þoly wiþ hym. we
schulle blissy wiþ hym. Nis þis good forward. wot crist nys he
no good felawe þat wil nouȝth als wel stonde to þe harme as to 25
þe byȝete.

Illis solis prodest sanguis christi qui voluptates deserunt ⁊
corpus affligunt. ⸿ God schadde his blode for alle ac to hem it
is worþ þat fleiȝen fleschlich likynges ⁊ pynen hem seluen fram
synne to wiþstonde it. And nys it any wonder. nys god oure 30
heued ⁊ we his lymes. þan his lyme nys he nouȝth þat ne haþ non
ache vnder so sore akeande heued. whan þe heued sweteþ alle þe
lymes sweten. And þat lyme þat | ne sweteþ nouȝth it is tokne þat
he leueþ in þe sekenesse. And oure heued swatt blody swette for

(M. 360)

p. 437b

7 venit, sic for pervenit. 8 resureccionis: first c by correction. 12 paulus.
in left margin in red ink. 19 paulus, in left margin in red ink. 20 sue:
u by correction on erasure 21 hele and, sic for heleand. 29 pynen:
traces of erased letter under p. y written above line and marked for insertion.
32 sweteþ: sw partially effaced. 33 Small hole in the middle of bottom
margin made by a round instrument. The hole was made on p. 464 and is found
on that page and all down to p. 437.

oure sekenesse to turne vs out of þe londe yuel þat alle londes
laien on ⁊ lyuen ȝutt many. þe lyme þat ne sweteþ nouȝth in
swynkful pyne for his loue. tokne it is þat he leueþ in his sekenesse. Nis þere no bet þan bot forto kerue it þeiȝ it þenche sore.
for bettere is fynger of þan it euer ake. Quemeþ he wel god þat 5
þus bilymeþ hym seluen, þat he nyl nouȝth swete nay god it wot
he.

O Portebat christum pati ⁊ sic intrare in gloriam suam.
   ℭ Seint Marie mercy it mote so be it seiþ þat crist schulde
suffre pyne ⁊ passioun ⁊ haue in gon in to his riche ⁊ on non oþer 10
wise and we wrecched synful wil wiþ eise steȝe to þe sterres þat
ben so heiȝe abouen vs. ⁊ so swiþe michel worþ. And Man ne
may nouȝth a litel cote areren wiþouten swynk. ne nouȝth a
paire schon haue wiþ oute buggynge. oiþer we ben conions þat
wenen wiþ liȝth chep bugge so heiȝe blis ⁊ alle þise holi halewen 15
bouȝtten it so dere Neren nouȝth seint Petre ⁊ seint Andrew
ystrauȝtt opon þe rode þerfore seint laurence on þe gredire ⁊
loþles maidens tetes ycoruen of ⁊ towiþered on wheles. ⁊
heuedes ycoruen of. Ac oure sotschipp is so mychel þat we
holde to wel by oure seluen ⁊ hij weren lyche to wis ȝep childer 20
þat han riche faders þat willes ⁊ weldes to teren her olde cloþes
forto haue newe. Oure olde kirtel is oure flesch þat we of Adam
oure olde fader han. ⁊ þe newe we schulle vnderfonge of god oure
riche fader in þe arising at domesday whan oure flesch schal be
briȝter þan þe sunne ȝif þat is totorne here wiþ wo. ⁊ wiþ 25
sorouȝ of hem þat her kirtel to teren on þis wise seiþ ysaye.

D Eferetur munus domino exercituum a populo deuulso ⁊
   dilacerato a populo terribili. ℭ Folk to lymed ⁊ to torne ⁊
wonderful schal to oure lorde make present of hem seluen.
þat ben Men ⁊ wymmen þat here wiþstonden her flesch likynges 30
⁊ folowen god in sorouȝ ⁊ in wo. wiþ good wille. Hij teren her
olde kirtel forto haue a newe of her fader þat is her Flessche. he

---

5 fynger: *traces of erasure on g.*   10 pyne ⁊ passioun: *MS.* passioun
⁊ pyne *with marks of transposition.*   in gon, *sic for* ingong.   11 wise:
ise *on erasure.*   steȝe: e¹ *by correction.*   15 blis: i *corrected from* l.
halewen: al *blotted.*   17 gredire: d *by correction.*   21 faders: ders
crammed together at end of line.   24 riche *written above line and marked
for insertion.*   25 totorne: to *written above line.* orne *crammed together
at end of line.* n *corrected from* e.   27 Ysayas *in right margin in red ink.*
deuulso, *sic for* diuulso.

clepeþ hem wonderful folk. For. for hem is þe fende adradd for
þi he mened hym Iob to oure lorde ⁊ seide.

p. 438a
(M. 364)

PEllem pro pelle et cetera. ⟨ þat is he wil ȝiue fel for fel. þe
olde for þe newe as þeiȝ he seide. ne schameþ me nouȝth to
assailen hym for he is of þe totorne folk þat tereþ his olde kirtel   5
⁊ to rendeþ þe olde pilche of his dedlich fel. | for þe vndedlich.
þat is þe new fel þat schal schine seuen fold briȝtter þan þe
sunne. Ese and fleschest þise ben þe deuels merkes. Whan he
seeþ þise in Man oiþer in womman. he wot wel þat þe Castel is.
þere in þe totorne folk he misseþ his merkes. for in hem he   10
seeþ goddes baneres yriȝtted vp and þerfore he haþ mychel
drede þere of as ysaye witnesseþ. My leue sir saien summe ⁊ is
it good now to Man oiþer womman to done hem seluen so wo.
⁊ þou ȝelde me answere of two Men þat ben seke. þat on forbereþ of mete ⁊ of drynk and drynkeþ bitter drynk and so wexeþ   15
hole. ⁊ þat oþer takeþ al þat his hert stondeþ to ⁊ sterueþ onon
riȝth. wheþer loueþ hym seluen more ⁊ is wiser of þise two who
is þat nys seke of synne. ⁊ god for oure sekenesse drank bitter
drynk on rode. ⁊ we ne wil nouȝth bitters biten for oure seluen.
Nis þere non oþer sikerlich his folower. we mote be wiþ pyne ⁊   20
wo. ⁊ elles ne come we noȝt þere he is. ⟨ Leue sir saien summe
wil god so wrekefullich wreken hym of synne. ȝe Man oiþer
womman look now hou he it hateþ. Hou wolde a Man bete þat
ilch þing self ⁊ he it hadde þat for gret hate bete þereof þe schadewe ⁊ alle þat hadde þerto any liknisse. God fader al myȝtty hou   25
bitterlich bete he his derworþe son Ihesu crist oure lorde þat

(M. 366)

neuere ne hadde synne. ⁊ we schul ben yspared þat beren on vs
his sones deþ. þe wepen þat slouȝ hym þat was oure synnes. ⁊
he ne hadde nouȝth of synne bot schadewe one. ⁊ he was in þat
ilche schadewe so wonderlich ⁊ so sorouȝfullich ypyned þat er   30
it com þerto for þretenynge þere of he bisouȝth his fader to
deliuer hym þer of.

TRistis est anima mea vsque ad mortem. pater mi si possibile
est transeat a me calix iste. ⟨ Sore quod he ich am adradde
aȝeins þis pyne. my fader ȝif it may be spare me at þis tyme.   35
þeiȝ꞉ þi wille be done ⁊ nouȝth myne euer his derworþe fader.

---

1 For. for: *dittography.*   2 of *omitted after* hym.   4 schameþ:
sch *on erasure.*   7 schine: *MS.* schinen *with* n² *expuncted.*   12 seiþ
crossed out after ysaye.   33 [domi]nus *in left margin in red ink. Traces
of letter* (d) *at edge of MS.*

for þi ne forbare he hym nouȝth þat. Ac laide opon hym so
bitterlich þat he bigan crie wiþ rewful steuen Heloy. heloy.
Lamazabathany. Mi god Mi god my derworþ fader hastow al
forsaken me þine on lepy son þattow betest so hard. For al þis
ne lete he nouȝth ac bete hym so longe ⁊ so swiþe grimlich þat 5
he starf on þe rode.

Disciplina pacis mee super eum. ⸿ þus oure betynge fel opon
hym. for he dude hym bitwixen vs ⁊ his fader þat þret vs
forto smyten as þe moder þat is rewful doþe hir bitwene her
p. 438b childe. ⁊ þe sternesse of þe fader whan he | it wil beten. þus dude 10
oure lorde Ihesus crist keped on hym seluen deþes dynt to
schilden vs þerfro blissed be mercy for whore so mychel dynt
is it bulteþ aȝein to hem þat neiȝ stonden. soþelich who þat is
neiȝ hym þat kepeþ þe heuy dynt it wil bulten opon hym ⁊ it nyl
neuere greue hym. For þerby he may see ȝif þat he stonde neiȝ 15
hym. ȝif it so be þat he suffre so sorouȝ ⁊ wo gladlich and þolemodelich for his loue þat þoled for hym so hard dyntes forto
brynge þe ⁊ me ⁊ alle Men. þat ben vnder his lawȝe to þe blis of
heuene ⁊ take vs fram þe pyne of helle, For al oure pyne þat we
may suffre al nys bot as a litel dust of bultynge. aȝein þe wo þat 20
he suffred, 3e seien many. what is god þe better þat i pyne for
his loue. Leue Man ⁊ womman god þencheþ good of oure good
for oure good it is ȝif we doo þat we owen. Nimeþ now ȝeme of
þis ensample. A Man þat were went in to fer cuntre ⁊ Men
com ⁊ telde hym þat his spouse were sore alonged after hym ⁊ 25
M. 368) wiþ outen hym ne miȝth noman gladen hir sche is so þouȝt opon
his loue þat sche were bicomen al lene nolde hym nouȝth
better liken þan Men seide hym þat sche were wedded to oþer
and forhored hym. ⁊ lyued after her delices.

⸿ Also þe lorde of þe soule spouse þat seeþ al þat sche doþe 30
þeiȝ he sitte heiȝe he is ful wel ypaied þat sche mourne after hym.
⁊ he wil hiȝe to hir mychel þo þe swiþer wiþ ȝeme of his grace.
oiþer fecchen hir along vn to hym to glorie ⁊ to blis wiþ outen
ende ne grope hem non to nesche ne to softe i rede to biswiken
hem seluen. for non ne schal witen hem clene in chastite for þing 35

---

4 on lepy, *sic for* onlepy.   5 longe *crammed together at end of line.*   7 mee,
sic for nostre.   12 his *omitted before* mercy.   13 bulteþ: *traces of erasuer*
on b.   19 fram: m *partially erased. Mark representing* ra *above* m *on erasure.*
24 ensample: a *by correction.*   25 were: ere *on erasure.* sore: re *on erasure.*
hym²: m *partially erased.*   26 ne: e *by correction.* gladen hir: ad *and* h
partially effaced.   33 along; cf. *Corpus* allunge *99 b: 12.*

þat hij mowen wiþ outen two þinges as seint Alrede seiþ ⁊ wrot
to his suster. on to þe body anoþer to þe soule. þat is pynsyng in
flesche wiþ fastyng wakyng ⁊ disciplines wiþ hard weryng ⁊
hard lair ⁊ grete swynkes. þat oþer is hert þewes þat longeþ to
þe soule. deuocioun. rewfuls loue. þolemodenesse ⁊ oþer swich 5
vertuez. Now here may a Man ask ȝif god selle his grace. nys
his grace to ȝiuen my leue childer þeiȝ clennesse of chastite be
nouȝth by meded ac ben ȝeuen of his grace þe vngracious stondeþ þere aȝein ⁊ makeþ hem vnworþi to haue so heiȝe þing þat
nilleþ nouȝth swynken þerfore. bleþelich þolen hard bitwene 10
delices ⁊ eise ⁊ flesch est who was euer chaste. who bred euere
fyre inwiþ hem bot ȝif hij brent. pot þat plaieþ nyl it ben ouer-
laden oiþer cast þerinne colde watere oiþer wiþdrawe þe
brondes. þe wombe pot þat walleþ of | Metes ⁊ more of drynkes
þise ben neiȝ neiȝbours to þat touȝ lym þat hij delen þer wiþ þe 15
brenne of her hete. Ac many þe more harme is ben so fleschlich
wise ⁊ dreden hem so gretlich þat her heued schal aken. ⁊ her
body schulde febli to swiþe and witien so her hele þat þe gost
vnstrengþes and wexes seek in synne. And þo þat schulde
lechen her soules wiþ birewsyng of hert ⁊ pynynge hij bicomen 20
Phisiciens ⁊ bodilich leches, dude so seint Agaz þat ansuered ⁊
seide to oure lordes sonde. þat brouȝth salue to hen her tetes.

MEdicinam carnalem corpori meo numquam adhibui.
⟨ þat is. Flesschlich medicine sche seide ne desired ich
neuere. Ne telleþ men of þe þre holy Men þat were duellande to 25
gedre. ⁊ þat on was ywoned for his colde Mawe to noten hote
spices ⁊ was squaymous of mete ⁊ drynk. ⁊ þe oþer to þeiȝ hij
weren seek nomen neuer ȝeme what was hole ne what was vn
hole to eten ne to drynken. Ac nomen euere forþ what so god
hem sent. ne maden hij neuere strengþe of cetewale ne of gyn- 30
giuer ne of clowes gilofre. And on a day hij alle þre were fallen
on slepe in her gardyn ⁊ he þat was oorne of mete ⁊ of drynk lay
bitwixen hem two. And an holy man fram fer seiȝ hou þat oure
lefdy com a doun fram heuene ⁊ tweie Maidens wiþ hir ⁊ þat on
bare as it ware a box wiþ letewarie wiþ a styk of gold ⁊ putt in 35
þat ones mouþe of þis letewarie. And þe Maiden ȝede to hym

p. 439a (left margin, before line 14)

(M. 370) (left margin, before line 20)

---

5 rewfuls, *sic for* rewful.   8 by meded, *sic for* bymeded.   15 þe
written above line and marked for insertion.   22 hen, *sic for* helen.
23 Agatha *in left margin in red ink.*   35 it: i *erased. Only thin hairline
visible above.*

þat lay a Midde. nay quoþ oure lefdy he is his owen leche. goo
ouer to þe þrid. An holy Man stode ⁊ bihelde al þis. Naþeles
whan þe seek han at honde þat wil done hem good hij it mowen
wel noten. Ac to desiren it gretlich ne schal noman ich rede.
For ȝif þat hij ben angri and desirand gretlich it nys nouȝth 5
good to queme god And his deciples speken of soules lechecraft. ⁊ ypocras ⁊ galian of bodilich lechecraft ac þat on was better
lerned of cristes lechecraft þan þat oþer ⁊ proued þat fleschlich
wisdom is deþ to þe soule.

PRudencia carnis et cetera. ⸿ Iob procul odoramus bellum. 10
⸿ Iob seiþ who þat dredeþ flesches yuel er it come þe soule
waxeþ seek þerþorouȝ ⁊ we þolen soule yuel to astirten flesches
yuel al day. as þeiȝ it were better to þole sekenesse. hede ache.
grindyng in þe wombe þan þole it nouȝth. For als longe as þe
flesche haþ his likyng ⁊ helþe. he is þral vnder synne. ⁊ þis ne saie 15
i nouȝth so þat wisdom ⁊ mesure be euere ykept in boþe parties
þat Moder is ⁊ norice of good þewes. Ac we taken oft wisdom ⁊
nys non. Forsoþe I saie wisdom is þat euere a Man do soule hele.
Ac whan Men mai nouȝth boþe holden it is better take þe soule
hele | ⁊ þat is riȝthwisedome bifore flessches hele ⁊ chese bodilich 20
hyrtt þan þorouȝ strong fondyng soule hirt Nichodemus
brouȝth to smeren oure lorde an hundreþ weiȝttes of Mirre ⁊ of
aloes þe bitter spices. ⁊ bitokneþ bitter swynkes ⁊ flessches
pynsyng. hundreþ. is ful tale. ⁊ noteþ þis ful. þat is to saie þat
Man schal fullich pyne his flesche als mychel as he may þolen. 25
And in þe weiȝyng is bitokned mesure ⁊ wisdom. And þat vche
Man ⁊ womman proue to wirche by wisdom ⁊ Mesure what þat
hij Mowen best done ⁊ hou seruen god. þat is pyne nouȝth þe
body to mychel ne make it nouȝth to craske, bot euere bitwene
two holde it as it mai best serue god. Now we han seide of 30
bitternesse outwiþ. seie we now of bitternesse inwiþ sumwhat.

RIȝth as Nichodemus brouȝth smeriels to smere wiþ ihesus
body riȝth so brouȝth þe þre Maries derworþe aromaunce

---

1 quoþ (*at end of line*): o *for* uo *written above line.*   6 queme (*at
end of line*): e *for* ue *written above line.*   soules: *above* o *curl of unfinished letter.*   10 procul odoramus bellum: *cf. Job XXXIX: 25*: procul odorator bellum.   11 Iob, *in left margin in red ink.*   16 ne
omitted before be.   20 riȝthwisedome: dome *was connected by hyphen
later.*   23 flessches: *MS.* felessches *with first* e *expuncted.*   27 ⁊
womman *written above line and marked for insertion.*   wirche, *sic for*
weiȝe.   wisdom ⁊ Mesure: *MS.* Mesure ⁊ wisdom *with marks of transposition.*   33 Maries: M *on erasure.*

for to smeren his body, Nimeþ now good ȝeme. þise þre
Maries bitokneþ þre bitternesses for synne. For þis name Marie
spelleþ bitternesse as Marath ⁊ Mariath done. þe first is bitternesse of forþenching of synne whan þe synful turneþ hym fram
synne. ⁊ þis is bitokened by Marie Maudeleyne þat þorouȝ 5
forþenchinge and bitternesse of dede bote þe synful is yturned
to oure lorde. And þis is vnderstonden by þe first Marie Maudeleyn. And by goode riȝth. For þorouȝ mychel bitternesse ⁊
birewsyng sche lete hir synnes ⁊ turned to god. And forþi þat
summe miȝtten þorouȝ to mychel bitternesse fallen in to wan- 10
hope Maudeleyn spelleþ toures. Heiȝenesse is to hir yseide.

(M. 374) þorouȝ þat is bitokned hope of heiȝe mede of heuene. þat oþer
bitternesse is wresteling aȝein fondynges ⁊ þis is bitokned by
þat oþer Marie iacobi. Iacob is als mychel to saie as wrestler. ⁊
is ful bitter to many þat ben ful forþ. in þe waie toward heuen. 15
for hij moten passen by many hilles ⁊ wrestlen aȝein many
fondynges for as seint Austin seiþ.

PHarao contemptus surgit in scandalum. ⸿ Whiles þat þe
folk of Israel were in Egipt vnder pharaoos honde ne ledde
he neuere ferde til þat hij fleiȝen fram hym. ⁊ þan wiþ al his 20
strengþe he went after hem. so doþe þe fende als longe as Man
⁊ womman lyen in synne he nyl nouȝth assailen hem Ac whan
hij departen fram hym ⁊ bigynnen to serue god þan he arereþ
his baneres þat ben many temptaciouns ⁊ fondynges boþe
bodilich and gostlich. 25

SAnguinem fugies ⁊ sanguis prosequetur. ⸿ Fleiȝe blode ⁊
blode wil euer folowe þe. by blode is bytokned synne. fleiȝe
synne ⁊ synne wil euer folowe þe þe good Man ⁊ womman is
euere siker of alle fondynges. sone so þat on goþ anoþer comeþ.

p. 440a þe þridde bit|ternesse is longynge toward heuene And in þe 30
endynge of þis lyf whan any is so heiȝe þat he haþ hertrist on
entes vnþewes ⁊ is as he ware in heuene ȝates. ⁊ alle werldelich
þinges hym þinkeþ bitter, And þis is þe þridd bitternesse. ⁊ is
vnderstonden by Salomee. for Salome spelleþ pes. ⁊ ȝut hij
þat han rest ⁊ pes ⁊ ben clene inwiþ ȝutt hij han in her hert 35
bitternesse of loue þat wiþholdeþ hem fram. For ȝif her loue

---

3 Marath ⁊ Mariath, *sic for* Meraht ⁊ Merariht.   17 for as *partially effaced.*
18 augustinus *in right margin in red ink.*   19 Israel *on erasure.*   ledde: dde
on erasure extending from Israel *above.*   20 *After* he *letter erased.*   26 ezehiel
in right margin in red ink. i *by correction.*   prosequetur, *sic for* persequetur.
27 bytokned: by *partially effaced.*   29 euere siker, *sic for* neuere sker.

here were ended þan hij miȝtten comen to blis þat hem longeþ
to. þus loo in eueryche state regneþ bitternesse þat a Man haþ
of werldelich þinges. ⁊ longynge. Nymeþ now good ȝeme after
(. 376) bitternesse comeþ swetenesse. for as þe gospel telleþ. þe þre
Maries brouȝtten swete Smerels aromauntz to smeren oure 5
lorde By aromauntz þat is swete is vnderstonden swetnesse of
deuocioun of hert. þe Maries it bouȝtten, þat is þorouȝ bitternesse a Man mote come to swetnisse. By þis name Marie nymeþ
euer bitternesse þorouȝ Maries boone atte Bridale was water
yturned in to wyne. þat is to vnderstonden þorouȝ boone of 10
bitternesse þat men mote dreiȝen. for god suffred bitternesse
for vs. ⁊ so mote we for oure seluen. And þan wil god make þe
hert þat werisch as watere. þat is whan he ne haþ no sauour in
nouȝth þat he doþe. þan þorouȝ trauaile of penaunce ⁊ of gret
biddinge god it turneþ in to wyne. þat is in to swetnesse of hert 15
⁊ delytt in god. forþi seiþ þe wise Man.

VSque in tempore sustinebit paciencia ⁊ postea reddicio
iocunditas. ⟨ þat is þolemodelich þoly bitternesse awhile
⁊ þou schalt sone þere after haue ȝelde in blisse, tobie seiþ.

QVi post tempestatem tranquillum facit ⁊ post lacrimacion- 20
em ⁊ fletum exultacionem infundit ⟨ þat is blissed be þou
lorde þat makes stille after tempest. ⁊ after weping waters makes
blisful myrþes.

SAlamon esuriens ⁊ amarum pro dulci sumit. ⟨ Ȝif þou art of
hungred after þe swete. bitterlich þo most byten first þe soure. 25

IBo michi ad montem mirre ⁊ ad colles thuris. ⟨ I wil goo
seiþ goddes spouse bi þe hille of rechels. by þe doune of Mirre.
By rechels is bitokned swetnesse. ⁊ by myrre bitternesse. þat is
to vnderstonden ȝif þat hij wil comen to þe blis of heuen. hij
mote suffre here sorouȝ ⁊ wo often he seiþ in þat loue book. 30

QVe est ista que ascendit per desertum sicut virgula fumi ex
aromatibus mirre ⁊ thuris. ⟨ Who is þis þat stiȝeþ vp
þorouȝ desert as a litel ȝerd smoky for þe smel of mirre ⁊
p. 440b rechels. Nou menen hem summe ⁊ saien hij ne mowen haue | no
swetnesse of god wiþinnen hem. ne ben hij noþing awondred 35
þereof. Hij it moten first abuggen wiþ bitternesse of sorouȝ ⁊ of

5 brouȝtten, *sic for* bouȝtten.   13 was *omitted after* þat.   17 tempore, *sic for* tempus.   paciencia, *sic for* paciens.   18 iocunditas, *sic for*
iocunditatis   30 often, *sic for* eft.   31 ex: e *by correction.*
35 wiþinnen: wiþ *on erasure.*   36 it *written above line and marked for
insertion.*

trauaile noȝt wiþ euerych bitternesse. For summe gon from-
ward god wiþ bitternesse ⁊ sorowȝ þat hij han. for hij nebeþ
nouȝth pacient in her anguisch bot chidande wiþ god ⁊ wrab-
bande aȝeins hym ⁊ saien whi fareþ god þus wiþ me. In sory
tyme was i borne. swich wordes hij seien ⁊ many oþer. And   5
þise suffren bitternesses ⁊ sorowȝes ⁊ gon from ward god wiþ
al. It is writen in þe godspel þat þe þre Maries comen to ward
þe sepulchre.

(M. 378) VT venientes vngerent ihesum non vt recedentes. ⸿ þise
Maries þat spelleþ bitternesse weren comande to smere 10
oure lord ⁊ nouȝth goande a waiward Al þat Men þolen for his
loue al streccheþ hym to vs ward ⁊ makeþ hym swete ⁊ soft. as
þing þat is smered is soft ⁊ liþe ⁊ nesche to hondlen. And nas
hym seluen bischett in a Maydens wombe þat is a narewe stede.
so mote vche Man bischetten hym þat wil wel kepen his soule. 15
þat is he mote bischetten his fif wittes streitlich þat hij ne go
nouȝth out bot al to goddes worschip. And þenche noman
longe þeiȝ he be schett fram werldelich þinges whan þe lorde
of heuene ⁊ of al þe werlde bischett so longe hym for oure note
⁊ þan after þoled many bitternesses for vs. It nys no wonder þan 20
þeiȝ we þole bitternes for oure seluen. And also he was laide in
a cradel. ⁊ opon þe rode he was bischett. Now þou may answere
me ⁊ saie he ȝede out of boþe. ȝe so do þou. go out as he dude
wiþ outen breche ⁊ left hem al hole. ⁊ so we scholde do whan þe
gost went out atte last endynge of oure lyf. whan þe soule 25
wendeþ out of þe body þat is his hous. þat is as þe vtter wal of
þe Castel wende out clene of synne ⁊ þan wende we wel out. Al
þis þat I saye of flesche pynsynges nys nouȝth yseide for good
Men ⁊ wymmen þat ben in clene lyf ac for Men ⁊ wymmen þat
lyuen in þe werlde ⁊ gropen hem to nesche. ⁊ for hem þat 30
bigynnen to goo to heiȝe lyf. For whan Men setten a ȝonge
ympe Men setten it aboute wiþ þornes for þat no bestes ne
schulde comen þerto. And so it is good þat vche Man ⁊ womman
(M. 380) sette summe hardschippes abouten hem lest þe deuel wil ouȝth
snacche to hem ward þat he may hyrt hym so þat he ne dar 35
nomore come to hem ward aȝein Ac I rede þat noman ne sette

2 nebeþ, *sic for* ne beþ.   9 vt, *sic for* autem.   19 so: *above*
s *the loop of an unfinished letter.*   25 lyf: y *partially effaced. Several
letters partially effaced below* lyf *on the following four lines.*   26 is[1]
partially effaced.   27 þe: e *partially effaced.*   wende[2]: de *partially
effaced.*   28 pynsynges: y *partially effaced.*

hym bot in Mesure ne charge hem nou3th to gretlich atte first. |
p. 441a Ac litel ꝫ litel. ꝫ so more ꝫ more, 3if þat hij taken al þing in
Mesure. Ac of al penaunce þan is biddynge good. ꝫ wiþ al wo
þat 3ou comeþ þan beþ glad ꝫ leteþ litel of 3oure seluen ꝫ 3if 3e
ben ysette wiþ þise two þan be 3e wel ꝫ 3e mowe þoly daungere 5
of 3oure vnderlinges bleþelich ꝫ louelich. ꝫ þan mowe 3e saie
wiþ þe lefdy þat seiþ in her loue book.

VEnit delectus meus saliens montibus ꝫ transiliens colles.
(My lef sche seiþ comeþ lepeande ouer þe dounes ꝫ ouerlepeþ þe hilles. By dounes is bitokned hij þat leden hei3est lyf. 10
And hylles ben hij þat ben in lower lyf. Now sche seiþ þat hir
lef comeþ lepeande ouer þe dounes. þat ben hij þat ben to
troden here vnder Mennes fete as ihesus crist was ꝫ suffren þolemodelich ꝫ wiþ goode wille scheme ꝫ pyne ꝫ ben glad þere of
And sche seiþ he ouerlepeþ þe hilles þat ben hij þat ben in 15
lower lyf þat mowen nou3 þoly scheme ꝫ pyne ne ben to troden
vnder Mennes feet her lef ouerlepeþ þise. for he ne trostes
nou3th to hem. for he feblesse ne may nou3th þolen swich
tredyng. ꝫ þerfore he lepeþ ouer hem ꝫ forbereþ hem til þat hij
ben hei3er ꝫ leteþ hem haue sum likenesse of hym as it were a 20
schadewe Astow seest þe hilles stonde vnder þe dounes. so
done hij. vnder fongen pyne ꝫ wo first Ac nou3th wiþ goode
wille for hem þencheþ þat it greueþ hem gretlich. naþeles alway
hij it suffren. ꝫ al þat nys bot as a schadewe to ihesu cristes
pyne. ac þe dounes ben gladde þat hij it hane ꝫ þonken it hym 25
fast þat he sendeþ it hem ꝫ þe gladder hij ben. þise ben euere
honged wiþ ihesu crist ꝫ felen þat he feled. Swich a doune was
þe good Poule for he sou3th euere þer he mi3th haue most
sorou3 for þi he seide.

M. 382) DEicimur set non perimus mortificacionem Ihesu in corpore 30
nostro circumferentes vt ꝫ vita Ihesu in corporibus nostris
manifestetur. (Al wo quoþ he ꝫ al schame we þolien ac þat
is oure self þat we beren on oure bodi ihesu cristes deþ liknesse
þat it be seen sotillich in vs. wick was his deþ on rode god it wot
þat þus doþe. he proueþ his loue toward oure lorde. Louestow 35
me. 3if þou loue me loue wil schewe hym wiþ werkes outwiþ.

PRobacio dileccionis exhibicio est operis. Item amor omnia
facilia reddit. ⟨ Ne be neuere þing so hard loue liȝtteþ it. ⁊
softeþ ⁊ sweteþ it. what þoleþ Man ⁊ womman for fals loue, ⁊
more wolde þolen, what is more wonder þan þis. þat siker loue
⁊ trewe loue ⁊ swete loue ne mowen nouȝth maistrie vs as loue 5

p. 441b   þat is fals. nouȝth for þan a goode | Man telleþ þat he knew sum
Man þat wered þe haire next hym ⁊ þe bryny abouen it. ⁊
bonde his myddel wiþ brode bondes of yrne ⁊ þicke so þat þe
swete þere of was passioun to þolen. ⁊ ȝut he fasteþ ⁊ wakeþ ⁊
swynkeþ ⁊ ȝut he meneþ hym þat it ne greued hym nouȝth ⁊ 10
bad his schrift fader often teche hym hou he miȝth his body
pynen ⁊ wepe to his schrift fader ⁊ seide god had forȝeten hym
for þat he sendeþ hym no michel sekenesse ⁊ al þat is bitter for
oure lordes loue al hym þencheþ swete. god it wot þat makeþ
loue. For as he seide oft for no þing þat god may do to hym of 15
harme þeiȝ he wolde casten hym to helle ne miȝth he neuere
finden in hert to louen hym þe lesse. And also it was swich a
womman þat dude litel lesse, þere nys nouȝth bot þonke god
þat ȝiueþ hem þat strengþe. And knowe we þolemodelich oure
feblesse Loue we oþers goode ⁊ so it is oure owen. For as seint 20
Gregori seiþ þat of so mychel strengþe is loue þat it makeþ oþers
good oure good wiþouten trauaile. Here is þe sext dele of þis book.

(M. 384)   SEint Poule seiþ þat alle oure hardschipes ⁊ alle oure fleschlich
pynsynges ⁊ all bodilich swynkes al is as nouȝth aȝein loue
þat schireþ ⁊ briȝtteþ þe hert.   25

EXercitacio corporis ad modicum valet pieatas autem valet ad
omnia. ⟨ þat is bodilich bisischippes is litel worþ ac swete ⁊
schire hert is good vpe al þing.

SI linguis hominum loquar ⁊ angelorum et cetera. Item si
distribuero omnes facultates meas in cibos pauperum carita- 30
tem autem non habuero nichil michi prodest ⟨ þat is þeiȝ i
couþe mannes langage ⁊ anngels ⁊ þeiȝ ich dude opon my body
al þe pyne ⁊ passioun þat body miȝth þolye ⁊ ȝaf my body to

---

5 as: *traces of erasure on* s.   6 goode: *traces of erasure on first* o.   *In
left-hand bottom margin hand in black ink with forefinger pointing to left
column.*   7 þe¹: þ *blotted.*   haire: a *corrected from* e.   20 feblesse:
l *written above line and marked for insertion.*   22 g[r]egorius *in right
margin in red ink.*   24 pau[lus] *in right margin in red ink. Right minim
of* u *cut off at edge of MS.*   26 pau[lus] *in right margin in red ink.*
EXercitacio corporis ad *on erasure.*   pieatas, *sic for* pietas.   30 pau[lus]
in right margin in red ink. u *in the shape of* n. *Traces of* l *at edge of MS.*
31 habuero, *sic for* habeam.   32 anngels, *sic for* aungels.

brennen. ⁊ þeiȝ ich ȝaf to pouer al þat ich hadde ⁊ i ne hadde
nouȝth loue þerwiþ to god ⁊ to myne euen cristen in hym ⁊ for
hym. al were yspilt. For als þe holy Abbot Moyses seiþ. Al þe
wo ⁊ al þe hard þat we þolien in oure flesche. ⁊ al þe good þat
we euer done. Alle swich þinges ne ben bot as loomes to tilen 5
wiþ þe hert, ȝif an ax ne corue. ne a spade ne dolue. ⁊ þe plouȝ
ne eriȝed who wolde holde hem. also as noman ne loueþ lomes
for hem seluen ac for þat Men wirchen wiþ hem. also no
fleschlich pynyng nys nouȝth to louen bot for þat god þe raþer
lokeþ þiderward wiþ his grace ⁊ makeþ þe hert schire ⁊ of briȝth 10
siȝth þat none ne may þat haþ any Moniyng of vnþewes of
werldelich þinges For þis loue ablindeþ so þe hert eiȝen þat he

M. 386)

ne may knowe god ne glady of his siȝth. Schire hert as seint
Bernard seiþ makeþ þise two þinges. þat is al þat þou doost do
it onelich for þe loue of god oiþer for oþers good ⁊ for his 15

p. 442a

biheue, | haue in al þat þou doost on of þise two ententes.
oiþer boþe ⁊ þan doostow wel. for þe latter falleþ in to þe first.
Haue euer schire hert þus ⁊ do al þat þou wilt. haue wleche
hert ⁊ al turneþ vn to yuel þat þou doost.

OMnia munda mundis. coinquinatis autem nichil est mun- 20
dum Apostolus Augustinus. habe caritatem ⁊ fac quicquid
vis voluntate videlicet racionis. ⟨ Ouer alle þinges beþ besy
forto haue schire hert. Ich haue yseide biforne þat ȝe ne loue
noþing bot god. ⁊ þat þing þat helpeþ ȝou toward hym, Austin
seiþ to oure lorde. 25

MInus te amat qui preter te aliquid amat quod non propter
te amat. ⟨ þat is lord þe lesse he loueþ þe þat any loueþ
bot þe. bot loue for þe ⁊ in þe, Schirenesse of hert is goddes loue
one. ⁊ þat is al þe strengþe of al Religioun ⁊ of al ordre. Pleni-
tudo legis est dileccio. ⟨ Loue filleþ þe lawȝe seiþ seint Poule. 30

QVicquid precipitur in sola caritate solidatur ⟨ Alle goddes
hestes ben sett in loue. Loue one schal be leide in seint
Miȝels weiȝe for hij þat most louen schullen be most in blis. ⁊
nouȝth hij þat lyuen hardest lyf for loue it ouerweiȝeþ Loue is
heuen stiward for his mychel frenesse for he ne wiþholdeþ 35
nouȝth ac ȝiueþ al þat he haþ ⁊ hym seluen. ⁊ elles ne kept
nouȝth god of þat hirs were. ⟨ God haþ agon oure loue mychel.

---

5 moyses *in right margin in red ink. Right part of* y *cut off at edge of MS.*
14 Bernard *in right margin in red ink. Letter* (n) *erased at edge of MS.*
33 Miȝels weiȝe *on erasure.*

he haþ ȝouen vs ⁊ more he haþ bihoten vs. ⁊ mychel ȝutt of-
(M. 388)   draweþ loue. ⁊ al þe werlde he ȝaf vs in Adam oure fader And
al þat is in þe werlde he warpe vnder oure feet bestes foules er
þat Adam forgylt it.

O Mnia sub pedibus eius oues ⁊ boues et cetera.   And ȝut   5
al þat þere is serueþ þe good to þe soule biheue. ⁊ ȝut þe
erþe. sunne ⁊ mone ⁊ al þat þere is serueþ þe mek. ⁊ ȝut he deþe
more. noȝt onelich ȝaf vs al þis. Ac ȝutt he ȝaf vs al hym seluen
þerto. so heiȝe ȝift nas neuer ȝouen to so lowe wrecches þe
apostle seiþ.   10

CH Ristus dilexit ecclesiam ⁊ dedit semetipsum pro ea.
  Crist seiþ seint Poule loued so his lemman þat he ȝaf
for hir þe prys of hym seluen. Nymeþ now good ȝeme whi Men
owen to louen hym as a Man þat woweþ as kyng þat loued a
lefdy of ferne londe ⁊ sent hire many sondes biforne þat weren   15
patriarkes ⁊ prophetes of þe olde testament wiþ lettres enseled
and on ende he com hym seluen ⁊ brouȝth þe gospelles as
lettres yopened ⁊ wrott wiþ his owen blood salutz to his lemman.
⁊ loue gretynge forto wowen hir wiþ. ⁊ hir loue forto han in
welde. Her to falleþ a tale a wreiȝen forbisen. A lefdy was wiþ   20
p. 442b   hir fon bisette al aboute ⁊ hir londe al destreued | ⁊ sche al pouere
wiþinne an erþen castel And al miȝtty kynges son was so vny-
mete swiþe his loue turned opon hir loue ⁊ sent hire sondes And
ȝaf hire many faire ȝiftes ⁊ socours of lyues help of his heiȝe
hirde to holden her castel, And sche vnderfenge al as reccheles   25
⁊ so was harded hire hert þat miȝth he neuer be þe neer of hir
loue. What wiltow more he com hym self on ende and schewed
hir his faire nebb as he þat was of alle Men fairest to biholden
(M. 390)   ⁊ spak to hir so swetelich ⁊ wordes so mery þat he miȝth þe dede
areren to lyue. and he wrouȝth many wonders. ⁊ dude many   30
maistries toforne her eiȝen. schewed hir his miȝth telde hir his
kyngdom. bede to maken hir quene of al þat he hadd. ⁊ al þis
ne halp nouȝth nys þis hoker wonder for sche nas neuer worþi
to ben his honde mayden. Ac so debonairte wiþ loue haþ ouercomen hym þat he seide on ende Dame þou art werred ⁊ þine   35
fon ben so stronge þat þou ne may nones waies wiþ outen myne
help atflen hem þat hij ne moten do þe to schame ⁊ to deþ. And

---

1 ȝutt, *sic for* ȝift.   9 þerto: to *on erasure.*   11 semetipsum,
sic for semet ipsum.   17 ende: n *corrected from* r. *Downstroke of* r
erased.   22 al, *sic for* a.   25 as: s *blotted.*

ichille for þi loue nyme þis fiȝth vpe me and so rede þe of alle
þine fon þat þi deþ sechen. And I wot wel þe soþe þat I schal
bitwene hem nyme deþes wounde. and ich it wil take wiþ gode
wille forto haue þi loue ⁊ þine hert my swete lemman. Now þan
biseche i þe for þe loue þat i kiþe to þe. þat þou loue me after 5
my deþ siþþen þou ne wilt nouȝth lyues, And þis kyng
dude al þis. redd hir of hir fon ⁊ was hym self so wonderlich
ytogged ⁊ pyned ⁊ þan sleyn on ende ⁊ þorouȝ Miracle aros
fram ded to lyue. Nere nouȝth þis lefdy ouer vnkynde bot ȝif
sche loued hym þere after in al þing.   10

Þis kyng is Ihesus crist goddes son of heuen þat al þus wouȝeþ
oure soule þat þe deuel hadde bisett in his bandoun. þan as
gode werrour auȝtt to done ihesus crist dude sent first many
messangeres ⁊ fele duden dede for his lemmans loue to proue his
loue ⁊ drawe hir loue to hym ward ⁊ schewed þorouȝ kniȝt-   15
schipp þat he was loue worþi As summe kniȝttes weren wonte to
done hem in to tournamentz for her lemmans loue. so dude
ihesus crist lete þirlen his scheld on vche half as kene kniȝth
His schelde þat wered his godhede þat was his likham þat was
ysprad opon þe rode brode as scheld abouen. his streiȝt armes ⁊   20
narewe byneþen. as by mannes wene þere was nouȝth o fote
brode opon þe erþe. Ac þis schelde ne had no sides. þat is
bitokned þat his deciples þat schulde haue stonden by hym ⁊
ben his sides flowen | fram hym ⁊ leften hym as fremed as þe
gospel seiþ.   25

Relicto eo omnes fugerunt. ⸿ Hij forsoken hym alle ⁊
fledden, away fram hym for he ne halpe nouȝth hym seluen
in þat gret nede þis schelde is ȝouen vs aȝein alle temptacions as
ieremie seiþ.

Dabis scutum cordis laborem. tuum. vt post scuto bone 30
voluntatis. coronasti. nos. ⸿ Nouȝth þis scheld on scheldeþ
vs fram alle yuels ac it crouneþ vs in heuene.

M. 392)

p. 443a

---

1 ichille: *second* l *blotted.*   7 of hir *written above line and marked
for insertion.   Small cross in black ink in right margin probably to emphasize
insertion.   8* ⁊¹ *blotted.*   11 heuen: *first* e *and* u *irregularly connected
by stroke at upper parts of letters. Second* e *partially effaced.*   13 werrour, sic for wowȝer.   14 fele: le on erasure.   18 þirlen: ir blotted.
Above* r *loop of unfinished letter* (l).   20 streiȝt: ȝ written above line and
marked for insertion.   21 was: s blotted.   24 his written above line and
marked for insertion.   flowen crammed together at end of line.   30 Ieremias in left margin in red ink.   32 crouneþ: c corrected from erased letter* (r ?).*

SCuto bone voluntatis tue coronasti nos. ℂ þat is wiþ þe
scheld of þi good wille þou haste ycrouned vs. Scheld he
seide of good wille for willes he þoled þe deþ.

OBlatus est quia voluit. ℂ He offred hym seluen for vs for
he wolde so. Now saien summe whi ne miȝttestow wiþ 5
lesse greue han yredd vs fram helle. Ȝis I wis wel liȝthlicher ac
he nolde for whi forto bitaken vs from euerych tellyng aȝeins
hym of oure loue þat he so dere bouȝth. Men buggen liȝth cost
a þing. þat men leten litel of. And he bouȝth vs wiþ his blode.
derrer þing nas neuer non bouȝth so dere ne neuer ne schal after 10
And al forto drawen oure loue to hym ward þat cost hym so
sore. In scheld ben þre þinges þe tre. þe leþer. ⁊ þe colours.
Also was ihesus cristes schelde. þe tre of þe rode. þe leþer of
his body. ⁊ coloured wiþ his blode, þat hiwed it so fair. Also
after kene kniȝttes deþ Men hongen his schelde in chirches in 15
tokne. Also þe croice is sett in chirches in swich stede as men
mowen sonest seen it for to þenche þerby on ihesu cristes
kniȝtschipp þat he dude on rode for his lemman, Biholde þere
on hou he bouȝth hir loue. He lete þirlen his schelde opon his
side to schewe hir his hert þat sche miȝth sen hou openlich he 20
loued hir ⁊ to drawen her loue to hym.

FOure heued loues Men finden in þis werlde Bitwene goode
felawes. Bitwene Man ⁊ womman. Bitwene wyf ⁊ childe.
(M. 394) Bitwene bodi ⁊ soule. þe loue þat crist haþ to his lemman
ouergoþ alle þise foure. Men seien he is a good felawe þat laiþ 25
his wedde in þe iewrie to aquiten out his felawe. God almiȝtty
leide hym self in þe Iewerie for vs ⁊ dude his derworþe body on
þe rode for vs to aquiten his lemman out of þe Iewen honden.
Neuer ȝut ne dede no frende swich a fordede for anoþer. Michel
loue is bitwene Man ⁊ womman. ac þeiȝ sche were ywedded 30
vnto hym sche miȝth bicome so wicked ⁊ so longe sche miȝth
bihoren hym wiþ oþer men þat þeiȝ sche wolde comen aȝein he
wolde hire nouȝth. For þi crist loueþ more his lemman. for
þeiȝ his lemman haue hored hym wiþ þe fende fele ȝeres ⁊
daies. his mercy is to hir euere ȝare whan þat sche wil comen 35
p. 443b hom ⁊ leten þe fende. Al þis he seiþ | hym seluen þorouȝ Ieremie
þe prophete.

---

1 dauid. *in left margin in red ink.*   3 þe *written above line and marked*
for insertion.   36 seluen: s *blotted.*

SI dimiserit vir uxorem suam et cetera. tu autem fornicata es cum multis amatoribus tamen reuertere ad me dicit dominus. (3ett he seiþ al day þei3 þou haue vnwrastlich done biturne þe ⁊ come a3ein welcom schaltow be to me.

YMmo ⁊ occurrit prodigio venienti. (3ut it seiþ he erneþ 5 a3ein hir 3ain come. ⁊ werpeþ his armes abouten her swire who wolde aske more mercy. 3ut more wonder is. Haue his lemman hored hym wiþ neuer so many dedlich synnes als sone as sche comeþ a3ein to hym he makeþ hir newe Maiden. seint Austin seiþ so Michel Departyng is bitwene knowleching of Man 10 ⁊ womman. and god ⁊ his lemman. þat is þe knowleching bitwene Man ⁊ womman þat Man makeþ of a Maiden wyf And goddes knowlechinge bitwiþen hym ⁊ his lemman makeþ of wyf mayden.

REstituit inquit Iob gen's integre. et cetera (Good werkes ⁊ trewe bileue. þise two Maken maydenhede in soule. Now 15 of þe þridd loue þat is bitwene wif ⁊ childe. þe childe þat hadd swich yuel þat it bihoued haue a baþþe of blode er þat it were hole. michel þe Moder loued it þat wold make it a baþþe in her blode forto helen it wiþ al, þis dude oure lorde to his lemman þat was seek of synne ⁊ so ysoiled þerewiþ þat noþing mi3th 20 clense hir bot blode for so it wolde his loue maken vs baþþe þere of yblissed be he euere. For þre baþes he di3th to his lemman forto wasschen hir inne white ⁊ fair to his clene clippynge. þe first is baptesme. þat oþer is teres inner oiþer vtter 3if sche be yfiled after þe first baþe. þe þridde is Ihesu cristes blood þat 25 holdeþ boþe þe oþer as seint Ion seiþ in þapocalips.

QVi dilexit nos ⁊ lauit nos a peccatis nostris in sanguine suo. (He loueþ vs more þan any moder doþ þe childe for he it seiþ hym seluen þoro3 ysaie.

NVmquid potest mater obliuisci filij vteri sui ⁊ si illa obliuis- 30 catur ego non obliuiscar tui. (May moder he seiþ for3eten

(l. 396) in left margin at line 20

maydenhede in soule *(right margin note at lines 14-15)*

---

1 Ierem[ias] *in right margin in red ink. Only first minim of* m *and traces of the second visible at edge of MS. Traces of strokes in the same ink above at edge.* 2 tamen reuertere: tamen re *on erasure.* 4 schaltow:l *blotted.* 6 a3ein: ei *partially erased.* his: s *blotted.* armes: s *blotted.* swire: s *blotted.* 8 synnes: *second* s *blotted and probably corrected.* 14 REstituit . . . etc.: *cf. Job XII: 23:* Qui multiplicat gentes, et perdit eas, et subuersas in integrum restituit. *Cleopatra:* Restituit inquid iob gentes inintegrum. *184ʳ: 4–5.* 15 maydenhede: ma *partially effaced.* 21 blode: de *partially effaced.* 27 Iohannes *in right margin in red ink.* 31 ysayas *in right margin in red ink. Right part of* s² *cut off at edge of MS.* May moder: y mod *partially effaced.*

hir childe. ac þeiȝ sche do i ne may nouȝth forȝeten my lemman
neuere. ⁊ seiþ þe resoun whi. In manibus meis scripsi ter, Ich
haue he seide ypeynted þe inwiþ myne honden. ⁊ so he dude
wiþ rede blode opon þe rode. A Man knitteþ his girdel forto
haue mynde opon a þing. Ac oure lorde forto haue vs in menyng 5
dude þirlen his honden ⁊ his fete ⁊ his side for þat h nolde
neuer forȝeten vs. Now of þe fierþe loue þat þe soule loueþ þe
body so strongelich wiþ alle ⁊ riȝth sori ben in departyng as
riȝth leue frendes whan hij schullen departen asundre. Ac oure
lorde wiþ his good wille departed his soule from his body forto 10
bringe his spouse in to þe blis of heuen, | to hym wiþ outen
ende þere to duellen. þus ihesus cristes loue passeþ alle loues
þat Men fynde on erþe. ⁊ wiþ al þis loue ȝut he woweþ hir more
on þis wise.

þI loue he seiþ oiþer it is forto ȝiuen oiþer it is forto sellen. 15
oiþer it is to take wiþ strengþe. Ȝif it is forto ȝiuen. where
mai þou better bisett it þan on me. Ne am ich kyng fairest ne
am ich kyng richest. ne am ich heiȝest in kynde. ne am ich
wisest. ne am ich Man hendest. ne am ich Man freest. for so
men seiþ by large Man. þat ne can nouȝth atholden. þat haþ þe 20
honde þirled as ich haue, ne am ich alder þing swettest. ne am
ich Man þat neuer schal dye. ⁊ þus alle þe resouns whi Men
owen to loue me. And þou may finde in me chastite ⁊ al manere
clennesse for non ne may louen me bot hij holden hem clene.
Ȝif þi loue nys nouȝth to ȝiuen ac wilt þat Men buggen it ȝif it 25
schal be selde it owe forto be bouȝth wiþ loue oiþer wiþ sumwhat elles. Men sellen wel loue for loue ⁊ so men owen to sellen
loue ⁊ for noþing elles ⁊ ȝif þine is to selle so ich haue bouȝth
wiþ loue. For þe hede loues þat ben ich haue ykidd toward þe
meste of hem alle. ȝif þou seist þou nylt nouȝth lete it so liȝth 30
chep ⁊ wilt haue more. þerfore saie what is schal be sett þereon
fere. for þou ne may noȝt nempny so mychel. þat i nylle ȝiue þe
more wiltow castels wiltow kyngdomes. wiltow al þe werlde.
ichille do þe better. ichille make þe quene in heuene riche blis.
þou schalt þi seluen fold briȝtter þan þe sunne. non yuel ne 35

1 may: m partially effaced.   2 ter, sic for te.   6 h, sic for he.   14 wise
crammed together at end of line.   17 mai written above line and marked for
insertion.   24 me: above m loop of unfinished letter.   28 ich partially
effaced.   29 it expuncted after ich.   þe omitted after second þe.
35 seluen: l touched up. be seuen omitted before fold.

schaltow felen ne no þing ne scheme þe. ne no welþe ne schal
faile þe. al þi wille schal be wrouȝth in heuene ⁊ in erþe. ȝe ⁊ ȝet
in helle. ne schal neuer þink so mychel þat i nille ȝiue þe more for
þi loue. vn metelich. vn euenlich. vn endelich al cressus wele.
al Absalon fairnesse þat als oft as he euesed hym. his her þat 5
was coruen of was selde for an hundreþ siches of siluer. as
asailes swifteschip þat strof wiþ þe hertes ernynge al Sampsones
strengþe þat slouȝ a þousande of his fon at o tyme wiþ outen
fere cesars prelais al Alisaundres praisyng Moyses hele. nolde
a Man for on of þise ȝiue al þat he hadd ⁊ al þis nys nouȝth worþ 10
a nedel aȝein my body þat i wil ȝiuen for þi loue. Ȝif þou arte so
wode ⁊ out of þi wytt þat þou forsakest al þis fair biȝete wiþ al
manere helpe Lo ich holde here griselich þe swerd of ven-
geaunce abouen þine heued to todelen lyf ⁊ soule ⁊ caste hem
boþe in to þe pyne of helle to be þe deuels hore wiþouten ende. | 15
in pyne ⁊ in sorouȝ. Answere now ȝif þou canst aȝein me oiþer
ȝiue me þi loue þat i desire so mychel nouȝth for my good ac for
þine owen goode. Loo þus oure lorde woweþ vs. To hard hert he
haþ þat ne may nouȝth wiþ swich awowȝer turnen ȝif hij wele
þenchen þise þre þinges what he is. ⁊ what sche is. ⁊ hou mychel 20
is þe loue of so heiȝe þinge as he is toward so lowe þing as sche
is for þi seiþ dauid

NOn est qui se abscondat a calore eius ⟨ Nis non þat he ne
mote louten to hym ward and louen þe soþe sunne þat
was stiewen vp on heiȝe opon þe hattest on þe day. forto sche- 25
wen hou hot his loue was to his lemman forto drawen her hert
to hym as þe godspel seiþ.

IGnem veni mittere in terram ⁊ quid volo nisi vt ardeat. ⟨ Ich
com he seiþ to bringe fire in to erþe. þat is brennande loue
in to erþelich hertes. And what ȝerne ich elles bot þat it 30
brenne. wleche hert is hym loþ as he seiþ þorouȝ seint Ion þe
ewangelist in þe Apocalips.

VTinam frigidus esses aut calidus set quia tepidus es incipiam
te euomere de ore meo. ⟨ Ich wolde he seide vn to his
lemman þat þou were al hote in my loue oiþer al colde. Ac for 35

---

6 siches, *sic for* sicles.   as: *probably anticipation of* asailes.   7 asailes:
i *written above line and marked for insertion.*   19 haþ: þ *corrected from* y.
awowȝer, *sic for a* wowȝer.   21 so² *on erasure.*   25 stiewen: i
written above line and marked for insertion.   32 ewangelist: a *written
above line.*   33 Iohannes, *in right margin in red ink.*   35 hote:
t *corrected from* l. *Upper part of erased* l *faintly visible.*

þat þou art al wleche bitwene two. þat is noiþer hote ne colde
þou makest me to wlaten. ⁊ i schal spew þe out bot ȝif þou bi-

(M. 402) come hatter. Now ȝe han herd my leue childer whi ⁊ hou god is
to louen.

FOrto tende ȝoure fyre þat bitokneþ loue gedereþ wode wiþ 5
þe pouere womman of Sarept þat burghȝ þat is on englysch
tendyng.

EN inquit coligo duo ligna. ⟨ Lorde sche seide to hely þe
prophete. Loo i gadre tweie trewes. þe two trewes bitokneþ
þe rode. þat o tre. þat stode vp riȝth. ⁊ þat oþer þat lay ouer 10
þwert wiþ þo trees weschule tenden fyre of loue inwiþ oure
hertes. þat is þenche hou he spredde his armes to taken vs to
hym. And boweþ adoun wiþ þe heued to grante vs þat we asken
hym. Sikerlich i saie ȝif hely þat is oure lorde finde vs so geder-
end trees to geder bisilich. he wil duellen wiþ vs ⁊ ȝiue vs many 15
folde his grace as hely dude wiþ þe pouere womman in sarept
þat he fonde þise two treen gederande. Fyre gregays men
maken of rede mannes blode ⁊ þat ne may noþing aquenchen
bot Mugge ⁊ aysil ⁊ seide as Men seiþ. Gregeys fyre is þe loue

p. 445a of Ihesu crist ⁊ ȝe it schulle maken of rede mannes blode | þat is 20
Ihesus crist yreded wiþ his owen blode opon þe tre þat schal
make sareptiens þat is tendyng fyre wiþ fyre gregeyns þat salamon seiþ þat no waters ne may quenchen, þat is no werldelich
tribulaciouns ne temptaciouns may deren a Man fro þat ilche

(M. 404) loue. ne hym quenchen ȝif it be wel ytended. Ac kepeþ ȝou 25
fram þise þre þinges Mygge ⁊ aisel ⁊ sonde. Mygge bitokneþ
stynk of synne ⁊ on sonde wexeþ no good þat bitokneþ ydelnesse. And þerfore stireþ ȝou quiklich in good werkes ⁊ dryueþ
out þise two. þe þridd þing is aysel ⁊ þat bitokneþ soure hert.
of nyþe ⁊ of onde. Vnderstondeþ þis word whan þe ondeful 30
iewes offreden oure lord þis soure drynk opon þe rode. þan he
seide, þis word Consummatum est, neuer er quoþ he was i ful

---

6 englysch: ly *blotted.* 9 *After* bitokneþ *vertical stroke of unfinished
letter. Lowest part of stroke possibly expunction mark.* 11 þwert:
traces of erasure on þ. 14 saie: s *blotted.* 16 folde: o *irregular. Traces
of stroke possibly from unfinished letter.* pouere: o *blotted.* 17 gregays:
y *partially effaced.* 18 maken: a *probably corrected.* may: a *corrected
from unfinished* e. 19 Mugge: *first* g *by correction.* seide, *sic for* sonde.
20 schulle: sc *corrected from it.* 22 wiþ: w *blotted.* 24 tribulaciouns:
o *blotted.* 26 aisel: sel *crammed together at end of line.* 32 þis word:
lower parts of letters partially effaced. was i ful *partially effaced.*

ypyned þat is to saie her ondeful hertes duden hym more
harme þan al his pyne. ⁊ ȝutt ȝif a Man haue sore swonken ⁊
atte nende haþ his hyre ȝut hym þencheþ his trauaile wel bisett.
Oure lord tyled here after oure loue mo þan þritty ȝere ⁊ swank
þerfore ful hard ⁊ for alle kept he bot loue for his hire Ac in þe 5
endyng of his lyf whan Man schulde ȝelde werkmen her hyre
look what hij ȝolden hym for pyement of hony loue eysel of
soure nyþe. ⁊ galle of bitter onde. oowe quoþ oure lorde. Consummatum est. Al myne swynkes on erþe. ⁊ al my pyne on rode.
ne schemeþ ne dereþ me aȝein þis. þat hij beden me þus soure 10
hyre of nyþe and onde. Now i saie ȝou for soþe alle swich Men ⁊
wymen þat han swich nyþeful hertes ⁊ ondeful to her euencris-
ten. offren ihesu crist þis bitter drynk and greuen god more þan
hij þat offreden hym þan þat drynk on rode. for þat most nedes
be done for god wold þat it were so. And þat Man oiþer were 15
ondeful now ne wolde he nouȝth And þerfore hij greuen hym þe
more. Ȝif oure enemyes greuen vs ⁊ done vs harme salamon
techeþ vs what we schullen done.

SI esurierit inimicus tuus ciba illum. si sitit potum da illi. sic.
enim. carbones ardentes congeres super caput eius. (⟨ Ȝif þi 20
M. 406) Foo hungreþ ȝiue hym mete. to his þrust ȝiue hym drynk of
þine teres wepe for his synne ⁊ so þou schalt seiþ salamon reclen
on his heued hote gledes. þat is to saie þou schalt tende his hert
to louen þe. For hert is in holy wrytt by heued vnderstonden.
For þus wil god saie atte dome. whi louedestow þe Man oiþer 25
þe womman. sir for hij loueden me. þere is ȝolden loue for loue.
I ne owe nouȝth þere mychel to ȝelden for þou ȝoldest þat þou
p. 445b auȝttest. Ȝif þou saie sir i | loued hym for þi loue. þat loue he owe
þe ⁊ he þe wil ȝelden. Mygge is as i seide þat aquencheþ gregeys
fyre. þat bitokneþ stynkeande flesches loue ⁊ þat aquencheþ 30
gostlich loue. And by gregeys fyre is bitokned hote loue in ihesu
crist as he hadde to vs ⁊ to his deciples.

NIsi ego abiero paraclitus non veniet et cetera. (⟨ þat is bot
ȝif i parte fram ȝou þe holy gost þat is my faders ⁊ myne
may nouȝth comen to ȝou. Ac whan ich am departed fram ȝou. 35

---

1 ondeful: f and l *partially effaced.*　　2 al *partially effaced.*　　3 þencheþ: *above* þ *traces of curl of unfinished letter.*　　5 kept: *small hole in*
MS. above k.　　*Hole in MS. after* he.　　15 womman *omitted after* oiþer.
19 salamon *in left margin in red ink.*　　sitit, *sic for* sitierit.　　33 dominus *in right margin in red ink.*　　34 ȝif *written above line and marked for*
insertion.

i wil sende ȝou þe holi gost. þat is loue. nymeþ now ȝeme hij
loueden so ihesu crist þat was her Maister bodilich þat hij ne
miȝth nouȝth hane þe holy gost for þe loue þat hij hadden to
hym er þat he was departed fram hem. Look þan þou Man
oiþer womman þat louest here fleschlich loue ⁊ han gret desire to   5
comen to gedre. hou schulde þan þe holy gost come to hem ⁊
dwelle wiþ hem, þat han sette her hertes on erþelich þinges ⁊
erþelich loues. whan þe holy gost miȝth nouȝth come to ihesu
cristes deciples whiles þat ihesus was wiþ hem. þat was hym
seluen boþe fader ⁊ son ⁊ holy gost. For hij loueden his body þat   10
hij hadden in present þere hij ne miȝtten nouȝth haue þe holy
gost tyl þat he was went fram hem. I rede Man ⁊ womman be
war here of þat hij setten her loue ariȝth. For bot ȝif hij hane þe
holy gost hij ne comen neuere in þe blis of heuene, And Als
longe as Man oiþer womman han sett her hert in any erþelich   15
þing hij ne mowen neuer haue þe holy gost. þat is to saie bot
ȝif he loue it for god. ⁊ in god, Loue þi frende in god ⁊ þine
enemye for þe loue of god and þe goodes in þis werld in god to
haue þi sustenaunce þere of astow seest þat þou may best serue

god. Haue þan schire hert ⁊ clene loue to alle Men. ⁊ þan make-   20
stow oþer mennes good þine owen. as seint Gregori seiþ. Charite
þat is cherete of lef þing ⁊ dere. vnworþi he makeþ god þat
any þing loueþ more þan hym. He þat wil loue riȝth. he ne may
loue bot hym one. for so he loueþ loue þat he makeþ loue his
euenynge. ȝe. ȝutt I dar saye more. He makeþ hir his Maister ⁊   25
doþe al þat sche biddeþ hym do as þeiȝ he nedes moste, May i
proue þis. ȝe.ʳ trewlich by his owen wordes. þat he seide to
Moyses þat hym moste loued

D Imisi iuxta verbum tuum. non dicit preces. ⟨ Ich had he
seiþ miȝth to wreke me of þi folk þat greuen me. ac þou   30
seist me i ne schal nouȝth ⁊ astow seist it schal be. Loo men
seien loue byndeþ witterlich. ⁊ soþlich it byndeþ god þat he ne
may noþing do bot by loues leue. þe proue here of for Men
þenchen wonder þerof ysaye seiþ.

D omine non est qui consurgat ⁊ teneat te. ⟨ Lorde wiltou | 35
smiten seiþ ysaye weileway þou miȝth wel smyten þere nys

---

1 hij: j blotted.   21 Charite: *traces of erased downstroke below* h.
26 sche: *above* c *curl of unfinished letter.*   30 miȝth, *sic for* imunt.
31 schall¹: a *by correction.*   33 here: *traces of erasure on* h.   35 ysayas
in red ink in bottom margin below wiltou. *Blotted* y¹ *has smudged MS.*

non þat þe holdeþ. as þeiȝ he seide ȝif any loued þe ariȝth he
miȝth holde þe ⁊ lette þe to smyten in genesis.

(. 410)　Festina et cetera. non potero ibi quicquam facere donec
egressus fueris illic. ⟨ þat is whan oure lorde wolde bisenchen
sodome ⁊ Gomorre þere Loth his frende was inne þerfore he 5
seide to Loth wende out of þis cite For þerwhiles þat þou art
here inne i ne may done hem bot good. Nas þis wiþ loue bounden whan he ne miȝth nouȝth wreken hym on swich a cite for
loue þat he hadde to o Man. And þat cite was more as Platon a
clerk seiþ þan Aufrike and Europe. ⁊ now it is cleped þe rede 10
see, what wiltow more Loue is his Chaumberleyn. his conseiler
his spouse. He ne may nouȝth wiþhele fram hir ac telleþ hir al
þat he þencheþ. þe proue here of in genesis.

NOn celare potero abraham que gesturus sum, Ne may ich
seide oure lorde helen wiþ abraham þing þat ich þenche to 15
done. nay he seide on non wise Nou can he loue þat þus spekeþ
⁊ þus doþe to alle þat hym louen. Ben hij nouȝth grete foles þat
leten his loue ⁊ his blis þat he haþ diȝth hem to. þat no tunge ne
may tellen. ne hert þenchen. ne eiȝe seen þat leteþ al þis for a
litel werldelich loue here seiþ ysaye. 20

OCulus non videt deus absque te. que preparasti diligentibus
te. ⁊ Apostolus. Oculus non videt. nec auris audiuit nec in
cor hominis ascendit et cetera. ⟨ þis loue is þe riȝth rewle þat
rewleþ þe hert.

COnfitebor tibi in direccione. id est. in regulacione cordis 25
exprobacione malorum. generacio que non direxit cor
suum ⁊ non est creditus cum eo et cetera. ⟨ þis is þe riȝth loue
þat reuleþ þe hert wiþinnen þat euere owe to ben in worschipp
ykept þis is þe seuenþe dele of þis book.

NOw ichil tellen on of þe siȝttes þat seint Iohn þe ewangelist 30
seiþ in þe Apocalips. An Angel seide vn to hym on of þe

4 ge *in left margin in red ink. Right minim of letter* (n *?*) *at edge of MS.* os
below ge *in the same ink. Before* o *right minim of letter* (n *?*) *at edge of MS.*
Original s *with abbreviation sign smudged by ink. The scribe's intention was to*
write [in]ge[ne]sis. *Another* s *with abbreviation sign written below in the same*
ink.　illic, *sic for* illinc.　　14 ge *in left margin in red ink. Right minim*
of letter (n *?*) *at edge of MS.* es *with abbreviation mark written below in the*
same ink. Faint traces of stroke before e. *The scribe's intention was to write* [i]n
ge[n]esis.　　19 leteþ: *upper part of unfinished letter above* þ.　　21 [Ys]a-
yas *in left margin in red ink. Traces of* s *cut off at edge of MS.* as *written below*
in the same ink. Left part of a cut off at edge of MS.　　26 exprobacione,
sic for exprobacio.　　30 þat *blotted.*　　31 Angel: A *possibly corrected.*
Last minim of an original m *now used for* g.

seuen aungels which þat bare þe seuen Phioles of goddes wraþþe
seide to me. Come wiþ me ⁊ i schal schewe þe þe Lombes
spouse ⁊ his wyf. ⁊ he lad me in my gost vp to an heiʒ moun-
tayne ⁊ schewed me þe Cite of Ierusalem comande adoune fram
heuene and it hadde þe briʒtnesse of golde, ⁊ his liʒth semed as   5
preciouse stones on iaspar ⁊ of cristal. ⁊ it had a gret wal ⁊ an
heiʒ þat hadde þe twelue kyndes of þe childer of israel þere opon
writen. And in þe Est side þre ʒates. ⁊ to þe westward þre ʒates.
And to þe north þre ʒates. ⁊ toward þe south þre ʒates. And þe
wal of þe cite hadd twelue foundementz. ⁊ in hem were twelue   10

names writen of þe apostles. ⁊ of þe lombe. And he þat spak | wiþ
me hadde a ʒerd of golde for to meten þe cite and þe ʒates. ⁊ þe
wal. And þe Citee was square and as brode as it was longe and
he mett þe cite wiþ a ʒerd of gold and þe lengþe of þe Cite was
twelue þousan pase abouten And þe lengþe ⁊ þe heiʒt ⁊ þe   15
brede ben euene. and he mette þe walles an hundreþ ⁊ foure ⁊
fourty coutes on heiʒth of Man ⁊ of Aungel.

Þat þe Aungel ledde me seint iohn seiþ to þe grete moun-
tayne ⁊ heiʒe forto see þe spouse of þe lombe bitokneþ hem
þat ben þorouʒ þe grace of god in heiʒenesse of lyf mowen haue   20
knoweynge of þe glorie ⁊ of þe blisse of holy chirche. þat liʒth
as of preciouse stones of iasper ⁊ of cris of iasper ⁊ of cristal
bitokneþ vertu of holy chirche þat is confermed in þe grenehed
of þe bileue ⁊ in clennesse of Baptesme ⁊ in hete of þe werk of
schrift. þe gret heiʒe wal bitokneþ ihesu crist þat to alle is keper.   25
þe xij ʒates bitokneþ þe xij apostles. ⁊ þe xij names writen
bitokneþ þe xij olde faders of þe olde lawe patriarkes ⁊ prophetes
þat prophecieden er þe apostles precheden. þe þre ʒates to þe
Eastward bitokneþ þe lawʒe of þe trinite þat was telde vn to þe
iewes of which he was born of as vn to his manhede. þe þre   30
ʒates of þe south bitokneþ þe prechinge þat was preched to þe
sarsines þe þre ʒates of þe norþ bitokneþ hem þat comen to
bileue siþþen þat ihesus crist took flesche and blode. þe þre

---

11 apostles: ostl *smudged.*   15 pase: s *blotted.*   18 to: t *partially
effaced.*   22 of jasper ⁊ of cris (*at end of line*), sic.   22–8 *This section
is thinner and darker than the rest of the page, which led Påhlsson (pp. xiii
n. 1 and 194 n. 4) to assume that it was a large erasure. It was pointed out to
Påhlsson by Anna Paues in a letter referred to in Påhlsson, p. xiii n. 1, that
this section is not an erasure. With the aid of the ultra-violet lamp I have been
able to corroborate the latter opinion.*   27–8 *Holes (mentioned at 175: 5)
can be seen below first* p *in* prophetes *and after* precheden.

ȝates of þe west bitokneþ þe prechinge þat hely ⁊ Ennok
schullen prechen ⁊ turnen þe folk to god. þe brede of þe Cite
bitokneþ þe faiþ of ihesu crist. þe xij foundementz þat þe xij
names were writen inne bitokneþ þe twelue apostles And þe
lombe bitokneþ þe xij Patriarkes þat helden vp þe faiþ of 5
ihesu crist þat in her tyme was to comen þat þe xij apostles
helden after his comyng. þat is þat we holde now. þe reed of
gold bitokneþ holy wrytt in which þe witt of god is ⁊ þat is
tokned by þe gold. þe mesure of þe citee bitokneþ þat oure
lorde ȝiueþ þe lawȝe in holy chirche as vcheon may bere ⁊ 10
ordeinde ⁊ deuised þe degre in holy chirche þe which vche Man
owe wel to kepen as maydenhode. ⁊ clennesse in widewehode ⁊
riȝthful weddynge. þe foure sides of þe cite bitokneþ þe stedfast bileue. hope. ⁊ charite. ⁊ good werkes. þe more þat Men
bileuen. þe more men taken. þe more þat Men hopen þe more 15
Men louen. þe more þat Men louen þe more men done in werk
And þis is þe lengþe ⁊ þe brede ⁊ þe heiȝtte þat ben euen. For
by þe lengþe is bitokned þe longe lastynge vn to his lyues ende.

p. 447a þat þe angel mett þe wal an hundreþ ⁊ four ⁊ fourty | Coutes
bitokneþ perfeccioun in good werkes after þe ten comaude- 20
mentes of god ⁊ þe gospelles þorouȝ which man comeþ to per-
feccion of aungel ⁊ þat is bitokned by þe mesure of Man ⁊
Aungel.

Þᴇ wal is of iasper ⁊ þe cite in hym self is al gold tried liche vn
to briȝth glas ⁊ clene. þe foundementz ben sette ful of al 25
manere preciouse stones. þe first foundement is Iasper. þe
secounde Saphire. þe þridde Calcedoyne. þe fierþe Emeraude.
þe fift Sardoniche. þe sext Sardyne. þe seuenþe Gristolite. þe
eiȝtteþ Beryl. þe nynþe Topas, þe tienþe Crisopas. þe elleuenþe
Iacynkte, ⁊ þe twelfþe Amatiste. 30

Þᴀt þe wal is of iasper ⁊ þe Cite of golde bitokneþ hem þat
schulden gouernen oþer in holy chirche schulden ben of
stedfaster bileue and of heiȝer lyf as þe iasper is aourned wiþ
gold þat þe foundementz of þe Cite weren bisett wiþ preciouse
stones bitokneþ þat þe Patriarkes weren alful of gode vertuz. 35
Iasper þat is vertuouse bitokneþ stedfast bileue As Abraham
was. Saphire þat haþ þe colour of þe ayre bitokneþ hem þat ben
in heiȝe hope as seint Poule was þat seide þat oure conuersacioun

---

3 xij²: *traces of erasure on* i.   18 his, *sic for* þis?   20-1 comau-
dementes, *sic for* comaundementes.   32 oþer, þ *by correction.*

was in heuene. Calcedoyne þat haþ þe colour of gold ⁊ wexeþ in
ynde bitokneþ hem þat ben in soþefast faiþ ⁊ charite ⁊ folowen
þe wayes of Ihesu crist þat comeþ out of þe est. Iacinkte þat
chaungeþ wiþ þe ayre Ac in briȝtnesse it is clere ⁊ amydward
derk bitokneþ þe wise Maisters in holy chirche þat cunnen 5
stable Men þat ben vnstable Amatiste þat is a purpre ⁊ haþ þe
colour medle of violet ⁊ of Rose ⁊ kastes a flambe fram hym
bitokneþ hem þat han Memorie of þe kyngdom of heuene and
desiren þe felawschippes of aungels ⁊ Martirs ⁊ confessours ⁊
þere of hij han þe colour medle as purpre. violet ⁊ Rose ⁊ putten 10
her charite to her enemyes and bisechen for hem. And in þe
tuelue ȝates ben tuelue Margarites And þe stretes of þe cite ben
of gold clere as glas. ⁊ i ne seiȝ no temple in þe cite. And þe
aungels of þe cite hane no myster of sunne ne of Moone for þe
briȝtnesse of god it liȝtteþ ⁊ þe lombe is his Lanterne. ⁊ þe folk 15
schal gon in his liȝth. And þe kynges of erþe schulle beren in
hym her glorie ⁊ her honoure. And þe ȝates ne schulle nouȝth be
schett on niȝth. for þere ne schal be no niȝth ne no foule þing
ne schal come þere inne ne non þat makeþ foule lesynges ne non
bot his name be writen in þe book of lif of þe lombe. 20

Þ At þere ben xij Margarites in þe ȝates bitokneþ hem which
oþer schul comen in to holy chirche schul ben clere of
p. 447b vertuz. þe stretes of þe cite bitokneþ | symple folk in holy chirche
þat ben abrode in þe werld ⁊ han her wyues ⁊ her riches.
Hij schulle ben als clene as gold þorouȝ werkes of charite þat hij 25
schulle comen to þorouȝ clere vnderstondynge. Hij schulle bene
clere as glas þorouȝ Innocence of baptesme. oiþer þorouȝ
verray schrift in riȝth bileue. þat he ne seiþ no temple þere inne
bitokneþ þat holy chirche schal haue no myster of orisouns ne of
sacrifise whan it is glorified ne it ne haþ no myster of sunne ne of 30
moone þat is to saie it ne schal haue no myster of prechour. ne
of prelate forto techen it ⁊ kepen it. þat þe Men schulle gon in
his liȝth and þe kynges schulle brynge to hem her glorie bitokneþ
þat aȝein þe endyng of þe werlde schal wexen religioun ⁊ schulle
forsaken erþelich blisses for hope of heiȝe blis þat euere schal 35
laste. And þe ȝates ne schullen nouȝth ben yschett on niȝth

---

6 a, *sic for* as.   8 han: *traces of erasure on* n.   16 schulle: ll
blotted.   28 bileue: *smudge under* b.   30 no: *originally* m
with last minim altered to o.   31 no: *the last minim of* m *changed*
into o.   33 hem, *sic for* hym.

bitokneþ þat no tribulacioun ne anguisch. ne destourbaunce as
oure lorde suffred here in þis lyf. þat no filþe ne schal come
þere ne non bot his name be writen in þe book of lyf of þe lombe
bitokneþ þat non ne schal entren bot he be clene þorou3 blode of
Ihesu crist ꝫ þorou3 þe sacrement of holy chirche. And bot 3if 5
he haue ordeynde his lyf to ihesu crist here in erþe þat was
writen for vs opon þe croice He schewed me a clere flode as
Cristal þat com out of þe sege of god ꝫ of þe Lombe Amyd þe
strete of þe cite. ꝫ a boþe halue þe Flum is þe tree of lyf þat
bereþ fair fruytt ꝫ vche moneþe 3eldeþ his fruyt. And þe leues 10
of þe tre ben to helþe of Men. And neuer after ne schal be no
malisoun. And þe sege of god ꝫ of þe lombe schal be þerinne.
and his seruauntz schulle ben seruande hym ꝫ hij schulle ben in
his face. ꝫ his name schal be in her forheuedes. And ni3th ne
schal nomore be. And it ne schal haue no mister of li3th. ne of 15
lanterne ne of sunne for þe lorde god schal li3tten it ꝫ hij schulle
regnen wiþ outen ende.

By þe Flum of þe water of lyf is bitokned þe ioye þat neuer
schal faile. By þe sege of god bitokneþ halewen þorou3
whiche þe oþer comen to grace ꝫ to glorie. And þat is þat þe 20
Flum comeþ fram þe sege of god ꝫ of þe lombe. By þe watere of
lyf þat is clere as cristal bitokneþ þe glorie Forþi þat þorou3
water of baptesme it was wunnen to Man. þat o party of þe
flum bitokneþ þe folk þat were bifore er cristendom come. And
þat oþer partie þe Men þat comen in þe newe lawe. And opon 25
boþe parties was þe tre of lyf for boþe þat on ꝫ þat oþer ben
saued þorou3 þe bileue of þe croice þat is preched þorou3 þe xij
apostles. þat it 3eldeþ vche moneþ his fruyt. bitokneþ þat
p. 448a   þorou3 þe patriarkes | ꝫ þe prophetes. ꝫ þe apostles in al tymes
were summe brou3th to þe ri3th bileue. þe leues of þe tre 30
bitokneþ þe comaundementz of ihesu crist in þe gospel. þat ben
worþe to helþe of men 3if hij ben ykepte þat neueremore ne
schal be no wariyng in þe cite bitokneþ þat neuer after ne schal
be no synne ne pyne for synne þat goddes sege ꝫ þe Lombe
schal ben in þe tre. bitokneþ þat alle we schulle ben saued þorou3 35
ihesu crist on þe croice. And none ne may come to blis bot þere

---

10 fruytt: y *by correction.*   11 of¹ *partially effaced.*   ne: n *partially*
effaced.   15 nomore: or *crammed together.* o *probably corrected from*
another letter.   16 for: o *partially effaced.*   20 whiche: he *smudged.*
28 3eldeþ: d *smudged.*   vche: vch *on erasure.*

þorou3 And we ben his seruauntz ⁊ þere we schulle seruen hym
wiþ aungels wiþ outen ende. þat he seide hij schulle seen his
face ⁊ his name schal be writen in her forhede. þat bitokneþ þat
is writen in þe gospel þat is lyf þat euer schal laste. þat he be
knowen of god þat is soþefast Ihesus crist þat þou sentest. And 5
in anoþer stede it seiþ he þat abow3eþ hym þoro3 me i schal
abow3e hym by fore my fader in heuen, And þat is þat he seiþ
hij ne schulle haue no mister of li3th ne of lanterne nc of sunne
as it is seide bifore. And þe Aungel seide me þise wordes ben
ri3th soþe write hem. And þe lord god of spiritz þat sent his 10
aungels to his prophetes. forto schewe to his seruauntz þing þat
sone most be done. ⁊ stonde þou i come hastilich. blissed he is
þat kepeþ þise wordes ⁊ þe prophecie of þis boke. And i ion
after þat i hadd herd þis fel adoune forto honouren þe aungel
þat hadde schewed me þis. And seide to me loke þat þou ne do 15
it nou3t for ich am goddes seruaunt astow art. Ioye ⁊ blis schal
be to hem þat kepen þise wordes of þis boke ⁊ worschipen god,
What it wolde menen may men sone vnderstonden by þat þat
is seide bifore ⁊ þerfore i nyl nou3th rehercen it. And seint Ion
seiþ in þat cite schal come none houndes. þat ben mysbileuand 20
Men þat done as þe hounde doþe. whan he haþ eten to mychel
he casteþ it ⁊ goþ a3ein ⁊ eteþ it. So done mysbileuand Men
schryuen hem ⁊ resceyuen ihesu crist ⁊ holden euere forþ her
synne. þise ne schulle nou3th comen in þat cite For hij ben wers
þan oiþer Iewe oiþer Sarazene and greuen god wel more. ne 25
Mansleers. ne lei3ers. oiþer þo þat dien here in dedlich synne.
hij ne come nou3th in þat cite. ne non bot 3if he entre in by þe
3ates. þat is bot 3if he do as holy chirche biddeþ hym he ne may
neuer come þere inne.

(M. 412) NOw to Men ⁊ wymmen þat ben bischett hij ne schullen ben 30
yhouseled bot fiftene siþes in þe 3ere. at Mid wynterday.
þe xij day. candelmes day. þe sonenday mydway bitwene þat
⁊ estre oiþer opon oure lefdy day 3if it be nei3 þat sonenday.
estre day þe þrid sonenday þere after. holy þursday. wytsonen-
p. 448b day. Midsomerday. seint Marie day þe Mau|deleyn. þe assump- 35
cioun of oure lefdy. þe natiuite of hir. seint Mi33els day. alle
Halewen day seint andrew day. A3ein alle þise dayes beþ clene

---

5 of blotted.   10 þat, *sic for* haþ.   25 greuen *written above line
and marked for insertion.*   26 lei3ers: *dot below first* e, *probably not
intended to be expunction mark.*

schriuen ⁊ takeþ disciplynes of ȝoure seluen and of none oþer.
⁊ forgoþ ȝoure pitaunce a day fram ester to holy þursday. In
heruest eteþ ilche day þries bot friday one ⁊ ymbryng dayes. ⁊
vigiles. þe goyng dayes ne in þe aduent ne schulle ȝe nouȝth bot
nede it make ete twies.   5

Þ E oþer half ȝere ȝe schulle fasten al out bot seuen daies ⁊ ȝe
ne schulle ete no flesch bot sekenesse it make. bot ȝe haue
leue ne fasteþ nouȝth to bred ⁊ watere. and summe ancres maken

I. 414) her boord wiþ her gestes ⁊ þat is mest aȝeins ancres ordre ⁊
vncomelich. Men han ofte herd þat þe ded spak wiþ þe quyk. Ac   10
þat hij eten wiþ hem hane men nouȝth herd of. Hij ne schulle
make no gestenynges. for it wolde oiþer while letten hem of
heuenlich þouȝttes. Hij han chosen Maries dele þe Maudeleyn
⁊ þerfore hij owen to ȝiuen her hertes to noþing bot to god. And
ȝif any blameþ hem god wil weren hem as he dude þe Mavde-   15
leyn. ȝif hij han rentes to lyuen by. sende hij þan out her almes
M. 416, priuelich. Bestes ne schulle hij none habben bot a cat. ne chaff-
I. 418) aren ne schulle hij nouȝth ne next ȝoure flesche ne wereþ no
lynnen cloþ bot it be þe grettere. Ne wereþ non yrne ne haire.
I. 420) ne beteþ ȝou nouȝth wiþ scourges bot it be wiþ schriftes red.   20
Kepeþ ȝou warme in wynter ⁊ doþe grete werkes. ne gadereþ
noþing to hoord of no rynges ne brooches ne non oþer þing. þe
gretter werkes þat ȝe don þe better it is. And ȝif ȝe may lyue by
ȝoure werk ne spendeþ non oþer while þat it lasteþ. bot sendeþ
it forþ as it comeþ and beþ non housbonde ne houswyf to holde   25
M. 422) noþing. Ȝiue ȝou al to ȝoure lemman Ieremye biddeþ. ne be ȝe
neuer ydel. ne lerneþ none children. ne sendeþ none lettres. ne
vnderfongeþ none lettres. beþ ypolled in þe ȝere fiftene siþes.
⁊ foure siþes yleten blode and ofter ȝif it is nede. And whan ȝe
ben yleten blode þre dayes resteþ, For better is rest o day   30
oiþer two. þan a seuenniȝth for mysȝemynge of ȝoure seluen.
M. 424) And þan takeþ wiþ ȝoure seruaunt ⁊ gladeþ ȝou. Ancre þat naþ
nouȝth to libben by. it nedeþ þat hij han two seruauntz. on at
home anoþer oute. ⁊ by þe waye as hij gon. ne done hij nouȝth
bot bidden her bedes. ne ne speken hij to noman by þe waie bot 35
þider þat sche is sent go. ne takeþ noþing to holde of noman ne
of no womman. ne noiþer of þe seruauntz ne bere non vncouþ

19 non: *first* n *probably by correction.*   26 Ieremye, *sic for* Ierome.
32 takeþ, *sic for* talkeþ.   36 ne² *written above line and marked for*
insertion.

p. 449a tales þat miȝth any þing stiren her hertes, | fram god ward. ne
beþ nouȝth leiȝynge ne lokyng to noman ward. ne geueþ nouȝth

(M. 426) ȝoure dame. And ȝif ȝe do.' beþ redy to take penaunce. þerfore

(M. 428) ȝif any stryf ariseþ bitwixe þe Maidens. chastise hem louelich.
ꝫ liȝthlich for þat is wommans chastisynge, and selde whan wiþ 5
sternesse. ꝫ þat þat sternesse be menged al wiþ loue. as Men done
in to a wounde boþe wyn ꝫ oyle ac more of þe swete oyle þan of

(M. 430) þe bitter wyne. Mete ꝫ drynk takeþ in Mesure ꝫ at certeyn
tyme. And al þat ȝe done look þat it be euere in mesure for
elles ne quemeþ it nouȝth god Hyre ne owe þe Mayden non to 10
chalengen ne mede bot of god ꝫ eueryche weke ones redeþ þis
book ꝫ it wil do ȝou good more þan ȝe badd ȝoure bedes. For in
þis book ȝe mowe knowen ȝoure defautes wel better þan in
biddyng. And þe ofter þat ȝe reden it þe more ȝe mowe lerne
þere inne. For þere ben inne many wordes þat ben schortlich 15
seide ꝫ beren gret charge And mychel þing may ben vnderstonden þere by ȝif it be often yloked ouer ꝫ bysilich, And god
for his mychel miȝth my leue breþeren and sustren ȝif it be his
swete wille, ne ȝiue ȝou no lesse hyre þan al hym seluen Amen.

And ȝif it be ȝoure wille als oft as ȝe it reden. oiþer heren 20
seieþ a pater noster to oure lorde. and an Aue Maria to his
moder Marie, for hym þat it drouȝe out in to þis langage and
for alle þat it heren. oiþer reden. oiþer writen oiþer done
writen. and for al cristen folk. ꝫ for alle cristen soules þat god ȝif
it be his suete wille haue mercy on hem for his dere Moder loue 25
Amen.

þis good book Recluse.' here now makeþ ende.
Vn to þe blis of heuen.' god graunte vs grace to wende.

2 geueþ, *sic for* greueþ.   6 al *written above line and marked for
insertion.*   23 reden *probably on erasure.*   26–7 *Between lines 26
and 27 the following words in Stephen Batman's hand in black ink*: the passion; Caulid the complainte of oure Lady   27–8 *The two lines of the
couplet connected by vertical stroke.*